INTRODUCTION

Series Editor: J

PROMOTING EQUALITY IN
SECONDARY SCHOOLS

BOOKS IN THIS SERIES:

PROMOTING EQUALITY IN SECONDARY SCHOOLS

Edited by Dave Hill and Mike Cole

CASSELL
London and New York

Cassell

Wellington House 370 Lexington Avenue
125 Strand New York
London WC2R 0BB NY 10017-6550

First published 1999

British Library Cataloguing in Publication Data
A catalogue record for this book is available from the British Library

ISBN 0-304-70256-0 (hardback)
      0-304-70257-9 (paperback)

Typeset by Kenneth Burnley, Wirral, Cheshire
Printed and bound in Great Britain by TJ International Ltd, Padstow,
Cornwall

Contents

Notes on contributors

Dave Allen taught Art and Media Studies in Hampshire schools from 1975 to 1985. He spent three years at the School Curriculum Development Committee/National Curriculum Council as a central team member of the Arts in Schools Project. In 1988 he returned home to Portsmouth where he teaches a range of Visual and Cultural Studies courses at the University of Portsmouth.

Peter Bailey is Head of Mathematics at Frankley Community High School, Birmingham, having taught in secondary schools for many years. He wrote *Multiple Factors: Classroom Mathematics for Equality and Justice* (1991) with Sharanjeet Shan. He has worked in Malawi and Botswana. Recently he has contributed to the 'Values' Project for the Qualifications and Curriculum Authority and is currently Chair of The Mathematical Association's Publications Committee.

Clyde Chitty is Professor of Policy and Management in Education at Goldsmiths' College, University of London, having previously taught at the University of Birmingham. His latest books include *The Education System Transformed: A Guide to the School Reforms* (1992, 1999), *Rethinking Education and Democracy: a Socialist Alternative for the Twenty-first Century* (1997) (co-written and co-edited for the Hillcole Group), and, with Caroline Benn, *Thirty Years On: Is Comprehensive Education Alive and Well, or Struggling to Survive?* (1996, 1997). He is co-editor of the education journal *Forum* (for promoting comprehensive education).

Gill Clarke lectures in Physical Education and Biographical Studies in the Research and Graduate School at the University of

Southampton. Prior to this she was Field Leader for PE at University College, Chichester. She has co-edited *Researching Women and Sport* (Macmillan, 1997) and published widely on lesbian physical education students and teachers.

Mike Cole teaches at the University of Brighton. He has written extensively on anti-racism and on equality and schooling. He co-founded the Hillcole Group of Radical Left Educators, and (with Sharanjeet Shan and Dave Hill) edited the companion volume to this, *Promoting Equality in Primary Schools* (Cassell, 1997). He is editor of *Professional Issues for Teachers and Student Teachers* and *Human Rights, Education and Equality* (both 1999).

Margaret Cox is Professor of Information Technology in Education at King's College London, and Director of the MODUS (computer-based modelling across the curriculum project). She was the director of the Computers in the Curriculum project (1982–1991) which published over 200 educational software packages for schools. She is a founder member of the London Mental Models Group and the National Energy Education Forum.

Anton Franks taught English and drama in London schools for ten years before teaching both subjects to trainee teachers at the Institute of Education and King's College, University of London. He has published articles and chapters including *Stories, Drama and Learning* (1994), *Report from Baghdad* (1995), *The Body as a Form of Representation* (1995) and *Drama, Desire and Schooling* (1997).

Dawn Gill taught Geography in Inner London secondary schools for twelve years before being seconded for three years to the ILEA Anti-Racist Strategies Team. The team developed anti-racist curricula and strategies for most subjects taught in schools, and produced and delivered a training course for teachers and school managers. After the ILEA was disbanded by a Conservative government, she worked as a freelance writer and editor. She was involved in setting up teachers' groups to publish and make videos on anti-racist education. Dawn is co-editor of *Anti-Racist Science Teaching* (Gill and Levidow, Free Association Press, 1988) and *Racism and Education* (Blair, Gill and Mayor, Open University/Sage, 1991). She is currently Humanities Inspector for Doncaster LEA, having worked for six years as Humanities Adviser in the London Borough of Hackney.

Dave Hill teaches at University College Northampton, having also taught at Tower Hamlets College and at Chichester Institute of Higher Education and at Stockwell Manor School in the ILEA. He is a former Labour Parliamentary candidate (in 1979 and 1987), former Labour Group Leader on East Sussex County Council, and regional higher education Chair of NATFHE, the lecturers' union. He has advised the Labour Party on teacher education from a Radical Left perspective; and, with Mike Cole, in 1989 he co-founded the Hill-cole Group of Radical Left Educators.

Tom Jackson teaches History and GNVQ at Heathfield Community College in East Sussex, where he also has responsibility for Sociology. He is committed to equality of access across all areas of school life and is involved in research into bullying among students and staff. He is also working on an A-Level Sociology reference book.

Ken Jones is a Lecturer in Education at Keele University. He previously worked at the London University Institute of Education and in London schools. He is co-editor of the journal *Education and Social Justice*, and is co-author of *Children's Television in Britain: History, discourse, politics*, ISFI (1999).

Ruth Mantin is a Senior Lecturer in the Study of Religions and co-ordinator of the PGCE (Secondary) in Religious Education at University College, Chichester. Prior to this she was a secondary schoolteacher of Religious Education for seven years. She has written articles on Religious Education and co-authored *Teaching Christianity* and *The Islamic World*, a Key Stage 3 textbook on Islamic civilization. Her research interest is in the feminist study and practice of religion.

Ian Newman was born in Liverpool and taught French and Spanish in Kent. He was Head of House then Head of English at the British Council bilingual school in Madrid. He was Head of Modern Languages, then Deputy Head in an Inner London comprehensive school. He is now Head of a comprehensive school (Raynes Park High School) in the London Borough of Merton.

Gareth Nutt lectures in the Faculty of Education and Social Sciences at the Cheltenham and Gloucester College of Higher Education where he is the Physical Education Subject Co-ordinator for the Gloucestershire Initial Teacher Education Partnership. His research interests include the study of innovation and change within physical education, and the changing nature of teachers' work. Before taking up his appointment at Cheltenham in 1989, he taught physical education in Berkshire for fourteen years. During this period he also held a variety of posts with pastoral responsibilities.

Rod Paton is a composer, arranger, horn player and improvising musician. He studied music and philosophy at Southampton University and in the Czech Republic, later gaining his DPhil from the University of Sussex. He has worked as a teacher, lecturer and community musician with a wide range of ages and abilities and is currently Senior Lecturer in Music at University College, Chichester.

Arleene Piercy is an experienced teacher and lecturer who has taught in further, secondary and special needs education and on a Fulbright exchange at a high school in the USA. She has experience of working on GNVQ in both secondary and further education sectors and is an external verifier for GNVQ. Having completed her own teacher training and masters degree as a mature student she is particularly interested in equality of access to education. She has held office in teachers' unions and local Left politics and is a member of the Fawcett Society.

Glenn Rikowski is a Research Fellow in the School of Education, University of Birmingham. His research work is principally within the field of post-compulsory education and training, and the main focus of his theoretical writing is the development of Marxist educational theory. He was previously a lecturer at Epping Forest College, Essex, where he taught sociology and philosophy. He is a member of the Hillcole Group of Radical Left Educators, and a member of the Social Justice Group at the University of Birmingham.

Sharanjeet Shan was invited to take up the post of National Executive Director of the Mathematics Centre for Professional Teachers in Johannesburg, South Africa. She has established seven centres throughout South Africa, for teachers and children from farming, rural and township communities. Her contributions to the South African education scene include many books and learning support materials for teachers and children. In 1997, the centre won an award from Education Africa.

Adarsh Sood is a curriculum team leader for Information Technology at Carshalton College of Further Education. She taught in secondary schools in south-east London for over ten years before moving into further education at Lambeth College. She is committed to widening access for non-traditional entrants into Information Technology. Her initial teaching experience was in humanities subjects.

Clifford Walker was born in England to an Indo-Irish mother and an Anglo-Indian father. He is an Italian citizen. He has worked in primary, secondary and tertiary education in nine countries. He has taught English, History, Geography, Religion, French, Italian, Spanish, ICT, Mathematics and Science in London secondary modern and comprehensive schools. He has been University Lecturer in English, Senior Lecturer in Education, Head of Languages and Head of Year. He is now Vice Principal of a comprehensive school (Orwell High School) in the port of Felixstowe.

Introduction

Education, education, education – equality and 'New Labour' in government

Dave Hill and Mike Cole

According to Tony Blair, 'education is the passion of my government'. While the passion may not be misplaced, in our view the use to which that passion is put – the policy direction of the 'New Labour' government – is substantially misplaced.

It is true that some New Labour measures are clearly in the social democratic tradition, in terms of redistributive policy and financing through the agency of the local and national state. Examples of such policies are nursery education on parental demand; reduced class sizes for 5–7-year-olds; a policy focus on reducing social disadvantage in schooling through a variety of funded schemes; education maintenance grants for further education students from poor backgrounds; increased expenditure in Education Action Zones (EAZs) – areas of particular social need (The Government, 1999).

However, it is evident that the 'New Labour' government has accepted the neo-liberal and neo-conservative settlement of Thatcherism. It has accepted both the competitive market and the neo-conservative National Curriculum in schooling, in initial teacher education, and in further education (Hill, 2000a,b; Nightingale, 2000). In a modified form, with some extra powers given to LEAs and an increased number of parent governors on school governing bodies, it has also accepted the lack of locally elected democratic accountability across much of the education system.

In his speeches both prior to and following his election victory, Tony Blair has constantly alluded to some new middle ground, 'the

Radical Centre', or the 'Third Way' beyond Left and Right. This, he suggested, could be managed by eliding aspects of both Old Left and New Right policy. However, we consider that this is a smoke screen to hide the real ideological position held by the New Labour leadership. Tony Blair's pre-election declaration in Hayman Island, Australia, to Rupert Murdoch and the world, that '[t]he era of the grand ideologies, all encompassing, all pervasive, total in their solutions – and often dangerous – is over' (1995:12) is unconvincing, euphemizing (for Blair) the end of socialism and thereby acquiescing with Conservative hegemony. The effect of such a statement is to euphemize, to hide, and ultimately to ditch egalitarian policies for schooling, whether such policies be concerned with what the government sees as 'standards' (i.e. the internal arrangements and organization – such as the curriculum – within schools) or whether they be concerned with 'structures' – the organization of the wider schooling system – such as the competitive market in schooling.

It is significant that Blair immediately followed his 'end of ideology' commitment to Murdoch with the reassurance that 'the battle between market and public sector is over' (*ibid.*), signalling that New Labour accepts the centrality of the 'free market', keeping the divisive competitive market in schooling, including selective grammar schools.

Indeed, in some major areas of policy, New Labour actually goes beyond – deepens – Conservative policy. Examples are: the unwarranted attack on mixed ability teaching; the impending implementation of PRP (Performance Related Pay) for teachers; the introduction of private company control over schools in EAZs and over 'failing' LEAs; and the extension of the Private Finance Initiative – whereby private companies build schools, lease them to LEAs – but thereafter own them outright (Whitfield, 1999). These last three policies may be seen as the beginning of the privatization of the education system (Cole, 1998; Hatcher, 1998; Whitty, 1998; Hill, 1999).

However, in schools, teachers have not stopped promoting equality and equal opportunities. Schooling, education in general, and teacher education should be concerned with issues of social justice and therefore actively combat racism, sexism, homophobia, discrimination against the disabled, and the systematic exploitation of and discrimination against the working class in society and in secondary schools. Only then can we talk realistically of raising standards for all.

Chris Searle has made a powerful critique of the direction of education policy begun under Margaret Thatcher – and continued with a vengeance by the New Labour government. It is worth quoting him at length:

> As the British system of state education is forced more and more into a market orientation; as the abolition of free university education is accompanied by spin that this is really good for working-class families; if teachers are dragooned into becoming more like classroom operatives there to 'deliver' prescribed and narrow curricula, rather than creating professionals who develop an internationalist dynamic of knowledge side-by-side with their students and communities; as 'National Curriculum' fast degenerates to curriculum nationalism; as schools become more and more functionalist, managerialist and behaviourist venues rather than ripe with imagination, the spark of student action, collective teacher insight and community power; as the number of excluded and disaffected students grows in direct relationship to the tedium of schools' institutional life and the irrelevance of constricted and often racist curricula, and as the cover-all pretext of 'standards' replaces the need to re-examine and transform inequitable educational structures and divisions based on class, economic circumstance and social placement; as the fundamental linkage between poverty and educational attainment is set aside – the need for provocative and stimulating text for study, active debate and the sustaining of hope and struggle in the many facets of public education becomes more and more essential. (Searle, 1998:30–1)

The revisions to the Secondary National Curriculum at Key Stage 3 give greater autonomy to teachers, thereby facilitating teachers' use of the various curricular interpretations and suggestions in this book. The May 1999 document *National Curriculum Review Consultation* (QCA, 1999) notes that 'flexibility has been increased across all key stages' (p. 6). It continues:

Greater flexibility should enable teachers to:

- Give more emphasis to nationally identified priority areas such as literacy and numeracy, when necessary; and
- Exercise greater professional autonomy when designing and shaping a school curriculum to reflect the needs of their pupils and to maximise local opportunities and resources;

- Teach aspects of individual subjects in greater depth to develop knowledge, understanding and thinking skills, particularly at Key Stage 3.

In order to create opportunities for flexibility in these subjects, revisions have included:

- Removing content by reducing the number of statutory requirements;
- Reducing prescriptive detail;
- Clarifying requirements by defining their scope more succinctly (QCA, 1999:6–7).

This is what David Blunkett, the Secretary of State for Education and Training, referred to in his letter '*Achieving Excellence in the National Curriculum*' as 'a light touch approach' (QCA, 1999:unpaginated).

The major change included in the secondary curriculum (and, indeed, the primary curriculum) has been to require schools to introduce 'Citizenship' into the formal curriculum. Here is not the place to engage in detailed critique of the Citizenship requirements (see Clay *et al.*, 2000), but what we can point out here is that these proposals do give space for a radical interpretation. Citizenship will become a foundation subject in the National Curriculum at Key Stages 3 and 4. The focus is that:

> Citizenship contributes towards the school curriculum by giving pupils the knowledge, understanding and skills to enable them to participate in society as active citizens of democracy. It enables them to be informed, critical and responsible and aware of their duties and rights . . . Citizenship promotes their political and economic literacy through learning about our economy and our democratic institutions, with respect for its varying national, religious and ethnic identities. It helps them to gain a disposition for reflective discussion. (QCA, 1999:28)

We laud this, while questioning the degree to which putative moves to school democracy might be inhibited by the focus on managerialism and top-down governance of schools (Allen, Cole and Hatcher, 1999). We also worry that the 'civics' approach that permeates the document might inhibit the development of citizens as radical activists in pursuit of a more egalitarian society.

For those teachers and student teachers wishing to 'teach for social justice', to act thereby as 'critical transformative intellectuals' (Hill, 1994; 1997, 2000a) and who do wish to enable their students to 'gain a disposition for reflective discussion' and to develop, *inter alia*, a 'respect for . . . varying national, religious and ethnic identities', the various chapters in this book can indeed help stimulate and help provide and develop theory and practice about a non-quietist citizenship across the curriculum. Citizenship – and the quest for a society and schooling system that does not demean and discriminate against people on grounds of their social class, 'race', sex, sexuality and/or special needs – should be the concern of all teachers, and the concern of all curriculum subjects.

We hope this text will be provocative and stimulating, and that it will sustain – and stimulate – hope and struggle within classrooms, within staffrooms and outside the school gates.

BIBLIOGRAPHY

Allen, M., Cole, M. and Hatcher, R. (1999) *Business, Business, Business: The New Labour Agenda in Education*. London: Tufnell Press.

Blair, T. (1995) Speech to the News Corporation Leadership Conference, Hayman Island, Australia, 17 July 1995.

Blunkett, D. (1999) Achieving Excellence Through the National Curriculum. In Qualifications and Curriculum Authority *The Review of the National Curriculum in England: The Secretary of State's Proposals*. London: QCA.

Clay, J. (2000) *Citizenship: a Critical Programme*. London: Tufnell Press.

Cole, M. (1998) Globalisation, modernisation and competitiveness: a critique of the New Labour project in education. *International Studies in Sociology of Education*, 8(3):315–32.

The Government (1999) *The Government's Annual Report 98/99*. CM4401. London: HMSO.

Hatcher, R. (1998) Profiting from Schools: Busines and Education Action Zones. *Education and Social Justice*, 1(1):9–16.

Hill, D. (1994) Cultural Diversity and Initial Teacher Education. In G. Verma and P. Pumfrey (eds) *Cultural Diversity and the Curriculum, Vol. 4, Cross-Curricular Contexts, Themes and Dimensions in Primary Schools*. London: Falmer Press.

Hill, D. (1997) Reflection in Teacher Education. In K. Watson, S. Modgil and C. Modgil (eds) *Educational Dilemmas: Debate and Diversity, Vol. 1: Teacher Education and Training*. London: Cassell.

Hill, D. (1999) *Half-way Where? 'New Labour' and Education*. In press.

Hill, D. (2000a) 'New Labour' and the Conservative Revolution in Teacher Education 1979–1999. In D. Hill and M. Cole (eds) *Schooling and Equality: Factual and Conceptual Issues*. In press.

Hill, D. (2000b) The National Curriculum as Ideological and Cultural Reproduction. In D. Hill and M. Cole (eds) *Schooling and Equality: Factual and Conceptual Issues*. In press.

Nightingale, P. (1999) Plus ça Change. Education Policy a Quarter of a Century after Ruskin: the National Curriculum in Concert. In D. Hill and M. Cole (eds) *Schooling and Equality: Factual and Conceptual Issues*. In press.

Qualifications and Curriculum Authority (QCA) (1999) *The Review of the National Curriculum in England: The Secretary of State's Proposals*. London: QCA.

Searle, C. (1998) Book review of Hillcole Group (1997) *Rethinking Education and Democracy: A Socialist Alternative for the Twenty-first Century*. London: Tufnell Press; *Forum*, 40.

Whitfield, D. (1999) Private Finance Initiative: The Commodification and Marketisation of Education. *Education and Social Justice*, 1(2):2–13.

Whitty, G. (1998) New Labour, Education and Disadvantage. *Education and Social Justice*, 1(10):2–8.

CHAPTER 1

Equality and secondary education: what are the conceptual issues?

Mike Cole and Dave Hill

EQUALITY AND EQUAL OPPORTUNITIES

This book is premised on the conviction that all those connected with the education of young people should have a sound awareness of equality and equal opportunity issues. In this chapter, we provide a conceptual overview of the issues of social class, 'race', sexuality, gender, and disability and special needs as a means of informing the chapters in the rest of the book which deal with these issues with respect to the various subjects of the Secondary Curriculum.

The book is aimed at teachers, headteachers, school governors, parents, student teachers, school mentors, non-teaching staff, teacher educators and trainers, and others involved in secondary schooling. Its purpose is to encourage and assist them in promoting equality in secondary schools. As far as the equality issues discussed in this book are concerned, a number of important points need to be made at the outset.

First, a distinction needs to be made between equal opportunities on the one hand, and equality on the other. Equal opportunities policies, in schools and elsewhere, seek to enhance social mobility within structures which are essentially unequal. In other words, they seek a meritocracy, where people rise (or fall) on merit, but to grossly unequal levels or strata in society: unequal in terms of income, wealth, lifestyle, life-chances and power.

Egalitarian policies (policies to promote equality) on the other hand, seek to go further. First, egalitarians attempt to develop a systematic critique of structural inequalities, both in society at large and at the level of the individual school; second, egalitarians are committed to a transformed economy, and a more socially just society, where wealth and ownership are shared far more equally, and where citizens (whether young citizens or teachers in schools, economic citizens in the workplace or political citizens in the polity) exercise democratic controls over their lives and over the structures of the societies of which they are part and to which they contribute. While equal opportunity policies in schools and elsewhere are clearly essential, we believe that they need to be advanced within a framework of a longer-term commitment to equality. Where they are not, the false assumption has been made that there is a 'level playing field', on which we all compete as equals. Plainly, there is not.

The second important point is that these equality issues are all social constructs, which reflect particular social systems; they are not inevitable features of any society but, rather, crucial terrains between conflicting social forces in any given society. In other words, we do not believe that societies *need* to be class-based, to have 'racialized' hierarchies, to have one sex dominating another. We refuse to accept that people are *naturally* homophobic or prone to marginalizing the needs of disabled people. On the contrary we believe that, in general, we are socialized into accepting the norms, values and customs of the social systems in which we grow up, and schools have traditionally played a major part in that socialization process.

Third, each of these issues under consideration in this book has a material and institutional parameter (differences in wealth and power, laws which disfavour certain groups) and a socio-psychological parameter (modes of thinking and acting by the exploiters and discriminators, and by those on the receiving end of exploitation and discrimination).

The fourth point is that these inequalities are interrelated, and need to be looked at in a holistic way. Every human being has multiple identities. To take a case in point: there are, of course, lesbians, gays and bisexuals in all social classes, among the Asian, black and other minority ethnic communities and among the white communities. There are gays, lesbians and bisexuals with disabilities and with special needs. This book is distinctive in that the authors of the various chapters in the book were asked to look at issues of social class and of sexuality, in addition to the issues of 'race' and ethnicity, gender, and disability and special needs, which are more widely discussed and represented in publications. The chapters of this book testify that all curriculum subject areas lend themselves to a serious consideration of all equality issues, often in an interrelated way. We recognize, for example, that teachers and educationalists attempting to analyse the curriculum and to develop and interpret it in order to promote, for example, anti-racism, can learn from the guidelines and practices of anti-sexist teachers and organizations. We also recognize that individuals and groups have multiple subjectivities, and are subject to multiple forms of oppression and discrimination, and that teachers and student teachers and others may, usually unwittingly, also demean, discriminate against, label and stereotype in all sorts of ways: children (and their parents and communities), for example, can be labelled on grounds of their perceived social class, as well as on grounds of their ethnicity or religion.

The fifth point is that, while recognizing the interrelatedness of various inequalities, at the same time we recognize that inequalities are also separate. Some *groups* of school students, and some *groups* of teachers and other education workers, experience systematic, wide-ranging and long-lived discrimination, the under-expectation of others, academic and subsequent career/vocational under-performance, and alienation on the grounds of one particular presenting characteristic. Some groups as a whole (though there are numerous individual exceptions) get a raw deal in society and in schooling. Examination of the extent and ways in which this happens is now almost removed from initial teacher education and training courses (see Hill 1994; 1997; 2000a).

Sixth is the need to challenge the existing *status quo*. Through the formal (National) Curriculum, via the knowledge and culture(s) validated by schooling (and, indeed, through the hidden curriculum, via the expectations of teachers and other school staff, by the respective roles of staff in the schools), the hierarchies of the wider society are reflected, reinforced and reproduced. However, those at the receiving end of the exploitation, oppression or discrimination have, along with their supporters, historically resisted and fought back in various ways. Secondary schools do not have to be places where students are encouraged to think in one-dimensional ways. Indeed, were this the case, there would be no point in this book. Schools can and should be arenas for the encouragement of critical thought, where young people are introduced to a *number of ways* of interpreting the world, not just the dominant ways.

We believe that progressive and egalitarian teachers, students, school students and others involved in secondary schools should use the spaces available in the National Curriculum to encourage critical thought (indeed the purpose of this book is to aid that process). However, we believe that they should also mobilize and agitate for structural and organizational changes in the schooling and education systems and for a new common curriculum throughout the compulsory education system.[1]

In the following section, for the sake of conceptual clarity, the issues of social class, 'race', gender, sexuality and disability and special needs will be dealt with one by one.[2] The issues are not dealt with in any order of priority. For examples of up-to-date empirical data aspects, and for school policy development, readers are directed to Hill and Cole (eds) (2000). Here we deal conceptually with these issues.

SOCIAL CLASS

In order to begin to understand the changes occurring in the economy, in society in general, within the environment and within education, an awareness is needed of the crucial relevance of the concept of social class. Almost the whole world is currently run on market capitalist lines. All students, we would insist, have a right to know that this is only one way of running economies, societies and education systems, nationally and globally. Economic and industrial understanding should form an essential part of the curriculum of every school pupil and student, including secondary school students.

Britain continues to be rigidly stratified according to social class, as does the education system in England and Wales (and, of course, elsewhere). Michael Barratt Brown and Ken Coates in *The Blair Revolution: Deliverance for Whom?* (1996) list some data on income distribution and capital ownership in the UK to show how much inequality, poverty and social exclusion have increased in the last twenty years:

In the last twenty years the top fifth of income earners have seen their incomes increase by 40% in real terms, while the bottom fifth have actually become poorer. As a result the top fifth of households were actually taking 51% of all original income in 1994 compared with 43% in 1979. Most of this change was caused by the rise in unemployment. The unemployed in the 1970s averaged around 700,000; in the 1980s and '90s there has rarely been less than two and a half million of them and on the old basis of calculation over 3 million – nearly 15% of the workforce. More than a million of those registered for work have been without work for over a year. Even among those employed, some 13 million, over 60% of the workforce, receive pay that is below half the national average. (1996)

How can these relationships be explained? Below, we discuss a variety of different perspectives. These are Marxist, sociological (as represented by the Registrar General's classification) and post-modernist.

Marx and Marxism

The history of all hitherto existing society is the history of class struggles . . . oppressor and oppressed stood in constant opposition to one another, carried on an uninterrupted, now hidden, now open fight, a fight that each time ended, either in a revolutionary re-constitution of society at large, or in the common ruin of the contending classes . . . Our epoch . . . has simplified the class antagonisms . . . into two great hostile camps, into two great classes directly facing each other: Bourgeoisie and Proletariat. (Marx and Engels, 1977: 35–6)

Karl Marx, more than anyone else, developed a comprehensive theory about the relationship between social class and social structures; in particular social class and capitalism. By capitalism, Marx meant that mode of production which followed feudalism and in which the means of production (raw materials, machinery and so on) are concentrated into a few hands, a world order predicated on a few owning the means of production, and the vast majority being forced to sell their labour power in order to survive. Marxists believe that the schooling system represents the interests of the ruling capitalist class in more or less reproducing the existing economic, social and political system. It does this by 'ideological reproduction' – by persuading new citizens and workers that the existing (in fact grossly unequal) system is fair and 'natural'. It also does this by 'economic reproduction', by educating and training different social groups to fill a variety of different economic places in the workforce. Marxists disagree over how much space or 'autonomy' state apparatuses such as secondary schools, teachers, school students and communities have in challenging the existing system and its values. Finally, the ruling capitalist class does this by 'cultural reproduction', by validating and affirming its own culture, and by disconfirming and invalidating other cultures, such as working-class culture (see Giroux, 1983; Whitty, 1985; Cole (ed.), 1988; Cole, Hill and Rikowski, 1997; Hill, 1999 for a discussion). Young people bring their social class backgrounds into school with them (as well as other aspects of their subjectivities). As such they tend to meet with socially differentiated (i.e. social class-related) teacher expectations. This is primarily through 'the hidden curriculum' of values and attitudes and desired social and work behaviours that are expected of them. Teenagers attending Hackney Downs School in London, or Ramsgate Secondary Modern in Kent, or The Ridings in Halifax tend to have different expectations, labelling and stereotyped work futures than those attending the London Oratory School or Benenden or Eton.

When discussing social class, however, care needs to be taken to make clear that not all the working class is poor, or living in poverty. But whether very poor or in relatively secure and well-paid work, they do not *own* the means of production. They do not own the shop, or the bakery, or the factory, or the office in which they work. They are in the category of paid wage labourers, whatever their skill level.

Issues of nomenclature are crucial in understanding the nature of social class. For example, the use of the terms 'upper class' and 'lower class' can imply a justification for the existence of differentiated social classes and says nothing about the relationship between these classes. 'Ruling' and/or 'capitalist class', on the one hand, and 'working class', on the other, however, implies a specific relationship between them.

Social class and the Registrar General's classification

While we believe that Marxism provides the best explanation of social class, in order to understand sociological (and other) analyses, we need to turn to the Registrar General's classification of occupations (used also for official government purposes). Since the census of 1911, occupational groups have been put into a number of broad categories. Unskilled, semi-skilled and skilled manual workers are denoted 'working class'. The 'working class' is differentiated from the 'lower-middle' class – employees such as those in 'routine', low-paid white-collar jobs, who are in turn differentiated from other, better-paid/higher status/more highly educated sections of the middle class. These official classes (Classes 1–5) are used as the basis for the A, B, C1, C2, D and E social class/consumption group indicators used by sociological research, market research bureaux, opinion pollsters and advertisers.

Table 1.1   The Registrar General's classification of occupations

Class 1	Professional	Accountant, architect, clergyman [*sic*], doctor, lawyer, university teacher	5%
Class 2	Intermediate	Aircraft pilot, chiropodist, MP, nurse, police officer, teacher	14%
Class 3a	Skilled non-manual	Clerical worker, draughtsman [*sic*], secretary	10%
Class 3b	Skilled manual	Driver, butcher, bricklayer, cook	44%
Class 4	Semi-skilled	Bus conductor, postman [*sic*], telephone operator	17%
Class 5	Unskilled	Labourer, messenger, cleaner, porter	6%

In November 1998 the Registrar General's classification was amended to take into account some recent changes in the occupational structure of the labour force. The new classifications shown in Table 1.2 will be used for the census in the year 2001.

There are manifestly different layers or strata among the working classes. Skilled workers (if in work, and particularly in

Table 1.2 The Office for National Statistics classification of
occupations (HMSO: 1998)
Source: Office for National Statistics

Class 1	Professionals; Employers, Administrators and Managers employing 25 or more people (e.g. doctor, lawyer, scientist, company director)
Class 2	Associate professionals; Employers, Administrators and Managers employing fewer than 25 people (e.g. supervisor, nurse, sales manager, laboratory technician)
Class 3	Intermediate Occupations in Administrative, Clerical, Sales and Service Work (e.g. secretary, nursery nurse, salesman [*sic*], computer operator)
Class 4	Self-Employed Non-Professionals (e.g. plumber, driving instructor)
Class 5	Other Supervisors, Craft and Related Workers (e.g. factory foreman [*sic*], joiner)
Class 6	Routine Occupations in Manufacturing and Services (e.g. lorry driver, traffic warden, assembly line worker)
Class 7	Elementary Occupations (e.g. fast-food waiter [*sic*], supermarket cashier, cleaner, labourer)
Class 8	Never Worked, Unemployed, Long-term Sick

full-time, long-term work) in general have a higher standard of living than semi-skilled, unskilled or unemployed workers. Their weekly and annual income is likely to be considerably higher, and their wealth is likely to be higher. They are more likely, for example, to have equity on an owner-occupied home. In contrast, poorer families, in poorer sections of the working class, may have no wealth whatsoever, and are far more likely to live in private rented accommodation or in council housing. Millions of adults in the UK have no savings whatsoever and are in debt, living poorly, running out of money for food and fares before the next pay-day or the next giro cheque. With reference to social class and education it is clear from empirical data that children from Sunderland or Southwark stand less chance of getting to university – or of learning to read – than children from Surbiton or Solihull. The reason for this is not essentially geographical; it is because of the social class difference between the populations of Sunderland and Southwark (which are relatively predominantly working class) as compared to the predominantly middle-class populations of Surbiton and Solihull. There is a stark relationship between occupational status and income, and education success, with higher qualifications being very closely related to and, in general, demanded by higher status and higher income jobs. It is also clear that there is an enduring relationship between schooling success and social class origin/background. Social class background is clearly (although obviously not totally) statistically related to educational achievement – as indeed are the annually published 'league tables' of various assessment and examination results for secondary schools, which in effect represent a social map of the UK. Marxists explain these data, these patterns of achievement, not in terms of differential intelligence but in terms of the economic, cultural and ideological reproductive function of schooling in perpetuating the capitalist scheme of things – the domination of the working classes by the capital owning/capital managing capitalist class.

The postmodern challenge

There has been a serious challenge to Marxism from postmodernism. This influential world-view questions the salience of the notion of social class. Postmodernism has infiltrated or is infiltrating virtually every discipline within the social sciences, to the extent that it is rapidly becoming an orthodoxy, both in research and in undergraduate and postgraduate texts. Student teachers, teachers and others concerned with the education of secondary school students are increasingly likely to be confronted with the ideas of postmodernism. Postmodernism, we believe, albeit unintentionally for many postmodernists, serves the interests of the current pro-capitalist and anti-socialist stance taken by New Labour. Postmodernism concentrates on the 'local' – ironically so, during a period when local government and democracy have suffered severely at the hands of centralizing tendencies, and local government functions are increasingly being put in the hands of undemocratic quangos or tendered out to the private sector; and this concentration on the local rather than on mass movements, gives support to the continuing programme of disempowering the trade union movement.

Postmodernists argue that we live in 'new times', that we are in a postmodern (some say post-capitalist) era, that social class is not a central issue any more, that socialism is no longer a viable proposition. We have elsewhere attempted an extended critique

9

of such postmodernist arguments (Cole and Hill, 1995, 1996a, b; Hill *et al.*, 1999; see also Callinicos, 1989; Epstein, 1997). Here we will summarize our views.

Postmodernism was born in the 1950s and 1960s, broadly speaking, as the confluence of three separate strands of thought. These can be distinguished as follows:

1. Cultural critiques of 'modernist' forms of art, in favour of a heterogeneity of artistic and cultural styles. These are derived both from the past and from popular culture (for example, certain architectural forms, Warhol's pop art, Rushdie's novels and the work of certain film directors, such as David Lynch).
2. The 'poststructuralist' writings of French theorists, such as Deleuze, Derrida and Foucault, which reject structuralist explanations of society – the power of central structures like capitalism or patriarchy – in favour of textualism (seeing the social world as text) and/or the privileging of multiple sites of power.
3. General theories of contemporary society, dating from the 1960s, which have redesignated advanced capitalist societies as 'post-Fordist', 'post-industrial' or 'post-capitalist' (Callinicos, 1989:2–3; see also Green, 1994:68).

The privileging by postmodernists of consumption, style and greed over production and solidarity also undermines the concept – and the occurrence – of solidarity and any large-scale fight-back by workers' organizations. This is because possibilities for 'radical politics' become centred on market choices. Though boycotts of products, 'buying with a conscience', 'ethical investments' and the like have some role to play in a radical political perspective, they do not have the direct social force of democratically organized collectivities of workers withdrawing their labour or taking over a work site. Strikes and occupations pose a direct challenge to capital accumulation and the rule of capital, whereas 'market choices' merely lead to differential shifts in the realization of surplus value. Furthermore, it is also more difficult to organize hundreds, thousands or millions of individual and individualized consumers who have no social connection with each other than through their own market behaviour and choices. The main problem with postmodernism is that it is unable to recognize a major duality in capitalist societies, that of social class (for an extended analysis, see Cole and Hill, 1995, 1996a, 1996b; Cole, Hill and Rikowski, 1997; Hill, McLaren, Cole and Rikowski (eds), 1999; Sanders, Hill and Hankin, 1999. See also Callinicos, 1989; Epstein, 1997). For this reason, we retain our conviction that Marxism provides the best means of understanding issues of social class and their relation to education in capitalist societies.

Composition of the working class in contemporary Britain

Arguing that the working class has changed, rather than declined, John Kelly has suggested that there are two definitions of that class in common usage:

1. A narrow definition which includes only those workers directly exploited by capital in the production process, where actual goods are produced, workers whose surplus labour yields surplus value.
2. A wider definition, which includes all those who are obliged to sell their labour in order to survive (the majority of whom, but not all, are indirectly exploited, i.e. not actually producing goods).[3]

On the latter definition, the working class is growing both absolutely and relatively (1989:26; see also Ainley, 1994).

Justifying this wider definition of the working class in the context of Britain, Kelly argues first that an increasing section of the workforce is employed in business services which directly contribute to the production of surplus value by helping capitalists extract ever more out of workers (such businesses include research and development, industrial engineering, computer hardware and software and other branches of consultancy).

Second, there is a growing service sector (retail stores, hotels, the leisure industry and personal services such as hairdressing – Kelly fails to mention the sex industry). The antagonistic relationship between, say, a supermarket checkout assistant or burger-chain worker and his or her employer is analogous to that of a factory worker and his or her employer, since both employers have a vested interest in keeping wages and salaries down, and therefore profits up.

Third, there are workers in the central state and in the local state who are essential for the political stability of capitalism, even though they are not directly exploited for surplus value, such as civil servants and local authority office workers/bureaucrats.

Finally, there is a large section of the workforce engaged in producing new workers and/or maintaining the working class, particularly in the health and education services. Teachers of course fall into this last category. The devolution of budgets, the marketization of schools, the setting up of hierarchical management structures, league tables and performance-related pay mean that working in schools more and more resembles working for ICI or American Express.

If it is the case that there has been a re-composition, rather than a demise, of the working class, could it still be that there has been a change in class identification? Is Eric Hobsbawm correct in arguing that everywhere solidaristic forms of consciousness have given way to 'the values of consumer-society, individualism and the search for private and personal satisfaction above all else' (cited in Marshall *et al.*, 1989:1)? In a comprehensive survey of social class in Britain, Gordon Marshall *et al.* show that 'social class is still the most common source of social identity and retains its salience as such' (1989:143).[4]

Postmodernism's refusal to recognize dualisms, such as the central tensions and struggles between an exploiting capitalist class and an exploited working class, and its stress on localized action rather than overall emancipation, mean that no major changes in societies are possible. In its rejection of human solidarity and socialism, it plays into the hands of those whose interests lie in the maintenance of national and global systems of capitalist exploitation and oppression (see Epstein, 1997).

Countering the postmodern position, we would refer postmodernists to a relatively recent example of mass human solidarity, namely the overthrow of the self-proclaimed 'socialist' states of Eastern Europe. If such regulated and dictatorial regimes can be destroyed by collective human agency, then the possibilities for major structural change remain firmly on the agenda. Ironically, there are currently indications that the new brutal market economies created in the former Eastern bloc are being met with growing resistance, with many even preferring the old way of life under communism, and voting for a return to aspects of it. In Britain, the revolt against the poll tax, and the subsequent demise of Thatcher, if not Thatcherism, show that human beings will only take so much before they are prepared to join together to try to effect change.

'RACE' AND RACISM

Robert Miles has argued cogently against the notion that there exist distinct 'races' (1982:9–16). After a review of the literature, and following Bodmer, he gives three reasons for this. First, the extent of genetic variation within any population is usually greater than the average difference between populations; second, while the frequency of occurrence of possible forms taken by genes does vary from one so-called 'race' to another, any particular genetic combination can be found in almost any 'race'; third, owing to inter-breeding and large-scale migrations, the distinction between 'races', identified in terms of dominant gene frequencies, is often blurred (Miles, 1982:16).

If 'race' has no genetic validity, it still has use as an analytic concept (in comparing and contrasting 'race' with other equality issues, for example). In addition it does, of course, also exist as 'a social construct' in discourse. It is therefore still necessary to use the term. When this is the case, for the reasons outlined above, we would argue that it should be put in inverted commas.

The (false) belief that there exist distinct 'races' is the genesis of the concept of racism. Racism has traditionally referred to a situation where people are seen as causing negative consequences for other groups or as possessing certain negatively evaluated characteristics because of their 'biology'. While this has seemingly been the dominant form of racism throughout history, following Cole (1997a) we would argue that it is necessary to extend this definition in two major ways. First there is a need to include 'seemingly positive characteristics' in any definition of racism (cf. Cole, 1996, 1997a, 1997b); second it is necessary to enlarge the definition to include cultural factors (cf. Cope and Poynting, 1989; Modood, 1992,[5] 1994; Cole, 1996, 1997a, 1997b, 1998). We will deal with each in turn.

Evaluated characteristics

Negatively evaluated characteristics include such instances of racist discourse as 'black people are not as clever as white people', but excludes such seemingly positive statements as 'black people are good at sports'.[6] While such assertions can lead to individual and/or short-term group enhancement (an unmerited place in the school football team for the individual, or enhanced status for the group as a whole in an environment where prowess at sport is highly regarded), it is potentially racist and likely to have racist consequences. This is because, like most stereotypes, it is distorted and misleading and typically appears as part of a discourse which works to justify black school students' exclusion from academic activities.

Distinguishing between 'seemingly positive' and 'ultimately damaging' discourse is important. Nazi propaganda portrayed Jewish people as alien and morally subhuman and, therefore, a threat to the Aryan 'race'; a description which was part of a process that led eventually to the Holocaust. However, Jews were also characterized as a clever 'race' and (at least implicitly) having superhuman ability. Thus, along with perceived threats of German 'racial degeneration' were fears that, through having superordinate skills of organization, the ability to dominate and act collectively as one entity, the Jews were able to control the world. This 'clever', 'super-able' stereotype, a perception which on the surface could seem positive, led to allegations that Jewish people were part of a conspiracy to take over the world, a notion which was also in part responsible for the Holocaust.[7]

To take another example, people of Asian origin tend to be stereotyped as having a 'strong culture', an attribute which is used to pathologize people of African/Caribbean origin, who are in turn stereotyped (ridiculously) as having a weak culture or as having no culture at all! While this may serve to enhance the status of the former at the expense of the latter, in the context of racist discourse it can result in accusations that people of Asian origin are failing to integrate or are 'taking over', which can lead to violence and other forms of hostility.

Cultural racism

While we agree that a belief in a biological notion of 'race' lies at the root of much contemporary racism, we do not believe that it provides a full explanation. Perhaps contemporary racism might best be thought of as a matrix of biological and cultural racism (cf. Cole, 1997a). In that matrix, we would suggest that racism can be based purely on biology (e.g. such statements as 'blacks are not as intelligent as whites') or purely on culture, as in the case of Islamophobia (e.g. in Peregrine Worsthorne's (1991) words, 'Islam . . . has degenerated into a primitive enemy' (cited in Richardson, 1992:xi).

Quite often, it is not easily identifiable as either. The racist term 'Paki' is a curious case in point. Relatively unrelated to Pakistan, it has become a generic term for anyone who is perceived to be from a specific alien stock and/or is believed to engage in certain alien cultural practices based, for example, around religion, dress or food. The fact that it is being written by racists as 'packy' in the singular and 'packies' in the plural (the *Guardian*, 17 February 1995) is indicative of how far it has become removed from the geographical area of Pakistan. Even when 'Pakistani' is used in racist discourse, it is highly unlikely that it is used in a knowledgeable way to refer to an (ex-)inhabitant of that particular South Asian country.

The issue of nomenclature, the way we refer to people, is important and is a hotly contested issue. The first point to make is that it is not to do with that invention of the Radical Right – 'political correctness'; it is to do with respect for people. The second point to make is that it is perhaps easier to establish terms that are not acceptable than those which are preferred. The nomenclature 'coloured', for example, is unacceptable to most people in Britain. The third point to make is that there are no accurate and fixed definitions of a minority ethnic group. Ideally, we believe in ethnic self-definition. However, there is, inevitably, disagreement over what is and is not appropriate (e.g. Modood, 1988, 1994; Mama, 1992). Since many people of Asian and other minority ethnic origin do not self-describe as 'black', and because the use of the term 'ethnic minority' has, in practice, meant that members of the dominant majority group are not referred to in terms of their ethnicity with the implication that they do not have ethnicity (Leicester, 1989:17), we suggest that, at the present time in Britain, the formulation 'Asian, black and other minority ethnic' is preferable (the sequencing of 'minority' before 'ethnic' does not carry the implication referred to by Leicester above).[8] 'Ethnic' or 'ethnics' should never be used in isolation and need to be prefigured by 'minority' (or 'majority') and followed by a noun such as community (ies) or group(s). It needs to be stressed that we all have ethnicity, whether we are a minority or the majority.

GENDER

Whereas sex refers to basic physiological differences between females and males (differences in genitalia and respective roles in human reproduction, for example), gender relates to social and cultural differences, relative to time and place. For example, what is considered the norm with respect to 'acceptable modes of dress' or body language for males and females varies dramatically through history and according to geographical location (this is not to say, of course, that everyone within a given society conforms to such norms).

There are a number of competing theories about how gender roles become established. First, there are those who argue that biology accounts for gender differences in society, that human beings possess a genetically based programme, a 'biogrammar', which predisposes them to behave in certain ways (cf. Tiger and Fox, 1972). The main problem with these explanations is that they fail to account for the aforementioned geographical and historical variations. If our gender roles are biologically determined, why is there not one universal form for each sex? (Measor and Sikes, 1992:7; see also La Fontaine, 1978).

Other explanations are based around socialization and can be grouped under the headings 'social learning theory' (roles learned from parents, peers and teachers), 'cognitive development theory' (roles established in the child's quest for competence in a world where such competence is linked to being 'male' or 'female'), and psychoanalytic theories. This last field focuses on the emotional aspects of a child's life. Rooted in a feminist critique of the work of Freud, specifically a challenge to Freud's deficit view of women, feminist psychoanalytic theory has emphasized femininity in a positive sense. In place of female/male inferiority/dominance, has come 'difference' and complementarity. It has been suggested too that boys can be jealous of girls' femininity, whereas Freud emphasized only girls' envy of boys. It has also been suggested that boys, unlike girls with respect to their femininity, have to struggle to become 'masculine' and this can involve the attacking of things that are feminine and the devaluing of girls and women (Measor and Sikes, 1992:11–12).

Measor and Sikes suggest socialization might best be seen as a combination of the above non-biological approaches (1992:10, 12). What they have in common is a belief that gender is by definition a social construct – unlike sex, which is a biological construct; that is to say appropriate gender roles are learned through socialization rather than genetically given.

As far as nomenclature is concerned, a growing number of people now accept the right of women to decide how they wish to be referred to, whether it is a preference for 'woman' over other forms of address, or a preference for 'Ms' over more traditional titles, or vice versa.

In the English language, there are many more derogatory terms in popular discourse to describe women than men, which perhaps vindicates feminist psychoanalytic theory; but it is definitely indicative of the patriarchal nature of the societies in which we live. Patriarchy has been defined by Adrienne Rich as:

> the power of the fathers: a familial-social, ideological, political system in which men – by force, direct pressure, or through ritual, tradition, law, and language, customs, etiquette, education, and the division of labour, determine what part women shall or shall not play, and in which the female is everywhere subsumed under the male. (Cited in Eisenstein, 1981:18–19)

Just how true this is can be gleaned from a cursory glance at who, in general, at national and international level, controls big business and finance, politics, the military, the police, technology, science and education.

Gender inequalities are reproduced, in large part, through the institution of the family, where gender roles are constructed through the socialization process, with respect to expectations, dress, household chores or lack of such chores, chosen toys and comics and so on.[9] Inequalities are also reproduced through, for example, peer pressure (often an effective counter to an enlightened family socialization), the media (cf. Cole, Maguire and Basowski, 1997), leisure and sport (cf. Tomlinson (ed.), 1997) and, of course, by the education system (discussed below).

So how have feminists and their supporters challenged gender inequalities? Traditional feminist perspectives have ranged from radical or revolutionary feminists (who see patriarchy as the principal form of oppression), through socialist feminism (targeting both capitalism and patriarchy), black feminism (an important corrective to those feminists who tended to be colour-blind), to those liberal feminists favouring reform, who envisage full equality for women under capitalism (something which socialists

17

would see as not feasible, because of capitalism's reliance on the cheap labour of women in the workforce and wageless labour in the household).

Unfortunately, the interests of girls and women are not served by the current spate of feminist theory based on poststructuralism or postmodernism (see, for example, Butler, 1990; Lather, 1991; Jones, 1997). We have written at length elsewhere on the dangers of the extensive appropriation of feminism by postmodernism (see, for example, Cole and Hill, 1995, 1996a, b; see also Kelly, 1992, 1994, 1999). Briefly, consistent with our general critique of postmodernism, we argue that in its rejection of a metanarrative of social change, in its concentration on the local, rather than the national and international, in its implicit acceptance of all voices as equally valid, postmodernism is not able to theorize, nor to advance the causes of women in the modern world.

In particular, as socialist feminist Jane Kelly (1992, 1994, 1999) has argued, postmodern feminists have nothing to say about the situation of working-class women in the 1990s. Without an 'overarching' theory, they are unable to explain the ways in which women's oppression, centred in the family, determines their entry into the workforce; unable to analyse why the majority of women workers are confined within a segregated labour market, are paid less and work in worse conditions than men; unable to understand the ways in which part-time work, seen as 'appropriate' for women, whose primary responsibilities are viewed as domestic, has been used in the restructuring of the workforce in Britain in the last decade; unable, finally, to decide which women's issues should take priority in campaigning.

SEXUALITY

As with 'race' and gender, the issue of nomenclature is important in reference to sexuality. The term 'gay' seems generally acceptable to gay men and to some gay women. Other gay women prefer to be referred to as lesbians. The term bisexual or 'bi' is still in common usage, for those people attracted to both sexes. Recently, former terms of abuse like 'queer', 'bent' and 'dyke' have been reclaimed as positive and assertive by some gay and lesbian activists and artists (in a similar way some rap artists, for example, particularly in the United States, have retrieved negative terms like 'nigger'). The golden rule, once again, is that we should take note of self-definitions but be aware of disagreements and different preferences and that we should bear in mind changing modes of self-referral. It should be noted that certain terms may not be appropriate in certain circumstances, for example the above-mentioned reappropriated terms in straight cultural settings.

Sexuality is firmly on the political, Christian religious, social and academic agendas. We will deal with each agenda in turn. As far as politics is concerned, there have been a number of campaigns for lesbian and gay rights (the one concerning the age of consent being an ongoing issue). In addition, British 'municipal socialism' in the 1980s (especially in London and Manchester) took the issues on board; there are varying degrees of commitment to lesbian and gay rights from local authorities today; and although the House of Commons' decision to equalize the age of sexual consent for homosexual acts as for heterosexual acts was reversed by the House of Lords in early 1999, it is likely that various legislative equalities will be enacted by the current Labour government.

With respect to the Christian religion, a number of clergy in the Christian Church have decided to 'come out' or have been 'outed', and Christianity has been reinterpreted by some Christians to encompass a love of all humankind, not just heterosexuals (for a discussion, see Babuscio, 1988:74–92). This is not to say that such a position is universal in the Christian Church. In fact, the Church seems to have three positions: outright condemnation of homosexuality; acceptance of the orientation, but not the practice of homosexuality; or total acceptance and affirmation.

As far as the social scene is concerned, there are now numerous lesbian, gay and bisexual clubs, pubs and other social venues. There is lesbian and gay theatre and cinema, lesbian and gay music, and lesbian and gay publications can be bought in the local newsagents and at high street bookshops. In addition, other issues of sexual diversity – such as fetishism, sado-masochism, transvestism and transexualism – are being more openly discussed.

Finally, academic publishers are marketing scores of books on sexuality, there are now degrees in lesbian and gay studies at British universities, and indeed at universities in many other parts of the world.

All this indicates most forcefully that acknowledgement of lesbians and gays and bisexuals is here to stay, and full acceptance of the inalienable right to sexual diversity will increasingly become the norm amongst all communities, including the community of the secondary school.

On the negative side, gay sexuality in the popular imagination is very much associated with the epidemic of HIV infection and AIDS. However, as Epstein points out, there are at least two key agendas in operation here. The first, dominant agenda, as spelt out in the popular press, has been that of the 'moral majority', with an emphasis on 'normal' family life as opposed to 'unnatural' homosexuality and the accompanying 'gay plague'; the second, counter-agenda, promoted by voluntary bodies such as the Terrence Higgins Trust, has celebrated diverse formations of sexuality (cited in Epstein (ed.), 1994:3), as has the lesbian and gay rights organization, Stonewall.

DISABILITY AND SPECIAL NEEDS

Through history, disabled people have frequently been seen as unclean and polluting. This is apparent, for example, in the Old Testament of the Bible. In the New Testament, however, charity is counselled for disabled people (Rieser, 1990:12–13). With the emergence of medical knowledge in the mid-nineteenth century, disabled people became individual objects to be 'treated', 'changed', 'improved', 'cured', made more 'normal'. 'The overall picture is that the human being is flexible and "alterable" whilst society is fixed and unalterable' (Mason and Rieser, 1990:14; see also Ford *et al.*, 1982; Tomlinson, 1982; Barton and Tomlinson (eds), 1984; and Slee, 1993).

In place of the 'religious model' and the 'medical model', a 'social model' has been suggested. Disability, according to this model, is seen as 'the complex system of economic and social constraints imposed on people with impairments by the organization of society' (Barton *et al.*, 1993:110). Mason and Rieser spell out the implications of such a view:

> . . . whilst we may have medical conditions which hamper us and which may or may not need medical treatment, human knowledge,

technology and collective resources are already such that our physical or mental impairments need not prevent us from being able to live perfectly good lives. It is society's unwillingness to employ these means to altering itself rather than us, which cause our disabilities. (1990:15)

As is the case with other issues of equality, nomenclature is of great importance with respect to disability and special needs (terms now more or less universally used, rather than 'handicap'), and some suggestions are given in Mason (1990:88) of both offensive and preferred terminology. (As always, this should be read in the context of a cultural climate subject to constant change and revision.)[10]

Mason (1990) has argued that 'special educational needs' came about as an attempt to de-medicalize the labelling of children with disabilities; in other words to replace offensive terms such as 'retarded', 'maladjusted' and so on, with what was hoped to be less negative labelling based on educational need. While Mason states that disabled people welcome the spirit in which this was done, she suggests that it overlooks the political dimension:

> We do not consider ourselves to be special. We consider disability to be a norm within every society, borne out by statistics, and we want our needs to be taken into account as normal human beings. It seems questionable that even 20 per cent of young people can have 'special needs'. It seems ridiculous that 45 per cent of young people within inner-city areas can have 'special needs'. Surely the question is how does the education system fail to answer the needs of 45 per cent of its users? (1990:88)

Mason suggests retaining the official terminology of 'special needs' for the present and for it to include disabled children, children with learning difficulties and children with emotional and behavioural problems; in fact, in the context of the compulsory school years, to include all young people with any physical and/or mental condition, be it permanent or temporary, who are affected in some way by the wider society's attitudes towards disability (*ibid.*:89).

THE STRUCTURE OF THE BOOK

Part 1 of the book examines the three core subjects of the Secondary National Curriculum, on a subject-by-subject basis. Each chapter gives an ideological analysis of the content of Programmes of Study, and goes on to show and suggest ways in which teachers can use the National Curriculum in order to transform it, or use spaces and suggestions within it to combat inequalities. Ken Jones examines English; Peter Bailey, mathematics; and Sharanjeet Shan, science.

Part 2 of the book deals similarly with the non-core foundation subjects of the National Curriculum. Margaret Cox and Adarsh Sood look at design and technology (including information technology); Tom Jackson, history; Dawn Gill, geography; Rod Paton, music; Dave Allen, art; Gill Clarke and Gareth Nutt, physical education; and Clifford Walker and Ian Newman, modern foreign languages.

In *Part 3*, Ruth Mantin examines religious education; Clyde Chitty, sex education; and Arleene Piercy and Glenn Rikowski, GNVQs.

As is to be expected in an edited collection, there are differences in perception, opinion and in emphasis between contributors, and individual chapters should not be read off as the precise academic or political views of the editors, either individually or jointly. Yet we all have in common a commitment to the resuscitation, invigoration and extension of equality and equal opportunities work in schools and in education for justice and equality.

NOTES

1. For proposed curricular changes to the primary school curriculum in England and Wales, see the various chapters in the companion book to this, *Promoting Equality in Primary Schools* (Cole *et al.*, 1997). The details of the education programme which we advance – the much wider-ranging organizational, curricular and pedagogic changes across the wider educational system – are spelt out in the Hillcole Group's two books, *Changing the Future: Redprint for Education* (1991) and *Rethinking Education and Democracy: A Socialist Alternative for the Twenty-first Century* (1997).
2. This section on conceptual issues draws on and develops some of the issues in Cole (1997a).

3. Kelly's analysis is an attempt to defend Karl Marx's concept of social class, where relationship to the sphere of production is the determining factor. The sociologist Max Weber, whose work is often cited as providing an alternative to Marxist theory, argued that it is differential life chances distributed by the capitalist market, rather than relationship to production, that distinguish social classes. As we have seen in government censuses and other surveys, and in academic and other empirical research, social class is defined according to occupation, ranked according to what are perceived to be a hierarchy of skills (for a critical discussion, see Marshall *et al.*, 1989, Chapter 2; see also Marx, 1976 and Weber, 1968). For a discussion of changing class relations in late capitalist economies see Hill, 1999 and Sanders *et al.*, 1999).

4. Sixty per cent of their sample claimed that they thought of themselves as belonging to one particular class, and well over ninety per cent could place themselves in a specific class category, when asked the follow-up question: '[s]uppose you were asked to say which class you belonged to, what would you say?' (1989:143, 166). (Respondents placed themselves in the categories, 'upper', 'upper-middle', 'middle', 'lower-middle', 'upper-working', 'working' and 'lower-working' class respectively (1989:144).) Marshall *et al.* conclude that 'modern Britain is a society shaped predominantly by class . . . no matter whether the phenomena under scrutiny are structural or cultural in nature' (1989:183). See Hill 1999 for a more detailed discussion of social class in contemporary Britain.

5. While we agree with Modood's arguments for racism having a cultural dimension, we are not in sympathy with his overall project in this book, which entails the wholesale rejection of historical materialism, and the privileging of functionalist analysis and a liberal concept of 'ethnic pluralism' (Cole, 1993a:23).

6. We are using the term 'black' in the British context to refer to children of African/Caribbean origin (see Cole, 1993b). We are indebted to Smina Akhtar for the following discussion of positively evaluated characteristics.

7. Thus, writing in 1941 for *Das Reich*, a German weekly controlled by Nazi propaganda minister Joseph Goebbels, Elizabeth Noelle-Neuman declared, with respect to the United States:

Jews write the newspapers, own them, and have close to a monopoly over the advertising agencies that open and close the doors to advertising for each newspaper. They control the film industry, own the big radio stations, and all the theatres. Due to their *cleverness* [my emphasis], Jew journalists are not the most noisy advocates for war. When they reach for public opinion, they don't move as a group, but instead come from various directions. (Cornwall, 1997:21)

8. For a fuller discussion of nomenclature in Britain, see Cole, 1993b.

For a discussion of nomenclature with respect to Britain and to some other (selected) countries in Europe, see Cole, 1996.

9. It is important to point out that, as the nuclear family of husband, wife and children together in one household becomes less and less universal, socialization processes *may* be changing.

10. Barton *et al.* unanimously agreed to change the title of the journal, *Disability, Handicap and Society* to *Disability and Society* as from Number 1 1994, because of the overtly negative and oppressive implications of the term 'handicap', used in relation to disabled people (Barton *et al.*, 1993:110).

BIBLIOGRAPHY

Abercrombie, N., Hill, N. and Turner, B. S. (1994; 2nd edn) *Contemporary British Society*. London: Polity Press.

Ainley, P. (1994) *Degrees of Difference: Higher Education in the 1990s*. London: Lawrence and Wishart.

Arnot, M., David, M. and Weiner, G. (1996) *Education Reforms and Gender Equity in Schools*. Manchester: Equal Opportunities Commission.

Babuscio, J. (1988) *We Speak for Ourselves: The Experiences of Gay Men and Lesbians*. London: SPCK.

Barratt Brown, M. and Coates, K. (1996) *The Blair Revolution: Deliverance for Whom?* Nottingham: Spokesman.

Barton, L. and Tomlinson, S. (eds) (1984) *Special Education and Social Interest*. London: Croom Helm.

Barton, L., Barnes, C., Booth, T., Borsay, A. and Oliver, M. (1993) Editorial. *Disability, Handicap and Society*, 8(2):109–10.

Bowles, S. and Gintis, H. (1976) *Schooling in Capitalist America*. London: Routledge and Kegan Paul.

Bowles, S. and Gintis, H. (1986) *Democracy and Capitalism*. New York: Basic Books.

Brown, S., Riddell, S. and Duffield, J. (1997) Classroom Approaches to Learning and Teaching: the Social Class Dimension. Paper presented to the ECER (European Educational Research Association) Annual Conference, Seville.

Butler, J. (1990) *Gender Trouble: Gender and the Subversion of Identity*. London: Routledge.

Callinicos, A. (1989) *Against Postmodernism: A Marxist Critique*. Cambridge: Polity Press, Cassell.

Cole, M. (ed.) (1988) *Bowles and Gintis Revisited: Correspondence and Contradiction in Educational Theory*. Lewes: Falmer Press.

Cole, M. (1993a) Widening the cricket test. *Times Higher Educational Supplement*, 26 March.

Cole, M. (1993b) 'Black and ethnic minority' or 'Asian, black and other minority ethnic': a further note on nomenclature. *Sociology*, 27(4):671–3.

Cole, M. (1996) 'Race', racism and nomenclature: a conceptual analysis. In U. Merkel (ed.) *Racism(s) and Xenophobia in European Football*. Aachen: Meyer and Meyer.

Cole, M. (1997a) Equality and primary education: what are the conceptual issues? In M. Cole, D. Hill, and S. Shan (eds) *Promoting Equality in Primary Schools*. London: Cassell.

Cole, M. (1997b) 'Race' and racism. In M. Payne (ed.) *A Dictionary of Cultural and Critical Theory* (2nd edn). Oxford: Blackwell Publishers – 2nd edition, paperback – please note that the first edition (hardback) has a serious typographical error which alters the sense of what Cole is saying.

Cole, M. (1998) Globalisation, modernisation and competitiveness: a critique of the New Labour project in education. *International Studies in Sociology of Education*, 8(3):315–32.

Cole, M. (1998) Racism, reconstructed multiculturalism and antiracist education. *Cambridge Journal of Education*, 28(1):37–48.

Cole, M. and Hill, D. (1995) Games of despair and rhetorics of resistance: postmodernism, education and reaction. *British Journal of Sociology of Education*, 16(2):165–82.

Cole, M. and Hill, D. (1996a) Resistance postmodernism: emancipatory politics for a new era or academic chic for a defeatist intelligentsia? In K. S. Gill (ed.) *Information Society: New Media, Ethics and Postmodernism*. London: Springer-Verlag.

Cole, M. and Hill, D. (1996b) Postmodernism, education and contemporary capitalism: a materialist critique. In M. O. Valente, A. Barrios, V. Teodoro and A. Gaspar (eds) *Values and Education*. Lisbon: Faculty of Science, Department of Education, University of Lisbon.

Cole, M. and Hill, D. (1997) New Labour, old policies: Tony Blair's vision for education in Britain. *Education Australia*, 37.

Cole, M., Hill, D. and Rikowski, G. (1997) Between postmodernism and nowhere: the predicament of the postmodernist. *British Journal of Education Studies*, 45(2):187–200.

Cole, M., Hill, D. and Shan, S. (eds) (1997) *Promoting Equality in Primary Schools*. London: Cassell.

Cole, M., Maguire, P. and Bosowski, J. (1997) Radio 1 in the 80s: day-time DJs and the cult of masculinity. In A. Tomlinson (ed.) *Gender, Sport and Leisure: Continuities and Challenges*. Aachen: Meyer and Meyer Verlag.

Cope, B. and Poynting, S. (1989) Class, gender and ethnicity as influences on Australian schooling: an overview. In M. Cole (ed.) *The Social Contexts of Schooling*. Lewes: Falmer Press.

Cornwall, T. (1997) In Goebbel's shadow. *Times Educational Supplement*, 19 September.

Eisenstein, Z. (1981) *The Radical Future of Liberal Feminism*. New York: Longman.

Epstein, B. (1997) Postmodernism and the Left. *New Politics*, 6(2).

Epstein, D. (ed.) (1994) *Challenging Lesbian and Gay Inequalities in Education*. Buckingham: Open University Press.

Ford, J., Mongon, D. and Whelan, T. (1982) *Invisible Disasters: Special Education and Social Control*. London: Routledge and Kegan Paul.

Giroux, H. (1983) Theories of reproduction and resistance in the new sociology of education: a critical analysis. *Harvard Educational Review*, 53(3).

Green, A. (1994) Postmodernism and state education. *Journal of Education Policy*, 9:67–83.

Guardian, 17 February 1995.

Halsey, A. H., Heath, A. F. and Ridge, J. M. (1980) *Origins and Destinations*. Oxford: Clarendon Press.

Haralambos, M. and Holborn, M. (1995; 4th edn) *Sociology: Themes and Perspectives*. London: Collins Educational.

Hill, D. (1994) Cultural diversity and initial teacher education. In G. Verma and P. Pumphrey (eds) *Cultural Diversity and the Curriculum, vol. 4: Cross-Curricular Contexts, Themes and Dimensions in Primary Schools*. London: Falmer Press.

Hill, D. (1997) Reflection in teacher education. In K. Watson, S. Modgil and C. Modgil (eds) *Educational Dilemmas: Debate and Diversity, vol. 1: Teacher Education and Training*. London: Cassell.

Hill, D. (1999) Social class and education. In D. Matheson and I. Grosvenor (eds) *An Introduction to the Study of Education*. London: David Fulton.

Hill, D. (2000a) 'New Labour' and the Conservative revolution in teacher education 1979–1998. In D. Hill and M. Cole (eds) *Schooling and Equality: Factual and Conceptual Issues*. In press.

Hill, D. (2000b) The National Curriculum as ideological and cultural reproduction. In D. Hill and M. Cole (eds) *Schooling and Equality: Factual and Conceptual Issues*. In press.

Hill, D. and Cole, M. (eds) (2000) *Schooling and Equality: Conceptual and Empirical Issues*. In press.

Hill, D., McLaren, P., Cole, M. and Rikowski, G. (eds) (1999) *Postmodernism in Educational Theory: Education and the Politics of Human Resistance*. London: Tufnell Press.

Hillcole Group (1991) *Changing the Future: Redprint for Education*. London: Tufnell Press.

Hillcole Group (1997) *Rethinking Education and Democracy: A Socialist Alternative for the Twenty-first Century*. London: Tufnell Press.

Jones, A. (1997) Teaching post-structuralist feminist theory in education: student resistances. *Gender and Education*, 9(3):261–9.

Kelly, J. (1989) Class is still the central issue. *Communist Review*, 3, Spring.

Kelly, J. (1992) Postmodernism and feminism. *International Marxist Review*, 14, Winter.

Kelly, J. (1994) Feminism and Postmodernism: A Productive Tension or an Incompatible Collusion? Paper presented to the British Educational Research Association Annual Conference, Oxford.

Kelly, J. (1999) Postmodernism and feminism: the road to nowhere. In D. Hill, P. McLaren, M. Cole, and G. Rikowski, *Postmodernism in Educational Theory: Education and the Politics of Human Resistance*. London: Tufnell Press.

La Fontaine, J. S. (1978) *Sex and Age as Principles of Social Differentiation*. London: Academic Press.

Lather, P. (1991) *Getting Smart: Feminist Research and Pedagogy With/In the Postmodern*. New York: Routledge.

Leicester, M. (1989) *Multicultural Education: From Theory to Practice*. Windsor: NFER-Nelson.

Lynch, J., Modgil, C. and Modgil, S. (eds) (1992) *Cultural Diversity and the Schools, vol. 3: Equity or Excellence? Education and Cultural Reproduction*. London: Falmer Press.

Mama, A. (1992) Black women and the British state: race, class and gender analysis for the 1990s. In P. Braham, A. Rattansi and R. Skellington (eds) *Racism and Antiracism*. London: Sage.

Marshall, G., Rose, D., Newby, H. and Vogler, C. (1989) *Social Class in Modern Britain*. London: Unwin Hyman.

Marx, K. (1976) *Capital: A Critical Analysis of Capitalist Production, vol. 1*. Harmondsworth: Penguin.

Marx, K. and Engels, F. (1977) *Manifesto of the Communist Party*. In Karl Marx and Frederick Engels, *Selected Works in One Volume*. London: Lawrence and Wishart.

Mason, D. (1994) On the dangers of disconnecting race and racism. *Sociology*, 28(4):845–58.

Mason, M. (1990) Special educational needs: just another label. In R. Rieser and M. Mason (eds) *Disability Equality in the Classroom: A Human Rights Issue*. London: Inner London Education Authority.

Mason, M. and Rieser, R. (1990) The medical model and the social model of disability. In R. Rieser and M. Mason (eds) (1990) *Disability Equality in the Classroom: A Human Rights Issue*. London: Inner London Education Authority.

Measor, L. and Sikes, P. (1992) *Gender and Schools*. London: Cassell.

Miles, R. (1982) *Racism and Migrant Labour*. London: Routledge and Kegan Paul.

Modood, T. (1988) '"Black", racial equality and Asian identity'. *New Community*, 14, 3:397–404.

Modood, T. (1994) Political blackness and British Asians. *Sociology*, 28(4):858–76.

Redman, P. (1994) Shifting ground: rethinking sexuality education. In D. Epstein (ed.) *Challenging Lesbian and Gay Inequalities in Education*. Buckingham: Open University Press.

Richardson, R. (1992) Preface. In T. Modood *Not Easy Being British: Colour, Culture and Citizenship*. London: Runnymede Trust and Trentham Books.

Rieser, R. (1990) Disabled history or a history of the disabled. In R. Rieser and M. Mason (eds) *Disability Equality in the Classroom: A Human Rights Issue.* London: Inner London Education Authority.

Sanders, M., Hill, D. and Hankin, T. (1999) Social class and the return to class analysis. In D. Hill, P. McLaren, M. Cole and G. Rikowski (eds) *Postmodernism in Education Theory: Education and the Politics of Human Resistance.* London: Tufnell Press.

Searle, C. (1996) OFSTEDed, Blunketted and permanently excluded: an experience of English education. *Race and Class,* 38(1):21–38.

Searle, C. (1997) *Living Community, Living School.* London: Tufnell Press.

Slee, R, (1993) The politics of integration – new sites for old practices? *Disability, Handicap and Society,* 8(4).

Social Trends (1998) 28:95. London: HMSO.

Tiger, L. and Fox, R. (1972) *The Imperial Animal.* London: Secker and Warburg.

Times Educational Supplement (1996) Why class is still a classroom issue. *Times Educational Supplement,* 4 October.

Tomlinson, A. (ed.) (1997) *Gender, Sport and Leisure: Continuities and Challenges.* Aachen: Meyer and Meyer Verlag.

Tomlinson, S. (1982) *A Sociology of Special Education.* London: Routledge and Kegan Paul.

Walkerdine, V. (1983) Sex, power and pedagogy. *Screen Education,* 38.

Weber, M. (1968) *Economy and Society.* New York: Bedminster Press.

Whitty, G. (1985) *Sociology and School Knowledge: Curriculum Theory, Research and Politics.* London: Methuen.

PART 1

FOUNDATION SUBJECTS KEY STAGES 3 AND 4: THE CORE SUBJECTS

CHAPTER 2

English

Ken Jones, with Anton Franks

The meaning of 'English' has been fought over for 100 years, and the battles are still going on. In this chapter we argue against aspects of the official English of the 1990s. We explore ideas that we think are useful in developing contemporary alternatives. The core of what we say is that the subject should develop in learners the full range of skills and capacities needed by people who are to become 'critical social actors'; and that in order to do this, English must be alert to the ideas and experience which learners bring with them to the classroom (Luke, 1994:x). Our criticism of the present National Curriculum is that it does not do this. Our assessment of earlier versions of English is that, in patchy and imperfect ways, they did.

The English of the 1970s, 1980s and early 1990s developed as a response to the difficulties and opportunities of comprehensive education. In those years teachers re-shaped the curriculum. In saying this, we do not mean that all English teachers were involved, or that all changes tended in the same direction. But we would argue that the subject was touched at many points by radical thinking. These points constituted its leading edge. What were they? What did they concern? Briefly, they focused on three topics: 'experience', cultural change and cultural criticism. Together, these topics added up to a version of English strongly marked by egalitarian purposes. 'Experience' involved attention to the languages and cultures of groups long overlooked in the school system. Cultural change meant an interest in changing modes of communication – especially the growth of new media – and the ways in which they demanded new skills of reading and production. Cultural (and social) criticism entailed a willingness to challenge existing ideas of what was valuable and necessary in language, literature and education.

Three examples will give some sense of what this re-shaping involved. The first has to do with changes in the teaching and learning of language. Educationalists in the mid-1960s coined the term 'oracy', and in doing so paved the way for speaking and listening to be seen as important parts of English – the written word was no longer completely dominant. With 'oracy' came a change in attitudes towards Standard English, which lost its status as the sole language of classroom learning. Class and regional dialects, patois and creoles gained an (always partial) legitimacy: they were recognized as means of exploring ideas and representing meanings and values that were centrally important to students. And the more seriously teachers took language diversity, the more seriously they came to understand other aspects of learners' lives. As Harold Rosen put it more than twenty years ago:

> Out there, in the 'social context' there is a culture which is alive and kicking. Just as we have discovered that children do not come to school to be given language but arrive with it as a going concern, we need to discover that children come with this too . . . Their language, the despised vernacular . . . is part of it. (Rosen, 1977:208)

The second aspect of change involved literature. Once the diversity of classrooms was understood, then the selection of texts for those classrooms had to be modified – hence the discovery of 'black writers' and the new prominence given to writing by women in (say) A-level syllabuses. But curriculum change did not end with the selection of a new group of texts; it went further, focusing on the reader as well as the read. In a recent article, John Yandell writes about teaching *The Merchant of Venice* in a Year 10 classroom in Hackney (Yandell, 1997). Usually, he argues, learners who encounter a text like this are made to feel ignorant: there is so much vocabulary they do not know, so many conventions and assumptions they do not share and are made to think they cannot understand. Yandell's intention, by contrast, was to get readers to feel knowledgeable and confident. He used an ICT-based prediction game, in which students reconstructed for themselves one of Shylock's speeches. Students' errors, here, were less important than their willingness to speculate, to make hypotheses, to figure out possibilities. In the process they learned two things: to read boldly and closely, and to understand that meaning is not just a property of texts, but an effect of the way in which they brought their own experience to bear on the text. Yandell encouraged students to bring their everyday familiarity with 'race', power, money, victimization and revenge – the issues at the heart of the play – to an interpretation of the text. 'Instead of being aware of their ignorance,' he writes, 'they can (thus) make use of their knowledge' (*ibid.*, 110).

The final set of changes centred on the post-1980 introduction of media studies into English. Media studies alters English in several ways. First, it highlights questions of *representation* – the link between the construction of images and issues of power, conflict and control. This has a particular importance for those who want to make the classroom a place where equality is a live issue. Images relating to gender or 'race' or to sexuality, disability, social class, are never neutrally descriptive. The production of images is always going to be dependent on the social interests of the people who make them; the way they are read will always be affected by the point of view of those who consume them. Media studies makes these issues central. But it does more than that: its alertness to the way in which the 'landscape of communication' is changing – the multiplication of TV channels, the growth of home video, the explosion of multi-media ICT – forces English to face the necessity of reinventing itself, as a broader discipline. It asks English teachers to recognize how complex human communication now is. Media studies suggests to them that the new forms of communication do not respect national boundaries, but link localities to global cultures. It maintains that students, immersed and skilful inhabitants of this culture, have skills, knowledge and attitudes which classrooms do not sufficiently recognize. And in doing so it calls into question the distinction between (acceptable) high culture and (debased) popular culture on which for a long period English was based.

Since the early 1990s, these developments have been slowed, drastically. Curriculum and assessment systems have changed in ways that discourage teachers from exploring once-important questions. The 1995 revised (Dearing) National Curriculum gives strong priority to Standard English and to the canon of English literature. The transformation of GCSE assessment to terminal exams – rather than coursework – sharply limits the room for negotiated, student-centred learning. The tiering of exams (decided upon before the New Labour government's opposition to mixed ability teaching, yet compatible with it, nonetheless) makes it more difficult for classrooms to be places where a wide range of student experience is brought together. In short, English has become conservatized. Like so much else in education, this conservatization was initially the work of the governments of Margaret Thatcher and John Major, but it has now been endorsed by a Prime Minister – Tony Blair – who makes his dislike of the slow, progressive reforms of earlier decades very clear. This chapter argues that English needs to be opened up again. More than any other school subject, it offers a space for the exploration of experience and the development of creative skills. But to do this, English has to be re-designed, and in ways that build on the positive elements in its history and that take account of present-day cultural change.

We do not think this re-designing can take place within existing curriculum and assessment frameworks. As we will show, there is some small space for innovation in GCSE – enough to allow for new approaches to Shakespeare, for media studies to retain a foothold, for texts from other cultures to be explored. But as Peter Thomas has recently made clear, for all the experimental energy which teachers and learners might expend in these areas, the total mark that can be obtained for them amounts to no more than about 10 per cent of the examination total (Thomas, 1997:26). These sharp constraints explain why the main focus of this chapter is not on the existing limits of the possible, but on the necessary expansion and re-designing of the subject. Given the vast and exciting potential of English, this seems to us a responsible thing to do: the future of the subject, and the part it could play in an egalitarian project, are too great for discussion to be confined within conservative horizons. But it is with these horizons that our argument will begin, in discussing the notions of tradition which have done so much to shape the English of the 1990s.

IDENTITY AND TRADITION

As a school subject, English shares with other aspects of the national culture a preoccupation with identity and tradition: its

emphasis on Shakespeare and other pre-twentieth-century literature, as well as on Standard English, should be understood in this
way. Tradition involves a concern with cultural authority, but
also with the customs and habits of everyday life. In modern societies, tradition does not arise spontaneously: it is designed,
invented, fostered and reinforced in ways that owe much to the
intervention of powerful social groups. Such interventions seek
to ensure that everyday life is conducted, as it were, in the shadow
of the past. As the conservative philosopher Roger Scruton
suggests, tradition involves 'all manner of . . . participation in
institutional life, where what is done is not done mechanically,
but for a reason and where the reason lies not in what will be done
but in *what has been'*. Moreover, Scruton continues, traditions do
not depend for their effect on the conscious, willing agreement of
those who adhere to them – 'It does not matter if the reason
cannot be voiced by the man who obeys it: traditions are enacted
and not designed . . .' (Scruton, 1984:40).

But no matter how powerful the forces which seek to ground
social life in a sense of what has been, they now face considerable
problems. Many of the most potent British traditions come out of
the period of industrialization and consolidation of the nation-
state in the eighteenth and nineteenth centuries. In many
respects, the institutions and habits which evolved in this period
– in fields as diverse as religion, monarchical rule, communications, sport and education – are threatened by social and
economic change. The irony at the heart of the process – an irony
which is slowly breaking apart the coherence of right-wing
politics – is that it has been the Conservative Party which has
accelerated the pace of such change, even while it continues to
support traditional and supposedly cohesive practices and institutions, particularly in areas of cultural policy. Major's
premiership, in particular, was distinguished by nostalgia combined with deregulation which ran down many of the institutions
underpinning national unity – the rail network, public service
broadcasting. Major used to invoke an 'England of the mind'. This
other England consisted of attempts to recreate or imagine a community organized around national pride, social hierarchy, and
stable, collective systems of belief. The value of familiar cultural
forms was reasserted, even while the validity of these forms was
being undermined by forces of change: as the momentum towards
European union grew, so the political Right sought to rally

support for traditional versions of national sovereignty and ethnic identity. It is another predictable paradox that these appeals to what is supposedly familiar and well-rooted were voiced in edgy and anxious tones: tradition was seen as both the powerful centre of cultural cohesion and something which is pressured, frail and untrustworthy. Conservatives, therefore, needed not only to preserve it, but also to prop it up – to reinvent and reinforce it. In doing so, however, they deprived tradition of its natural and timeless qualities. No longer something that was unquestioningly inherited, it became instead a set of practices and beliefs that could be argued over. The attempt to reassert tradition was thus self-defeating.

In education, traditionalism was made concrete, though not as firmly as Conservatives hoped, in a national curriculum giving priority to authoritative, familiar forms of knowledge. Asked to choose between alertness to change and the pull of nostalgia, Conservatives chose the latter almost every time. True, the 1995 English curriculum did eventually make some mention of non-traditional aspects of English: it now acknowledges that there is a place for the study of non-print texts, that bilingualism is in some limited sense an educational asset, that writing in English from other cultures merits study. But the predominant bias of the curriculum, strongly reinforced by GCSE syllabuses, is towards more traditional features of English. The non-traditional practices of teaching and learning which developed in the 1970s and 1980s, and which flourished in the early years of the GCSE exam, were curtailed. Instead, tradition, embodied in the fixed and largely non-negotiable form of the National Curriculum, confronts learners not so much as a set of resources which they can transform or from which they can make selections, but as a canonical and authoritative force, to which they must acquiesce. As such it reverses earlier trends to inclusiveness: it contributes to the exclusion from the classroom of certain kinds of experience, and of the interests of particular groups of learners.

The period of Conservative Party government is over, perhaps for many years. But there is still a contemporary point in writing about the philosophies that motivated it, since many of its positions have been adopted by New Labour. It is true that New Labour is not searching for a curriculum which incarnates the idea of the nation; but it has ceased to challenge Conservative curriculum policies. It talks very little now of altering the established patterns of curriculum and assessment (Labour Party, 1995). It has taken to citing – as models for a post-Conservative future – types of education developed in the period before the major, 1960s-initiated changes in curriculum and school organization. Important in this respect is its hostility to mixed-ability teaching, and its preference for streaming and setting (Blair, 1996:173–7). Left-of-centre reformers in earlier decades were often motivated, like those who in the 1960s pushed forward the work of the Schools Council, by the belief that successful mass education depended in part on changing the curriculum to make it relevant and appealing, and changing systems of in-school organization to the same end (Stenhouse, 1967). Contemporary Labour, by contrast, seems to believe that a mass, inclusive system of education can be constructed on the basis of traditional forms of knowledge and selective forms of organization.

The argument of this chapter is that traditionalism hinders us from facing important issues of educational change, and that its failures are apparent in the way that National Curriculum English is put together and defended. To develop this argument, we will initially refer to two sources. The first is a piece of writing by a student in North London, composed in 1995. The second is a speech made in the same year by Nicholas Tate, Chief Executive of the School Curriculum and Assessment Authority (Tate, 1995). We hope to show how these examples embody different understandings of tradition and of the ways in which people should relate to it. Later in the chapter, we broaden the discussion, and in doing so we adapt some of the ideas of a writer with a strong though unconventional sense of educational purpose – Bertolt Brecht. We hope to make use of Brecht's work to address the complex issues around nation, value, learning and forms of communication which tradition, in an educational context, has come to represent. This we do in order to contribute to the debate on re-designing English in the period that will follow the ending of the moratorium on curricular change in 1999/2000. Finally, we suggest ways in which such ideas can be implemented – though in a constrained way – within the classrooms of the present.

Yuksel

Yuksel, a Year 10 student, wrote some chapters of her autobiography for a GCSE assignment. They begin like this:

My mother explained to me what happened on the day when I was born: 'When I was pregnant with you, I went for six months to another village. It's called ——. On the night you were born your father went to your uncle's house to sleep, because the farm was a bit far from our house, and in the morning the sheep were going to market and he was going to get up early . . . And you were born on that day – correctly, in the middle of that night. And someone went to tell your father that you had been born and you were a girl.' My father explained what happened when that man arrived there to tell him that I had been born:

'I slept and I saw my mother. I never saw her in my life because when I was born she died, because of me. I killed her and that's why I hate myself a bit. She said, "Your daughter Yuksel is born today. She's going to be a nice girl and you have to look at her very nicely. You should think that she is me." And when the man came to tell me that you were born I said before he spoke, "It's a girl." And I forgot about everything – about farm, sheep and myself. And I am still calling her mother because of my mother who said, "You have to look at her as me," and I am doing that . . .'

Many things could be said about this powerful piece of writing. One concerns the cultural continuity which so preoccupies current policy-makers, and centres on the immediacy with which the piece brings together different generations. The past is a living force: the effect of the writing is to render the narrator, her parents and her grandmother simultaneously present. The use of direct speech is important in this respect: the characters in the story – especially the narrator and her father – take care not to interpret or mediate strongly the voices they quote, so that the speakers are as 'present' as the narrator herself. Likewise, there is a strong sense of what could be called intimate address: the characters to whom the stories are told (the girl, her father) are intent, close listeners, sometimes overwhelmed by the stories they hear.

It is possible to infer from this form of narrative a kind of society in which generational links remain close. The re-telling of family tales in such a context is a way of binding the youngest generation tightly to family histories, in particular through the figure of the daughter who is the very image of her grandmother. The content of the story also serves to evoke a society of which the term 'traditional' can fairly be used: it depicts a pre-capitalist pattern of rural life, in which time is experienced differently, and dreams have a direct truthfulness. Far more than the often-invented and authority-centred traditions to which conservatives pay homage, tradition in Yuksel's writing has popular origins: created by subordinate groups, it embodies a memory that is not committed to writing or enshrined in official ritual, but instead serves to convey the most intimate of continuities and to reassert the common experience of generations, in the face of all that makes their grip on life a fragile one.

But this view of what the text involves is only a partial one. In *The Age of Extremes* Eric Hobsbawm describes one of the greatest social and demographic changes of the post-war period (Hobsbawm, 1994:289–93): pushed from their land by economic compulsion or military force, tens of millions of peasants have become city dwellers, either in their own countries or in the metropolises of the West. The process still continues, but rather than creating communities that have resettled themselves (albeit tenuously) it tends to produce enormous populations of refugees, who even more plainly than their predecessors lack jobs, stable homes and legal rights. Yuksel belongs more to this second group than the first. She is Kurdish, from Turkey. Her farm was burnt by soldiers and the farm animals were killed. Her father was in prison for two years, where he was tortured. He left for London, and the status of a refugee. Later, Yuksel and her mother joined him. In doing so, they left traditional society, probably for ever. 'I never asked to come here', Yuksel wrote; but she does not think that she can go back. Even if she does manage to return, her displacement will not end. As a report on Kurdish migration tersely states: 'returning to the village is not always easy, for new ideas do not reconcile themselves with traditional ones' (McDowall, 1989:14).

Yuksel and her family have moved to a different country and to a different zone of historical time, to a city which is immensely wealthy and cruelly poor, a city in which, within walking distance of each other, both sweatshops and finance-houses go about their business. Yuksel's cultural experience is now hybrid: it includes her family, their stories and her remembered experience; it also embraces pop videos, some knowledge of political texts, arguments about the meaning of Islam, marches against asylum laws, and romance. One of the many places where this particular diversity will be engaged is in a classroom with other students, most of whose lives have likewise been shaken by the effects of economic change, family break-up and cultural admixture. And in this classroom Yuksel and her fellow-students encounter a cultural form which is meant, across all their differences, to integrate them, to offer them a shared experience of a national culture, and to enable their participation in a wider society. The experience is that of learning English, as set out in the National Curriculum.

Nicholas Tate

Nicholas Tate has been a history teacher and a lecturer in teacher education. He was SCAA's Chief Executive, and in 1999, leads its successor body, the Qualifications and Curriculum Authority. Over the last few years, he has made a number of speeches – including the one from which we quote here – which seek to relate curriculum development to what can fairly be called cultural politics. Tate's concern is with the protection of stable identities and cultures, particularly of a nation-related kind, in a world where 'economic globalisation and the revolution in communications and information technology have the potential for sweeping aside national identities in a way few had anticipated' (Tate, 1995). Education has a key role in Tate's project of maintenance and repair.

Tate is someone who recognizes – almost as much as a Kurdish refugee – the depth of cultural change, and the strength of the forces which drive it. He speaks often of 'social and geographical mobility, frequent job changes, and family breakdown'. At the same time, however, he expresses a yearning to hold on to what has been lost – 'a sense of place, belonging, tradition and purpose, of those things that bind people into distinctive communities'. It is this combination of recognition and nostalgia that takes him into the ranks of what Anthony Giddens calls neo-conservatism (Giddens, 1994:30–3). Neo-conservatives are social critics of a particular kind. They accept free market economic principles, but at the same time think the market is destroying the traditional symbols and practices on which a meaningful social life depends. They regret that the fixed social roles on which cultural identities were based in pre-capitalist societies – such as rural Anatolia, perhaps – have been erased, largely through the operation of market forces. The market on its own cannot supply replacements for the cultural continuity and cohesion that these roles supplied. Neo-conservatives try to assist it by establishing, or bolstering, practices and institutions which can provide cultural and social defences against the upheavals of economic life. Central to this work, in the view of many neo-conservatives, is the attempt to establish authoritative, nation-centred value systems.

It is in this context that we can best make sense of Tate's ideas and prescriptions. He wants schools to establish a 'common culture', whose features are strongly anglo- (or at least euro-) centric. All children in England must have the English language at the centre of their curriculum. They need to be 'introduced to the English literary heritage, to English history (in all its cultural diversity) and to the study of Christianity and to the classical world'. These things, he maintains, are at 'the heart of our common culture and our national identity'; every student, whatever their background, is entitled to possess them, as 'at least one of their cultural identities'.

This last phrase is important: Tate is signalling a belief in cultural pluralism which is unusual among neo-conservatives. Nevertheless, there are problems with what he says. He understands cultural diversity as a matter of addition. There exists a 'majority' culture, organized around the attributes listed above. And then there exist various 'minority cultures' which reproduce their own distinctive 'customs and traditions'. His intention is not that students should in some postmodern way pick and mix elements from these various cultures; it is more that, securely anchored in one kind of culture, they should be able to respect and understand others. For all its pluralistic drift, however, this way of understanding contemporary cultural relations is problematic; in order to understand why this should be so, we need to turn back to Yuksel's writing.

Refugee students like Yuksel know many things. Where they come from is a place of sharp and often violent confrontation, of a cultural (linguistic and religious) as well as a political and military kind. Where they have come to is a country in which cultural differences take a less acute form but are nonetheless pervasive. Yuksel's story evokes a moment in which cultural cohesion is very strong. But she knows that moment to be irrecoverable: she can't go home again; she lives amid an irreducible cultural complexity. It is not that she inhabits a 'Kurdish' culture, while partaking also, as another one of her identities, in an 'English' one. The boundaries aren't as easily drawn as that, and there are no spaces that can be defined in simple, national terms. Whichever aspect of cultural experience is highlighted – gender, political activism (a feature of much Kurdish life), music, religion – each reveals a mixing of cultural influences which it is neither possible nor helpful to disentangle. And the point can be extended beyond this particular piece of writing to the cultural experience of Yuksel's classmates: it is thoroughly hybrid, in the sense that it mixes together different national influences, and reflects on top of it all the influences of commercially generated youth culture. The outcome of all this cannot be captured by Tate's additive formula; moreover, the approach to curriculum policy which his understandings generate does not adequately respond to the complexities of identity experienced by learners. Because of this, the approach does not facilitate that dialogue between the formal, organized knowledge of the school and the everyday cultures of students upon which successful learning depends. Even so, some of the problems Tate raises, especially those which concern the relation between present and past, mainstream and marginal cultures, are important: a successful re-designing of the curriculum depends upon resolving them.

BERTOLT BRECHT

Bertolt Brecht (1898–1956) wrote poems, plays, film scripts, stories, novels, critical and polemical pieces; he kept a scrapbook and wrote diaries and journals. More often than not he worked with others, usually with women writers whose contributions he rarely acknowledged (Fuegi, 1994). This work – collaborative, endlessly revised, often unfinished – amounts to no fixed set of commandments. If it did, it would be less useful to us. 'His' texts (we'll stick to the singular pronoun, misleading as it is) are worth returning to because they engage with problems still central to cultural policy and, by extension, to educational policy as well. These engagements provide resources for the rethinking of contemporary issues, and we will argue that they are particularly important in addressing the future of English.

Brecht was interested in the ways in which drama and other kinds of cultural production could represent social life so as to make more possible a general popular understanding of its 'causal complexes'. Issues of learning and teaching were thus a central and explicit part of his work: reality had to be reinterpreted, and literally re-presented, in ways which were of relevance and use to mass audiences. This overall project led him first of all to a re-thinking of questions of form and to experiments with a number of artistic methods, from the use of new technologies (involving for instance the integration of drama and film) to the recycling of traditional tales and dramatic styles. It also led to a rethinking of ways in which cultural production related to audiences. The conventional theatre, he argued, addressed audiences as if they had no power to change the social relations which it represented. Brecht's 'epic' theatre would do otherwise: it would address audiences as people who were accustomed to change, not just as people who had experienced rapid transformation, but who also were capable of bringing change about. (The contrast with Scruton's stress on the inarticulate, obedient ways in which the mass of people absorb tradition is striking.) Brecht emphasized the productivity of everyday life. Through daily labour, people learn skills and attitudes which help them change one thing into another – the harvest into bread, iron ore into finished steel and so on. Theatre and other kinds of art should try to develop this 'productive' disposition further, from the world of nature into the realm of the social. Art forms should make audiences more aware that larger social arrangements, too, can be transformed: these arrangements do not last for ever, and purposeful human activity can change them.

These interests – in form, in audiences and the ways in which they can be related – are constant in Brecht's mature work, although the precise expression they are given oscillates considerably. Some of the most notable oscillations occur around the meaning of tradition. Brecht had a strong sense of the shaping force of history but was not in any ordinary sense a traditionalist. He was often hostile to the idea that artistic forms generated in previous historical periods, and by extinct or redundant social classes, could serve any useful present purpose. Tied down himself by what he saw as the drudgery of film-studio work in wartime Hollywood, he poured scorn on the assumption that the exhausting lives of workers could be improved by a programme of classically based cultural uplift. In the same spirit, he dismissed the concerns of liberal anti-Nazis who hoped that the restoration of classic German literary traditions would provide the major means of cultural reconstruction after Hitler. Such efforts, he wrote, sent him to sleep (Brecht, 1994:249 and 255).

Likewise, the arguments of Georg Lukacs in defence of the

great traditions of nineteenth-century realism against the fragmented modernism of the twentieth century left him cold (Brecht, 1977). Proposals such as these to raise the cultural 'level' of the workers seemed to him based on an ignorance of the real conditions of people's lives, both economic and cultural. In particular, assumptions about the uplifting powers of culture had as their counterpart a belief in the degradation and passivity of working-class life. On such a basis, a dialogue between cultural producers and audiences could not happen.

It is not difficult, then, to set up Brecht as Nicholas Tate's polar opposite, as someone with no time for cultural continuity, and with little interest in the past except as something to break from. Yet this is not the whole story. Much of Brecht's theatrical work involved the reworking of earlier texts – many of them in some sense 'traditional' – rather than the invention of something new. So what divides Brecht from Tate or Scruton? The division rests on Brecht's understanding that 'tradition' is something transformed by each new generation, whereas the major difference between Brecht and Tate is that Brecht separates the issue of tradition from that of nation. Tradition becomes something that is not so much inherited from a national past as recomposed from a variety of resources in a way that respects neither national boundaries nor conventional distinctions of 'high' from 'low' culture. In this reconstruction, questions of belonging take second place to those of cognition. The demand Brecht makes of past forms is not 'Will they tell us who we are and where our roots lie?', but 'Can they be used to help us understand the world we live in?'.

Brecht's question led him to search through a wide range of resources, from fable to modern radio and film, from China to Hollywood. He regarded film and folk culture as potentially of equal value: either the gangster story or the Shakespeare play could be reworked so as to reveal the causal complexes of society and to give pleasure as they did so. Nothing is privileged by nature of its origins. Shakespeare's plays may offer delights, but they are 'barbaric' (Brecht, 1964:189); the devices of artistic modernism may be developed as tools that are useful to the propaganda of oppressors (Brecht, 1976:386). Traditional culture can often carry progressive meanings, but there is no value in the loving reproduction of archaic popular forms (Brecht, 1964:153). So whereas John Major found tradition a source of beliefs and values which are largely beyond questioning (Major, 1993), for Brecht tradition is a set of resources which can be used according to purposes which are themselves open to debate.

So far, this brief summary of Brecht's interests has centred on issues of form. As we have suggested, however, form in Brecht cannot be understood outside his thoughts about the purposes of cultural production, and about its audience. At the core of his project is a belief in members of the audience as producers of meaning and agents of social change. It would be easy, but misguided, to think that this understanding was just wishful – that it made a set of assumptions about 'the people's' innate yearning for enlightenment which overlooked the real difficulties of a cultural programme aimed at the mass of the population: Brecht's project was much more complex and awkward than that. He recognized that people do not like what they are supposed to like, and frequently reject what dominant opinion thinks is good for them. He had a keen sense of the boredom and the lack of pleasure which supposedly great art could induce in contemporary audiences. Set alongside appreciative and indeed marvelling comments about Mozart, Shakespeare, Schiller and others, Brecht's writings register a sense of learning and enjoyment as contradictory (Brecht, 1964:27). Knowledge in current society is not pleasurable; and what gives pleasure does not illuminate. Conventional theatre offered no way out of this dilemma. The challenge Brecht set himself was to make the link between knowledge and pleasure in the context of popular theatre.

The ability to bring together pleasure and learning became for Brecht a touchstone of worthwhile artistic work, and depended on re-making the ways audiences relate to plays. Most of Brecht's technical innovations stem from attempts at such a remaking. Most radical in this respect are certain types of *lehrstucke* (learning, or teaching, plays) in which audiences become actors and are invited to argue with and modify texts. There are also significant innovations of other kinds: alienation effects, for instance, which work by presenting in a new framework what is in one sense already known to audiences, so that everyday, familiar actions become things to be thought about in different, historicized terms (Barthes, 1977). Finally, and most comprehensively, the idea of a 'smokers' theatre' (Brecht, 1965) evokes a relationship between play and audience which combines pleasure, detachment and a lightness of touch: at its simplest, this envisages an audience free to move around; at a more complex level, this lack of physical constraint marks a new relationship between audience and cultural production – perhaps the dramatic equivalent of John Yandell's teaching, encouraging students to participate in Shylock's speeches by using their own knowledge and experience.

Why Brecht?

The account we have just presented has stuck fairly closely to Brecht's ideas and their drama-based context. Their relevance to educational practice has been hinted at, but not in any substantial way developed. In this section, without labouring arguments which we think are already there in Brecht, we want to consider some of the lessons which can be drawn from a translation of his ideas into an educational context. Or, to put things another way, what is in Brecht's work for Yuksel?

Two points stand out. The first is the way in which working with Brecht's ideas allows a different approach to questions of tradition. Brecht encourages us to think about tradition across national boundaries, in ways which do not depend either upon literary canons or notions of folk culture, but which are alert to the constant transformations of cultural legacies occurring within the process of social and technological change. From a Brechtian perspective, it would be possible to respond to the traditional elements in Yuksel's cultural experience, and also to the ways in which they are mixed, hybridized, with what is new.

Secondly, Brecht alerts us to the difficulties that exist between those whose main social function is the production of texts and those whose main social function is their consumption. To translate his perceptions into an educational context here is an illuminating exercise. They need reformulating, of course: educators are in some sense cultural producers, but they are also bureaucratic functionaries, in a way that most writers are not. Certainly the generation of 'original' texts is not among a teacher's main functions. Likewise learners, positioned as they are by legal compulsion and the need for certification, are very different from theatre audiences. Nevertheless, Brecht's work draws attention to what is often overlooked, not least in National Curriculum English – namely, the extent of variation in audience response to an authoritative text, which can range from pleasure to boredom, indifference to critical stimulation. Securing a productive relationship between curriculum and learner demands sensitivity to these reactions, and to the social interests from which they spring.

A Brechtian viewpoint implies, then, an alertness to overall social and cultural patterns and to the ways in which they affect the experience of learners; to the innovations such alertness promotes in content and in pedagogy. And, one should add, the purpose of such a project is clear – to develop the kind of knowledge of the world which allows a sense of its transformability, and to develop the skills which enable people to participate in such change.

The necessity of this approach is demonstrated every time there is a conflict between the attitudes of learners and the demands of the formal curriculum. Recent work by Roger Hewitt underlines both the scale of the problem here, and the failure of official curricular approaches to deal with it:

> For young people in some schools the presentation of multi-cultural variety can seem strangely alienating. For ethnic minority students the representations of 'their' culture can seem somewhat removed from their daily and family experience. Schools' celebration of diversity approaches can seem like a pageant of some stereotypical ethnicity . . . For some white students, the celebration of cultural variety actually seems to include all cultures but not their own. It is not surprising that white children – especially, it seems, young people from working-class homes – experience themselves as having an invisible culture, even of being cultureless (Hewitt, 1996:40)

No simple notion of culture can grasp the complexities of this situation. As Hewitt suggests, multicultural approaches overlook the 'mixed, hybrid and fragmentary nature of all societies' (Hewitt, 1996:39). Alternatively, Tate offers a version of national culture which does not touch the experience of these white students, 'cultural ghosts' in the richly decorated corridors of multicultural society. Only an approach which accepts the complex cultures of learners as its starting point is likely to engage them in any useful way.

English as it is presently formulated allows only some small and tenuous footholds for an educational approach based on these insights: its (restricted) licensing of media studies allows some space to rethinking the text–audience relationship. Likewise, the space allowed to texts from cultures other than England's offers room for a partial internationalization of the English curriculum. But, as we argued in the first section of this chapter, these are not the areas in which the main emphases of the present curriculum lie. To re-weight the curriculum by drawing from a reading of Brecht requires an approach based less on taking advantage of such limited opportunities as presently exist – though such work does need to be done – than on redesigning the whole curriculum, and on rethinking its institutional context.

These latter changes are difficult, and we will discuss them first. Both the Conservatives and now New Labour are committed to strong forms of selection, between or within schools. These commitments involve an implicit rejection of the idea that learning involves significant cultural interaction. To put it more simply: the immense contribution that Yuksel offers to any group of learners who are discussing cultural change, or questions of history and memory, would not be available in a selective system. As a learner of English at a fairly early stage of her development, Yuksel would be confined to the lower sets, or to a withdrawal group. The consequences for her own learning, and for the learning of other students who might otherwise interact with her, should be plain. Rethinking English in ways that would overcome this mutual exclusion involves institutional change: in one bold phrase, no selection.

Other changes are also required (Jones, 1996). Cultural and economic change matter for English. The growth of knowledge-based industries, the commercial and cultural importance of electronic media, the globalization of culture and the emergence of multi-modal forms of communication are transforming what Gunther Kress calls the 'semiotic landscape' of people's lives (Kress, 1995). These changes must be reflected in curricular redesign, and also in the way in which we think about learners. As most English teachers would agree, learners bring with them to school certain cultural resources, which teachers have often designated by the term 'experience'. The nature of this resource is changing: 'experience' is not what it was. Youth cultures are lived out in a polycultural society, greatly marked by cultural divisions and the break-up of old occupational patterns. They have a complex relationship with commercial cultural forms and are thoroughly enmeshed in new technologies of communication. Schools, though, operate in ways which overlook most of the cultural resources to which students now have access. While students evolve cultures in which visual, musical and bodily elements are strongly present, the English curriculum is shy of contact with the popular and the non-verbal. Consequently, it overlooks what could be called the cultural agency of students: their ability to make, out of the resources they encounter, new meanings and new systems of representation. By inattentiveness to cultural change the curriculum encourages the underestimation of students' cultural capacities. To explore these areas of change, in which global processes encounter the development of individual subjectivities, is to move a long way from the terms of contemporary policy debate. Yet to do so is to establish a position from which a productive return to discussion about policy is possible.

First, the global-subjective encounter imposes an insistent stress on what is culturally new – its scale, pace of development, its deep effects on the way we think and communicate – which can counteract the nostalgia which influenced the presentation of English during the 1990s. Second, an emphasis on popular culture in its many forms can contribute to arguments for an inclusive curriculum: English as presently designed brings together a non-inclusive curriculum with an assessment system that has clear, segregating effects. Drawing attention to the involvement of learners – all learners – in complex cultural activity is one means of bringing about a change in current arrangements. To emphasize engagement with what learners know, and what they can do, is to move away from the tiering of students on the basis of their degree of comfort with quite narrow cultural forms. Third, to emphasize the uncertainty and complexity of the relationship between cultural change and curriculum design involves reasserting something about the role of teachers. If attentiveness to the relationship between 'form' and 'audience'/'curriculum' and 'learner' becomes the touchstone of productive educational change, then the present stress on teachers as curriculum deliverers will be replaced by a concern for the role of teachers as thinkers, experimenters, curriculum negotiators.

USEFUL WORK

Innovation is not dead; nor have the traditions of English teaching described at the beginning of this article completely lost their dynamism. Yandell's piece demonstrates how new tools can be used to organize the encounter between students and prescribed texts; Yuksel's work shows that a space can still be found for the critical exploration of 'experience'. This chapter concludes with some suggestions for developing such approaches further. To do this, we will cite a few brief examples of recent classroom practice. We do not offer such examples just as 'good ideas' – though they are that, certainly; rather, we want to read them as particular instances of a coherent overall approach, one that relies considerably on the framework we have derived from Brecht.

Our examples are chosen to illustrate a number of issues and approaches. First, they represent work at different key stages of the National Curriculum. Second, each example shows how the elements separated out into the different attainment targets of National Curriculum English – reading, writing, speaking, listening – are in practice all integral and related aspects of classroom activity. Third, in each of the activities we describe, students use both old and new cultural forms and combine them in innovative ways to produce texts and 'learning events'. Finally, we suggest how in these examples the concepts of 'experience', 'cultural change' and 'cultural criticism' operate in practice. Here the immediate experience and social interests of learners are permitted to sit beside, or stand against, familiar and 'official' cultural forms – the recommended texts of the National Curriculum.

Vivi Lachs, an advisory teacher in Hackney, has worked with primary and secondary students to produce a CD-ROM called *Reaching for the Stars* (Hackney Professional Development Centre, 1996). The particular project which caught our attention is *Wartime Women*, devised by a group of 11-year-old girls at De Beauvoir School. Their work is organized around stories taken from the experiences of three women. One is Joan Miller, once a dinner helper at the school, whom they interviewed about her experience as an evacuee; extracts from her account are introduced by and interspersed with the girls' own commentary, and the sound-effects of war. A second strand is the story of the British spy Odette Samson, which is presented through dramatization and through animating an exchange of letters between Odette and her husband. We hear them agonize over Odette's decision to leave their young children and go to war. The third strand is the story of Anne Frank, based on the girls' reading of her diary.

The project is so striking in the way it combines the girls' own voices, their verbal dramatizations of source material, witness accounts, archive photographs, their own drawings and graphic animation: it moves without difficulty between texts of different kinds, and of differing status, from the exam-sanctioned *Diary of Anne Frank* to popular song and autobiography. There is a strong sense of the girls' ease with these combined media – a comfort and competence which raise many questions about the value of a curriculum for English very firmly centred on the written word. This ease gives their production a coherence, vivacity and creativity which is rarely found in commercially produced CD-ROMs. Likewise, the sense of detachment, indifference or boredom which too often accompanies the whole-class reading of a text, or the completion of project work, is entirely absent. Instead there is an engagement with received texts, and a willingness to ask questions of them, to rewrite them in new forms, and to set them alongside the writers' experience of the 1990s. This surge of productivity is combined with a critical attitude: through the girls' choice of topic – women in wartime – and their advocacy of women's active, participatory experience, they raise implicit criticisms of conventional representations of women, which tend to define them as workers on the home front, as spectators, or as people confined to a domestic scene.

The second example we use is taken from a lesson with a class of 15-year-old boys in a London comprehensive. In one sense, it constitutes a conventional classroom activity; viewed from another perspective, it reveals the extent of the cultural resources from which learners draw, and in which any pedagogy worth the name should be interested.

In this instance, the students had spent four weeks working on Arthur Miller's play, *A View from the Bridge,* which is set in New York. The play is a staple of GCSE classrooms; it relates to issues of immigration and immigrant communities, as well as masculinity, family relationships, old and new moral codes. The students had read the play and were now embarking on that familiar activity, the improvised trial scene; the main protagonists were about to be put on the witness stand and subjected to an interrogation, so that the class could examine, weigh and judge the characters' actions and motivations. The boys had spent the previous lesson selecting the main parts and preparing their cases in small groups. The defendant in the scene was to be Marco, a migrant worker from Sicily, accused of stabbing his cousin's husband Eddie Carbone, the play's main character. The witnesses included Marco's brother; his cousin Beatrice (married to Eddie); Catherine, Beatrice's niece and an object of Eddie's tangled affections; and the lawyer Alfieri, a kind of chorus figure. Beside these characters from Miller's play were others of the students' own devising – lawyers, a judge and a jury. The teacher played little part in the process by which these parts were selected and devised: this particular learning event was run by the students.

Perhaps the event was especially tight and orderly because there was an observer present (Anton Franks), taking copious notes and sharpening the students' sense of performance and audience. At any rate, the occasion was impressively theatrical. The lawyers spoke in measured, formal tones, probing with questions, summarizing and evaluating the responses. The witnesses were thoughtful, upset and indignant; the boys playing Beatrice and Catherine wept without embarrassment and without raising a giggle; the jury exchanged whispered comments and earnestly discussed their response to the evidence. The 'play' lasted for over an hour, and as the students left the classroom they were still discussing it.

Teachers set this kind of activity because it is an enjoyable way of consolidating and sharing knowledge of a text and response to it. Learners are encouraged to speculate on themes and issues, and are able to explore character extensively. From the observer's point of view, the lesson achieved these objectives, and in the process satisfied important GCSE criteria; but it also achieved much more. The boys had made their own play to set beside *A View from the Bridge*. This second play was concerned, just as much as Miller's, with realizing in language and action issues involving power, conflict and control. In the dramatized trial, they were considering what it is like to represent one's case and a version of events in the powerful and formal setting of a courtroom. Throughout, the boys were bringing to bear more than their knowledge of the play: they were drawing also from what they knew of courtrooms and legal processes, experiences which were gathered from life and from television and film. The pleasure of the activity lay in the process of exploration – of coming to understand a social order that extended beyond the boundaries of the play itself. This process was not a simple one. The attitudes of many students to the courtroom were affected by their experience within migrant communities and youth sub-cultures – they were not uncritical observers of the legal scene, and did not always accept the frames it offered for understanding and judging the actions of the characters. As their value systems changed, so the language they used shifted from classroom vernacular to court-room formality, and back again.

To say all this is to describe a classroom activity valuable in its own right. From the point of view set out earlier in this article, we want to take matters one stage further: the 'event' produced by the students offers rich material for conscious reflection on issues of power, language and the varying judgements about 'truth' which are produced in different social situations. To enable such reflection seems to us an activity that is both socially and intel-lectually worthwhile. In keeping with Yandell's approach, this activity offers a way of placing learners in powerful positions: it affirms their knowledge and experience, and at the same time asks that they question it, in the process of making sense of and responding to a particular text. It draws from experience, but does not hesitate to cross its boundaries.

Our final example of practice illustrates another approach to the teaching of Shakespeare and offers a foundation from which to approach authoritative texts in the classroom. Rather than focus on a specific learning event, we describe a single element in a framework for teaching, based on approaches developed by Jane Coles (Coles, 1991) and 'tested' with groups of PGCE student teachers. Again, the purpose here is to encounter the text in a way which will draw on learners' knowledge, and this involves making the text familiar and making it strange. Consider, for example, *A Midsummer Night's Dream*, and the characters of Demetrius and Helena. At the start of the play, Helena is infatu-ated with Demetrius but he is unmoved. ('Hence, get thee gone, and follow me no more.') The task set for students was to drama-tize an early scene between them – again, a conventional activity. But, drawing on Coles' Brecht-based approach, the task went one stage further. The students were asked to split the scene into its constituent 'gests' (moments, or incidents) and give each of these moments a title – a caption – which would underline its social point. To attempt such a task is to engage instantly with argu-ments about status, gender and power. This is what Helena says to Demetrius, in Act 2, Scene 1, 203–10:

> I am your spaniel; and, Demetrius,
> The more you beat me, I will fawn on you.
> Use me but as your spaniel, spurn me, strike me,
> Neglect me, lose me; only give me leave,
> Unworthy as I am, to follow you.
> What worser place can I beg in your love, . . .
> Than to be used as you use your dog?

Can a caption be placed under a moment like this 'Helena abasing herself'? Or is Helena merely playing with language? And is Demetrius appalled? Or does he take Helena's metaphor to be nothing out of the ordinary? Answering such questions and trying to find an appropriate caption not only engages learners in an argument about interpreting the play, but also goes beyond the boundaries of the text, and crosses the dividing line between high culture and popular experience. It requires students to draw from their cultural knowledge, in this case of the powerful connotations that surround the word 'dog', and the issues that arise when a word that is usually (in the context of this play) the property of men, is used by a woman.

Approaches of these three kinds demand a lot from teachers – their attentiveness to students' language and cultures, a willingness to read old texts in new ways, a willingness to bring low-status texts into the classroom. In the present climate, these skills are undervalued. We look forward to a time when they are not.

BIBLIOGRAPHY

An earlier version of parts of this chapter appeared in *Changing English*, Vol. 4. No. 1 March 1997.

Barthes, R. (1977) Diderot, Brecht, Eisenstein. *Image-Music-Text*, trans. Heath. London: Fontana.

Blair, T. (1996) A new vision for comprehensive schools. *New Britain: My Vision of a Young Country*. London: 4th Estate.

Brecht, B. (1964) *Brecht on Theatre*, ed. and trans. Willetts. London: Methuen.

Brecht, B. (1965) *The Messingkauf Dialogues*, trans. Willetts. London: Methuen.

Brecht, B. (1976) New ages. *Poems Volume Three*, eds Mannheim and Willetts. London: Methuen.

Brecht, B. (1977) Against Georg Lukacs. In Bloch *et al.* (eds) *Aesthetics and Politics*, trans. Livingstone. London: NLR.

Brecht, B. (1994) *Journals 1934–1955*. London: Methuen.

Brooks, H. F. (ed. 1979; rep. 1989) *The Arden Shakespeare: A Midsummer Night's Dream*. London: Routledge.

Buckingham, D. and Sefton-Green, J. (1994) *Cultural Studies Goes to School*. London: Taylor and Francis.

Coles, J. (1991) Teaching 'Shakespeare'. Unpublished dissertation. Institute of Education, University of London.

Fuegi, J. (1994) *The Life and Lies of Bertolt Brecht*. London: Methuen.

Giddens, A. (1994) *Beyond Left and Right – The Future of Radical Politics*. Cambridge: Polity.

Hewitt, R. (1996) *Routes of Racism: The Social Basis of Racist Action*. Stoke-on-Trent: Trentham.

Hobsbawm, E. (1994) *The Age of Extremes: The Short Twentieth Century 1914–1991*. London: Michael Joseph.

Jones, K. (1996) Rhetorical hope and little faith. *The English and Media Magazine*, 34.

Kress, G. (1995) *Writing the Future: English and the Making of a Culture of Innovation*. Sheffield: NATE.

Labour Party (1995) *Diversity and Excellence*. London: Labour Party.

Lachs, V. (1996) *Reaching for the Stars*. London: Hackney Professional Development Centre.

Luke, A. (1994) Series editor's preface. In Freedman and Medway (eds) *Genre and the New Rhetoric*. London: Taylor and Francis.

McDowall, D. (1989) *The Kurds*. London: Minority Rights Group.

Major, J. (1993) Conservatism in the 1990s: our common purpose. Speech to the Carlton Club, 3 February.

Rosen, H. (1977) Out there, or where the Masons went. In Hoyles (ed.) *The Politics of Literacy*. London: Writers and Readers.

Scruton, R. (1984; 2nd edn) *The Meaning of Conservatism*. London: Macmillan.

Stenhouse, L. (1967) *Culture and Education*. London: Nelson.

Tate, N. (1995) Speech to Shropshire Headteachers Annual Conference. London: SCAA Press Release.

Thomas, P. (1997) GCSE English: planning for 2000. *The English and Media Magazine*, 36:24–6.

Times Educational Supplement (1996) 21 June.

Yandell, J. (1997) Sir Oracle: The Merchant of Venice in the classroom. *Changing English*, 4(1):105–22.

RESOURCES

In recent years, much of the planning of practical work in English has slowly succumbed to official pressures. Nevertheless, some useful work – and forward thinking – carries on.

The English and Media Magazine remains the most accessible and stimulating source of new ideas for the teaching of English. The copious output of the English and Media Centre, 136 Charlton Street, London NW1 1RX is invaluable for planning classroom work. It produces a source booklet on *A View from the Bridge*, from which the trial exercise was taken.

The journal *Changing English*, published from the English Department at the Institute of Education, University of London, 20 Bedford Way, London WC1H 0AL, aims to connect classroom practice to debates about new perspectives in the teaching of English.

Cambridge University Press produces a series called *The Cambridge Schools Shakespeare* under the general editorship of Rex Gibson, which alternates pages of play-text with suggestions for a variety of accessible and practical workshop techniques which open the play to study and interrogation by students.

DRAMA: The Journal of National Drama is a forum for the discussion of a variety of issues to do with drama teaching; it always includes a photocopiable section of resources for classrooms. (*DRAMA*, London Drama, c/o Central School of Speech and Drama, Eton Avenue, London NW3 3HY.)

The magazine *New Internationalist* is a source of accessible articles on issues of globalization as they affect everyday life, including education.

Two Internet sites which contain valuable resources for the teaching of English – and debate about its purposes – are those of the Australian Association for the teaching of English (accessible through the Education Department of Monash University http://www.education.monash.edu.au); and the International Federation for the Teaching of English, whose conference report is published at http://www.nyu.edu/education/teach-learn/ifte).

Some academic writers continue to produce invaluable studies of learners, their experiences and ideas. Two recent, challenging works in this tradition are David Buckingham and Julian Sefton-Green, *Cultural Studies Goes to School* (Taylor and Francis, 1994) and Roger Hewitt, *Routes of Racism: The Social Basis of Racist Action* (Trentham Books, 1996).

CHAPTER 3

Mathematics

Peter Bailey

Learning is a place where paradise can be created. The classroom, with all its limitations, remains a location of possibility. In that field of possibility we have the opportunity to labor for freedom, to demand of ourselves and our comrades, an openness of mind and heart that allows us to face reality even as we collectively imagine ways to move beyond boundaries, to transgress. This is education as the practice of freedom. (bell hooks, 1994:207)

We are living in the golden age of Mathematics and every day brings marvellous new ideas. (Ian Stewart, 1996)

OVERALL PERSPECTIVES

Why teach mathematics?

Within the National Curriculum, mathematics is a core subject which gets a larger share of time on schools' timetables than many other subjects. Teachers of mathematics should be clear about the central purposes of teaching mathematics.

In the wider world, mathematics is used in commerce, industry, government, in research and at home. There are few who use mathematics for pleasure, despite the large number of puzzle books and games on sale at newsagents; it is mainly used to control, to organize and to plan. Mathematics is therefore, in part, a tool for creating and distributing wealth in society.

Mathematics is also used to describe the world. People need a grasp of figures to get to grips with matters of concern such as the environment and unemployment. Without an understanding of figures, voters in a modern society are unable to make a considered choice, and would fall prey to distorted statistics. Indeed the situation in Britain is so bad that several years ago a powerful group within the Mathematical Association set up the Maths Roadshow which toured several British cities attempting to raise the profile of numeracy and wider mathematics. D'Ambrosia (1990) argues that mathematics is becoming the 'primal discipline in the variety of intellectual tools that characterize the modern world, and the most central among all the disciplines in all the school systems which sustain, in every modern society, the current style of life'.

Mathematics education should prepare students for full citizenship. D'Ambrosia argues that mathematics too often is used to filter out losers and failures rather than to give each individual the satisfaction of their own creativity.

The revised (1995) Mathematics National Curriculum does not give reasons why students should learn mathematics, although the document does say they should be taught to use and apply mathematics in practical tasks, in real-life problems and within mathematics itself. Until pressed to consider it, many teachers of the subject would probably think that the mathematics curriculum has been devised to teach pure mathematics, with a nod in the direction of simple real-life problems, especially for those who find the subject difficult. The GCSE examination system has included more real-life contexts than the previous O-level papers, but many questions in GCSE still remain abstract.

In 1989, Ernest suggested three aims for the teaching of mathematics: the utilitarian aim (acquisition of utilitarian mathematical skills); the personal development aim (concerned with the growth and development of the whole individual); and the mathematical aim (transmitting mathematical knowledge and academic discipline to students).

Those interested enough to consider the purposes in teaching mathematics will select different proportions of these aims to suit their view of society. The National Curriculum very much focuses on the third aim, transmitting knowledge. Students receive a fixed body of mathematical knowledge prescribed by the government with external tests and assessment at ages 7, 11, 14 and 16. Socialists are more concerned with the development of talents and skills in all young people, putting the second aim as a priority. We wish to empower students, who will lead active lives, using and enjoying mathematics for the benefit of all. Students are not pots into which teachers pour skills at the behest of government and industry. Good mathematics education will enable young people to build their own confidence and ability to understand the world, and to use mathematics to define and to build their own and the wider society.

Secondary mathematics teachers work hard at achieving the best examination results at 16+, particularly for students at the higher levels. With the public emphasis on higher GCSE grades, they have not been so ready to be accountable for students getting lower grades or for those not entered for the examinations at all. Early leavers have mostly had a raw deal. In coming to judgements about a mathematics department's performance, not only examination results should be taken into account, but also the performance of those students who have dropped out of school, those who have not taken public exams, the future career patterns of students, and the ability of the students to use their mathematics to understand and play an active part in the world.

The chapters of this book make it clear that all students are entitled to the education which will lead them to develop fully as human beings. The fact that so many adults fear mathematics may reflect very poor teaching in the past. Too many young people are still being put off the subject by inappropriate lessons. Truancy and lack of motivation are still too often part of the mathematics classroom ethos. Students come to the classroom with different skills, knowledge, interests and plans for their future. In the past, the mathematics department's scheme of work consisted of a series of chapter numbers which teachers followed, often with little regard for the students in their classes. In order for all students in the class to be involved in their mathematics, teachers should now plan approaches to topics which engage the interest and energies of all the young people in their lessons.

Numeracy is a key skill which is vital to full participation in the modern world. Access to college courses and professions often depend on a qualification in mathematics, and a lack of confidence in basic numeracy will discourage young adults from further training. Not all young people leave school with these necessary skills and knowledge.

The report of the National Commission on Education (1993:8)

states that there has been little change over the years in the proportion of entrants to higher education who come from working-class families. Later in the report is the view that England's top-ability students at age 17+ are among the highest scorers in mathematics, and this country's below-average students do less well than students in many other 'developed' countries. The report states that 'at secondary school level the design of the curriculum has been dominated by the needs of the minority who are being prepared for further study at an intensive level' (1993:7). An Adult Literacy and Basic Skills Unit (ALBSU) survey (1993) shows that a substantial number of 21-year-olds have serious problems in reading, writing, spelling and basic mathematics. Many more seem to perform at a lower level than is required by the demands of everyday life and work in this country (ALBSU, 1993). This lack of numeracy should be a matter of great concern to all mathematics teachers; but too often the main aim of mathematics departments is to focus on GCSE results and not on numeracy. Teachers might argue that to concentrate on numeracy is to deny students opportunities to understand mathematics. Here is a conflict of aims. Should teachers be more concerned about the teaching of academic mathematics than the development of utilitarian skills? The role of mathematics teachers must be to empower their students with the knowledge and skills which they need to play a full part in our modern world. They need mathematics to interpret the nature of society with its social divisions and greed, to understand when politicians and businessmen and women are lying, to debate important matters at and between elections, and to be able to challenge inequities. Socialists will not wish merely to give their students the numeracy knowledge and skills to participate in the capitalist economy which the Radical Right, the industrial trainers, would wish us to do. They will also wish to develop in their students the power to use mathematical skills in order to be critical of the system as it is now, so that they can work for a world of greater equality.

Teachers concerned with the individual will provide a variety of learning opportunities which will motivate, engage and develop the many different individuals in the class. The planning for these lessons must take into account the needs of all students in the class. The course planning should also introduce each student to the many different applications of mathematics which are used to describe and develop society. Teachers must provide opportunities for the students to raise their knowledge and skills in these applications.

Dimensions of Discipline (DFE, 1993) talks of building students' engagement in lessons. How can mathematics teachers really engage the 25 to 30 young people in their class? Is it possible to motivate and interest the truant, the quiet, the street-wise, the noisy, those who like to be told what to do and those who prefer to do what they like?

Howard Gardner (1983) raises the idea of 'multiple intelligences'. The notion of each person having one fixed 'intelligence' is rapidly changing to ideas of variety in people's ability to think and learn. In addition there is the understanding that individuals can and do change. No longer can we label a student permanently slow. Professor Gardner regards himself as 'part of a small but growing movement that places students' individual interests and strengths centrally in the education equation', and points to evidence that schools adopting this principle are 'on any criteria you look at . . . doing a better job' (TES, 1995:24). (Gardner's ideas are more fully explained in his book *The Unschooled Mind*, 1993.)

Teachers will have students who may be partially sighted and hard of hearing; others will have family problems. Some will be keen to develop arithmetic skills; others may have artistic tendencies. Some may be concerned about the environment, others about racism. There may be some with problems in manipulation of rulers and compasses. Some will beg for more work while others may do exactly what the teacher asks and no more; others will do less! The class, gender, sexuality, racial, cultural and disability aspects of life will be reflected in the students of our classrooms. All these students are entitled to appropriate mathematical learning opportunities.

There must be three main thrusts in planning a mathematics curriculum which will develop the entitlements of all the students in the class: the approach to content, variety of teaching style, and motivating assessment. But these three can only be successfully delivered if the teacher really knows the students, their culture, history, and likes and dislikes. The best teachers will be aware of the students' families and their aspirations. They will know the skills and aptitudes which each student brings to the learning in the classroom.

The mathematics National Curriculum

There has been criticism of the concept of a single National Curriculum for all. Foster and Tall (1996) write that the present National Curriculum is a ladder which 'demands too much of the less successful so that they reach various plateaux where their cognitive structure is no longer able to cope with the increasing complexity, yet fails to support the mathematically able' (1996). Whereas Foster and Tall remark that university mathematicians and schoolteachers may be focusing on different forms of mathematical need, Pyke (1996) wrote an article in the *Times Educational Supplement* asking 'Who owns maths A-level?' There are accusations that the universities have hijacked the syllabus for their own traditionalist ends to the detriment of business and industry! The project leader for the Mathematics in Education and Industry Project said: 'Underlying this is a debate about who owns school Mathematics: the university maths departments . . . or . . . the users of maths A-level as a whole'. While university lecturers on the one hand, and those teaching for business and industry on the other hand, argue about A-level mathematics, who is arguing for the less academically gifted students who leave school at 16? Jaggar (1996) argues for two GCSEs in mathematics: one for life skills and the other as a foundation for developing logical thought. She writes that society seems to be demanding two distinct aims for 16+ students – to develop numeracy and special awareness, and to teach mathematics as a subject in its own right. Our National Curriculum, with its single ladder of levels, cannot provide what is required to give every student an appropriate mathematical education.

Before the revised National Curriculum came into place there was considerable discussion on the first Attainment Target 1 (AT1): 'Using and Applying Mathematics'. Right-wingers who were more concerned with the third of Ernest's aims (the transmission of mathematical knowledge) urged the Schools Curriculum and Assessment Authority (SCAA) to abandon AT1. Teachers who are on the political Left and who are concerned with both the utilitarian and the personal development aims will be pleased that AT1 is still to be taught. It is now the duty of teachers to include opportunities for students to develop skills in applying mathematics to practical tasks and to real-life problems. Admittedly it is not easy to put these aims fully into practice in secondary classes, and many have avoided these links between classroom mathematics and life outside school. Much of the exemplar material for mathematics coursework tasks provided by examining groups has focused on abstract mathematical investigations rather than real-life problems (for example, the exemplar material for Northern Examinations and Assessment Board Syllabus A, published in Spring 1996, contains no real-life mathematics at all). It is sometimes easier to teach what can more easily be assessed. Teachers wishing to provide opportunities within AT1 for their students to develop skills in using mathematics in the wider world have to keep the assessment criteria much in mind.

Cultural diversity has never been a feature of the mathematics curricula provided by the government. The 1985 Department for Education considered that a multicultural approach to mathematics could confuse young people and could be considered patronizing. Many teachers now agree with the thinking expressed in the Swann Report *Education for All* (HMSO, 1985). They will build into mathematics lessons opportunities for students to understand the contributions of many cultures to the development of mathematics (for examples at primary level, see Shan, 1997). They will also seek to use and build upon students' own cultural heritage(s). Further, students should have opportunities to develop their own interests and ideas during mathematics lessons. Bishop (1988) and Joseph (1990) show how mathematics has been developed through differing cultures. The Swann Report itself has been criticized for a failure to address racism in education and to promote anti-racist strategies. Teachers concerned with social justice will develop students' awareness of cultural issues by including classroom contexts concerned with 'race' and culture in exercises and projects. Shan and Bailey (1991) develop ideas on culture, equality and justice within the classroom and through mathematics itself.

Further criticisms on the concept of a single mathematics National Curriculum are given in Dowling and Noss (1990).

Learning strategies

There are many problems in mathematics education which teachers concerned with equity issues have to face. The pressure caused by league tables of assessment results for all students at the ages of 14 and 16 is encouraging teachers to spend more time on practising for the examinations, and less time on practical work which could lead to deeper understanding. There is now a 'no calculator' paper in the tests at Key Stages 3 and 4 which will mean more time on basic arithmetic. Many teachers are choosing to assess Attainment Target 1 ('Using and Applying Maths') during formal GCSE examinations rather than in coursework, thereby limiting students' experience of applying mathematics in their 'real' worlds.

Recently there has been much discussion on the performance of boys and of some Asian, black and other minority ethnic students (see, for example, Young, 1996). Other reports consider an 'underclass' of 100,000 young people being marginalized from society by exclusion from school (and, effectively, from the education system). Often these young people feel they are failures in mathematics, as in other subjects. They have been let down by their teachers and by the schools. There are many outside pressures which these young people bring into schools each day, yet it is very sad that, after several years in mathematics lessons, they feel so bad about their mathematical abilities. The students in slower mathematics groups should not receive a boring diet of arithmetic and vocationally orientated skills, but an interesting mix of practical mathematics solving real problems combined with practice in developing arithmetic skills.

In 1981, John Head reported that undergraduate mathematics students were by far the most 'syllabus-bound' and least questioning of all undergraduates. Those that did well in the subject tended to be conformist and obedient in school (Head, 1981). It would be interesting to find out if this is still true. Perhaps mathematics teachers have adapted less than those in other curriculum areas to more modern approaches aimed at capturing the imaginations of our students.

Many students suffer a lack of real understanding, and make very slow progress. For some, motivation is low. Without an enthusiasm for learning, there will be little mathematical development. For city students, this challenges many teachers from the middle class as we often choose to live away from the city area and do not share the pressures of urban life. Neither do we speak a 'second' language and understand the interests and aspirations of the many cultures present in our classes. In 1987 Moll and Diaz wrote that under-performance in students' attainment in mathematics can be attributed increasingly to institutional failure rather than to the cultural limitations of working-class people, of women, of students with a first language other than English, or of students who have particular needs.

There is, however, one encouraging point which simplifies our work. Research indicates that all children, no matter what their cultural background, learn mathematics in similar ways (see Carey *et al.*, 1995). There are 'universal' similarities in how children learn mathematics, similarities which cut across cultures, although this does not mean a single curriculum and teaching style for all, because students start from different situations and have different aspirations:

> Building a mathematics programme that enables each child to construct connections between his or her own informal knowledge and new knowledge requires that several things be taken into consideration: the background culture of the child, so that the context in which mathematics is embedded is meaningful to the child; the kind of mathematical problems the child is able to solve informally so that he or she can see relationships between out-of-school knowledge and in-school requirements; and the tools the child intuitively uses to solve problems, such as fingers or other counters. Thus, the culture of each child is used to structure the learning environment so that he or she is able to construct relationships and learn mathematics with understanding. (Carey *et al.*, 1995:90)

The last major government report into the teaching of mathematics, *Mathematics Counts* (HMSO, 1982) seemed forward-looking at the time, with the famous paragraph 243 (1982:71). In a section on teaching methods, this paragraph advocated a variety of classroom practice: exposition by the teacher, discussion, practical work, consolidation and practice, problem-solving (including application to everyday situations) and investigation work. GCSE syllabuses and the first Mathematics National Curriculum built on some of these ideas, although many teachers were slow to build them into their classroom strategies.

In the United States, a report titled *Everybody Counts* was produced by the National Research Council (1989). In a major section on learning through involvement, the report urges:

Teachers' roles should include those of consultant, moderator and interlocutor, not just presenter and authority. Classroom activities must encourage students to express their approaches, both orally and in writing. Students must engage Mathematics as a human activity; they must learn to work cooperatively in small teams to solve problems as well as to argue convincingly for their approach amid conflicting ideas and strategies.

There is the further observation:

> Myth: Students learn by remembering what they are taught. Reality: Students construct meaning as they learn Mathematics. They use what they are taught to modify their prior beliefs and behaviour, not simply to record and store what they are told. It is students' acts of construction and invention that build their mathematical power and enable them to solve problems they have never seen before. (1989:61)

Mathematics is a major tool in the rapid development of technology, capitalism and globalization. Bishop (1988) suggests an acceptance by many educators of a mathematico-technological (MT) culture which embraces a universal applicable mathematics working hand-in-hand with the growth of applicable technology. This is challenged by many, including Gerdes, Fasheh and Nebres. It is only fairly recently that the arguments against the idea of value-free mathematics has been presented. For example, Bishop (1993) states: 'The established social order within any society has a vested interest in controlling mobility within that society, and academic educational control (of mathematics) is an increasingly powerful vehicle for achieving this' (1993).

Suggesting a possible gap between the culture of the mathematics classroom in some schools (largely accepting the MT values and ideas) and the students, who may have other values and ways of thinking, Bishop states: 'It seems reasonable to conjecture that mathematics learners whose immediate home cultures relate more closely to the structure and character of the school culture will have less difficulty in reconciling the messages coming from the two cultures, than will learners whose home cultures are a long way from their school culture' (1993:23).

Bishop builds on the work of Coombs (1985) in suggesting formal mathematics education (FME), informal mathematics education (IFME) which covers any organized systematic educational activity outside the framework of the formal system, and non-formal mathematics education (NFME) which is the lifelong process by which every person acquires and accumulates knowledge and skills, attitudes and insight. He suggests that the most important prior knowledge may have been learned by students *outside* the school context, and will therefore be embedded in a totally different social structure. He writes that those of us who work in mathematics education need to be more aware than we have been of developments in students' NFME and IFME.

In 'The socio-cultural context of mathematical thinking' (1993), T. Nunes contrasts the mathematics which some young people have learned through out-of-school activity with the mathematics of school. The examples show how the out-of-school mathematics often requires modelling, the need to retain the real-life context, and imprecision, whereas school mathematics can be a process of manipulating numbers, often unrelated to students' understandings. Nunes writes that people using oral methods in real-life situations retain the context to the problem, whereas often students in classrooms see a separation between the problem and the mathematics. She also observes that Higino (1987) was able to show that connecting everyday experiences with classroom learning of addition and subtraction produces better results than teaching without regard for children's previous knowledge (Nunes, 1993).

More recently, OfSTED (1995) has produced a review of recent research into mathematics education. This important document raises several issues, which include the mathematical 'ethos' in school, the need to move on from using simple (i.e. fingers) techniques to remembering number bonds, and the difficulties many face in moving from practical work to more formal mathematics. Further, learning is more effective when students are given opportunity to raise and discuss issues which may need correcting, and to work on a wide range of problem-solving situations which will require general skills and specific knowledge. The culture of the classroom, the mathematical concepts and activity all need to be integrated, with activity arising from work rather than being imposed. There needs to be an emphasis on *ill-defined tasks* carried out in a social setting, probably with group work and with several possible solutions and methods. These tasks reflect the reality of life, rather than the traditional problems with neat and unreal solutions; they encourage discussion so that students build ideas into their construct; and they allow opportunities for students to relate more closely to the contexts than to the problems.

At the heart of these ideas is a focus on the learning opportunities for each student. The notion is of a classroom where students support each other, where they are actively engaged in tasks which have developed from previous work. For all attainment levels, students develop strategies in mathematical thinking to assist in solving problems as well as the required knowledge. Silver, Smith and Nelson (1995) write:

> In such communities, students would be expected not only to listen but also to speak mathematics themselves, as they discuss observations and share explanations, verifications, reasons and generalisations. In such classrooms students would have opportunities to see, hear, debate, and evaluate mathematical explanations and justifications. (1995:31)

For a steady development of mathematics, the teacher must know each student well. The teacher will also know how children learn and what difficulties children face as they get to grips with their mathematics. For better motivation and for the transference of understanding from inside the classroom to outside, the problems should arise from previous discussion, be interpreted by the students and be real. Students should be willing to engage in problem-solving and take responsibility for learning. This approach will mean that textbooks are not the main resource for learning, though they will still have many uses. Ladson-Billings (1995) gives an example of teaching by 'Mrs Rossi', who motivates, stimulates and provides all her students with learning by problem-solving. Students are all involved, in groups. She encourages and provides questions which assist in students' thinking. The point is that lessons such as these show how students who are treated as competent are likely to demonstrate competence, and how providing instructional scaffolding for students allows them to move from what they know to what they do not know. Also, the major focus of the classroom is instructional, and effective pedagogical practice requires in-depth knowledge of students as well as subject matter. Creativity is important in mathematical thinking and is sadly lacking in many classrooms. Higgins (1993) discusses some sad consequences of the deprivation of creativity in the classroom, indicating that it is one of the many reasons why children fail to develop as well as they could.

Stemming from these ideas are real issues of equality for mathematics classrooms. If students in poor cities, small towns and rural areas are to work together supportively on problems from their experiences, then their mathematics teachers will not be transmitting dilute versions of middle-class mathematics, but engaging in activities which stem from the neighbourhood of the school, to empower the students both in mathematical learning and also in the confidence to fulfil ambitions. Gender and sexuality issues will emerge from such problems, while the importance of providing for all students in the class, able-bodied or otherwise, will be self-evident.

Changing the system?

There have been criticisms of ideas such as the above in the US, not because the ideas are flawed, but because there are dangers that equality issues will still not be addressed. Neither the National Council of Teachers in the US nor the OfSTED document in the UK has indicated how the new ideas should be used to address inequality. Unless consideration is given to helping to provide their entitlement to all students, what is likely to happen is that teachers will find it easier to assist bright academic students along these lines, leaving others missing precious opportunities.

In other chapters of this book and elsewhere (e.g. Cole *et al.*, 1997) it is argued that the present education arrangements support the elite, the class system and inequity, and that, in Britain, the Conservative governments of 1979 to 1997 showed little real concern for equity – as indeed do New Labour's strategies (see the Introduction to this book, also to Cole *et al.*, 1997). In Britain the examination focus on the success of the higher GCSE grade students, combined with the lack of official validation for low-attaining students, marks one aspect of a biased system. Education as a whole will merely reproduce existing prejudices unless there are active steps taken by everyone to ensure it does not. Many believe that in order to really give their entitlement to all students, big changes in the schooling system are needed. See *Changing the Future: Redprint for Education* (Hillcole Group/ Chitty (ed.), 1991) and *Rethinking Education and Democracy: a Socialist Alternative for the Twenty-first Century* (Hillcole Group, 1997).

Teachers of mathematics must be clear about how children

learn their maths. The debate over the transmission and the constructivist ways of learning has yet to reach classroom teachers fully. Yet this matter is vitally important when considering equal access to mathematics.

Davis (1994) argues that traditionalists place great emphasis on the basics of number, and the idea that mathematics is 'out there, independent of us' and to be taught. But he supports Ernest (1991) in that 'objective knowledge of mathematics is social, and is not contained in texts or other recorded materials, nor in some ideal realm. Objective knowledge of mathematics resides in the shared rules, conventions, understandings and meanings of the individual members of society, and in their interactions (and consequently, their social institutions)'.

Davis writes that a child digesting mathematics will need gradually to acquire ownership of complex networks of concepts, symbols and terms. But already in the child's mind are emergent and maybe erroneous complexes of mathematical concepts. In an example, Davis describes how a child's maths 'will have much in common with that of her friends, but it is also likely to be individual and idiosyncratic to some degree'. So teachers need to search for activities which seem likely to enhance the 'interconnectedness of learners' knowledge; and to facilitate the development within each child of their personal and idiosyncratic networks of concepts'. Explanation and exposition have their place, yet we also 'need to consider listening, discussing, questioning, hypothesizing, inviting students to hypothesize or speculate, demonstrating, acting as a reference book, refusing to answer, joining in children's play and many other forms of behaviour'.

Nunes (1993) shows that Brazilian children with little or no formal education can invent their own methods of carrying out calculations. These mental calculations make sense to the child. The young street-vendors who had some schooling were far more successful with their street mathematics than they were in attempting to solve the same problems using school maths. Sometimes, children keep the meaning of the problem in mind when using oral mathematics, but disregard the meaning when using written arithmetic to find the solution (1993:306). Children come to teachers with their own constructions. A major reason why many children fail to achieve lasting learning and confidence in their mathematics is that the knowledge was never comprehensively grasped when taught. Transmission learning often achieves limited success. In the last resort knowledge has to be constructed by each individual learner if it is to be an integrated part of the knowledge held by the individual. As Noddings (1990) argues, 'in order to teach well, we need to know what our students are thinking, how they produce the chain of little marks we see on their papers, and what they can do (or want to do) with the material we present to them' (1990:15). Teachers concerned with equalizing opportunities need to understand how their students are learning their mathematics, and provide appropriate learning experiences for them.

Freire (1972) argues for a rejection of a 'banking concept' of schooling, and for acceptance of 'problem-solving' education, in which students and teachers 'become jointly responsible for a process in which they all grow' (1972:53). Not only will teachers need to understand the skills that poor street vendors have, but they will work side by side with the oppressed in pursuit of full humanity and in a spirit of fellowship and solidarity.

On issues of gender and the learning of mathematics, much has been written. A wide-ranging account of concerns can be found in *Girls into Maths Can Go* (Burton, 1986), while the recent publication *Women in the History of Mathematics* (Rothman, 1996) provides details of the lives and works of nine female mathematicians. Reports by the Monitoring Sub Committee of the Mathematical Association show that the lack of concern for gender issues by the 1989 GCSE Mathematics examiners has been changed by the provision of a better gender balance in recent years. Girls' examination results in mathematics have been steadily improving, despite a lack of discussion on sexism/gender issues in classrooms.

The improvement in girls' results, as against those of boys, takes place in a time during which National Curriculum mathematics, GCSE papers and league tables of school test/exam results have been consolidated. Little thought has been given to gender-related curriculum issues. The competitive élite male-dominated abstract ethos which has alienated so many students must be replaced by a mathematics which is owned by the individual, giving confidence and enabling that person to play a full part in society. For example, Becker (1995) mentions women's ways of knowing. She gives examples of 'connected teaching' using voice, first-hand experience, confirmation of self as knower, problem-posing, believing versus doubting, support versus challenge and structure versus freedom. On another front, the gap between the vocational and academic must fall as the new consensus emerges: all students must have opportunity for mathematical approaches to problems rather than a stifling narrow arithmetic which some now face. Lessons must be co-operative, with opportunities for all to learn in classes which challenge oppression, the class system and the structural divisions currently in society. The attitudes of many teachers, both male and female, must change to allow boys and girls to work constructively together. There must be publicly funded research on which aspects of education hold some students back, whether boys or girls, and on how teachers can develop their skills and knowledge further, to allow all to participate.

There must be national and local concern for the effectiveness of the teaching of mathematics. The present narrow view of success in written tests must be replaced by a wider vision in which there are many different ways to succeed. Support systems to enable some in society to succeed need to be funded rather than reduced. It has been recognized that present funding is not just. OfSTED (1995) recognizes that without intervention, students in richer schools could benefit from the computer revolution while others cannot.

> Students in economically disadvantaged areas, those from ethnic minorities, and females have less access to computers both at home and at school. Unless these issues of access are resolved, computers, despite their significant potential for remedying inequality, may serve only to reinforce it. (1995:35)

So greater resourcing must be channelled into the mathematics classrooms with students who are currently underachieving. This, of course, extends a wider challenge to the structure of schooling.

SUCCESS FOR ALL

In this section, practical issues concerning the different aspects of equality are raised. Relating mathematics to cultures and to the real world provides opportunities for some class and cultural issues to be addressed. Special needs and disability issues (for many students in mainstream classes as well as those in special schools) are considered. Many cultural and class issues concern language and mathematics. Using mathematical problems as a way of both using mathematics and understanding the world raises many ideas about inequality and injustice as well as gender and cultural matters. Finally a section on assessment mentions issues of inequality in testing and examining.

Interesting and motivating all teenagers in mathematics will require more than good textbooks and the single ladder of a sequential national curriculum. Accepting responsibility for the failure of some young people (including those truanting and others who are excluded) and engaging them in mathematical learning is a start. Problems arising out of personal experience can develop mathematical skills and knowledge if handled well by the teacher. Using textbook problems is not sufficient; but neither, it seems, are 'relevant' problems written by the teacher. Boaler (1993) points out difficulties with contexts, and subsequently mentions (Boaler, 1994) the possibility of female underachievement when particular contexts are used. She states:

> Links between school mathematics and the real world will not be demonstrated by perfectly-phrased questions involving buses and cans of paint. These misleadingly suggest that similar problems with a comparative simplicity exist in the real world, rather than arising out of the learner's interaction with the environment. If the student's social and cultural values are encouraged and supported in the mathematics classroom, through the use of contexts or through an acknowledgement of personal routes and directions, then their learning will have more meaning for them. (1994:17)

This research pinpoints a problem for traditionalist mathematics teachers: more often than not, problems in the real world do not work out simply. Simple interest is not used – compound interest is. So is it not dangerous teaching simple interest?

Consider this question:

A 200 gm jar of coffee costs £2.92. A 100 gm jar of the same coffee costs £1.98. Which is the best buy?

Using ratio, the best buy is the large jar. But some reasons for buying the smaller jar include 'My family is collecting the 100 gm jars', 'The small jars fit under the shelf', 'I like the smell when I open a new jar of coffee and I'll choose the small jars every time' or simply, 'We cannot afford the large jar'.

Teachers have to allow time for a discussion of the context to a problem, allowing the mathematics to be drawn out by the students themselves. And some lessons have to encourage students to bring problems for solution. Perhaps the mathematics department can run the school breaktime shop, with students doing the books and ordering. The end-of-year outings could similarly be a mathematical exercise for students. Time must be allowed for project work, developing AT1, linking with social issues in Personal and Social Education, and creative subjects such as art. Imaginative teachers will have the confidence to give students rein and see what problems of their own they can solve.

There seem to be social class issues here as well. Research in Scotland by Brown *et al.* (1996) showed that students in predominantly working-class secondary schools appear to be given many more time-consuming reading and writing tasks than children in middle-class schools, and have less opportunity for classroom discussion. It is these children in particular who need opportunity for discussion, for using the mathematical vocabulary and for working mathematical concepts into their understanding of life. The researchers felt that teachers were using the time-consuming tasks in a desire to maintain control of the students in the classroom. They also felt that teachers did not think the students could really manage to discuss things among themselves. These researchers feel that social class has recently been pushed off the research agenda by school effectiveness issues, but that it still needs investigation.

There are many gender matters concerning young men and women and their mathematics. These raise concerns about teacher/student interaction in the classroom, assessment, differences in attainment in various aspects of mathematics, and point to a humanizing and co-operative approach to learning and to the contexts of problems. Despite girls' achievement levels closing on and sometimes surpassing those of boys, there are still many issues yet to be resolved. These include the 'maleness' of present mathematics (coming from mostly male academics rather than from both women and men in wider society) and the progression of girls from school to higher mathematics courses and into professions.

Mathematics teachers should understand and relate to cultures within the school area, such as Irish, Bengali, working and middle classes, rural and city lives. Issues include the logic systems used in different cultures and languages, difficulties with words (see below), monocultural textbooks and examination papers, contexts to mathematical situations and setting arrangements. Again:

> Unless the Mathematics curriculum includes real contexts that reflect the lived realities of people who are members of equity groups and unless those contexts are rich in the sorts of mathematics which can be drawn from them, we are likely to stereotype Mathematics as knowledge that belongs to a few privileged groups. (Secada, 1991:49)

Parents and students expect schools to challenge the racist values within and outside the education system. The mathematics classroom can and should play a full part in this. For a full discussion on multicultural and anti-racist mathematics see Shan and Bailey (1991).

Some students come to school with particular special needs and difficulties. The Code of Practice is designed to support those having particular needs. Its emphasis in providing entitlement should encourage mathematics teachers to try to provide real learning opportunities.

Teachers of students with physical disabilities may need specialist advice in providing equipment which best provides for the learning of mathematics. Discussion with the students themselves, their parents and support staff may lead to physical support and advice which assists. This might include a laptop computer, a large calculator or special geometry equipment. As in other curriculum areas, mathematics teachers need to seek advice and respond to advice from the colleague in charge of special needs.

In many classes there are students with other disabilities which impair the students' learning of mathematics. Too often, the diet of mathematics lessons for students who seem to be making little progress is restricted. Problems are simplified and cut into small sections so that students rarely get their teeth into anything interesting.

> Students who have even the most acute deficiencies in basic skills need to experience the intellectual excitement of higher-order

thought processes. Instructional time devoted to basic skills deficiencies should never pre-empt the opportunity of students to explore the cutting edges of thought and feelings embedded in the subject matter of the core curriculum. (California State Department of Education, 1987:67)

Recognizing individual difficulties, teachers should provide every student with rich, thoughtful and creative learning experiences. They must be aware of their students' needs and skills levels. For many students with physical and learning difficulties, we must not spend all our time trying to correct deficiencies but to developing skills and talents, say Mason and Rieser (1994). Mathematics teachers will find the journal *Equals – Mathematics and Special Needs* (published by the Mathematical Association) very helpful. For example Inglese (1997) describes work she has done in National Curriculum Mathematics with mainstream students with Autistic Spectrum Disorders (ASD).

Language difficulties in learning mathematics may be an added problem for hearing-impaired students. Barham and Bishop (1991) give evidence of mathematics underachievement in hearing-impaired students and suggest that language difficulties contribute to this underachievement. One difficulty might be in distinguishing words such as 'ten' from 'tenths'. Further, they suggest that hearing-impaired students have extra difficulties with logical connectives and sequencing. There is also evidence for a series of problems which may seem to be unrelated to language impairment, such as hyperactive lack of control, preoccupation, aggressiveness and anxiety. Barham and Bishop (1991) give a valuable list of practical points which will assist mathematics teachers in meeting the needs of hearing-impaired students. These include the avoidance of providing a reduced mathematical curriculum whilst recognizing that hearing-impaired young people may need particular skills for survival in the harsh world outside the classroom; also, access to fun and puzzle mathematics, and provision of microcomputers which can offer so much to individual students. Another observation is that developing practical skills will give confidence to hearing-impaired children in unfamiliar situations, especially since mathematics can assist such young people in understanding cause and effect. Finally they suggest that there must be a determined avoidance of acquiring 'learned helplessness' and that 'decision-making activities' can be offered.

Goodstein (1994) also makes eight recommendations on the teaching and learning environment to provide for the learning of mathematics by hearing-impaired young people. In summary, these are:

1. Bilingual/bicultural programmes (involving sign language and English, and cultural approaches) should be employed as far as possible.
2. Before they can develop precise mathematical reasoning in a formal fashion, deaf students must overcome three obstacles: use of sign language, learning and understanding the mathematics concepts and properties involved through visual communication, and reading and writing about these concepts and properties while learning English.
3. Teachers of deaf students must realize that there is more to education than precision in English. Such students need experience in rational thinking, number sense, measurement sense, concepts of fractions, etc. in the development of the students' cognitive schemas.
4. Teachers of deaf students must at least be competent in sign language to ensure that communication barriers are not created.
5. Better courses are required for teachers of deaf students, so they are able to develop mathematical understanding, problem-solving, reasoning, etc.
6. The sooner the deaf child and parents accept the deafness the better.
7. In order to understand story problems fully, visual communication, acting out and co-operation are recommended until the problem is fully understood.
8. Writing journals or logbooks can be helpful in encouraging students to express their mental images of certain mathematical concepts or relations.

Nunes and Moreno (1997) report on evidence that deaf students are on average 3.4 years behind their hearing counterparts in mathematical achievement tests but that, in another study, 15 per cent of the profoundly deaf children scored at or above their chronological age in mathematical ability. For Nunes and Moreno, hearing impairment is a 'risk factor' rather than a cause of difficulties in learning mathematics, and they discuss the development of numerical concepts, and extra challenges for hearing-impaired children who have to use signing and finger counting at the same time. They suggest that carefully designed instruction is likely to have a significant impact on mathematical learning.

Some students have visual impairment which presents them with particular problems. Teachers must find out from parents whether glasses are to be worn for lessons – many young people are reluctant to wear them! Ducker (1993) describes a project for visually impaired students which allowed them to create their own graphs. She describes work on the National Curriculum with Thermoforms and German films. The special school in which she worked uses the SMP scheme, and two students, aged 14 and 15, were expecting to sit the intermediate GCSE Mathematics examination.

Pepper (1997) gives details of some mathematical games for use by visually impaired children with talking calculators, the SMILE game 'Junior Counting' with dice, and games by Anita Straker (1996).

Another difficulty which some students face is dyslexia. Short-term memory can give added problems in subtraction (with 'carrying') and in learning multiplication tables. There may be difficulties in expressing mathematical ideas in written form. Some practical guidance for mathematics teachers of dyslexic students is given in Thomson (1991), of which the following is a summary:

- The need for a fully structured teaching programme for these dyslexic students, crucially starting with the basics and building slowly to more complex concepts.
- Realistic expectations and avoidance of 'over-learning'. A variety of ways in presenting material is required to avoid boredom.
- An integrated approach to teaching tables (advice on these approaches is given in Thomson).
- Providing success in areas of strengths.
- Circumventing difficulties by 'concretizing' problems using materials and by relating problems with money.
- Rewarding correct responses.
- Undertaking small sequential steps and recognizing that there are many routes to the same objective.

Other causes of failure in schools are discussed in *How and*

Why Children Fail (Varma, 1993). This author does not write solely about teaching maths, but teachers of mathematics need to understand many of the causes of failure if they are to provide experiences which help young students. The book considers lack of opportunity for creative thinking, fear, boredom, limited intelligence, confusion, child abuse, 'chaotic families', lack of proper social relationships and inappropriate teaching methods.

Language

Language in the mathematics classroom is becoming a focus of attention when equity matters are being considered. Reasons for the low attainment of many mathematics students are numerous, and in past years the major explanation has been characteristics of the individual student, followed by attributing failure to cultural differences. Students come to classes with a variety of influences and these two are important. But increasingly, language is being seen as an important factor in relation to failure – for example, the inadequate or inappropriate development of language in mathematics classes. Secada (1992) shows how students with limited proficiency in English can be marginalized in mathematical discussion even with a good mathematics teacher. However, Moll and Diaz (1987) are optimistic about the education of young people because their work suggests that 'just as academic failure is socially organized, academic success can be socially arranged'.

The issues in language which seem to be linked with poor achievement centre on five points:

1. The use of language to convey mathematical ideas.
2. The use of logic and argument.
3. Lexical ambiguity.
4. Word problems.
5. Classroom methodology.

First, language is used to convey mathematical ideas from one person to another. Without the vocabulary of many words required to convey these ideas, learning becomes impossible. Further, internalizing the mathematics is difficult without the use of these words. Khisty (1995) writes that success involves 'fostering the internalisation of the subject, and enculturating the learner into mathematical activity' (1995:290). Others have described using language to 'own' their mathematics, thereby building confidence and self-empowerment.

The second point concerns logic and argument. Strevens (1974) pointed out that there are difficulties if the teacher and student do not 'share the same logic and reasoning system'. Languages vary in the way in which arguments are transmitted, added to which cultures within countries use language differently to convey an argument.

The third point is about lexical ambiguity (see Durkin and Shire, 1991). Students whose language is less developed will have more difficulty in overcoming the many ambiguities in their lessons. Examples from mathematics are 'interest', 'mean', 'leaves', 'tables', 'product'. These and other problem areas, such as the audible similarity of English words (such as sum, some), will slow the development of mathematical understanding.

Fourth, 'word problems' can cause real difficulties. As previously mentioned, the contexts to problems can lead people up different avenues (note the example on coffee prices earlier). But language itself can cause real problems. The Cockcroft Report *Mathematics Counts* (HMSO, 1982) mentions difficulties with 'simple' Janet and John problems. Two examples are given in which the word 'more' is used in each – one problem leads to an addition sum, the other to subtraction (1982:90). De Corte and Verschaffel (1991) have worked on student successes and failures in seemingly simple problems given in words. In one part of their research they provide twelve varying word problems. Here are two:

Joe had 3 marbles; then Tom gave him 5 more marbles; how many marbles does Joe have now? 97 per cent correct.

Joe has 3 marbles; he has 5 marbles less than Tom; how many marbles does Tom have? 38 per cent correct.

(1991:120–1)

There are equity issues here. Young people in families with an interest in vocabulary, in reading, who visit libraries and who read so-called 'quality' newspapers will find such problems easier to untangle than many other students, who find them very hard. Research indicates that word problems can be situated along a 'reality' dimension ranging from stereotyped, content-lean problems at one end to more realistic rich problem situations on the other. The authors suggest three strategies: a variety of word problems should be used, more explicit and systematic instruction should be given, and writers of texts and word problems should give more attention to the appropriate formulation of the problems.

Finally, more research is needed on classroom methodology for students whose first language is not English. Use of the first language can help but many teachers are unable to teach in this way. Khisty (1995) mentions that variation in tone and volume can be effective, as can the 'recasting' of mathematical ideas. The translation of words is not always straightforward, and because acquiring proficiency in academic language takes several years to develop, teachers must develop verbal skills of discussion and argument in students so that they are engaged in higher-level critical thinking in mathematics rather than in superficial and ultimately lower-level thinking (1995:295). Khisty makes the point that talking within lessons can be encouraged in different ways. Poor classroom practice will lead students to a feeling that they cannot really 'participate in mathematics, that the subject is beyond them and that this knowledge is something that someone else has to give them'. Good practice will lead students to the opposite feeling – that mathematics is participatory, socially constructed, and a skill that all students can achieve (1995:294). Many of these ideas can assist in classes of mainstream language speakers, not all of whom by any means find the particular styles of language required for mathematics easy. Mathematical styles of language have to be taught and used confidently by students if they are to embrace mathematical ideas fully.

Mathematics teachers must not be isolationist

Students should be attracted to mathematics lessons because they interest and excite, and do so not merely by showing the wonders of the subject but by relation to the thrills, the ups and downs of life itself. Students need to build confidence in their own mathematical skills and also in their development as full human beings. Mathematics classes can be popular for all students if the lessons are good. Teachers need to take risks and to involve their students in decisions.

Many have argued for mathematics lessons to be humanized (e.g. Guting, 1980). Each student's voice, according to bell hooks (1994) should be heard in lessons: 'Just the physical experience of hearing, of listening intently to each voice strengthens our capacity to learn together' (1994:186). Stories have been used to interest, and to link mathematics to the world, for which examples are given in Carey *et al.* (1995), Griffiths and Clyne (1991).

Mathematics lessons can contribute fully to a school's interpretation and implementation of cross-curricular themes, such as environment and health education with lessons on topics such as dying species, smoking, trade and low pay.

A recent report shows that parents in Britain and France rely on school to teach morals more than the parents of any of the other ten OECD countries (OECD, 1995:10). More researchers in our country use mathematics to create weapons of war than do so to provide food for the hungry. Mathematics is being used for good and evil in the world. Students must be given opportunity to practise mathematical skills on real-life information allowing feelings and values to enter the classroom. Sexist and racist aspects of society can be examined through statistics, as can the concerns of young people. Rather than survey the colours of cars at the school gate, teachers and students could plan a survey on more serious topics.

Global statistics can be used to look at life in different countries around the world. For example, a database by Worldaware Software (1995) gives students an opportunity to examine statistics on infant mortality, life expectation, education, environment, trade and debt issues. Data can be presented graphically with students looking for correlation between the figures. For example, they can identify the few countries with both a high Gross National Product and high infant mortality. A discussion on the equity within those countries could follow. Care must be taken to avoid the 'developed' and 'undeveloped' mentality, and to see behind the figures for different lifestyles, as well as the reasons why many countries remain very poor despite trading with rich countries for centuries. Students can observe that poverty is not inevitable – they can try to spot the political actions which would reduce inequality across the world.

An instructive three lessons can be spent taking students to the school library and asking them to find some examples of mathematics being used in different situations (and expressly not in mathematics books!). The students show they are interested in so many aspects of life – cooking, sport, space, slavery, art. More examples of classroom mathematics for equality and justice are given in six chapters of *Multiple Factors* by Shan and Bailey (1991). There are also ideas on using a global perspective in the teaching of ten topics within the mathematics curriculum given by Nelson *et al.*, in *Multicultural Mathematics from a Global Perspective* (1993). Christian Aid and Oxfam produce excellent materials. Grant (1991, 1995) uses statistics which can be of use in classrooms.

Assessment

The first and central recommendation of the TGAT Report (DES, 1988) was that 'the basis of the national assessment system should be essentially formative, but designed also to indicate where there is a need for more detailed diagnostic assessment. At the age of 16, however, it should incorporate assessment with summative functions' (1988:paragraph 227). Appendices D and E of the same report give examples of different styles of assessment, many of them in mathematics.

Exploring Assessment (Association of Teachers of Mathematics, 1989) considers different strategies for classroom assessment of mathematics. The central feature of classroom assessment is that it should assist both student and teacher in learning. Many classrooms use tests for summative purposes and for reporting. A variety of strategies should normally be used to assist learning because different aspects of mathematics require it (assessing facts will take a different form from assessing problem-solving) and because students can learn in different ways.

It is important to set clear targets. Students can then self-assess, taking responsibility for themselves. Assessment which is limited to marking right or wrong offers little support for getting things right in the future if mistakes are not discussed. It is in talking through issues that the positive side of assessment comes through.

Assessment strategies can include verbal questioning, observing activity, student–student assessment, commenting on written work, assessing group work and a student's own assessment against agreed targets. Marking written work only assists learning if the teacher provides enough information for the learner to move forward; and in the majority of cases this requires discussion.

There are many issues of class, culture and gender in this

discussion. If teachers really know their students, they will also be aware of the approaches which will best assist learning. If all students, with their different cultures, skills and motivations are to learn effectively, the teacher must choose from the assessment strategies available to best assist learning.

It is difficult for the equity-minded mathematics teacher to approach GCSE assessment without feeling that the system has inbuilt bias. For example, the mathematics papers do not reflect minority cultures (the Mathematical Association, 1995). There seem to be differences in the ways boys and girls approach examination questions (Joffe and Foxman, 1988; Buchanan, 1987). According to Abrams (1991) the GCSE examinations have failed to narrow the gap between different ethnic groups and between the sexes. There are concerns that coursework has widened gaps rather than narrowed them. Haylock (1985) is concerned that rigid assessment does not encourage creativity in mathematics.

Other issues relate to language (readability, especially for English learners), to problems associated with the real-life contexts for questions, and to choice by teachers for entry to the different levels in GCSE. A wider issue is the whole purpose of mathematics assessment at age 16. No one is clear exactly what is being measured in GCSE mathematics examinations. It could be described as the ability to succeed in written tests. This examination hurdle, which shows little indication of how mathematics is used in life outside the classroom, offers real bias in favour of quiet, academic young people. Teachers must campaign for a system of assessment which is more just than the present system. If the recommendations of the TGAT report (DES, 1988) were implemented, many of these criticisms in mathematics assessment at 16 would be reduced.

CONCLUSION

Teachers of mathematics can play a crucial role in making the world a fairer place. Providing all young people with confidence in numeracy and using examples from the real world can give the next generation of children the tools to change things, to make things happen.

Mathematics is used by many people in places of work. Knowledge and skills learned in schools can be used for personal greed or for co-operative ventures. Many use mathematics to maximize profit and to undertake research into warfare (our so-called defence industry). At the International Congress on Mathematical Education in 1988, Chandler Davis, a Canadian delegate, suggested that mathematicians should discuss their social responsibilities in the same way as doctors, chemists and scientists. As he put it: 'They call World War 1 the chemist's war, World War 2 the physicist's and World War 3 the mathematician's – isn't it time that there was an ethical statement, a pledge for mathematicians, analogous to the Hippocratic oath in medicine?'

Teachers of mathematics should accept their responsibilities in providing all students with the basic numeracy needed to understand the world, and also the ways in which mathematics can be used to improve peoples' lives directly. Discussions between students and teachers on the morality of the various uses and abuses to which mathematics is put will increase the critical awareness of these students in their world.

Many students come into secondary schools unable to recite their multiplication tables. They need these tables in order to gain confidence in arithmetic and statistics. Many young people excluded from schools have low attainment in numeracy. Some reports indicate an underclass being created, in which young people face their future without numeracy skills and without academic qualifications. Each one of these young people has been failed by the education system, and teachers of mathematics must accept their part in that failure. Secondary school mathematics departments should put basic numeracy as a priority, with cross-school policies similar to those on oracy and literacy.

A qualification in English and mathematics is often required for access to higher education and entry to various professions. Fewer students get these high grades in mathematics than in English, so it is often the mathematics teacher who holds the key to the future of his or her students. Teachers of mathematics have to be very aware of equality and equal opportunity issues. For some years now the government has been monitoring examination performance by gender, but has only recently been concerned about the performance of Asian, black and other minority ethnic students. League tables have shown differences in performance between schools. The government should concern itself with an analysis of performance by class. As the white population has moved from the big cities to the suburbs, there is a greater concentration of young people from the ethnic minorities in working-class areas. There must also be clarity of thought in identifying variations of performance in mathematics examinations with respect to class, gender, 'race', disability and special needs issues in order for the education service to provide the educational entitlement to all young people.

Teachers of mathematics who are concerned about the injustices in society will understand that they can play a real role in the classroom in preparing all young people for their lives ahead, giving them the skills and the confidence to use their talents for good. The cross-curricular themes of the National Curriculum (Environment, Health Education, Economic and Industrial Understanding, Citizenship, Careers) provide ample opportunity for mathematics teachers to address issues of injustice. The School Curriculum and Assessment Authority is planning to provide guidance for the promotion in schools of students' spiritual, moral and social development. This is expected to be in the form of guidance material and a matrix provided in 1998 to assist schools in detailing how they intend to develop 'values education', based on values already agreed (see SCAA, 1996). Mathematics departments should fully contribute to their school's policy on Values Education, indicating how the learning programme will try to meet aspects of injustice in their students' lives, and allow students to see how mathematics can be used to explain and to change the world.

Mathematics teachers also need to be involved in the politics of education, pressing for a fair distribution of resources, for just assessment systems (particularly for changes to the government mathematics tests at 7, 11 and 14 years, and GCSE examinations) and for changes in the next mathematics curriculum due in the year 2000.

BIBLIOGRAPHY

Abrams, F. (1991) Better grades or odious comparisons. *Times Educational Supplement*, 15 February.

ALBSU (1993) *Basic Skills in Colleges: Assessing the Need*, and *The Basic Needs of Young Adults*. London: The Basic Skills Agency.

Association of Teachers of Mathematics (1989) *Exploring Assessment*. Derby: ATM.

Barham, J. and Bishop, A. (1991) Mathematics and the deaf child. In

K. Durkin and B. Shire (eds) *Language in Mathematical Education.* Buckingham: Open University Press.

Becker, J. R. (1995) Women's ways of knowing in mathematics. In P. Rogers and G. Kaiser (eds) *Equity in Mathematics Education: Influence of Feminism and Culture.* London: Falmer Press.

Bishop, A. (1988) *Mathematical Enculturation: A Cultural Perspective on Mathematics Education.* Dordrecht, Holland: Kluwer.

Bishop, A. (1993) Influences from society. *Significant Influences on Children's Learning of Mathematics.* Paris: UNESCO.

Boaler, J. (1993) The role of contexts in the mathematics classroom: do they make mathematics more 'real'? *For the Learning of Mathematics,* 13(2).

Boaler, J. (1994) When do girls prefer football to fashion? An analysis of female underachievement in relation to 'realistic' mathematic contexts. *British Educational Research Journal,* 20(5).

Brown, S., Riddell, S. and Duffield, J. (1996) *Classroom Approaches to Learning and Teaching: the Social-class Dimension.* Stirling: The University of Stirling.

Buchanan, N. K. (1987) Factors contributing to mathematical problem-solving performance: an exploratory study. *Educational Studies in Mathematics,* 18:399–415.

Burton, L. (1986) *Girls into Maths Can Go.* London: Cassell.

California State Department of Education (1987) *Caught in the Middle.* Sacramento, CA.

Carey, D. *et al.* (1995) Equity and mathematics education. In W. G. Secada, E. Fennema and L. B. Adajian (eds) *New Directions for Equity in Mathematics Education.* Cambridge: Cambridge University Press.

Christian Aid (1995) *The Globe-trotting Sports Shoe.* PO Box 100, London SE1 7RT.

Cole, M. and Hill, D. (1997) New Labour, old policies: Tony Blair's vision for education in Britain. *Education Australia,* 37:17–19.

Cole, M., Hill, D. and Shan, S. (eds) (1997) *Promoting Equality in Primary Schools.* London: Cassell.

Coombs, P. H. (1985) *The World Crisis in Education: The View From the Eighties.* Oxford: Oxford University Press.

D'Ambrosia, U. (1990) The role of mathematics education in building a democratic and just society. *For the Learning of Mathematics,* 10(3):20–3.

Davis, A. (1994) Constructivism. In A. Davis and D. Pettitt (eds) *Developing Understanding in Primary Mathematics.* London: Falmer Press.

Davis, C. (1988) *A Hippocratic Oath for Mathematics?* A paper for ICME-6 (International Congress on Mathematical Education), Budapest.

De Corte, E. and Verschaffel, L. (1991) Some factors influencing the solution of addition and subtraction word problems. In K. Durkin and

B. Shire (eds) *Language in Mathematical Education.* Buckingham: Open University Press.

DES (1985) *Education for All (The Swann Report).* London: HMSO.

DES (1988) Report. *National Curriculum: Task Group on Assessment and Testing.* London: Department of Education and Science and the Welsh Office.

DFE (1993) *Dimensions of Discipline – Rethinking Practice in Secondary Schools,* D. Gillborn, J. Nixon and J. Rudduck. London: HMSO.

DFE (1995) *Mathematics in the National Curriculum.* London: HMSO.

Dowling, P. and Noss, R. (1990) *Mathematics Versus the National Curriculum?* Lewes: Falmer Press.

Ducker, L. (1993) Visually impaired students drawing graphs. *Mathematics Teaching,* MT144:23–26.

Durkin, K. and Shire, B. (1991) *Language in Mathematical Education.* Buckingham: Open University Press.

Ernest, P. (1989) Social and political values. In P. Ernest, *Mathematics Teaching – The State of the Art.* Lewes: Falmer Press.

Ernest, P. (1991) *The Philosophy of Mathematical Education.* Basingstoke: Falmer Press.

Foster, R. and Tall, D. (1996) Can all children climb the same curriculum ladder? *Mathematics in Schools,* 25(3):8–12.

Freire, P. (1972) *Pedagogy of the Oppressed.* London: Penguin Books.

Gardner, H. (1983) *Frames of Mind.* New York: Basic Books.

Gardner, H. (1993) *The Unschooled Mind.* London: Fontana Press.

Goodstein, H. (1994) Teaching mathematics and problem-solving to deaf and hard-of-hearing students. *Selected Lectures from the 7th International Congress on Mathematical Education.* Quebec, Canada: Les Presses de l'Université Laval.

Grant, J. P. (1991 and 1995) *The State of the World's Children.* UNICEF, Oxford: Oxford University Press.

Griffiths, R. and Clyne, M. (1991) The power of story: its role in learning mathematics. *Mathematics Teaching,* 135.

Guting, R. (1980) Humanising the teaching of mathematics. *International Journal of Mathematics Education in Science and Technology,* 11(3):415–25.

Haylock, D. W. (1985) Conflicts in the assessment and encouragement of mathematical creativity in schoolchildren. *International Journal of Mathematics Education in Science and Technology,* 16(4):547–53.

Head, J. (1981) Personality and the learning of mathematics. *Educational Studies in Mathematics,* 12:339–50.

Higino, Z. M. M. (1987) Por que e dificil para a crianca aprender a fazer continhas no papel? Master's thesis, Mestrado em Psicologia, Universidade Federal de Pernambuco Recife, Brazil.

Higgins, R. (1993) Creativity and underfunctioning. In V. Varma (ed.) *How and Why Children Fail.* London: Jessica Kingsley Publishers.

Hillcole Group (1997) *Rethinking Education and Democracy: A Socialist Alternative for the Twenty-first Century.* London: Tufnell Press.

Hillcole Group (1991) *Changing the Future: Redprint for Education.* London: Tufnell Press.

HMSO (1982) *Mathematics Counts (The Cockcroft Report).* London: HMSO.

hooks, bell (1994) *Teaching to Transgress.* New York: Routledge.

Inglese, J. (1997) Teaching mathematics to pupils with Autistic Spectrum Disorders: exploring possibilities. *Equals,* 3(2).

Jaggar, J. (1996) Two strands that can't be straddled. *Times Educational Supplement Mathematics Extra,* 24 May:vi and vii.

Joffe, L. and Foxman, D. (1988) *Attitudes and Gender Differences: Mathematics at age 11 and 15.* London: APU, DES.

Joseph, G. G. (1990) *The Crest of the Peacock: Non-European Roots of Mathematics.* London: Penguin Books.

Khisty, L. L. (1995) Making inequality. In W. G. Secada, E. Fennema and L. B. Adajian (eds) *New Directions for Equity in Mathematics Education.* Cambridge: Cambridge University Press.

Ladson-Billings, G. (1995) Making mathematics meaningful. In W. G. Secada, E. Fennema and L. B. Adajian (eds) *New Directions for Equity in Mathematics Education.* Cambridge: Cambridge University Press.

Mason, M. and Rieser, R. (1994) *Altogether Better Comic Relief.* Available from Charity Projects, 74 New Oxford Street, London WC1A 1EF.

Mathematical Association (1995) *G.C.S.E. Mathematics Papers – An Analysis of Contexts for Gender and Culture.* The Mathematical Association, 259 London Road, Leicester LE2 3BE.

Moll, L. and Diaz, S. (1987) Change as the goal of educational research. *Anthropology and Education Quarterly,* 18:300–11.

National Commission on Education (1993) *Learning to Succeed.* London: Heinemann.

National Research Council (1989) Everybody Counts. Report to the nation on the future of mathematics education. Washington DC: National Academy Press.

Nelson, D., Joseph, G. G. and Williams, J. (1993) *Multicultural Mathematics from a Global Perspective.* Oxford: Oxford University Press.

Noddings, N. (1990) Constructivism in mathematical education. *Journal for Research in Mathematics Education,* Monograph Number 4. Virginia: National Council of Teachers of Mathematics.

Nunes T. (1993) The socio-cultural context of mathematical thinking: research findings and educational implications. In *Significant Influences on Children's Learning of Mathematics.* Paris: UNESCO.

Nunes, T. and Moreno, C. (1997) Is hearing impairment a cause of difficulty in learning mathematics? *Equals,* 3(1).

OECD (1995) Survey. The *Independent,* 12 April.

OfSTED (1995) *Recent Research in Mathematics Education,* 5–16. London: HMSO.

Pepper, M. (1997) Mathematical games for visually impaired children. *Equals,* 3(1).

Pyke, N. (1996) 'Who owns maths A-level?' asks the rewrite team. *Times Educational Supplement*, 18 October:3.

Rothman, P. (1996) *Women in the History of Mathematics*. University College London: Department of Mathematics.

Schools Curriculum and Assessment Authority (1996) *Consultation on Values in Education and the Community*. London: SCAA.

Secada, W. G. (1991) Agenda setting, enlightened self-interest, and equity in mathematics education. *Peabody Journal of Education*, 66(2).

Secada, W. G. (1992) Race, ethnicity, social class, language, and achievement in mathematics. In D. A. Grouws (ed.) *Handbook of Research on Mathematics Teaching and Learning*. New York: Macmillan.

Shan, S. (1997) Science. In M. Cole, D. Hill and S. Shan (eds) *Promoting Equality in Primary Schools*. London: Cassell.

Shan, S. and Bailey, P. (1991) *Multiple Factors – Classroom Mathematics for Equality and Justice*. Stoke-on-Trent: Trentham Books.

Silver, E. A., Smith, M. S. and Nelson, B. S. (1995) The QUASAR Project: Equity concerns meet mathematics education reform in the middle school. In W. G. Secada, E. Fennema and L. B. Adajian (eds) *New Directions for Equity in Mathematics Education*. Cambridge: Cambridge University Press.

Stewart, I. (1996) *From Here to Infinity*. Oxford: Oxford University Press.

Straker, A. (1996) *Mental Mathematics for Ages 5 to 7, Teachers Book*. Cambridge: Cambridge University Press.

Strevens, P. (1974) What is linguistics and how it may help the mathematics teacher? An introductory paper prepared for the 1974 Conference, UNESCO, Paris.

Thomson, M. (1991) Mathematics and dyslexia. In K. Durkin and B. Shire (eds) *Language in Mathematical Education*. Buckingham: Open University Press.

Times Educational Supplement (1995) In V. Makins, *Machines of the Mind*, 17 March.

Varma, V. (1993) *How and Why Children Fail*. London: Jessica Kingsley Publishers.

Worldaware Software (1995) *World Development Database*. 1 Catton Street, London WC1R 4AB.

Young, S. (1996) Black boys 'fall behind in maths'. *Times Educational Supplement*, 21 June:3.

CHAPTER 4

Science

Sharanjeet Shan

This chapter has three aims:

1. To present a range of practical activities set into a multi-cultural context, which could be used in any secondary classroom, whatever the 'race', gender, ability, social class and sexuality component of the students.
2. To encourage low achievers in science to understand and experience the joy and the power of the subject so that they will feel inspired to choose it as an area of study for higher education.
3. To present science as a *truly* universal activity.

The list of resources recommended will enable the teacher to obtain suitable and appropriate material, some of which is not easy to come by. However, a little effort would be well rewarded and open an exciting new world of evidence that science is a universal activity. It must be acknowledged to be so.

The theoretical rationale in which the author's arguments are embedded has been discussed in detail elsewhere (Shan, in Cole *et al.*, 1997). This chapter is a continuation of that thought process and elaborates on the variety of ways in which ethnocentric bias is communicated to secondary students within the context of a science lesson. Science teachers tread a very thin line between acting as the 'neutral teacher', following the syllabus and being a critical transformative educator who changes herself and her students in the process of classroom delivery. Both the student and the teacher should feel free in influencing publishers and examination boards. At present, though, the Association for Science Education UK does not have a specific student wing – maybe it should establish a network to encourage students to participate creatively in the development of videos, posters, games, materials, etc.

Throughout this chapter, National Curriculum links are established to specific topics within the curriculum. However, any science syllabus, anywhere in the world, should find these ideas useful. While visiting India and Kenya in search of literature on black scientists, I discovered that 'local' texts were not local at all: they were almost all imported from the West. As a result, local scientists and mathematicians were confined to the archives in the Institute of Science, New Delhi.

HOW TO MOVE FROM AN ETHNOCENTRIC VIEW OF SCIENCE TOWARDS 'SCIENCE FOR ALL'

By studying, exclusively, examples of scientific discoveries made by white scientists, students may come to the conclusion that white groups are innately better at science. A secondary school student is at a stage where he or she is constructing values, attitudes and beliefs – not only the knowledge that they will eventually believe in – and using the mathematics and science learnt in the classroom to make sense of the wider world, to connect their school experiences to daily, real life and gain the ability to review and choose interpretations presented to them.

At secondary level, students are old enough and must collaborate with the teachers in learning to recognize hidden as well as overt forms of bias. Teachers have a huge choice in the manner in which they will present the curriculum to their students: they define the context, they choose the environment. Recently, science schemes have recognized the need to connect experiments – particularly in biology and chemistry – to real names, to avoid 'race' and gender bias and to use photographs from a variety of cultural backgrounds. This is a good start; however, it is a small beginning and needs to go much further. Teachers should note that by providing real-life, diverse examples to set the syllabus into context, they are also helping to make friendlier the very complex, often alienating and threatening language of science.

GCSE programmes of study available at the time of writing this chapter do not, generally speaking, indicate the study of specific examples. While some examples are suggested by the Non-Statutory Guidelines, in my view this is avoiding responsibility. There is no direct encouragement to ensure the use of diversity and broaden the context of teaching and learning. Either the teacher uses only familiar examples, or has the liberty to choose such examples as will have meanings for the majority of their particular students.

At a time which pre-dates Stonehenge, the Chinese used ploughs, studied astronomy and were skilled in the art of paper-making. Many of these inventions required greater inventiveness than is required of scientists in modern times, given the absence then of science laboratories, technicians, computers and other appropriate appliances. The following are just three, very brief perspectives on diverse contributions to science from different parts of the world.

Islamic contributions to science

Study of the history of science at any level almost completely ignores the achievements of Islamic, Chinese and Indian science. Most school students in Britain will know of the oil-producing Arab world but will not have any idea at all of the rich heritage of science that Islam has given to the Western world, dating from as far back as the seventh century. A number of projects during the early 1980s raised awareness of these contributions: for example, an issue of the popular magazine *New Scientist* (23 October 1980), was devoted to 'Islamic Science: A New Renaissance'. Referring to the work of the Turkish science historian Fuat Sezgin, the article states:

> Fuat Sezgin's *Geschichte des Arabischen Schrifttums* – six out of the planned twenty volumes have now been published . . . ample evidence that the medieval Western world diligently imitated, copied and plagiarised the works of Muslim scientists. As early as the 12th century, a decree was issued in Seville, forbidding the sale of scientific writings to Christians because the latter translated the writings and published them under another name.

Sezgin's research includes a survey of 1.5 million manuscripts from all over the world. The article continues:

> Achievements of Muslim scientists continue to be attributed to Western scientists. For example, the discovery of planetary motion to Kepler and Copernicus, of the circulation of blood to Harvey, and of gravity and various discoveries in Optics to Newton.

Clearly, serious rectification has to be made in all areas of the history of science: for whether they discovered the lesser pulmonary circulation; invented spherical trigonometry in the late tenth century; measured the circumference of the earth and values for specific gravity correct to three decimal places almost 1,000 years ago, or used the camera obscura 300 years before Europe, there is scarcely a field where Muslim scientists did not invent or think out something exemplary.

In a series of articles in the *Aramco World Magazine* (1982), entitled 'Science: The Islamic Legacy', Paul Lunde provides further evidence of the very close connection between Greek, Indian and Arab scientists and mathematicians; it is also an interesting discourse on the conflict between religion and science, reason and philosophy. One of the books that illustrate the wealth of scientific knowledge on animals – the *Book of Animals, Kitab-al-hayawan* – runs to seven volumes. Al-Jahiz, the writer, offers an evolutionary theory, discussions on animal mimicry, and writes at length about habitat adaptations of humans as well as animals.

In the modern Arab and Asian world, science is focused on development, for example the vast reserves of crude oil in the Arab world; on the other hand, there are huge problems to be overcome in terms of harsh weather conditions and difficult terrain, where the growing of disease- and drought-resistant crops requires innovations in agricultural science. There is, of course, the most pressing problem of the drifting sand, which is a constant threat to billions of dollars-worth of infrastructure. Water desalination is another crucial field of research. Students of science would find much of real-life interest from a very different perspective in looking at science in Islamic countries.

Chinese contributions to science

While it is common knowledge that printing in China has been in use for well over 1,000 years, and that the Chinese invented paper, the history of science and medicine in China continues to remain a difficult and mysterious field, as there are few works of comprehensive translation and these are not easily available. To translate a work as authentically as is humanly possible can only be achieved if the translator is immersed in and familiar with the context. Chinese culture, ancient and modern, is rich, complex and involves very different experiences from those of Western scientific historians. It is therefore as great a problem to explain Chinese scientific concepts as it is to explain the Arabic, using the English vocabulary.

However, there are some well-known and well-documented traditional medical practices which science students can study. This study must be undertaken as a serious project rather than simply skimming the surface. Most young people would have heard Confucian sayings proclaimed by TV presenters, often in cryptic, sarcastic ways, and sometimes in very bad taste. Also, most ordinary people know limited and simplified notions such as *yin and yang, t'ai chi* etc. For the Chinese, as with Indians, all medical treatment was to do with bringing about harmony in various parts of the body and the mind. Ted Kaptchuk on 'Medicine East and West' in his book *Chinese Medicine: The Web that has no Weaver* (1983:4) states:

> The two different logical structures have pointed the two medicines in different directions. Western medicine is concerned mainly with isolatable disease categories or agents of disease, which it zeroes in on, isolates, and tries to change, control or destroy. The Western physician starts with a symptom, then searches for the underlying mechanism – a precise cause for a specific disease – the physicians' logic is analytic – cutting through the accumulation of bodily phenomenon like a surgeon's scalpel to isolate one single entity or cause. The Chinese physician, in contrast, directs his or her attention to the complete physiological and the psychological individual. All relevant information, including the symptom as well as the patient's other general characteristics, is gathered and woven together until it forms what Chinese medicine calls a 'pattern of disharmony'. The logic of Chinese medicine is organismic or synthetic, attempting to organise symptoms and

signs into understandable configurations. The total configurations, the patterns of disharmony provide the framework for treatment.

Acupuncture, moxibustion, herbal medicine are all governed by the principles of *yin and yang*. Channel 4 television shows some excellent documentaries and teachers should approach the educational broadcasting department for a list. One of the most authentic works is Ted Kaptchuk's (cited above), a most readable book with comprehensive illustrations about the meridians and the patterns of the body landscape. The writer is a consultant for the BBC television series *The Healing Arts*, also available as a book from Channel 4.

Indian contributions to science

There was considerable exchange of scientific information between Arab and Indian scientists during the seventh century. Most Indian scientists remained unknown in the West until the end of the eighteenth century when the translations from Sanskrit into European languages began to be made. Children in cities such as Birmingham, Leeds and London may be quite familiar with the excavations at Harappa and Mohenjo-daro in 1921–2. Teacher packs on Indus Valley Civilization (2500–1500 BC) can be obtained from the Ethnic Minority Support Services in these three cities.

It is interesting to read that the most remarkable findings have been those of well-planned cities with efficient water supply and drainage. People were expert potters and metal-workers. These are mysteries of science and technology that deserve further investigation in order to acknowledge and understand the total history of science and not a narrow, Eurocentric vision.

From about 1500 BC India was invaded by Aryans, who came from the north west and believed in the doctrine of the body being made up of five elements. The science of Ayurveds – the science of life – was developed over many centuries and was popular until the eighteenth century. Earth, water, fire, air and a non-material substance are the five elements whose balance and equilibrium in the body is crucial to good health. Plant extracts, and later minerals and alchemical practices, were popularized to cure diseases. Blood was also an important factor in the curing of diseases. The elements are present in the human body as three humours: *vata* (breath), *pitta* (bile), *kapha* (mucus). Sources show clearly that

India had not borrowed her surgery or anatomy or medical sciences from anywhere else in the world.

By 1510, with the establishment of the Portuguese colonies on the west coast of India, the decline of science and medicine had begun. The Dutch in 1595 and the East India Company in 1608 were keen to learn about tropical conditions, local plant life, their uses in the curing of scurvy, etc. It is hard to believe today that three to four hundred years ago, Europeans used ancient Hindu methods and diet to make their blood more like the Indians so that they could be immune to local diseases and ailments.

In the eighteenth century, standards of science and medicine in India were probably the highest in the world. The British studied and documented these (Ainslie, 1826). During the early nineteenth century, the Westernization of India began with full force, with the adoption of English as the official language in 1835. The study of Ayurvedic medicine was banned; but it was restored much later, early in the twentieth century. By the end of the nineteenth century, important scientists such as J. C. Bose (biology), C. V. Raman (physics), Meghnad Saha (physics) and P. C. Ray (chemistry) had begun to establish international reputations as modern scientists. Keen physicists should know of C. V. Raman and Meghnad Saha who are associated with the theory of thermal insertion and its application to the stellar spectra in terms of the physical conditions prevailing in the stellar atmospheres. The most comprehensive work available on the subject is *Collected Works of Meghnad Saha* (Chatterjee, 1982). His theory is known to have revolutionized astro-physics.

In the Introduction to his well-known *Theoretical Astrophysics* (1936) Rosseter observed:

> Although Bohr must thus be considered the pioneer in the field, it was the Indian physicist Meghnad Saha who (1920) first attempted to develop a consistent theory of the spectral sequence of the stars from the point of view of atomic theory. Saha's work is in fact the theoretical formulation of Lockyer's view along modern lines, and from that time on the idea that the spectral sequence indicates a progressive transmutation of the elements has been definitely abandoned. From that time dates the hope that a thorough analysis of stellar spectra will afford complete information about the state of the stellar atmospheres . . . The impetus given to astrophysics by Saha's work can scarcely be overestimated, as nearly all later work in this field has been influenced by it and much of the subsequent work has the refinement of Saha's ideas. (cit. Chatterjee, 1982:6)

THE SCIENCE SYLLABUS AND STUDENT EXPERIENCE

Every science syllabus should examine the critical outcomes relevant to the broader real life of secondary students. All of the following examples connect to the new National Curriculum targets in science, particularly Attainment Target 2.

1. Challenging the myth of second-class proteins

It is a well-known fact among students in science classes in a secondary school that proteins are essential for tissue growth and function. From time to time, newspapers, food magazines or nutritionists engage in debate about the quality of the proteins offered by the vegetarian diet. There is no conclusive medical evidence to suggest that vegetarians will suffer if they do not supplement their diet with eggs or commercial protein preparations. Vegetarians are often labelled as cranks who cannot eat meat because their religion is against animal consumption. Few believe that one may be a vegetarian on the real scientific basis that being a vegetarian often means a healthier life.

The term 'second-class proteins' used in conjunction with vegetable proteins has given rise to the myth that a vegetarian diet will always be lacking in some essential nutrients, vegetarian food being incomplete and second class as opposed to a carnivorous diet. These opinions are outdated and have no scientific credibility. Indeed, science classrooms should study the miraculous effects of soya bean and fibre. Together these must have saved thousands of lives. Plant proteins such as soya are often the basis of diets for children or adults suffering from allergy to milk (in the case of infants); for asthma sufferers; heart patients; arthritis; certain cancers and the like. Plants, with their fibre content, aid digestion while plant fats are less saturated. The lack of fibre is also known to be a contributory factor to cancer of the large intestine in people consuming large quantities of meat. The saturated fatty acids of animal fat contribute to the risk of coronary heart disease. Soya beans and chickpeas contain 38 per cent protein as opposed to 19 per cent in beef. Lentils have twice as much protein as eggs. Most green legumes are very rich in minerals and vitamins. In addition, animals are notoriously inefficient at converting plants that they feed on into protein as they use 90 per cent of the feed for their own warmth and body function requirements. A large proportion of primary energy is sacrificed in order to make a few grams of animal protein. Thus one acre of agricultural land can sustain one person's protein requirement for:

- 77 days by grazing beef cattle;
- 236 days by grazing cows for milk;
- 773 days by growing corn;
- 2,224 days by growing soya beans.

It is encouraging to note that in Britain, food technologists have been engaged in developing a large variety of plant foods rich in protein, full of natural flavours and colourings. Health-food shops are opening in many places, valuing the traditional recipes and the traditional diets of peoples of non-white cultures. Science teachers should have no difficulty in acquiring a range of pulses and beans from the national supermarket chainstores. These include black-eyed beans, aduki beans, chickpeas, continental lentils and red, white and brown kidney beans.

Another little-known grain that students could investigate is amaranth, one of the most important and basic foods of the 'New World' in pre-Columbian times. Once thousands of hectares of farmlands in Aztec and Inca empires were covered with this tall red, leafy plant. The plant is being examined today for its essential amino acids and rich protein content. The two crucial amino acids present in amaranth protein are lysine and methionine (see National Research Council, 1984:7). The crop is widely known and grown in India and West Africa.

Activity
Any of the vast range of bean seeds could be used as a basis for:
- germination and mineral requirements;
- balanced diet;
- energy content of foods;
- structures of seeds;
- testing of foods for proteins, carbohydrates and fat.

At the early stages of germination, most pulses are rich in vitamins, minerals and proteins; examine the easily available bean sprouts grown from Moong beans. Most green shoots can be eaten raw, a crisp delight with the best ingredients for health.

2. Whole food and processed food

Activity
- What is the difference? Investigate.
- Why is *whole food* so expensive?
- What are the chemical physical processes that convert *whole food* into *processed food?* What is lost in the processing? What is gained?
- Make an assessment of the differences under the following headings: dietary fibre; texture; taste; nutritional value; variety.

You can get most of the information from the packets or the manufacturers.

Activity
Have you ever wondered why bread made from wheat is such a staple food all over the world? Investigate how many different forms of 'bread' are being made and consumed in your local community.

3. Where does our daily food come from?

Activity
- List the ingredients of your favourite meals over a week.
- List the names of the countries where they were produced.
- Getting the food from the farm to your table is complex. It includes:
    – producing: arable land, farmers;
    – processing: preserving, cooking, sorting;
    – packaging: tins, cardboard boxes;
    – distribution: lorries, ships.
- Do a project on the life of a banana, coffee beans or a loaf of bread.

4. Energy requirements per day in Britain

Activity

Analyse the actual consumption of different people over a week (see Table 4.1) and see if they are over-fed or under-fed.

Table 4.1   Daily consumption by various groups of people

Age/sex/occupation	Kilojoules	Calories
New-born baby	1,700	408
Six-month-old baby	3,220	770
University student (male)	12,300	2,950
University student (female)	9,600	2,300
Factory worker (male)	12,600	3,020
Factory worker (female)	9,700	2,320
Agricultural worker (male)	12,600	3,020
Agricultural worker (female)	10,000	2,400
Clerk (male)	10,500	2,510
Clerk (female)	8,900	2,130
Pregnant woman	10,450	2,500
Lactating mother	11,300	2,700
Elderly retired (male)	9,700	2,320
Elderly retired (female)	8,300	1,990
Teenage boy	14,212	3,400
Teenage girl	11,286	2,700

Malnutrition – bending the truth

Images and references to black people (if any) are often presented in the context of poverty, diseases and natural disasters, with a focus on commonly understood ailments, such as beriberi and kwashiorkor. Not so long ago, children in Britain were sent up the chimneys and suffered from rickets. More importantly, the concept of malnutrition is rarely linked with gluttony, yet over-consumption and greed for food cause many of the commonest health problems for British people. Obesity is malnutrition and can lead to heart attacks and diabetes.

5. The ongoing saga of Bhopal – the story of the humble human mucus membranes

An excellent activity in which to demonstrate the power of gas leaks, chemical plant explosions such as the Bhopal disaster, tear gas used to disperse people in demonstrations, etc. is to engage students in peeling some strong onions and then asking them to write about their feelings and experience. It is a most powerful experiment to bring home the truth of the damage that is done to the mucus membrane of the nasal passages and the eyeballs. Osmic acid contained in onions is a harmless irritant to the eyes; chemicals leaked in Bhopal made people blind for ever. Students can do their own research on chemical and biological warfare and make up their own minds if human beings should be engaged in the production of such lethal weapons.

6. Continuous or discontinuous variation? Genetics in a multicultural society

Why do schools avoid the issues of 'race', intelligence and gender, issues of origins, definitions and theories? Rarely do schools in Britain look at how the theories of 'race' were constructed and who constructed them; the myths and the acceptance of those myths by politicians and religious leaders alike to exploit two-thirds of humanity. At the same time, books are silent about the pseudo-scientific basis of the positioning of women for hundreds of years in Britain, and how they were not allowed to vote, not allowed to study medicine, etc. IQ debates labelled peoples of lower socio-economic status, young and old alike, as being of less intelligence. This topic is ideally suited to at least one whole criterion in the new National Curriculum Orders for Key Stage 3 (HMSO, 14:3c) which states: 'The nature of scientific ideas: relate social and historical contexts to scientific ideas by studying how at least one scientific idea has changed over time.'

At secondary level students should begin to unfold Newton's phrase 'Whatever I have learnt, I have done so by standing on the shoulders of giants.' There is a scientific reality behind this statement. The theories that are accepted and respected today emerged from many that were formulated before and have been superseded. The list of books cited in the notes should be compulsory reading for all science teachers.[1]

The word 'race' continues to be abused over and over again. Feeble excuses are made that one is referring to ethnicity, that people are aware that there is only one 'race', the human 'race'. Science teachers could contribute a lot to redressing the balance if they engaged students in the power of language and how statements such as 'people of different "races"' are not simply scientifically incorrect – they are dangerous. Genetics is the most important part of the syllabus when it comes to looking at scientific constructions of racism. Students must engage in close scrutiny of some of the most obvious evidence of continuous variation in human beings. Instead of going over the outmoded and dangerous ideas about the different 'races' – Caucasian, Australoid, etc. – it would be much healthier to look at the benefits of diversity in nature and at continuous variation as an established scientific reality. Simply ignoring the teaching of 'race' is in fact a sin of omission.

Aims of the following activities are:

- To make children challenge their own constructs of 'race', racism and different 'races'.
- To look at classification, variation and natural selection – scientific evidence of essential features that establish the reality of human 'race' – one 'race'.
- To look for bias and unintentional messages in the teaching of genetics.

Activity
Skin colour is an excellent example of *incomplete dominance*. Suppose the gene for dark skin colour is D and for light skin colour is d.

- Take two parents with DD and dd as the gametes.
- What will happen in F1?
- Is either gene dominant?
- Find out when the combination DD and dd will occur. Perform a back cross.
- What will you have to do to keep a dominant group dominant?

Blood groups, hair colour, height, colour of eyes, facial features are some more examples of *incomplete dominance*. Find out if there are any features of complete dominance in human beings.

- Find out the difference between *inherited* and *acquired* characteristics.
- Collect a variety of hair and eye colours from catalogues. Build a collage.

- Vitamin D and melanin: is there a connection?
- Sunlight and melanin: is there a connection?

Activity: Classification
- Homo sapiens: what are the variations in our species?
- Collect photos of a variety of children from different backgrounds.
- Look for differences and similarities. Group these under:
  – physical features and styles such as clothes, hair styles;
  – languages (spoken and sign), scripts in different languages;
  – genetic differences such as colours of eyes and hair;
  – names in different cultural groups, different ways in which people greet each other;
  – popular clothes for celebrations, popular make-up for different occasions, etc.

It is hoped that this type of activity, taken seriously, will help celebrate differences in a healthy environment and destroy stereotypes.

Activity: Variation
- Select approximately twenty of your schoolmates – some from similar and some from different backgrounds. Include yourself.
- Write down their names and in front of each name accurately describe their skin colour. Can you do it? Can you truthfully say that they are all white or cream or pink or brown or black? What do you think is the problem?
- After sunbathing (with suitable skin protection) with your friends for a week or so, observe what has happened to the skin colour.
- Can you say if skin colour is an example of continuous or discontinuous variation?
- Read about *melanin* in your science textbook. Melanin is present in varying degrees in the skin of all human beings except those who suffer from *albinism*. Make up a genetic cross for an *albino* sufferer and an albino carrier.

The following are some of the comments by 15-year-old students after a week-long session on genetics. The comments are unedited.

'I don't know if I think white or black, in full colour or in white and black. I am confused.'

'My dad's cousin married a black person. He used to think wogs are stupid. Now he says there is good and bad in every kind.'

'Skin colour makes no difference. We know all black people are aggressive.'

'You are different, Miss Shan. You are one of us.'

'I was going on my bike. This black boy tripped me. I will never make friends with black boys.' (When asked by another student what he would have done if it had been a white boy, this student replied, 'That is different. You got to take some flack from your own kind.')

'English is white. Isn't it?'

'It is stupid to say: Chinese English, Black English, English Muslims – don't you think? Only English are English.'

In language, history and geography lessons, students can explore how the world was carved up using 'race' in the first instance to dominate and cruelly kill human beings. Some 20 million people of colour have been killed in the slow holocaust of slavery, colonialism and apartheid.

Activity: Natural selection
This type of research must only be done after a climate of non-racist and non-sexist science has been established. Students could check out if environmental factors make a difference to the physical features such as hair colour, eye colour, skin colour, etc. Extreme sensitivity is required.

7. Sickle-cell anaemia

A lot has been written and researched regarding this disease, which is confined to peoples of African, Afro-Caribbean, Asian and Mediterranean origin. Because of this, there is a lot of myth and mystery attached to sickle-cell anaemia and many sufferers have been victims of discrimination (Prashar *et al.*, 1985:49). Sufferers have been known to be socially stigmatized by their communities. It is important for students of science to understand that this particular trait evolved as a result of a particular response in the body. The general awareness of this disease and other associated disorders is very poor. The disease is similar to any blood disorder and is not contagious; neither is it infectious and you cannot pass it on to anyone. Similar to haemophilia, it is a blood disorder which is inherited. A person born with such a disorder has inherited a gene for sickle haemoglobin from both their parents. There is no known cure and since the patient needs to attend hospital for up to a week at a time, employment penalties can be high. Yet there are very few situations which can prove to be hazardous to the carriers and sufferers of this trait, other than perhaps diving and sub-marine activities. No other exclusions can be justified. However, in Britain Her Majesty's Armed Forces exclude individuals with sickle-cell trait (Franklin and Atkin, 1986). An example of a genetic cross is if both the mother and the father carry the trait but do not suffer from the disease; this will result in a 25 per cent chance that the children will suffer. Red blood cells containing the sickle haemoglobin can change from the usual round shape to a sickle-cell shape. This leads to many problems associated with the absorption of oxygen and its transport through the body, leading to serious health problems. School work may suffer if the victim is a student. It is not clear how the disorder manifested itself in the first place, though it is well known that sufferers have some protection against a most severe kind of malaria; this has allowed sufferers to survive and pass on the trait to their children.

8. The gene pools and the Vavilov Centres around the world

Students of science need to understand the role that wild plants play in our lives. Wild plants are the traditional source of food as well as medicines. Over 40 per cent of manufactured drugs sold as prescriptions are derived from plants; modern medicine is heavily dependent upon plant materials, mostly taken from the rainforests. When it comes to food an astonishing number of varieties have been developed – wheat, rice, maize, barley, beans, etc. No one variety of any grain or legume can withstand pests and blights; sooner or later a variety becomes resistant to strains of fungi, viruses, bacteria and pests.

Conservation and development must go hand in hand. It seems as if the agribusiness of the world has learnt nothing from the disaster of the Green revolution in India. Students can learn that every plant and animal species has a gene pool from which a large number of individuals can be selected for breeding. The commonest examples known to students would be that of the dog and the cat, and in plants, that of the cabbage family: the wild cabbage gives us cauliflower, brussels sprouts, kohlrabi, cabbage and kale. Many children's lives have been saved due to a tiny plant called rosy periwinkle, as its extract is known to help in conditions of leukaemia. Not many students will be aware that the humble aspirin was developed from the willow bark.

And yet, instead of protecting the wild species and unlocking the potential to alleviate human suffering, many of the species have been wiped out, due to the short-sighted, rapid destruction of the rainforests. Regarding the gene pools of the crops and medicines, we may be standing at the brink of a major disaster. Here is a list of disasters as a result of monoculture and the destruction of crops blighted by a single pest that they had no resistance against:

- Irish potato famine (1840) – 2 million people died.
- Rice crops destroyed (1942) – millions of Bengalis died.
- Wheat stem rust (1950) – devastated US harvest.
- Maize fungus (1970) – 80 per cent of the corn crop was threatened.

The products of agri-technology are displacing the source upon which the technology is based. It is analogous to taking stones from the foundations to repair the roof.
(Professor Garrison Wilkes, University of Massachusetts)

Activity
Design experiments to check claims for the antiseptic properties of many plants. Investigate antibacterial activity of chemicals in the plants listed below. A health-food shop should be able to assist with a list of plant preparations that have antibacterial properties. Garlic and ginger capsules are commonly available from the pharmacist.

- Neem – *Azadirachta*: commonly used in India for cleaning teeth, instead of toothpaste. Neem toothpaste is also available from Indian shops.
- Garlic – regular use lowers cholesterol and cures colds and coughs.
- Ginger – regular use cures throat ailments.

9. Cracking of oil

An excellent topic to look at the dependence of human beings on nature. Examine all areas of the curriculum: make links with mathematics, geography, general studies, economics, politics, social studies by asking questions such as:

- Where does oil come from?
- What is the cost to the environment?
- Which countries are oil-rich and which are oil-poor?
- What are the politics of oil companies' price-fixing?
- Why is it such a convenient fuel?
- Are there alternatives to oil?
- Contact oil companies and agencies such as Greenpeace, Earthscan, Friends of the Earth. Seek their views for understanding further the socio-economic context. Do they produce any leaflets? Put on a display.
- Research to find out about major disasters linked with oil around the world in the last ten years. Put on a display.

Teachers should guard against materials which form patronizing and condescending accounts of what goes on in the name of science in Asia and Africa, where it is often depicted as ordinary people using 'appropriate technology' – described as low-level technology and applied science. Both continents are rich with works that are, in many cases, the precursors of modern-day scientific theories and inventions.

CONCLUSION

Science teaching and learning for a multicultural society requires whole departments to have a shared vision and a shared commitment. It is not simply a question of including some images about black people and some artefacts: it is about believing that solutions for a fair and just society really do lie in science for people and science for society.

The science departments can lead the way

Science for equality and justice can only make sense if students are learning in an atmosphere of enquiry where they are allowed to be critical learners and thinkers. At the same time, teachers are required to be critical educators. Teachers need to:

- Understand that simply including foodstuffs, artefacts and information from a variety of cultures will not produce results. A critical dialogue about any incidental happening of abuse in relation to 'race', gender, ability and sexual orientation must be challenged.

- Review the content of the curriculum and the learning materials being used as a resource.
- Recognize and eliminate destructive myths and misconceptions.
- Connect all science teaching to real people; avoid presenting it as a 'pure and neutral, Western high-tech' discipline, full of facts and concepts, which has nothing to do with real life. Quality of life is affected on a daily basis using inventions of science, their use and abuse. Science in a classroom should be presented as such.
- Disabuse self and students of the notions of biological determinism and of genetic differences between 'races'.
- Give students and staff the opportunity of placing science in a social, political and economic context; make 'race', class and gender connections; test the validity of scientific theories in a broader spectrum.
- Ensure that images displayed in the classroom reflect a balanced view. Show all peoples – both able-bodied and those with disabilities – doing science. Show positive uses and advantages of science as well as real-life disasters that have happened as a result of the greed of those abusing scientific inventions and technology.

In order to ensure a shared understanding of science for a multicultural society, involve teachers and students in making decisions about policy and practice. Science, mathematics and technology are connected, related, interdependent areas. There is no existence of one without the other, which has any meaning for real life.

Brainstorm and check out student views and images of science and scientists:

- How many black and female scientists can they name?
- Do they question derogatory images and incomplete information which may be often out of context about people from other parts of the world?

Check out your own views and images of science and scientists as a teacher:

- How many black and female scientists can you name?
- Do you believe in or reject the myth of the neutrality of science and mathematics?
- Do you question demeaning terminology such as the 'Third World', 'primitive', 'under-developed', 'ancient', 'developing'?

Present science from a constructivist approach, rather than delivering a set of instructions that students have to follow. Let students plan their experiments, choose apparatus and choose their own method of presenting conclusions and inferences. Relate the study of metals and non-metals to the consequences of their use and extraction and the effect on people's livelihood and socialization. For example, would Apartheid in South Africa have taken a different shape if gold and diamonds had not been found? Would it have come about at all?

Produce a display on scientists from around the world: black and white, dead and alive, modern and ancient, young and old, male and female. As a whole department engage in the understanding of thinking skills appropriate for developing attitudes which are conducive to critical thinking (see Table 4.2).

ACKNOWLEDGEMENT

I would like to thank John Clay for his helpful comments on this chapter. As always, any inadequacies remain mine.

NOTE

1. *Not in Our Genes: Biology, Ideology and Human Nature* (1984) Rose, Kaman and Lewontin. Harmondsworth: Penguin Books. *The Panda's Thumb: More Reflections in Natural History* (1980) Stephen Jay Gould. Harmondsworth: Penguin Books. *The Mismeasure of Man* (1997) Stephen Jay Gould. Harmondsworth: Pelican Books (a brilliant and controversial study of intelligence testing). *Perspectives on Gender and Science* (1986) Jan Harding (ed.). Lewes: Falmer Press. *The Violence of the Green Revolution: Third World Agriculture, Ecology and Politics*, Vandana Shiva. London: Zed Books Ltd. *Science or Society: The Politics of the Work of Scientists* (1982) Mike Hales. London: Pan Books.

Table 4.2   Attitudes and skills conducive to critical thinking

Process	Attitude	Skill
Problem-solving	Curiosity.	
Collecting information	Is open to a variety of resources, new and old. Keen to put forward ideas.	
Hypothesizing	Independence of thought and originality.	Open to understanding and interpreting the holistic nature of the process of living.
Experimenting	Challenging different perspectives without dogma or indoctrination.	
Decision-making	Open-mindedness. Accepts collaborative effort. Acknowledges everyone's contribution; aware of social consequences.	Group work. Consensus.
Communicating	Able to criticize self. Socially aware.	Ability to communicate in many different ways.
Apply findings	Links all findings with impact on the environment. Understands true cost and is not afraid to reject findings. Responsible for social consequences.	

BIBLIOGRAPHY

Advisory Committee on Technology Innovation (1984) Modern Prospects for an Ancient Crop: AMARNATH, Report for International Development Office of International Affairs National Research Council. Washington DC: National Academy Press.

Ainslie, W. (1826) *Materia Indica or some Accounts of those Articles which are Employed by the Hindoos and other Eastern Nations, in their Medicine, Arts and Agriculture*, 2 volumes. London: Longman, Rees, Orme, Brown and Green.

Basham, A. L. (1985) *The Wonder that was India: A Survey of the History and Culture of the Indian Sub-continent Before the Coming of the Muslims*. London: Sidgwick and Jackson.

Bose, D. M., Sen, S. N. and Subbarayappa, B. V. (1971) *A Concise History of Science in India*. New Delhi: Indian National Science Academy.

Chatterjee, S. (ed.) (1982) Collected Works of Meghnad Saha. New Delhi: Orient Longman. Available from: Saha Institute of Nuclear Physics, Calcutta.

Cole, M., Hill, D. and Shan, S. (eds) (1997) *Promoting Equality in Primary Schools*. London: Cassell.

DFE (1995) *Science in the National Curriculum*. London: HMSO.

Dharampal, S. (1971) *Indian Science and Technology in the Eighteenth Century, Some Contemporary European Accounts*. New Delhi: Impex.

Franklin, I. M. and Atkin, K. (1986) Employment of persons with Sickle-cell disease and Sickle-cell trait. *Journal of the Society of Occupational Medicine*, 36:76–9.

Kaptchuk, T. J. (1983) *Chinese Medicine: The Web that has no Weaver*. London: Rider.

Keswani, G. H. (1980) *Raman and His Effect*. New Delhi: National Book Trust.

Lunde, P. (1982) Science: The Islamic Legacy. *Aramco World Magazine*, 33(3), May/June. These articles are copyright free and teachers can get this magazine free of charge from 4 Uxbridge Street, London W8 7SZ.

Myers, N. (1985) *The GAIA Atlas of Planet Management for Today's Caretakers of Tomorrow's World*. London: Pan Books.

National Research Council Report (1984) Washington DC: National Academy Press.

Prashar, U., Anionwu, E. and Brozovic, M. (1985) *Sickle-cell Anaemia – Who Cares?* London: Runnymede Trust. Information also available from Organization for Sickle-cell Anaemia Research (OSCAR), 22 Pellatt Grove, Wood Green, London N22 5PL.

Prescott-Allen, R. and C. (1982) What's Wild Life Worth? Economic Contributions of Wild Plants and Animals to Developing Countries. International Institute for Environment and Development. London: Earthscan.

PART 2

FOUNDATION SUBJECTS KEY STAGES 3 AND 4: THE NON-CORE SUBJECTS

CHAPTER 5

Design and technology and information technology

Margaret Cox and Adarsh Sood

> Technology is, and always has been, about the realisation of appropriate solutions to human problems, problems which arise in every sphere of human activity.
>
> (Leslie Thompson, 1989)

INTRODUCTION

Technology was included in the original list of subjects in the National Curriculum when it first became part of the New Orders in 1989. At that time each National Curriculum subject order included lists of attainment targets supported by extensive programmes of study. Included in the technology curriculum was information technology, identified by a list of specific themes for Attainment Target 5, although it was not intended that information technology should only be taught or used within the technology curriculum. All other subject teachers were encouraged to include information technology within their own teaching.

However, as reported by many writers, for example Cox (1993a), Underwood (1997), and in a review of inspection findings (OfSTED, 1995), information technology has not been adequately taught in schools and therefore when the revised National Curriculum was launched in January 1995, technology was split into two separate subjects: design and technology, and information technology.

The proposals for the IT curriculum published in May 1999 (QCA, 1999) recommend a further change of name for the IT curriculum to Information and Communication Technologies (ICT), but since the Welsh, Scottish and Northern Ireland curricula still use IT rather than ICT, and since there are now 603 university IT not ICT courses, we shall continue to refer to the IT curriculum, rather than ICT, in this chapter. This chapter discusses the ways in which both design and technology and information technology can be used to promote equality in teaching and learning in schools, and to teach students about ways of overcoming inequalities in our society.

Of all the National Curriculum subjects, design and technology and more particularly information technology are often regarded as relating to the technological change in the Western world; yet at the same time these very subjects provide perhaps the best opportunities for helping to bridge the gap between the different cultures, between different sexes, ranges of ability and income levels. Both design and technology and information technology are subjects based on skills and processes rather than tied to content (as in history or geography) and therefore provide more freedom for the teacher to incorporate ideas discussed in this and the other chapters. Since design and technology and information technology are perceived now by most schools as being two separate subjects, this chapter will consider them separately but will include ways in which teachers can apply IT also within the technology curriculum. There are, however, important historical factors relating to the original establishment of the technology curriculum before the split in 1995. We will discuss these briefly, to provide the reader with the background to the way in which the technology subjects have evolved and where their application has often been restricted to a very narrow view of technology.

DEVELOPMENT OF THE TECHNOLOGY CURRICULUM

In 1988, as the only new subject in the National Curriculum, technology brought together a number of divergent traditions, from metal work to home economics. On this basis, the new subject had the potential to address some of the weaknesses of the traditional approaches in regard to equality issues, specifically in the teaching and learning processes involved in the delivery of these subjects. technology subsumed the predominantly boys' subject of craft, design and technology (CDT) and the predominantly girls' subject of home economics. The new single subject of technology therefore posed for teachers a real equal opportunities challenge regarding the sexes: how to retain the active interest of those students whom they had seldom taught in the past. Many people's efforts to provide equality between the sexes 'have been designed to give girls and women access to areas of study that have traditionally been thought to be "masculine" and to areas of work that have traditionally been occupied by men. This assumes that what boys and men have is best, while conversely, by implication, that which girls and women have is worst' (Hilton, 1992). Over many years, girls' lack of interest in physics, technology and related mathematics had been a general cause of concern. Their preference for biological rather than physical sciences, for example, has been a long-standing feature of secondary education. It has been established for some years that girls are more attracted to subjects in which there are clear social applications rather than those traditionally more abstract.

Even before the formation of the technology curriculum there was widespread disagreement amongst educators as to the focus and content of CDT: 'the consensus view of the media and the general public seems to equate technology with specific industry products, for example, aerospace, micro-electronics, telecommunications, computers and so on, yet to link it exclusively with the narrow range of the products of the age in which we live is myopic and misses the point. Technology is, and always has been, about the realisation of appropriate solutions to human problems, problems which arise in every sphere of human activity' (Thompson, 1989).

In the rest of the National Curriculum subjects, curriculum knowledge and content rather than processes were increasingly stressed. The subject was therefore not only seen as new, but as fundamentally different from the rest of the National Curriculum, being directly concerned with generating ideas, making and doing. In emphasising the importance of practical capability and providing opportunities for students to develop their powers to innovate, to make decisions, to create new solutions it can play a new role. Central to this role is the task of providing a balance of a curriculum based on academic subjects – a balance in which the creative and practical capabilities of students can be fully developed and inter-related.

However, because of its origins, technology is still perceived by many schools as being less academic than science, mathematics and history, for example. Yet because of the uncertainties as to what and how it should be taught, this provides important opportunities for teachers to build in activities which promote equality among students.

In spite of the optimistic hopes for the new technology curriculum (see Paechter, 1993), in practice the hope for radical change failed to recognize that the groups of teachers introducing the new curriculum, coming mainly from CDT and home economics departments, were already the most traditionally oriented of school teachers. The subjects they taught were those which in their histories and certain aspects of the then current practice, contributed most explicitly to the maintenance of some aspects of the *status quo*. This applied not only to sexual biases, but the subject was historically tied to a Western culture with very little curriculum support for students from diverse cultures and incomes, nor for those with special needs. Although the technology order, unlike orders for other subjects, stressed the importance of human purposes and values in an interdisciplinary student-centred learning environment, little help was given to teachers to embrace equality and equal opportunities in the delivery of the technology curriculum.

In 1995, the revised National Curriculum could have provided an opportunity for a fundamental change for the better. In practice this has been slow to happen, hence the need for this chapter.

DESIGN AND TECHNOLOGY

The Design and Technology Curriculum for secondary schools (Key Stages 3 and 4 and beyond) has two main attainment targets: designing and making. These are the same for both primary and secondary education but differ in that secondary teachers are often more constrained by the requirements of national examination syllabuses compared to their primary colleagues. We are therefore providing examples of class activities which will address our purposes of promoting equality within the current secondary curriculum mostly dominated by the attainment targets of the National Curriculum and exam syllabuses.

Ideas provided within the other secondary subject chapters can also be considered here since 'students should be given opportunities to apply skills, knowledge and understanding from the programmes of study of other subjects, where appropriate, including art, mathematics and science' (DFE, 1995a). As a basis for our design and technology activities, we have selected two from those provided by the Schools Curriculum and Assessment Authority (1996a), although we shall redress the balance by removing the bias and extending the very narrow examples provided. The reason we have chosen this approach is because the *Exemplification of Standards* is sent to every design and technology school department in the country and it is therefore important that all those teachers can expand the officially recommended activities into those which will foster an egalitarian pedagogy.

Designing and making a food container

At each stage of the activity described in this section the teacher should consider teaching resources and methods appropriate to communicating these ideas to students whose mother tongue is not English, and to students with disabilities and specific learning difficulties.

The processes of designing and making a food container for a lunch box are given as an activity in the SCAA guide to assess students' abilities at Levels 2 to 5. The task is divided into the following activities for the *design* stage: generating ideas, applying knowledge and understanding, modelling and evaluating. For the *making* stage: planning, applying knowledge and understanding, working with materials and evaluating. To enhance the stages outlined in the guide we have included ideas to embrace different cultures, abilities and economic backgrounds, and to promote collaboration between students and to show how this activity can be extended to include higher levels of attainment.

However, it is important before the students start on this activity that they have the opportunity to consider issues such as whether all children and young people in England and Wales can afford lunch, what kind of school day requires students to have lunch outside the home, what other patterns of meal-times might there be in other countries. In many countries schools either have two sessions, with one set of students in the morning and another in the afternoon – as in Yemen – or all going home at lunch time, as in Greece.

Generating ideas

In order to decide on ideas for the lunch box, students can be given a research task, based at first in the classroom, for which the goal is to find out what kinds of lunch their classmates have. This should result in a list of foods and drinks which the students can then group into categories according to texture, hot and cold foods, perishability, and the range of foods used to make a lunch. If the class has students from a variety of cultural backgrounds, then this list can act as a focus for discussion about different foods eaten across the world and how these foods need to be packed and stored to be able to provide lunch. Issues which should be included are:

- nutritional value;
- cost of food;
- special diets (vegetarian, high fibre, low fat);
- religious requirements such as Kosher, Halal;
- handling requirements for those students with visual or manipulative impairments.

If the class is mainly monocultural, students should either be given a homework task of finding out what foods children from other countries eat, by researching this in the school or local library, or on the Internet to discover the main foods eaten by different cultural groups. The Internet can also be used for communicating directly with children in small rural villages, for example, through the Miranda project in Chile (Preston, 1995). (Further information about the cross-cultural Miranda project can also be found on the web.) An increasing number of countries now have some schools which make regular use of the Internet to communicate with schools in the UK, such as those in Russia, the Czech Republic, Brazil and Australia.

Further ideas can be obtained from the CD-ROM package *Distant Places* (details given in Resources list at end of chapter) which has information about meals eaten by people in many countries. This CD-ROM is accompanied by worksheets with ideas for studying the lifestyles of different peoples and also the food grown in different countries. It is also important to consider the range of incomes of the students' families and therefore get the students to think of economical foods as well as those pre-packed foods which are easily transportable but therefore expensive.

The National Curriculum orders state: 'appropriate provision should be made for students who need to use means of communication other than speech, including computers, technological aids, signing, symbols or lip-reading, as well as non-sighted methods of reading and non-visual or non-aural ways of acquiring information' (DFE, 1995a).

For students who are partially sighted, many of the web page texts can be enlarged to help with reading, and many now have speech as well as visual displays, both of which can provide alternative modes of communication.

The 1994 Special Needs code of practice (see reference at the end of this chapter) makes frequent reference to the value and use of information technology to support students with special needs. There are three types of roles that IT can play in assisting access to learning design and technology for students with special educational needs, in addition to contributing to the students' own personal development of IT capability. Information technology can provide:

- *physical access:* many students who have sensory or motor impairments can use a concept keyboard with an overlay, to prepare their list of foods, thereby producing quality written materials which they can share with fellow-students.
- *cognitive access:* students with learning difficulties can access relevant information in pictorial as well as written forms, enabling them to research the necessary information and overcome the handicaps of limited reading and writing skills. This also applies to students whose mother tongue is other than English.
- *experiential access:* profoundly disabled students do not have the same opportunities to experience much of the world firsthand. Using CD-ROM encyclopedias, *Distant Places* and the Internet can help those students who are unable to visit their local library or interview fellow-students to gather information about foods from a range of different countries.

Applying knowledge and understanding
The SCAA guide gives student examples on 'Applying knowledge and understanding' as follows:

- 'She discussed possible materials with her teacher, choosing plywood for strength and ease of cutting' (Level 2);
- 'He chose an appropriate material from the three available, and explained why it fitted the design proposal he had drawn up. He realised after discussion that the plywood would need to be varnished' (Level 3);
- 'She discussed what finishes would be suitable using information provided on health and hygiene' (Level 4);
- 'Drawing on information on food hygiene, he decided to add a polystyrene-lined compartment to keep the temperature constant' (Level 5). (SCAA, 1996a)

It is clear from these ideas that each student's work is being done and assessed individually, yet the design and technology curriculum also requires students to work in teams. Many studies have shown that, particularly for females, where talk is encouraged and collaboration is the norm, many of the fears of technological, mathematical and scientific subjects disappear. In a study of women learning mathematics, Isaacson found:

> the effect on the women of working in groups has been more dramatic than anything else this year, as these comments, all written at the end of a lesson, indicate:
> 'It was useful because we could argue until we all agreed (or agreed to disagree) on a point. As we are teaching each other we all get a better understanding of the subject matter'.
> 'Group work also inspires confidence, and enables the time to pass quickly and pleasantly'.
> 'I'm really enjoying it . . . it's so much fun working in groups, just in groups . . . it's really eye-opening'. (Isaacson, 1989)

The application of knowledge and understanding of individual students can be extended to include students working in teams using the list of foods produced earlier, with each team being given a particular goal such as designing the lunch box for a hot lunch for an elderly person, a lunch in a very hot climate, or a Western economical lunch. In considering the different needs of a variety of users, this is regarded as an activity at Level 8.

Modelling
At the modelling stage, Level 5, an example describes how 'he used scrap PVC to see if his ideas would work using material

thicker than the card used in his initial model. He tried and tested different sizes and shapes for folds and flaps using scraps of PVC in order to find the best design' (SCAA, 1996a). This shows that the modelling stage provides an ideal point in the project for students not only to consider the usual types of materials to use for their container, but to consider recycled materials, materials which do least harm to the environment and require the lowest expenditure of energy. At the Earth Summit in 1992, over 150 countries drew up Agenda 21, which states:

> Education is critical in promoting sustainable development and improving the capacity of the people to address environment and development issues . . . Education can lead to action, support and develop alternative policies that improve the environment, and empower individuals and communities to participate in changing their world. (Council for Environmental Education, 1996)

Students can be introduced to the importance of responsible management of resources through this design and technology activity and learn about low-tech alternatives for making a food container. For example, a 'take-away' in many Far Eastern countries is wrapped in vine or other leaves, and the container therefore is entirely biodegradable. Each team of students could be asked to consider two alternative models, a high- and low-energy model, the latter being made of existing products or the container being edible – the original idea behind the sandwich!

Evaluating
Students at this stage can evaluate their own design given appropriate criteria but to include the many factors relating to the range of different needs. This will require the students to consider and prioritize the production time, limitations of tools and equipment, properties of the materials, use of energy, minimization of waste, and flexibility of design to accommodate the range of users. At this stage students could create a spreadsheet, using EXCEL, for example, to incorporate anticipated costs of the product. For students at Levels 8 and above the spreadsheet can incorporate additional factors such as relationship between amount and shape of food and the amount of material required to make the container, the estimated energy costs to make the materials, the rate of cooling for hot foods in relation to the insulation thicknesses, and the physical and chemical properties of the materials.

Making the product

Similar teaching approaches can now be used during the students' activities to make their food containers, with each stage relating to the teams' different design plans. Throughout this and the design stage the students work individually and in their teams to consider:

- how far it meets a clear need;
- its fitness for purpose;
- whether it is an appropriate use of resources;
- its impact beyond the purpose for which it was designed, e.g. on the environment (DFE, 1995a).

One of the student examples describes how 'he gave the finished container to a relative to use on a day trip, with a simple questionnaire asking for feedback on how easy it was to use and clean and how acceptable it was in terms of appearance' (SCAA, 1996a). This approach can be followed for different types of food containers for different cultural groups and people with special needs. Students from lone-parent families or with very few relatives should be advised to exchange their food containers with others in their class team for evaluation. Where students have designed a container for another person with a particular physical disability, then organizations such as those listed at the end of the chapter may be willing to collaborate in the evaluation.

There are other examples and topics given in the SCAA guide, and in earlier guides such as the INSET resources produced by the National Curriculum Council of 1991 which can be adapted to provide many equal opportunities in the secondary design and technology curriculum. Ideas for incorporating information technology are discussed in the following section as well as providing equality of opportunities within IT itself.

One group of learners who are often disadvantaged but cannot be considered in great detail here, due to the specific focus of this book, is the children of occupational travellers. We feel they should not be forgotten although it is not possible to present many ideas here for addressing their specific needs. There are many children whose education is regularly interrupted because they are 'on the road' during the summer months. It is now possible for schools who, in the past, have provided them with distance learning packs, to keep in more regular contact with them through the use of the Internet. Access to Internet connections for students will increase significantly during the next few years, including access in local libraries, cafes and youth centres. Teachers and non-travelling students will then be able to communicate with travelling students in joint projects and collaborating teams through Internet communications, and/or access to school Web sites. This will reduce the isolation that many of these students feel and the periods of disruption to their formal education.

INFORMATION TECHNOLOGY

Information technology is one of the most difficult subjects for teachers to tackle because of many important historical, social and technological factors. For detailed literature about the growth of the use of IT in education and about research into its uptake and use and effects on learning, the reader is referred to Cox (1993a, 1997a), Passey and Samways (1997), the *Journal for Computer Assisted Learning, Computers and Education* and *Education and Information Technologies* and publications by the British Educational Communications and Technology Agency (BECTA).

IT access and training

Despite a steady flow of different government initiatives and programmes since the *National Development Programme for Computer Assisted Learning 1974–1978* (Hooper, 1978) and the current requirements for the teaching of IT as a foundation subject in the National Curriculum, the majority of teachers have received insufficient training to be able to teach it to the depth and quality required. Information technology (DFE, 1995b) is like any other subject in the National Curriculum in that schools are required to teach it up to and beyond GCSE level. The major themes for IT are information and computer systems, communicating and handling information, measurement and control, and simulations and modelling.

Insufficient funding for the IT curriculum over many years, in schools, LEAs and colleges, means only a minority of practising teachers have been able to embark upon the extensive training required to achieve the levels of knowledge and understanding to be able, for example, to teach modelling using spreadsheets, or designing a system to monitor the temperature, humidity and lighting in a greenhouse. Many headteachers still believe that as long as students learn a bit of word processing, produce a school newsletter, and send a few e-mails, then the school is meeting the requirements of the National Curriculum. This attitude is not surprising, however, since to equip schools adequately, train teachers and constantly innovate creates a daunting and very expensive prospect for any school. As a result, this is one subject in the National Curriculum where there are serious inequalities of access and opportunity between students in the same class, between classes and between schools (Cox, 1993a, 1997b). Studies of school provision and practice by many researchers, as well as reports from the OfSTED inspections, show that only a minority of students have the opportunity to study IT up to and including GCSE level, and only a very small number in the Sixth Form, even though there are now 600 courses in IT offered at university.

Possibly, because of the variations between schools in teaching IT, with some teaching IT as a separate subject and some across the curriculum, and some hardly at all, the present government has allocated over £1 billion of Lottery money to be spent on education, with a significant amount going on ICT in education, including training for 400,000 teachers. For ideas of how to use ICT in different subjects see, for example, Leask and Pachler (1999) and Cox (1999). How that will be interpreted by training providers is not yet known. Although there is inequality of access between students, classes and schools, there is some awareness among teachers of the need to try and provide equal access for girls and boys, although much of the earlier educational software did not address the needs of different cultures. However, there has been extensive effort made to provide IT resources for students with special needs, including the establishment of four special-needs centres in the early 1980s; a list of those still in existence is given at the end of the chapter.

Information technology works

The National Council for Educational Technology (renamed the British Educational Communications and Technology Agency in 1998), the government-funded body which promotes IT in schools, produced the report *IT Works* (NCET, 1994) in which it pinpointed how IT can motivate some children who have disabilities or who have previously failed in education (see also Singh Cooner and Loveless, 1997:30). The report spells out the advantages of having sources of information available at the press of a button that previously only a library could provide. It also highlights how IT can enhance understanding by adding visual or even moving images to a wide variety of subjects. Part of the acknowledged power of IT is its impersonality, and the report suggests that it is the fear of being wrong or being ridiculed for being wrong that prevents many children from learning. The report goes on to suggest that some of the most remarkable strides are being made in schools with children who have the most difficulty in learning. It is further suggested that well-designed software programs do not become impatient if the learner is slow, and that there is no pressure to keep up with quicker children. Only the computer program and student know about the mistakes being made. The Council makes a strong case for the use of IT in schools, with claims that it can hone skills of writing and drafting, because correcting mistakes is made easy. It increases motivation generally, making difficult ideas more comprehensible, at the same time as encouraging analytical and divergent thinking (Cox, 1997a).

The exponential growth in the use of the Internet, which evolved from the early academic and military networks of the 1960s and 1970s, will also have a major impact on equality and equal opportunity for students in schools. In this chapter we therefore also consider the significance of electronic information exchange for the secondary school classroom. Since mid-1993 with access to the World Wide Web the multimedia potential of the Internet has allowed users to travel the network with pictures, sound and video, simply by pointing and clicking a mouse. The potential for schools becomes apparent as teachers realize that the Internet is a 'place' to visit, and is full of people and ideas in 'cyberspace'. To many it is a new medium, based on broadcasting and publishing, but with another dimension added: interactivity.

At present there is no coherent development of electronic communications as a key educational resource, partly due to the costs involved, and also due to the concern of many schools on how to manage a range of information to which students have access. Several companies provide managed access for schools, but few have developed the service to provide 'walled garden access' to the Internet, bringing a vetted, but still extensive, information store for students on-line with passwords required for full Internet access. The provision of e-mail accounts for all students at Key Stages 3 and 4 would provide a significant way forward, enabling students to engage in meaningful research and providing a medium for maintaining contact with their teachers and peers outside lesson time. Equality of access to the facilities provided by electronic media should be encouraged and fostered within the school curriculum, as well as through the use of information technology in computer clubs and open access sessions.

Some commentators have argued that with the slimmed-down Dearing curriculum and the promised period of stability, schools need to decide on new directions in the use of the Internet for the support of teaching and learning. Schools already on an internal computer network are equipped to link into the Internet via an ISDN connection, and a number of computers can be used for information-seeking at the same time. We have provided examples of activities for the teaching of IT to provide equal opportunities and also refer the reader to Singh Cooner and Loveless on information technology in *Promoting Equality in Primary Schools* (Cole *et al.*, 1997:363–86).

When working in teams in an information technology classroom, students should be encouraged to extend and develop the examples provided in the SCAA exemplification of standards at Key Stage 3 (SCAA, 1996b). They could gather their own information on breakfast foods for a spreadsheet project to calculate the total protein and energy provided by different breakfasts, differentiating the information gathered at all stages to take account of the wide diversity of breakfast choice available (SCAA, 1996b:46–7). Similarly a database project on data handling need not be eurocentric if a world perspective on data collection is encouraged from the beginning, and students working as part of a team could begin to gather data on a given topic from across the world. For example, students may investigate the countries of origins of British people and do a survey of the origins of students in the class and other classes. This helps students to learn about the rich diversity of cultures in the UK, and the range of languages spoken and religions followed. As with the design and technology ideas, there is now a range of software for students with different abilities and special needs which helps them to investigate sets of data using different methods of input.

An important aspect of investigating data is interpreting its relevance to the particular context and topic. The examples provided by the SCAA guide can also enable students to investigate patterns in the relationships between data: students could investigate the data further to identify the location of all the Roman Catholic European countries, to learn how religions might spread, and how people from different places come to share different beliefs and knowledge through migration and communication. This would also extend the activity to Level 8 and beyond, and help students develop more advanced data analysis skills, for which IT has been shown to make an important and unique contribution (Cox and Nikolopoulou, 1997:105–20).

The scope and potential to extend the boundaries of student knowledge are realized in practice when students are engaged in defining the subject base of their own projects. At the same time, it is important to extend student thinking through exposure to concepts and topics beyond the realms of their own experience. By using existing sources of information such as *Save It and Stay Comfortable – A Guide to the Efficient Use of Electricity in the Home*, published by the Institution of Electrical Engineers (1995), it is possible to engage students in all aspects of the information technology and design and technology curricula and at the same time encourage them to think about environmental issues such as the importance of saving energy and how to save electricity in the home. For example, such data can be used as a foundation on which students can build their own spreadsheet models, or extend the activity further to the use of other modelling environments to investigate the effects of energy consumption on carbon dioxide emissions, discussed later in the chapter.

Once again the scope for teamwork could be established and developed through a brainstorming activity with students by asking them to identify different electrical devices used in the home. This activity is likely to produce a long list of examples such as: cookers, hobs, microwave ovens, conventional ovens, washing machines, tumble dryers, refrigerators and freezers, dishwashers, televisions, vacuum cleaners, irons and kettles, electric space heating and water heating. These can be related to the actual figures for UK domestic consumption of electricity (for example, about 22 per cent for space heating, 19 per cent for refrigeration, 14 per cent for water heating, and 9 per cent for cooking).

In considering the range of electrical appliances and their purposes, value decisions may be called for not only in relation to the specific design criteria – i.e. aesthetic, ergonomic and economic judgements, suitability of purpose and ease of manufacture – but also in relation to the right or wrong of a particular solution in ethical terms. Use of electricity contributes to carbon emissions and perhaps global warming, and students can be encouraged to consider how such use can be reduced; for example by keeping hot water, once boiled, in a vacuum flask to save energy; using low-energy light bulbs; hanging clothes outside to dry, and so on. In a case study approach based on saving electricity in the home, there is scope for collection of data from a variety of sources and sectors: domestic, commercial and industrial.

The use of real data sources with students can be a useful way of extending their curiosity to investigate independently. Providing them with statistics for the UK can open up the possibility for them to gather their own information on the same topic from a global perspective. At the same time, by encouraging them to study different designs of appliances such as electric hobs it is possible to encourage them to produce their own designs which reflect a concern not only for environmental issues but also provide a sound solution to problems encountered by people with disabilities when provided with standard designs. This helps to emphasize the relevance of people and their quality of life in an everyday setting or in less common settings which may be of specific interest to groups and individuals with varying requirements and needs.

Although modelling can be done through the use of general purpose software – such as the spreadsheet package EXCEL or data handling package ACCESS – planning National Curriculum activities around these packages is often very time-consuming and difficult since they were designed for the adult commercial market. There are alternative and comprehensive modelling packages which have been developed specifically for education. For example, *Model Builder* (Booth and Cox, 1997) has been designed for use with students aged from 10 years up to adulthood and includes a simple modelling language (incorporating natural language), plus graphs, tables and pictures. By using this environment either the student or the teacher can build models, with illustrations if preferred, to enhance the students' understanding of particular concepts. This resource enables teachers to select topics which are of particular interest and relevance to individual students.

Modelling packages such as these enable students to investigate and construct their own conceptual relationships within the context of environmental studies. Examples of models built by students in the past include a house model, where students constructed the relationships between factors which contribute to energy consumption and those contributing to better insulation. Different models can be built based upon the same topic with drawings of homes from different countries and showing alternative methods of keeping warm. *Distant Places* enables students to access pictures of homes in Tanzania, Niger, Peru, St Lucia and many other places around the world.

Other *Model Builder* models are included in the curriculum pack *Energy Expert*, which was designed to teach students about the important issues of energy use, environmental impact and alternative ways of maintaining a constant temperature inside the home, including keeping a home cool in a hot climate. It is an ideal resource for students to explore the ways houses used to be kept cool without the need for expensive and wasteful air conditioning. Students can then progress to build models such as the *Carbon Cycle*, which enables them to model the processes of the carbon cycle to investigate the amount of carbon dioxide produced in the atmosphere by industrial combustion of fossil fuels, also taking into consideration the rate of absorption by plants and the oceans.

CONCLUSION

Information technology includes topic-specific software, open-ended generic software, communications software, sensors, switches, hardware and virtual reality. It is impossible for any person to become an expert in all these domains, especially as the technology is moving faster than most people can. For ICT the future is not limited by the present. It is clear, however, from the overwhelming evidence of the last twenty to thirty years, that when used wisely and with a clear purpose and context, the use of IT and other technology can provide almost limitless opportunities for all children. IT is no longer the prerogative of the privileged few, but the economic basis of access to it could still bring about another great division in our global society between the 'haves' and 'have-nots' (Singh Cooner and Loveless, 1997). The challenge for the teachers is that in order to prevent this new inequality and to provide a technology curriculum which facilitates the realization of appropriate solutions to current human problems, they need, somehow, to find the time and resources to learn about the positive aspects of information technology as a subject and within technology and other curriculum subjects, and to harness them for the benefit of all their students.

BIBLIOGRAPHY

Booth, B. and Cox, M. J. (1997) *Model Builder: Creating Models. The Modus Project.* 1 St James Road, Harpenden AL5 4NX.

Cole, M., Hill, D. and Shan, S. *Promoting Equality in Primary Schools.* London: Cassell.

Council for Environmental Education (1996) *Our World – Our Responsibility: Environmental Education, A Practical Guide.* Reading: CFEE.

Cox, M. J. (1993a) Information technology resourcing and use. In D. M. Watson (ed.) *Impact – An Evaluation of the Impact of the Information Technology on Children's Achievements in Primary and Secondary Schools.* London: King's College London.

Cox, M. J. (1993b) Technology enriched school project – the impact of information technology on children's learning. *Computers Education,* 21(1/2).

Cox, M. J. (1997a) The effects of information technology on students' motivation. London: King's College London.

Cox, M. J. (1997b) Identification of the changes in attitude and pedagogical practices needed to enable teachers to use information technology in the school curriculum. In D. Passey and B. Samways (eds) *Information Technology: Supporting Change Through Teacher Education.* London: Chapman and Hall.

Cox, M. J. (1999) Using Information and Communication Technologies (ICT) for Pupils' Learning. In G. Nicholls (ed.) *Learning to Teach.* London: Kogan Page.

Cox, M. J. and Nikolopoulou, K. (1997) What information handling skills are promoted by the use of data analysis software? *Education and Information Technologies Journal,* 2(2), June.

Department for Education (1995a) *Design and Technology in the National Curriculum.* London: HMSO.

Department for Education (1995b) *Information Technology in the National Curriculum.* London: HMSO.

Hilton (1992) Girls and women in education: are the challenges they face today different from those they faced a hundred years ago? Master's Dissertation. London: King's College London.

Hooper, R. (1978) *NDPCAL – Final Report.* London Council for Educational Technology. London.

Institution of Electrical Engineers (1995) *Save it and Stay Comfortable – A Guide to the Efficient Use of Electricity in the Home.* IEE.

Isaacson, Z. (1989) Are you going to be a motor mechanic or something? Women learning mathematics for science and technology. In J. Head (ed.) *Girls and Technology.* London: King's Education Papers No.1.

Leask, M. and Pachler, N. (1999) *Learning to Teach Using ICT in the Secondary School.* London: Routledge.

National Council for Educational Technology (NCET) (1994) *IT Works.*

National Council for Educational Technology (NCET) (1996) *IT Disability and Lifelong Learning.* NCET.

OfSTED (1995) *Information Technology: A Review of Inspection Findings.* London: HMSO.

Paechter, C. (1993) Power, Knowledge and the Design and Technology Curriculum. Ph.D. Thesis. London: King's College London.

Passey, D. and Samways, B. (eds) (1997) *Information Technology: Supporting Change through Teacher Education.* London: Chapman and Hall.

Preston, C. (1995) Best Defence. *Times Higher Education Supplement,* 7 April.

Schools Curriculum and Assessment Authority (1996a) *Design and Technology. Consistency of Teacher Assessment. Exemplification of Standards. Key Stage 3.* London: HMSO.

Schools Curriculum and Assessment Authority (1996b) *Information Technology. Consistency of Teacher Assessment. Exemplification of Standards. Key Stage 3.* London: HMSO.

Shan, S. and Cox, M. J. (1997) Design and technology. In M. Cole, D. Hill and S. Shan (eds) *Promoting Equality in Primary Schools.* London: Cassell.

Singh Cooner, T. and Loveless, A. (1997) Information technology. In M. Cole, D. Hill and S. Shan (eds) *Promoting Equality in Primary Schools.* London: Cassell.

Thompson, L (1989) Technology education in schools. In J. Head (ed.) *Girls and Technology.* London: King's Education Papers No.1.

Underwood, J. (1997) Breaking the cycle of ignorance: information technology and the professional development of teachers. In D. Passey, and B. Samways (eds) *Information Technology: Supporting Change Through Teacher Education.* London: Chapman and Hall.

RESOURCES

Educational Software:

Distant Places (1994) AU Enterprises Ltd, 126 Great North Road, Hatfield, Herts AL9 5JZ.

Model Builder – The Modus Project; Expert Builder – The Modus Project; Energy Expert – The Modus Project. 1 St James Road, Harpenden, Herts AL5 4NX.

Our World – Our Responsibility: Environmental Education (1996) A practical guide. Council for Environmental Education (CFEE). Reading.

PUBLICATIONS

Information Technology – Exemplification of Standards, Key Stage 3. SCAA Publications, PO Box 235, Hayes, Middlesex UB3 1HF. Tel: 0181 561 4499.

Design and Technology – Exemplification of Standards, Key Stage 3. SCAA Publications, PO Box 235, Hayes, Middlesex UB3 1HF. Tel: 0181 561 4499.

Save It and Stay Comfortable – A Guide to the Efficient Use of Electricity in the Home (1995) The Institution of Electrical Engineers.

SUPPORT SERVICES – DESIGN AND TECHNOLOGY AND INFORMATION TECHNOLOGY

Special needs:

ACE Centre Advisory Trust, Wayneflete Road, Headington, Oxford OX3 8DD. Tel: 01865 763508. e-mail ace-cent@dircon.co.uk.Ace Centre – North: http://ds.dial.pipex.com/town/terrace/ac969/index/htm

ACITT, National Association of Information Technology Co-ordinators and Teachers of Information Technology, IAS, The Westbury Centre, Ripple Road, Barking, Essex IG11 7PT. Tel: 01342 715682. http://www.acitt.org.uk

British Educational Communications and Technology Agency (BECTA), Milburn Hill Road, Science Park, Coventry CV4 7JJ. Tel: 01203 41669. Fax: 01203 411418. http://www.becta.org.uk

Cenmac, Eltham Green Complex, 1a Middle Park Avenue, London SE9 5HL. Tel: 0181 850 9229. Fax: 0181 850 9220. e-mail cenmac@cenmac.demon.co.uk

Computability Centre, PO Box 94, Warwick CV34 5WS. Tel: 0800 269545. Fax: 01926 311345.

Inclusive Technology Ltd, Saddleworth Business Centre, Oldham, Greater Manchester OL3 5DF. Tel: 01457 819790. Fax: 01457 819799. e-mail inclusive@inclusive.co.uk

Mental Health Media, The Resource Centre, 366 Holloway Road, London N7 6PA. Tel: 0171 700 0100 Ext. 204. Fax: 0171 700 0099. http://www.mediafirst.org.uk

The SEN Code of Practice. DFEE, Special Educational Needs Division, Sanctuary Buildings, Gt Smith Street, London SW1P 3BT. Tel: 0207 925 6363. Fax: 0207 925 6986.

For IT and other teachers:

British Educational Communications and Technology Agency (BECTA, address as above).

Council for Environmental Education, 94 London Street, Reading, Berks RG1 4SJ. Tel: 0118 950 2550. Fax: 0118 959 1955. e-mail info@cee.i-way.co.uk. http://www.cee.org.uk

Design and Technology Association (DATA), 16 Wellesbourne House, Walton Road, Wellesbourne, Warwickshire CV35 9JB. Tel: 01789 470007. Fax: 01789 841955. e-mail data@data.org.uk. http://www.data.org.uk

Information Technology in Teacher Education Association (ITTE). http://www.itte.ntu.ac.uk

National Association for Co-ordinators and Teachers of IT (ACITT, address as above).

National Grid for Learning (NGFL), http://www.ngfl.gov.uk

Scottish Council for Educational Technology (SCET), 74 Victoria Crescent, Glasgow, Scotland G12 9JN. Tel: 0141 337 5000. Fax: 0141 337 5050. e-mail: enquiries@scet.com. http://www.scet.com

CHAPTER 6

History

Tom Jackson

... the lives and actions of the common people ... the very stuff of history.

(George Rudé, in Krantz, 1988:4)

INTRODUCTION

N.B. There will be very few Dates in this History.

(Jane Austen, *The History of England*, in 1978:67)

As created by the Conservative government in 1991, the National Curriculum (History) can be viewed as a nationalistic 'Well done': not purely to great men and their successes in wars and industry, as Frances Morrell would have it (Morrell, 1989), but to Britain's progressive development towards her apparently inevitable superpower status. Morrell does not exaggerate, however, when pointing out that the development of the United Kingdom is regarded by many as a story of initiative, exploration, individual daring, and conflict (Morrell, 1989). Older history textbooks tended to focus on these aspects and were consequently negative in their attitudes towards Asian and black peoples; women, the disabled and other oppressed groups were barely mentioned. Such texts, and the lessons in which they were used, served to reinforce the hidden curriculum, which teaches children 'to know their place and to sit still in it' (Illich, 1973). However, under the influence of *annaliste* historians such as Marc Bloch and Lucien

Febvre, twentieth-century historical research has shifted to focus much more on public events and the masses. Even so, as late as 1944 Trevelyan still felt the need to remark, 'Social history might be defined negatively as the history of a people with the politics left out' (Trevelyan, 1944:vii). The influence of the *annaliste* school on historical writing can easily be seen in the change in school textbooks. (And, having been taught history by plodding through Snellgrove (1968, 1972) that is no bad thing!)

The effective history teacher will select content and facts from the National Curriculum (History) which are appropriate to the purpose of the lesson(s). One only has to glance cursorily at the Programme of Study for Key Stage 3 and Key Stage 4 to appreciate the necessity of this. Given that in most, if not all, schools – including those in the private sector – history (as a separate subject) occupies merely one or two hours of the weekly timetable, it follows that all aspects of the Programmes of Study (PoS) cannot be given equal weight – or, indeed, be dealt with. It is therefore unsurprising that teachers/departments will select areas of the PoS which are best suited to the time and resources at their disposal, as well as the interests of both themselves and their students. The advantage of the revised (1995) National Curriculum for History (DFE, 1995) is that the field from which the selection can be made – in both core and supplementary units – is wide. That such a wide choice may not be possible to implement is due to the lack of time and, above all, resources. It is quite possible that such a dilemma cannot be worked out by the classroom teacher or even the department.

One is then left with two choices: either view history through the eyes of those modern Mr Gradgrinds, Conservative education policy-makers,[1] as nothing more than 'facts'; or accept that knowing (or not knowing) the date of the abolition of slavery is of little importance except as an isolated historical fact in a series of such. To continue with this latter example, what is surely of greater importance in a gendered, multicultural, racist and class-based society of diverse races is to know that the British Empire was built on slavery, the abolition of which was at best partial and initiated largely for economic reasons; also that slavery continues, under a variety of guises; and that an understanding of slavery, its 'abolition' and its effects requires an understanding of the historian's art and epistemological position.[2]

Traditionalists (who appear to include many Conservative and

New Labour MPs) still seem to hold the nineteenth-century Rankean view of history: *wie es eigentlich gewesen* (how it really was). This implies that history is 'the past' and the task of the teacher is to present it to the students. However, the National Curriculum (NC) recognizes that history is *more* than simply knowing 'how it really was': Key Element 3 focuses on interpretations of history, Key Element 4 on historical enquiry. Link these to the analysis of social, cultural and ethnic diversities allowed for in Key Element 2, and one begins to appreciate how the content and demands of the Key Stage 3 Programme of Study can be used in a progressive manner. (Key Stage 4 must be treated separately and within the confines of what is most important for the students – the end product, a GCSE grade.)

For all societies, a historical framework is both a necessity and a meeting ground for different disciplines, and so it is hardly surprising that, as Marwick (1989) points out, all societies have history in some form as an aspect of their educational system, formal or informal. This 'history', however, is always designed to meet what the designers feel are national needs. The NC in England and Wales is no different. That the teacher is, as yet, allowed to interpret it in such a way that different concerns can be emphasized and important points made is, no doubt, as far as Radical Right ideologues are concerned, an oversight. Hobsbawm (in Krantz, 1988) is surely correct in arguing that the past reasons for written history have been variously for the glorification, justification and use of ruling authorities: he cites the biographies of modern 'neo-Victorian' politicians as a current example. A National Curriculum designed by a breed of politicians who write such biographies is clearly open to the charge of ignoring, or at best playing down, the contributions of the working classes (however defined), women and Asian, black and other minority ethnic peoples.[3] For such a curriculum, popular or grass-roots history (for want of a better all-embracing term) is only seen to be relevant and necessary for students to study when it connects to the grand narrative: the making of political and/or military decisions and events which reveal the development (from a ruling class perspective) of all aspects of the United Kingdom. This view should, indeed must, be challenged. What better way to do so than via the study of contributions made by the working class as a whole, by women, by Asian, black and other minority peoples, with the overriding aim being always to stretch students of *all* abilities?

CLASS ISSUES

> The history of all hitherto existing society is the history of class struggles.
>
> (Marx and Engels, *The Communist Manifesto* (1967) [1848])

Sara Delamont is correct to observe that the (NC) History curriculum relates to the dominant political and economic ideology (Delamont, 1983). In such an ideology, certain events and individuals are seen as important. A political ideology which emphasizes industrial and economic development as indicators of individual and national success will be largely exclusive; not only women, Asian, black and other minority-group peoples would be excluded from a central place in the curriculum, but also the working classes. Such an ideology led to the compensatory educational practices influenced by cultural deprivation theory, in which the assumption is that the culture(s) of the working classes is/are inferior to that of the ruling class. In criticizing this theory, Bourdieu argues that the education system is biased towards the culture of the ruling class, which is different from but not inherently better than working-class culture(s). Hence we can see in the history curriculum historical aspects of the culture of the dominant classes which are defined as 'worthy of being sought and possessed' (Bourdieu, in Haralambos and Holborn, 1995:757). For example, the focus of NC History of the Nineteenth Century is on industrial and economic development. There is no reason why the history of that century could not be studied by giving equal space to, or indeed focusing on, social history and popular protest.

Just as it is important not to give the impression of Asian, black and other ethnic minority peoples as victims, or of women as only impinging on history as atypical individuals, so teachers should avoid presenting the working classes of the Industrial Revolution as an homogenous, unthinking, pitiable, autonomous mass, which occasionally rose up in a futile attempt at betterment, until released from their bondage by middle-class radicals with a conscience. The jenny, water frame and mule may arguably have been bad news for spinners, but one wouldn't have found many hand-loom weavers on the picket lines with them! The simple fact is that teachers must allow students to study the range and variety of the working classes. If any stereotypical assumptions can be made, they should be regarding the inherent self-aggran-dizement of government. Thus an issue such as popular protest in the nineteenth century can be seen not as repeated working-class failures (Luddism, Swing Riots, Chartism and so on) but as differ-ent aspects of public pressure on a landed gentry government which gave way as infrequently and with as little as it dared. Trade unions may have been legalized in 1824, but the Tolpuddle Martyrs could still be transported to Australia for seven years in 1830. Arguably the first truly successful strike – the Bryant and May matchworkers' strike led by Annie Besant – did not take place until 1888.

The matchworkers' strike itself is a useful means of teaching a variety of issues. Primary sources can be utilized to look at issues of motive and bias. They can also serve to illustrate the fact that the dockworkers' strike of the following year was successful because of the adoption of tactics used during the matchworkers' strike which had gained public and press support. Teachers can raise class *and* gender issues here. I emphasize 'and' because it is important for students to be aware that issues of equality sur-rounding gender (for example) apply *within* topics focusing on class (and Asian, black and other minority ethnic groups) as well as separately from them. A more modern parallel which could be utilized is the Polish trade union Solidarity, whose leader Lech Walesa became President of Poland after the Solidarity-led over-throw of the Soviet-backed government. Solidarity was started through the actions of Anna Walentynowicz, who suffered greatly at the hands of the communist government because of her actions. Despite her key role in modern Polish history, she now lives in forgotten poverty: a prime example of women being written out of working-class history by men.

'DOING WOMEN'[4]

History is 'represented as that of men, written by men'.
(Sue Sharpe, 1994:139)

Anyone with half an eye on the various education debates over the past decade or so will be aware of the political minefield through which teachers of history must pick a careful path. However, ideological arguments over the nature of history are of little relevance to the day-to-day life of the classroom teacher except insofar as any outcome may influence the curriculum. The NC has struck a kind of balance between the two extremes, allowing for 'know how' as well as 'know that'. Obviously historical *knowledge* is cumulative and requires context(s) created by previous study. Historical *narrative* is only to be fully created and understood through the study of the causal chains and related events which can be forged into development themes (Rogers, in Portal, 1987). Such a process is exemplified in Key Stage 4 by the Schools History Project's *Medicine Through Time*, described by the subtitle as a 'study in development'.[5] The implication is that one cannot simply 'do women', for example, without context. True, one could teach both Florence Nightingale and Mary Seacole as part of the *Medicine Through Time* course, but to do so outside the context of time, place, ethnicity, class, the reduced role of women in medical provision and the reduced role for some classes of women in wider society would be missing the point not only of what they did, but how they did it.

Mary Seacole is an excellent example of a woman involved in medical provision in a way which was, until the 1700s, quite normal. The fact that Mary Seacole was something of an anachronism in middle-class Victorian society played an important part in her role in the Crimea. When teaching the 'facts' of what she did, this has to be taken into account. In other words, students must grasp the context in which Mary Seacole operated.

The context is that women had always been providers of medical care due to their knowledge of herbs and other plants – this in turn linked to their roles in most, if not all, societies. Examples can be drawn from a variety of past and modern societies to illustrate this point. In Europe, at least three important events occurred which led to the declining and sometimes illegal role of women in medicine in the 1700s. First, the use of obstetric forceps, invented by Peter Chamberlen in 1620, required anatomical knowledge. Such knowledge could only be gained from a university education, something from which women were excluded. Second, their lack of access to university education meant that male surgeons had better education than women, particularly in Latin and Greek. Link this to the third factor, the fashion amongst middle-class families in Georgian Britain for highly educated doctors, and the significance of Mary Seacole's contribution can be more fully understood.

The past contains a lengthy supply of analogies by which students may more fully understand contemporary events, particularly events related to issues of equality. Rogers correctly argues that history has a 'capital benefit' which no other subject provides: the study of history creates for students a 'frame of reference', a 'set of working assumptions in terms of which *present* experience may be rightly understood' (in Portal, 1987:3). Both Mary Seacole and Florence Nightingale are an integral aspect of this frame of reference. Hence the teacher should not 'do women', but ensure that women are an integral part of the course.

Bourdillon urges caution, though. In *On the Record. The Importance of Gender in Teaching History* (1994) she argues[6] that *History of Medicine,* in the Schools History Project series (SHP), is presented as a developmental history of scientific ideas and inventions, religious and public beliefs. Domestic medicine – that is, medicine practised primarily by women – is presented as being continuous but superseded. Again this can mean that, if the teacher is not careful, women could be presented in isolation. (The successful teacher will, naturally, avoid this by ensuring students have a context to study.) Bourdillon gives the example of Jacqueline Felice De Almania as an example of one of the 'intellectual weapons to question intolerance and propaganda' (Bourdillon, 1994:68–9). There are many other examples: Elizabeth Blackwell, Elizabeth Garrett Anderson, Sophia Louisa Jex-Blake to name just three. Move beyond the history of medicine and its development, and the field becomes much larger.

Teachers should encourage students to question the role of women in historical events which are being studied perhaps for other 'equality issues'. Specific examples such as Sojourner Truth spring to mind. Escaping from slavery in 1827, Sojourner Truth not only spoke at meetings about the sufferings of slaves, but also campaigned for women's rights. Students can study Sojourner Truth alongside, say, Frederick Douglass, as an example of women being as significant in a social and political movement as men. When studying the late nineteenth/early twentieth centuries' suffragette movement in Britain, Sojourner Truth is just one example of the wider context of that movement's history. Anne Frank could be referred to for work surrounding the issue of tolerance so that students become aware they are using primary material created by a female, rather than a male.

HMI identify sexism as one of three particular concerns in

school history (the other two being 'history in a multicultural society' and 'bias, prejudice and indoctrination' (DES, 1988:30–2).) The HMI finds that when women are studied in traditional areas of the syllabus it tends to be as exceptional leaders, in the struggle for legal rights, and women's work in industrial societies; so HMI's view is that this focus, coupled with the absence of women in political and military history, leads to the creation and reinforcement of stereotypes.

The most damaging of these stereotypes is 'that women have not been agents of change in history' (DES, 1988:29), from which HMI rightly conclude that such a view transmits and underpins the low status of women and women's concerns in modern Britain. Moreover, there are, as HMI indicate (DES, 1988:29), many examples of female involvement in military history and political struggle. HMI identify the Ladies Land Leagues in 1880s' Ireland and female involvement in establishing Republican Clubs in Revolutionary France. When teaching the English Civil War, good use can be made of the example of Lady Harley – not only to highlight the rather obvious but easily overlooked fact that if husbands and sons were off getting killed in battles, then women had to run the home, whether this be a humble hovel or an elegant estate – but also to show that such a role was not unusual. The letters of Margaret Paston to her husband during the Wars of the Roses can be used either as support for this point or, if already dealt with earlier, can be referred to and the appropriate conclusions drawn.[7]

ASIAN, BLACK AND OTHER MINORITY ETHNIC PEOPLES' HISTORY

> Fortunately for serious minds, a bias recognized is a bias sterilized.
> (A. Eustace Haydon, quoted in Fitzhenry (ed.), 1990:292)

There are many examples of Asian, black and other minority ethnic peoples' history available for schoolteachers, and they can be broadly categorized for the purposes of enquiry into three areas. Of chief importance is that the teacher, and hence the students, recognize that there is not a separate 'black history' or 'Asian history' to be studied, just as there is no independent 'women's history'. Students, through their work, should be aware that if what they are studying is British history, then Asian, black and other ethnic group British and non-British histories are integral aspects of it. The reasons why some sections of society today may *feel* less British than others, and why they may be *viewed* as less British than others, can only be explored in this context – not without it. So the question of how the links that other countries have with Britain affect its cultural, economic, political and social development is integral and often central to a topic. Thus the areas of enquiry in such topics should be centred on the effects *on* Britain and the effects *of* Britain in relation to Asian, black and other minority ethnic peoples who are part of it. Those who advocate more 'British' history should realize that by dealing with these issues in connection with West African civilizations, for example, one is still 'doing British history'.

In *Liberating the National History Curriculum*, Josna Pankhania (1994) argues that in the various histories of oppressed groups, Britain and the colonies should be viewed as contiguous. She adopts a black socialist feminist perspective as being the least flawed perspective through which the links between, and unity of, the various oppressed groups can be taught. Whilst accepting that many teachers will not hold such a perspective, I maintain that Pankhania's central assumption – the contiguity of different histories – is correct, and therefore schemes of work and lesson themes should ideally reflect this. Similarly, Jared Diamond (1991) presents a strong case for the interconnectedness and inter-relationship of all peoples, and thus their histories, at some point in time. He argues persuasively for the predominant effects of bio-geography as a central reason for the dominance of Western Europe.

Essentially, the rationale for teaching aspects of Asian, black and other minority ethnic peoples' histories is the same as that for women's history – to bring these histories into mainstream class-room history with the aims of helping to further understanding and tolerance and influencing future behaviour. As with women's history, it is important to avoid merely teaching, for example, 'famous black people' without a frame of reference or context.

This aspect of the history curriculum is of central importance in all schools. HMI state that all teachers have to face up to the question, 'In what way should the history syllabus in this school be different because my pupils live in a multicultural society?' (DES, 1988:30). The success in tackling this question is, in part, dependent on the support of a whole school anti-racism policy and also on the acceptance that teaching Asian, black and other minority ethnic peoples' history means going beyond post-1945 studies of Africa, the Caribbean or the Indian subcontinent. HMI point out that such history teaching must not assume that all Asian, black and other minority ethnic students will have an affinity with this history (DES, 1988). It is also important to avoid only teaching Asian, black and other minority ethnic peoples' history in terms of conflict and oppression. To do otherwise is to foster unintentional and institutional racism by presenting these people as victims.

Let us put all these arguments into context by using the example of the Industrial Revolution. NC History requires the teaching of the Industrial Revolution, including the role of the slave trade and popular protest. However, as Pankhania asks (1994), how much scope is there to study how and why slavery, indenture and colonialism helped Britain to become 'Great'? A further restriction is identified by HMI (DES, 1988) and the Rampton (DES, 1981) and Swann Reports (DES, 1985) which indicate how unintentional racism can be promoted if slavery is taught as something bad done *by* Britain *to* Africans (thus ignoring the variety of African cultures in the process), and stopped by a few enlightened Englishmen. If the actuality of slavery is taught from this perspective, then black peoples' role as victims – and by implication as helpless – will be reinforced.

The teaching of slavery can be given a more positive context as part of the Supplementary Unit 'Black Peoples of the Americas'. Here the focus is shifted away from slavery as the totality of existence for black people in the southern USA. The origins of both the indigenous populations of the Americas and of the practice of slavery can be examined: the latter will help students to understand better the contribution of institutionalized mass slavery to British economic and social life. The variety of experiences of slavery can be more fully explored. Life for a household slave in Alabama in the mid-nineteenth century was very different from that of a field slave on a sugar plantation in seventeenth-century Barbados. Such an approach should avoid the seemingly ubiquitous 'Diary of a slave' approach in which students describe the sufferings of a field hand on a US cotton plantation – the black person as victim. Perhaps more importantly, resistance to slavery by the slaves themselves can be studied in some depth. Work done by students on the Jamaican maroons and the successful slave revolts on Saint Domingue – which can be used to highlight the influence of the radical ideas of the French Revolution – will reveal the wide range of roles played by slaves, ex-slaves and free blacks in the eventual abolition of slavery. Similarly, the struggles for freedom of slaves in the USA can be studied through the activities of black and white abolitionists. The different motives of those involved should be highlighted as well as the patronization of blacks by whites, even when on the same side. Students should be made aware of the positive aspects of slave culture: this could include looking at the influence of Negro spirituals and field songs on most Western popular music.

Obviously, for many teachers this is going to be a sensitive area. However, an exploration of these issues could be used to define and examine ideas related to tolerance and discrimination, 'race' relations and so on. It is essential that the teacher takes into account the particular circumstances of their school and class, adopting appropriate teaching strategies. A final point on this issue (and perhaps the most important): the history of the black peoples of the Americas did not stop with emancipation. In many ways – social, political and economic – it was only just beginning.

OTHER EQUALITY ISSUES

When teaching equality issues relating to sexuality, partial ability and special needs, history teachers face two central problems. First, and with regard to sexuality, teachers are bound by the vague, homophobic, and potentially wide strictures of Section 28 of the Local Government Act 1988. Essentially, Section 28 prohibits local education authorities from 'intentionally promoting' homosexuality, or promoting 'the teaching in any maintained school of the acceptability of homosexuality as a pretended family relationship'. The National Union of Teachers, however, does not see Section 28 as banning teachers from dealing with homosexuality in an objective and factual manner. If teachers follow Union advice in conjunction with their school policy on sex education, educating students against prejudice and discrimination on the grounds of sexual orientation is clearly within the law (National Union of Teachers, 1991:6). As one of their election promises, the current New Labour government stated that this legislation would be repealed.

Second, the equality movements for the disabled, as well as gays, lesbians and bisexuals are recent enough to be embroiled in the history/current affairs debate. Some, generally on the political Right, argue that anything which has happened within the last 30 years is current affairs, not history. The argument is that as we do not yet know the outcome of these events, they cannot be taught as history. It is not my intention to run through the many arguments against this position; suffice to say that schools and colleges would not be able to carry out a modern-world study on the conflict in Ireland as, amongst other events, we do not know the outcome of Bloody Sunday. Neither of these two problems are insurmountable when it comes to including gays, lesbians, bisexuals and the disabled in classroom history lessons. The arguments put forward by this author apply as much to these other equality issues as to those already discussed.

Equality issues relating to sexuality and disability can be included in both Core and Supplementary Units. The easiest and most effective methods would be to raise such issues when dealing with the variety of civil rights movements which can be studied at Key Stage 3 in Core Study Unit 4 or in Supplementary Study Unit 6, when Stonewall could be discussed. The 1969 riot outside the Stonewall Inn, Greenwich Village in San Francisco was a significant moment in the Gay Liberation movement and was almost certainly influenced by the then current climate of civil rights protests and the hippie movement.

The concern for history teachers must be that they are teaching history and not personal, social and moral education. So, although the history of black peoples of the Americas puts their civil rights movement into a valid (NC) context, this is not the case with the lesbian and gay movement, which is a much more recent phenomenon. Similarly, although the treatment of homosexuals in Nazi Germany can be raised, it cannot realistically be studied in detail. Here, then, lies the failing of the NC History. Because of its structure it is difficult to include the histories of certain sections of society if they do not neatly fit into one of the Study Units.

The Core Study Units in Key Stage 3 are chronological; the Supplementary Study Units focus on a turning point and a non-European society. Gays, lesbians , bisexuals and the disabled need to be included as individuals wherever possible, however briefly. At Key Stage 4 teachers should consider these equality issues when designing their 'Modern World' and 'History Around Us' studies.

CONCLUSION

> Most history is a record of the triumphs, disasters and follies of top people. The black hole in it is the way of life of mute, inglorious men and women who made no nuisance of themselves in the world.
>
> (Philip Howard, quoted in Fitzhenry (ed.), 1990:344)

This is neither the time nor the place to discuss the relative importance of the different equality issues being dealt with in this book. Suffice to say that all are *equally* important – the lessons which need to be learned regarding all aspects of inequality, oppression and exploitation are just easier to teach via some of these issues. The bases of the arguments already put forward apply to all equality issues.

NC History can be used for 'socialisation, with transmission of heritage' (Visram, in Bourdillon, 1994:54). Such a view was adopted by Lewes Priory School, Sussex in the late 1980s. The History Department at Lewes Priory appeared to be suggesting that the history curriculum should create a feeling of nationhood and common cultural identity. Whilst the NC History does appear to be designed with these aims in mind, such a view is Anglo-centric and assimilationist. HMI, in Curriculum Matters 11, hold a different view: 'History should give pupils not only the knowledge to make sense of the *many* heritages they inherit . . . but also the skills to interpret their history critically. In this way they will be able to resist interpretations . . . which filter or distort the record of the past' (DES, 1988:1, my italics). Visram (in Bourdillon, 1994:54–5) gives further examples of HMI's support for a history curriculum which pays 'greater attention than was formerly the case to the position of minority groups and the role of women in history' (DES, 1988:6).

If one is to present the material and skills necessary for students to be able to understand the world around them – locally, nationally and internationally – then British histories cannot, indeed must not, be separated from those of Asia, Africa and the Americas. To fail to include the histories of women, Asian, black and other minority ethnic peoples, working classes, the disabled, gays, lesbians and bisexuals for example (where relevant, appropriate and useful), is to deny the 'existence of (sections) of the British population, giving an incomplete understanding of British society and its development, its values and its culture' (Visram, in Bourdillon, 1994:57).

In attempting to deal with equality issues, the classroom teacher will run up against a variety of problems, time and resources being only the two central ones. The easiest issues to confront under these restrictions are, for the majority of teachers, those surrounding gender, ethnicity and class. Teachers also have to consider the historical skills which must be taught, as well as the suitability of material for a range of abilities. Consequently, the opportunities for teaching other equality issues (such as sexuality and disability) are fewer. This does not mean they should be avoided – if anything, the opposite applies.

TOPIC OPPORTUNITIES

A teacher affects eternity; he can never tell where his influence stops.
(Henry Adams, quoted in Fitzhenry (ed.), 1990:344)

The revised PoS and attainment target for History became legal requirements from 1 August 1995, for Key Stage 3, and for Key Stage 4 from 1 August 1996. Key Stage 3 is divided into six Study Units, of which 1, 2, 3 and 4 are Core Units, and must be taught chronologically. Units 5 and 6 – an era or turning point in European history before 1914, and a non-European society, respectively – allow teachers to make their own choices of topic. As already argued, although Units 1, 2, 3 and 4 focus on British history from 1066, there is plenty of scope for dealing with equality issues. This scope is greatly increased by Units 5 and 6.

The Key Elements, which need not all be dealt with in each Study Unit, are chronology; range and depth of historical knowledge and understanding; interpretations of history; historical enquiry; organization and communication. The breakdown of these, given in *History in the National Curriculum* (DFE, 1995:11), highlights the possibilities for teaching equality issues which the statutory guidance allows. The eight levels (nine, including the 'Exceptional Performance' level) of the single Attainment Target *expect* students to deal with equality issues from Level 2 onwards (which is not to say such issues should not be studied at Level 1): 'They are beginning to recognise that there are reasons why people in the past acted as they did' (DFE, 1995:15).

An important first question when devising a scheme of work asks which topics should be taught. The implication is that a decision must be made as to what is considered important (Rogers, in Portal, 1987). If one aim of education is to be emancipatory then clearly topics which allow study of (and, dare I suggest, empathy[8] with) oppressed groups are important. As implied in the Introduction to this chapter, the mass of content and the lack of time means that a patchwork approach must be adopted – a patchwork approach which must be hung on to a narrative framework. Defining specific areas of study is not the purpose of this chapter – content will depend upon the range of factors already mentioned. Yet having said that, I would like to offer readers *some* suggestions for topics in which the various histories of oppressed groups can be usefully studied – that is, studied for the lessons and understandings which can be drawn from them, not because these oppressed groups, and consequently their histories, have some inherent nobility. Any teaching of them in this manner would be both patronizing and discriminatory.

So the purposes of history in schools are numerous and varied. The subject should allow students to access the past in order to contextualize the present and provide platforms for the future. It should help students to develop a variety of skills, in particular the ability to handle and use a lot of information. It should teach ideas, which have a greater long-term impact than the hurly-burly of 'great events'. It should have a moral dimension, allowing students to discover what is fair, wise, right and then just (Fines, in Portal, 1987). Students should study and discuss a variety of human behaviour so that they can draw their own moral conclusions.

Key Stage 3: Study Unit 1: Medieval realms: Britain 1066–1500

- *The Domesday survey*: a local study could be carried out, raising gender and class issues relating, for example, to land ownership.
- *Feudalism*: fairly complex class relationships can be explored here.

- *Magna Carta*: this is often viewed nationalistically as the beginnings of parliamentary democracy. Students can investigate who gained what from Magna Carta.
- *The Peasants' Revolt:*[9] this provides an excellent opportunity to look at class differences by drawing modern-day comparisons. (Students will now need to be told about the Poll Tax protest of the late 1980s.) Students could explore the motivations of different groups of people for actions taken during the Revolt. Why, for example, would indentured villeins burn written records in manor houses?
- *The Crusades*: students can explore the difference between myth and reality, particularly as regards the image of Richard Coeur-de-Lion and Saladin. Students should also look at what Europe gained from the Arabic world.
- *Arts*: the key questions here focus on 'Whose art?' and 'Whose literature?'.

Key Stage 3: Study Unit 2: The making of the United Kingdom: crowns, parliaments and peoples 1500–1750

- *The poor*: comparisons can be drawn with modern attitudes to the homeless and unemployed.
- *The Civil Wars*: students can study the role of women as head of the household. (There is useful material about Lady Harley in the SHP textbook *Societies in Change*: 53–4.)
- *Radical politics*: students can investigate the motives and aims of the different radical groups (including women) and make comparisons with today's environmental campaigners. Teachers should ensure that students realize that these groups were to a large extent motivated by religion and would not automatically agree with the aims or motives of modern radicals.
- *The growth of science*: an ideal opportunity to look at the removal of women from medical provision and the attitudes surrounding witch-hunts.

Key Stage 3: Study Unit 3: Britain 1750–circa 1900

- *Overseas trade and the creation of Empire*: this offers a wide range of possibilities to raise class, gender and ethnicity issues, ideally with an element of local history if possible.

- *Popular protest*: again, local history can help make this topic very relevant to students, as does the drawing of modern comparisons.
- *Political change*: in particular students may study the role of different classes and sections of society.
- *Working and living conditions*: it is possible to study a variety of class and gender issues. It is important that students realize that the reduction in working opportunities for women and children was not universally welcomed by the working class.
- *Slavery*: if departments teach 'black peoples of the Americas' in Study Unit 6, then a focus can be made on what Britain gained from slavery and why slavery in Britain and the colonies was abolished. Such a focus will avoid repetition later on.
- If you must teach 'famous men', look for opportunities to include examples which allow the interrogation of equality issues. Nelson, for example, was disabled.

Key Stage 3: Study Unit 4: The twentieth-century world

- *War*: students should study the contribution of Britain's colonies and of women, as well as the consequences of their involvement for them. Students can also look at the class make-up of the army in the Great War (there may be opportunities for local history here).
- *The suffrage movement*: issues of class can be brought out here.
- *The General Strike*: to a large extent the failure of the General Strike was due to the opportunity it presented to the middle classes to realize, in many cases, ambitions to drive buses and trams, act as security guards, and so on.
- *The Russian Revolution*: offers a number of possibilities, not least the opportunity for students to look at what communism is all about.
- *Nazi Germany*: from the rise to the defeat of the Nazis, there are limitless possibilities for work on issues of class, gender, ethnicity, disability, special needs and sexuality. Local history and oral history can be used very effectively here. (The Spiro Institute[10] can arrange survivors' talks.)
- *Arts*: issues of class, gender and sexuality (with care) can be usefully raised.

- *The break-up of Empire*: focus in particular on how the colonial peoples freed themselves.

Key Stage 3: Study Unit 5: An era or turning point in European history before 1914

This Unit allows for a wide choice of topic, and the opportunities for raising equality issues are many and varied. Study of the Crusades or the Ottoman Empire allows students to explore what Europe gained from the Arabic world, especially in art, architecture and science. The French Revolution contains many opportunities to raise issues of class (e.g. different classes' complaints about the Ancien Regime), of gender (e.g. Louis XVI being brought back to Paris from Versailles by thousands of women), disability (Marat) and ethnicity (the influence of revolutionary ideas on slaves).

Key Stage 3: Study Unit 6: A past non-European society

As with Unit 5, the choice of topic will give ample scope for developing lessons focusing on equality issues, particularly societies which had significant contact with Britain and Europe.

Key Stage 4

As stated above, the main aim in this stage must be to enable students to achieve the highest GCSE grade of which they are capable. This does not mean that equality issues should be reduced in importance. Schools will choose their own topics, and teachers should raise equality issues as appropriate. Schools following the Midland Examinations Group syllabus have the opportunity to develop their own topics on local history and the modern world, and should work within appropriate equality issues. The SCAA Regulations and the Subject Criteria for History are incorporated into the syllabuses available from the various Examination Boards. This means that the opportunities for raising equality issues will be many and varied. The rationale behind their inclusion is the same as for Key Stage 3.

The following examples are from the course followed by GCSE students at Heathfield Community College, East Sussex.

The Study in Depth taught is *The American West, 1840–1895*.

The role of women in the settlement of the Great Plains is of prime importance, and is frequently the focus of examination questions, often in comparison with Plains Indian women. The treatment of the Plains Indians, an ethnic minority by the period of study, is a central theme of the course and allows teachers to raise questions regarding the treatment of other cultures. (A useful comparison can be made with the Roma (gypsies) who, like Plains Indians, have a way of life which is incompatible with that of the dominant culture.) Class issues can also be raised at various points throughout the course, particularly when looking at the social and geographical origins of settlers. Many ex-slaves settled the Plains, and it must not be forgotten that many cowboys were Mexican, black and mixed race.

Medicine Through Time, the Study in Development taught, contains many opportunities to teach the contributions of non-European societies and individuals. The influence of Arabic scholars in the development and dissemination of medical knowledge cannot be ignored. There are numerous examples from other African and Asian societies which can be utilized to inform students that the West was frequently not first with new ideas, and that Western medicine is not the only possibility.

The Modern World Study taught is *Northern Ireland*. This involves tracing the outline of Irish history from earliest times, becoming more detailed from the seventeenth century onwards. Aside from the treatment of religious minorities, this course also allows teachers to look at class issues. The Penal Laws of the eighteenth century essentially made most, but not all, Catholics second-class citizens. To some extent this was still the case after Partition, and resulted in the civil rights marches, culminating in Bloody Sunday. The role of women in the Peace Movement of the 1970s should also be looked at.

The History Around Us topic, *Bodiam Castle*, is only relevant to Heathfield Community College, but nevertheless serves as an example of what can be done with this coursework element. In setting Bodiam Castle into a developmental context, and by investigating the reasons why it was built, students are expected to look at the role of a variety of sections of late Middle Ages society, as well as the influence of other societies on English history.

Choose your own historical content, then, but know above all what you want it to do for your children. (Fines, in Portal, 1987:113)

Oh, yes. And make it interesting.

ACKNOWLEDGEMENTS

I would like to thank Cindy Duchesne for doing most of the typing; Frank Flood for doing the proof-reading and providing supportive comments and Kate Ridley for letting me use her printer.

NOTES

1. Although we now have a New Labour government the National Curriculum is primarily a Conservative document.
2. What the historian counts as valid historical knowledge is dependent upon their ideological position. Hence, *annaliste* historians would include the lives and actions of ordinary people as valid historical knowledge; Whig historians would not.
3. The adoption of this term follows the argument that the other commonly used terms 'black' and 'black and ethnic minorities' are problematic in a variety of ways. The nomenclature used here is not necessarily without problems.
4. The Schools History Project series 'Discovering the Past' contains *The Changing Role of Women*, which can be used at any point of Key Stage 3 and Key Stage 4. Containing a rich variety of source material, the book allows students to investigate women's history (in Britain) from the Middle Ages through to the present day.
5. There is a danger that by drawing out developmental themes one may give the impression that modern societies are in all respects better than previous ones, which therefore have little to offer us.
6. Bourdillon argues with the slight exaggeration sometimes seen in the writing of non-school teaching academics, who do not have to interpret material – partly through interaction with students – for daily use in the classroom, and can miss possible uses and interpretations of that material.
7. The examples of women cited can be found variously in all the newer mainstream texts, particularly the SHP books for Key Stages 3 and 4. A lot of information can be downloaded from Internet Web sites, such as the BBC education site (http://www.co.uk/education/histfile/index.htm).
8. Ashby and Lee argue that empathy is: 'Entertaining the beliefs, goals and values of other people or . . . other societies . . .' (in Portal,

1987:63). We reach this achievement every day, despite gaps in our knowledge and understanding. To develop this conceptual understanding in children is a long-term process. The implications for the teaching of equality issues are clear.

9. A number of historians refer to this event as the 'Great Revolt' due to the involvement of others outside the villein class. This author does not hold to this view because the trigger of the Revolt was a third Poll Tax, felt most keenly by the villeins. Minor gentry and other non-villeins who became involved peripherally had other motives such as local rivalries.

10. The Spiro Institute: The Old House, c/o King's College London, Kidderpore Avenue, London NW3 7SZ.

BIBLIOGRAPHY

Austen, J. (1978) *The History of England in Love and Freindship* (sic) *and Other Early Works*. London: Women's Press.

Bourdillon, H. (ed.) (1994) *Teaching History*. London: Routledge.

Cole, M. (1997) Equality and primary education: what are the conceptual issues? In M. Cole, D. Hill and S. Shan (eds) (1997) *Promoting Equality in Primary Schools*. London: Cassell.

Delamont, S. (1983; 2nd edn) *Interaction in the Classroom*. London: Methuen.

DES (1981) *A Report of the Committee of Enquiry into the Education of Children from Ethnic Minority Groups (The Rampton Report)*. London: HMSO.

DES (1985) *Education for All (The Swann Report)*. London: HMSO.

DES (1985) *History in the Primary and Secondary Years*. London: HMSO.

DES (1988) *History from 5 to 16*. London: HMSO.

DES (1991) *History in the National Curriculum (England and Wales)*. London: HMSO.

DFE (1995) *History in the National Curriculum*. London: HMSO.

Diamond, J. (1991) *The Rise and Fall of the Third Chimpanzee*. London: Vintage.

Fitzhenry, R. I. (ed.) (1990) *Chambers Book of Quotations*. Edinburgh: Chambers.

Haralambos, M. and Holborn, M. (1995; 4th edn) *Sociology: Themes and Perspectives*. London: Collins.

Illich, I. D. (1973) *Deschooling Society*. London: Penguin.

Krantz, F. (ed.) (1988) *History From Below*. Oxford: Blackwell.

Marwick, A. (1989; 3rd edn) *The Nature of History*. London: Macmillan.

Marx, K. and Engels, F. (1967) [1848] *The Communist Manifesto*. Harmondsworth: Pelican.

Midlands Examination Board (1996) *History Syllabus A (Schools History Project)*. MEG.

Morrell, F. (1989) *Children of the Future: The Battle for Britain's Schools.* London: Hogarth.

National Union of Teachers (1991) *Lesbians and Gays in Schools. An Issue For Every Teacher.* London: National Union of Teachers.

Pankhania, J. (1994) *Liberating the National History Curriculum.* London: Falmer Press.

Portal, C. (ed.) (1987) *The History Curriculum for Teachers.* London: Falmer Press.

Schools History Project (SHP) (1993) Discovering the Past. London: Murray.

Sharpe, S. (1994; new edn) *'Just Like A Girl'. How Girls Learn To Be Women.* Harmondsworth: Penguin.

Snellgrove, L. E. (1968, 1972) *Longman Secondary Histories* (series). London: Longman.

Trevelyan, G. M. (1944) *English Social History.* London: Longman.

CHAPTER 7

Geography

Dawn Gill

A main assumption behind any argument for equalities education through geography is that the future is ours to create: schools should strive to make the world a better place. The children in our care will inherit the earth. How can we educate them so that they value the earth and hold it wisely in trust for their own children and those who come afterwards? How can we support them in developing attitudes towards themselves and others which will help sustain peace and harmony and justice in their families and communities, and at a global scale? Equalities education is at the centre of such a debate. The content and methodologies of geographical education give the subject a key role in the process of educating for a wise inheritance and stewardship of the earth and its people. This chapter places the National Curriculum at Key Stage 3 within the twin contexts of equalities education and the nature of geography as an academic discipline. The central premise is that an understanding of inequalities must underpin any understanding of human geography. Geography teaching which fails to take this into account is little more than schooling for the acceptance of an unequal *status quo.*

Key Stage 3 has been taken as the focus for this chapter because the National Curriculum in this Key Stage outlines the only statutorily taught geography curriculum in Britain. The National Curriculum has been suspended in Key Stages 1 and 2 and geography is an optional subject in Key Stage 4.

WHAT IS GEOGRAPHY?

Geography is, as geographers do. The subject knowledge is the body of information produced by geographical research: this is accomplished by a variety of techniques which include mathematical and scientific investigation, and the techniques of social scientists. There is nothing peculiarly geographical about the research techniques themselves: what distinguishes geography from other disciplines is that its central concern is with mapping. If you can map it, it's geography. Although this sounds very simple, geography is currently a discipline with an identity crisis. In examining this crisis, interesting questions are raised about the subject's multiple roles in the political and economic system which it serves.

The discipline has a fascinating history which was linked directly with the growth and expansion of Britain as a world power in the nineteenth century. Initially the geographer's job was to explore, map and describe the world's physical and human features. The Royal Geographical Society's president of 1842 proclaimed that geography

> . . . is the mainspring of the operations of war, and of all the negotiations of a state of peace; and in any proportion as any one nation is the foremost to extend her acquaintance with the physical conformation of the earth, and the water which surrounds it, it will ever be the opportunities she will possess, and the responsibilities she will incur, for extending her commerce, for enlarging her powers of civilising the yet benighted portions of the globe, and for bearing her part in forwarding and directing the destinies of mankind. (Quoted in Cook, 1984)

Because the discipline's early history was intimately bound up with Britain's own history as a colonizing power, it was bound up also with the history of racism and the exploitation of black people by white in a developing global economy. Britain's Industrial Revolution depended to a large extent on wealth and commodities from the colonies. Transport systems and the distribution of settlements in colonized countries reflected the priorities of exporters, not the needs of the indigenous populations. The spatial patterns in the 'new world' were developed as part of a growing 'interdependence' between the countries which

Geography: the National Curriculum, Key Stage 3

The prescribed content of the Key Stage 3 Geography curriculum is as follows:

Pupils should be given opportunities to:

1. Investigate places and themes across a whole range of scales.
2. Undertake studies which focus on geographical questions: for example, 'What/where is it?', 'What is it like?', 'How did it get like this?', 'How and why is it changing?', 'What are the implications?'.
3. Explain geographical patterns, and physical and human processes.
4. Consider the issues that arise from people's interaction with their environments.
5. Become aware of the global context within which places are set, how they are interdependent, and how they may be affected by processes operating at different scales: for example, how a locality is affected by a regional economic policy or a world trade agreement.

Two countries, other than the United Kingdom, should be studied. They should be in significantly different states of development. One country should be selected from list A (Australia; New Zealand; Europe; Japan; North America; Russian Federation) and one from list B (Africa; Asia, excluding Japan; South and Central America, including the Caribbean).

In addition, nine themes should be investigated. These are tectonic processes; geomorphological processes; weather and climate; ecosystems; population; settlement; economic activities, development and environmental issues. Taken together, the studies should involve work at local, regional, national, international and global scales, and provide coverage of different parts of the world and different environments. (DFE, 1995)

The National Curriculum prescribes the geographical skills which pupils should be taught to use in investigating these places and nine 'themes'.

produced crops and minerals traded on the world market, and the countries in which these were consumed or manufactured into finished goods and re-exported (Rowling, 1987). Geography as an activity (exploring, describing and mapping) and as an academic discipline (which describes and theorizes about the patterns revealed in maps) has played a strong role throughout history in shaping the economic and power relationships between peoples who live in different parts of the world. These relationships are now reflected in the relationships between people who live in multicultural British society (Gill, 1993). Geography as a school subject has a role in promoting or preventing an understanding of social and economic relationships locally and globally: currently prevention predominates over the promotion of such understanding.

Exploration and description have been the tools of the geographer since the discipline first became an accepted academic study. In the early 1960s these tools were highjacked by a radical thinker and began to acquire new meaning. William Bunge, working in Detroit, had written a PhD thesis which attempted to reinterpret human geography as spatial science. This was not published in the USA, but eventually in Sweden. Bunge believed that it was the geographer's task to explore and map not 'Darkest Africa', but 'Darkest America'. He set up an expedition with community activists in inner-city Detroit and produced a series of distribution maps entitled 'Rat-bitten babies'; 'Toyless zones'; 'Rat sitings'; 'Skin-lacerating soils' (with a high content of broken glass and sharp metal) (Bunge, 1962). By 1971 he had been sacked from the teaching post which he held at Wayne State University, allegedly for swearing in lectures: he claims that he was sacked for his political views.

At about this time, in the 'mainstream' of academic culture, the descriptive phase in geography had begun to give way to 'the quantitative revolution'. In the late 1950s in the USA, and in the 1960s in Britain, the application of quantitative methods of analysis, and the construction of various spatial models designed to explain aspects of reality became the hallmarks of geographical research.

It is now understood – but not fully taught at school level – that geography is essentially the study of spatial patterns and the processes which have produced (and continue to reproduce) them. A spatial pattern is a pattern in space. Patterns can be shown on maps and by aerial photographs. There are physical spatial patterns, such as the distribution of oceans, mountain ranges, volcanoes or desert, for example. The processes involved in producing and reproducing the *physical* patterns are physical, in the main, although particular kinds of economic activity can have an effect. The extent of a desert is determined mainly by the amount of rainfall, and this depends on its nearness to an ocean and the direction of the prevailing winds. There may be desert in the middle of a large land mass, far away from a coast, or where winds blow *from* a continental land mass *towards* an ocean, instead of from the ocean onto the land. However, the extent of a desert can also be affected by the way that the land is used. If not well managed, deserts can spread. If people or their goats remove vegetation cover from the borders of a desert there is no ground cover to slow down the evaporation of moisture from the surface, and further 'desertification' can occur. Similarly with rainforests: if trees are removed, the soil may become so badly leached by heavy rain that it turns into laterite, a hardened mineral substance on which nothing will grow. If vast areas of rainforest are removed, this will affect the water cycle locally and globally; and because trees are the 'lungs of the earth', converting carbon dioxide to oxygen, the global supply of oxygen could be diminished.

In addition to physical patterns there are patterns to do with people and their activities, for example the global or local distribution of population, settlement patterns or the patterns of trade relationships. The global *human* spatial patterns are, in the main, superimposed on the physical world. Relatively few people live in deserts or high mountains unless there is a good supply of oil or gold to be mined. Population density tends to be lower in inhospitable environments than it is in places which have warm weather, a plentiful supply of rainfall and rich soil. The patterns of low and high population density can be seen from above; broadly, these reflect aspects of the physical world.

But the global picture, the view that can be seen from a satellite, does not tell the whole story. Telling the story of the human spatial patterns involves an attempt to understand the processes which produce and reproduce them. These processes are largely political and economic. For example, if we were to study the global distributions of infant mortality, or malnutrition, or average life expectancy, and to examine the processes which have produced and continue to reproduce these, we would begin to unpack a world history of exploitation of the poor by the rich, unequal trade relationships, racism, sexual oppression, the exploitation of children; a present in which disabilities are created by poor medical care and the disabled face discrimination; where racism, class inequalities and sexual oppression are woven into the very fabric of the global economy. We would begin to examine the history and functioning of capitalism itself, and the role of inequalities in maintaining its existence as a global system. This is the intellectual territory of 'radical' geography, which developed in the 1970s and throughout the 1980s, and which has yet to permeate the content of geographical education in schools.

During the 1970s and early 1980s the study of 'processes' became important in physical geography course units taught in British secondary schools. The questions 'How did it get that way?' and 'How and why is it changing?' were asked about volcanoes, mountains, rivers, sand dunes, coasts, the climate and all sorts of physical phenomena. Many complex statistical techniques were invented and linked with efforts to answer questions based on enquiry into issues such as why sand dunes move in this direction or that, why the north-facing slope of a river valley is often steeper than that facing south. Physical form and spatial pattern became the focus of intense scrutiny: the processes which produced the physical phenomena were investigated in great detail. In relation to human spatial patterns, however, the fundamental questions were not asked. Somehow it was not considered appropriate for school students to ask detailed and searching questions about the patterns of wealth and poverty within the world's cities, within and between countries. While physical geography became analytical, developing a concern with process, human geography has remained a descriptive discipline.

In some universities the questions 'How did it get that way?' and 'How and why is it changing?' began to be asked of human spatial patterns in the 1970s. Such interrogation inevitably leads to speculation – 'How could it be different?', 'What could we do to make a difference?'. This 'radical' debate was reflected in the British educational press through the pages of *Contemporary Issues in Geography and Education* between 1984 and 1988, when the journal's publication ceased. Such debate, which is fundamental to the equalities discourse, continues to be largely neglected in geographical education.

The Western city shows a particular and typical pattern in

which the central business district is surrounded by an 'inner-city' zone of relatively poor housing – although some patches are 'gentrified' nowadays, mainly by the teachers and social workers who cannot afford to travel daily from the suburbs to do their work. This is surrounded by a zone of relatively rich residential areas occupied, generally, by the middle classes. The zonal pattern may be distorted by major roads, so that the central business district and inner city grow outwards along the roads, to form a star shape. There may also be vast council estates in the outer suburbs, of people relocated from the inner area as competition for land in the central business district results in its spread to the surrounding zone; these estates provide a storage system for 'the industrial reserve army', a currently unpopular Marxist term for the supply of unemployed people who can be brought into employment or shed from it at convenience, and whose presence serves to keep wages down and workers in fear of their jobs.

It is not possible to explain a human spatial pattern like that of the Western city without reference to power and inequality. The central location of banks and big business, surrounded by a zone of relatively poor people and a zone of the rich, is a spatial pattern which exists only because of inequality. Within the city there are smaller patterns, more minute processes in which social inequality is again and again reflected in spatial form. British cities are a concretization of the social class structure. The built environment provides part of the mechanism through which inequalities are reproduced, as the communities in which children live provide access to opportunities and information which may restrict or enrich their life chances. Racism is also reflected clearly in the built environment: concentrations of black people can be found in the poorer areas of inner cities, in places like Brixton and Hackney, for example. A racially stratified class structure creates ghettos in most of Britain's major cities, as it does in the United States and South Africa and many other parts of the world (Gill, 1985; Potts, 1985).

Other aspects of inequality are also mappable: for example, if we were to map people's journeys we would find great differences between the methods of transport used and distances travelled by the rich and the poor; where black people form a disproportionate percentage of the poor, there would be manifest differences between the journeys of black and of white people; distinctive patterns of travel by women and by men, 'disabled' and 'able-bodied' people would also be mapped (Oliver, 1987). If we were to explain inequality in the uses made of the built environment we would need to explore the causes and effects of poverty and racism, men's attitudes towards women and the social conditioning which may result in one half of the population being experienced as a threat by the other half. In *explaining* the spatial patterns, as opposed to simply describing them – a process which, by itself, suggests a sort of inevitability about the patterns themselves – we are faced with the inevitable task of describing and attempting to explain inequalities and the attitudes and social processes which create and recreate unequal relationships.

School students may be encouraged to challenge their existing perceptions of the world. Their understanding of spatial patterns and the social relationships reflected in them could be illuminated by questions such as 'How did it get this way?', 'What are the processes at work?', and 'How could it be different?'. Students may be taught to question and think critically about the world in which they live, or they may be encouraged to accept as immutable the spatial patterns and social relationships which they have inherited. This depends on the teachers' views of geography, their own political perspectives and the degree of consciousness with which they hold these perspectives. It also depends, to some extent, on the quality and availability of appropriate resources.

GEOGRAPHY: THE NATIONAL CURRICULUM, KEY STAGE 3

Equalities education strives to enable young people to describe and challenge inequalities based on racism, sexism (including heterosexism), social class, religious intolerance, ageism and disability. It strives to support students in understanding the assumptions on which their own attitudes, and the attitudes of others in society, are based. It enables young people to see how attitudes and values affect reality. In short, it aims to uncover the social function and social effects of ideas or ideologies. Anderson defines ideologies as 'systems of ideas which give distorted and partial accounts of reality, with the objective and often unintended effect of serving the particular interests of a particular social group' (Anderson, 1973).

The National Curriculum in Geography can be used either to support and sustain or to challenge inequalities (Gill, 1993). The subject's content and social function are not prescribed to the extent that radical approaches are excluded. The problem is one of interpretation. Many teachers present the content as they themselves learned it, and as it is presented for them in textbooks; there is little evidence that teachers approach the subject from radical or critical perspectives. There is even less evidence that they explore with students a range of alternatives to the *status quo* as represented in the human spatial pattern; they seldom ask the fundamental questions 'How did it get this way?' and 'How could it be different?'. And more seldom still do they ask 'What could *we* do to bring about change?'.

The structure of the Curriculum

It is interesting that the language of the National Curriculum neatly sidesteps problems of terminology to do with global wealth and poverty. 'First World' and 'Third World' are terms that now seem to have bitten the dust in most official publications. 'Developed' and 'underdeveloped' have been embarrassing since the Guyanese writer Walter Rodney pointed out in *How Europe Underdeveloped Africa* that 'underdevelop', in this context, is an active verb (Rodney, 1974). 'Developed' and 'developing' are clearly euphemistic, as it becomes increasingly obvious that tariff barriers and patenting laws, price fixing in the commodity markets, and land ownership patterns prevent development in large parts of the world that were once the colonies of European powers, and which clearly are not developing much at all (Scannel, 1984; Simpson, 1984; Simpson and Sinclair, 1984). The National Curriculum simply lists countries that may be studied as 'A' or 'B', which are 'in significantly different states of development'. Nevertheless, there is an invitation to describe inequalities within a country and explain 'how it is interdependent with other countries': there is anti-racist potential to be exploited, if teachers have the wit to see it and the will to exploit it. There are also many opportunities to consider and question inequalities of class, gender and other types of inequality.

The Key Stage 3 National Curriculum (as shown above) can be put together in many ways. Geography courses in schools can be constructed – and often are – with no explicit rationale and no clear organizing framework. However, the way in which the curriculum is structured can be of great significance in affecting young people's understanding of inequalities. The list of nine prescribed 'geographical themes' includes three about physical geography (tectonic processes, geomorphological processes, weather and climate) and three about what is generally categorized as human geography (settlement, economic activities and population). The remaining three (development, ecosystems and environmental issues) focus on subject content in which human and physical geography are clearly linked. The National Curriculum in Geography offers many opportunities to educate about inequality and towards equality. Inequalities based on racism, sexism, social class and other forms of inequality can easily be explored, described and explained in relation to the prescribed content at Key Stage 3; there is nothing inherent in the National Curriculum itself which would prevent this. First, though, the curriculum should be structured according to this purpose. Sequencing the sections in some ways may lead to an unquestioning acceptance of popular misconceptions, leading to problems in building students' understanding of inequality. Sequencing in other ways may offer greater potential for critical questioning and intellectual challenge.

There are nine terms in Key Stage 3 and, conveniently, nine themes to consider. The themes themselves can be used as a framework for the curriculum; case studies of specific places can be built into this framework. Both the themes and the place-specific case studies of them should be explored using geographical skills. Consider the framework in Table 7.1.

Table 7.1 Framework of Key Stage 3 themes

	Term 1	Term 2	Term 3
Year 7	Weather and climate	Settlement	Ecosystems
Year 8	Geomorphological processes	Economic activities	Environmental issues
Year 9	Tectonic processes	Development	Population

This curriculum framework achieves balance by including in each year a physical unit, a unit which is broadly 'human geography', and a unit in which the complex links between human and physical processes are explored. There is a clear progression in the complexity of ideas, insofar as it may be possible to achieve this. This way of structuring the curriculum is intended partly to increase the possibility that students will see population within the context of economic development, which begins to explain why it is that people in 'list A' countries have faster rates of population growth than the 'list B' parts of the world. Without the economic context it is possible that a study of population could be perceived in terms of swarming masses of 'list B' peoples, breeding irresponsibly and putting pressure on the world's resources. The emphasis could so easily be cast on to high birth rates, exponential growth, the pressure put on the world's resources by having too many mouths to feed, an ever-growing number of children born each day. Malnutrition? It's the result of the population explosion. If only the poor could be persuaded to have fewer children!

If population is studied alongside or after a unit on economic development, for example, the chances of explaining high birth rates in economic context are greater. Some explanations may lead to racist perceptions of population growth, whereas some may help students to develop anti-racist attitudes, or to see how racism in the global economy, past and present, has led to particular trade relationships, particular patterns of wealth and poverty, health and sickness, and particular trends in reproduction and population growth. The effect depends in part on the structure of the curriculum. What is actually taught, and what understanding the students come away with, depends partly on how the curriculum is put together, partly on whether the teacher sees what the issues are, and partly on what resources are used.

Settlement

The structure of the curriculum and the textbooks are not the only problems, however. Geography, if well taught, is taught through an investigative, enquiry-led approach. Geographical skills are part of the investigative methodology: the content of geography can be shared with students through carefully structured investigation and analysis. Unfortunately, this seldom happens. Most teachers and most resources neglect investigation and analysis in favour of description. Often description masquerades as investigation: students are encouraged to employ geographical skills to reach their 'own' conclusions that badly flawed 'theories' are valid. Sadly, the caricature which follows is not far from what happens in many classrooms.

Textbooks, videos and CD-ROMs tell students that there are models which explain city growth. There is the model developed by Burgess (of the so-called Zonal Theory, described above), and the model developed by Hoyt (which is like the Zonal Theory, except that it acknowledges that roads and rivers may distort the zonal pattern): this is known, rather grandly, as the Sector Theory. Why such obvious and pedestrian descriptions are allowed to parade as 'theory' in the geography textbooks is a question never asked in their pages and seldom in the classroom where teachers seem unembarrassed by this trite nonsense. None of the books go as far as to suggest that in order to explain a spatial pattern which depends for its existence on social inequality, we have to acknowledge and explain inequality. The books and the teachers simply put forward these uninteresting models as information to be copied in diagrammatic form and learned: inevitable and unquestionable fact.

The resources themselves, as well as the teachers, tend to pose questions such as: 'What are the features of your own town? Is your own town more like the Burgess model or the Hoyt model? Zonal or Sector?' And teachers get students to test these so-called theories by doing transects through urban areas, mapping land use. They hold class discussions, often illustrated by data which students have collected, about whether the area conforms to one or another of these so-called theories. Afterwards the students write up fieldwork case studies based on 'hypotheses' such as 'Town X conforms with (or does not conform with) the Zonal (or Sector) Theory.' Students describe the so-called theory, they write about the method of testing it, and about their results. Then they write a conclusion which says that town X does, in fact, conform – or it doesn't – with the 'theory'. The theories themselves are never questioned. Spatial patterns such as those described by Burgess and Hoyt are found in most Western towns and are the result of a particular economic system and the social relations within it. There may be alternative economic structures, and alternative social realities: speculation on alternatives is rare indeed.

'Theory' which merely describes spatial 'reality' as it currently exists, without explaining how it got that way, is very much a part of that reality. Intellectual effort aimed at description – but falsely described as 'theory' – has the effect of reproducing the kinds of attitudes which will ensure an unquestioning acceptance of the *status quo* as natural and inevitable. '*Status quo* theory' in geography helps to reproduce the reality it seeks to explain; it therefore supports and helps to reproduce social inequality. By failing to speculate about alternative forms of spatial and social organization, geography teaching is part and parcel of the socialization into acceptance of an unequal *status quo*; and on the way, it supports an intellectual passivity and flabbiness of which educationalists should be ashamed.

The National Curriculum offers enormous potential for critical thinking which might enable students at least to become aware of inequalities and to challenge the apparent inevitability of human spatial patterns (see Hill, 1994, 1997 for a consideration of critical reflection in education). Despite this, what happens in the classroom is usually the reiteration of inadequate 'theories' followed by unimaginative investigations which support them. Students at Key Stage 3 are generally taught to absorb information uncritically as if it were fact. Geography, as currently taught at Key Stage 3, does very little to promote critical questioning. In fact inequality is hardly mentioned in most textbooks or in the lessons based on them. The textbooks of the 1990s are less overtly racist than they were in the 1970s (Gill, 1983), but in most other respects little has changed.

DIFFERENT SPATIAL PATTERNS?

The interrelationships between individuals, families, communities, local and national economies and the global economy are extremely complex and may be conceptualized in very different ways, by individuals whose political perspectives differ. The most fundamental difference in perception hinges on political perspective or belief; very broadly there are two mind-sets as far as belief is concerned. These sometimes become extremely tangled and confused when individuals shift from one to another without realizing it, during discourse or attempted explanation. One belief system is built on the assumption that there is such a thing as 'human nature'. Particular kinds of human social relationships are 'natural' and therefore the social, economic and political structures found in human society are also natural and inevitable – they cannot be changed. Human nature is selfish, acquisitive, driven by the urge to survive. Survival of the fittest is what we see reflected in human spatial patterns and the processes which have produced them.

An alternative belief system is based on the notion that human social behaviour is learned; the expression of human sexuality, and the operation of sexual and social relationships, are determined largely by social conditioning. If human relationships are socially conditioned, they can be different. There is nothing God-given, natural or inevitable about the non-physical aspects of sexual behaviour, for example, so that attitudes towards sexuality, and about individuals' roles within the family and society are what determine the nature of those roles. Similarly, there is nothing natural or inevitable about the trade relationships between richer and poorer parts of the world, or between black and white people, between disabled people and the restricted world that they inhabit. Values and intentions, attitudes towards gender, skin colour, disability, special needs, age, poverty, economic systems are what determine social reality: there is nothing fixed and immutable about it. Life is what we make it.

The anarchist Russian geographer, Prince Kropotkin, began to outline these alternative perceptions in 1913; his work has been given little recent attention, except in the pages of *Antipode*. Kropotkin argues that human spatial patterns could be very different, given a very different social system emphasizing equality of access to the earth's resources, and an equalization of power. According to this belief system, it would not be impossible to devise means of socializing people so that their attitudes towards themselves and others reflect not the imperatives of (global) capitalism but the agreed priorities of a very different global political and economic system, emphasizing values of community, 'mutual aid' and equality. He argues that mutual aid and collaboration are necessary for survival and that the Darwinian notion of 'survival of the fittest' should be reinterpreted in relation to human society. Collaboration, not competition, is in the best interests of human society. Competition for resources and the resulting inequality and concentration of power in the hands of the few will, argues Kropotkin, damage the survival chances of the many – and ultimately of the whole human race (Kropotkin, 1913). This debate, complex as it is, lies at the very heart of education; it is particularly relevant to geographical education and to the sustainability of life on earth.

WE CAN SAY 'NO'

Empowering pedagogies are based on critical questioning. Education could aim to ensure a critical questioning of the subtleties and interconnectedness of all aspects of power and the attitudes which confer this power on some and not on others. It could expose the extent to which our everyday actions and behaviour can either bolster and support, or subvert and undermine the whole complex edifice of inequalities. The idea that we can say 'No' is in itself very powerful. We can say no to bullying, racist or sexist abuse. We – and the students we teach – can say no to the sexualization of ourselves as male or female through clothing and conditioning and the idea that we'll be attractive if only this or that, and unfeminine or unmasculine, or unattractive if we fail to conform; no to gender conditioning of male children through the media, toys and games, through the subtle bullying that says boys ought not to cry. No to the bullying of boys through language and suggestion that they are like girls – and we can ask what purposes are served by such bullying, such praise, such encouragement to conform.

We can say no to 'fashion' clothing made by child labour in the sweatshops of the Philippines; no to the products of a world trade which disadvantages the farmers while enhancing the wealth of the coffee companies and those dealing in stocks and shares; no to the investment of our savings in manufacture and trade which we might consider unethical. No to clearing tropical forests for beef farming to support the burger industry. No to low-paid work for women; no to gender conditioning in the home which results in unequal divisions of labour and leisure; no to the abusive relationships which may be exposed if such inequality is challenged. We each have a personal power which is nothing more than saying yes or no. But this is power indeed. It is the saying yes – of billions of individuals in millions of homes and streets and shops and hundreds of thousands of farms and factories and thousands of army barracks and police stations and hundreds of stock markets.

Or saying no; recognizing that there are alternatives, if not now, tomorrow.

Geographical education as currently practised in secondary schools is part of what helps to perpetuate unequal relationships, simply by virtue of the fact that it peddles *'status quo* theory' – description as theory. Secondary school geography fails to promote critical questioning of contemporary spatial patterns and the processes which reproduce them; it fails to encourage the exploration of possible alternative futures. Within the framework of the National Curriculum, geography teachers and geography textbooks could so easily make a difference. An understanding of equalities is at the heart of geography as both an academic discipline and a subject in the curriculum. If only this were more fully recognized, the geography of the future – the spatial patterns themselves, the academic study of these, and the content of geographical education – could be very different from the geography of yesterday and today. Although geographical education is part of the society that has produced it, it can promote a critical understanding of that society. Both geography and education have purposes and consequences: these need to be recognized and made explicit. There is nothing 'natural' or inevitable about human spatial patterns or the processes which have produced them. The future is ours to create. There is no need to re-create the past.

BIBLIOGRAPHY

Anderson, J. (1973) Ideology in geography: an introduction. *Antipode*, 5(3):1–7.

Bunge, W. (1962) *Series C: Studies in Geography: General and Mathematical Geography.* Lund: Sweden: Royal University of Lund.

Cook, I. (1984) Colonial past: post colonial present. Alternative perspectives in geography. *Contemporary Issues in Geography and Education*, 1(2).

DFE (1995) *Geography in the National Curriculum.* London: HMSO.

Gill, D. (1983) Geographical education in a multi-cultural society. Research report commissioned by the Schools Council. London: The Commission for Racial Equality.

Gill, D. (1985) South Africa: apartheid capitalism (editorial). *Contemporary Issues in Geography and Education*, 2(1).

Gill, D. (1993) In G. Verma and P. Pumfrey (eds) *Cultural Diversity and the Curriculum: The Foundation Subjects and Religious Education.* London: Falmer Press.

Hill, D. (1994) Cultural diversity and initial teacher education. In G. Verma and P. Pumfrey (eds) *Cultural Diversity and the Curriculum, 4.* London: Falmer Press.

Hill, D., Cole, M. and Williams, C. (1997) Equality and primary teacher education. In M. Cole, D. Hill and S. Shan (eds) *Promoting Equality in Primary Schools.* London: Cassell.

Kropotkin, P. (1913) Fields, factories and workshops. In R. Peet (1977) *Radical Geography.* London: Methuen.

Oliver, K. (1987) Women's accessibility and social policy in Britain. *Gender and Geography.* London: Association for Curriculum Development.

Potts, D. (1985) The geography of apartheid: the relationship between space and ideology in South Africa. In *South Africa: Apartheid Capitalism,* a special edition of *Contemporary Issues in Geography and Education,* 2(1).

Rodney, W. (1974) *How Europe Underdeveloped Africa.* Harmondsworth: Penguin.

Rowling, N. (1987) *Commodities: How the World was Taken to Market.* London: Free Association Books.

Scannel, H. (1984) World trade. *Contemporary Issues in Geography and Education,* 1(3).

Simpson, A. (1984) The rich as a minority group. *Contemporary Issues in Geography and Education,* 1(2).

Simpson, A. and Sinclair, A. (1984) Multinationals. *Contemporary Issues in Geography and Education,* 1(3).

CHAPTER 8

Music

Rod Paton

This chapter will address issues of equality in relation to music at Key Stages 3 and 4 of the National Curriculum, and will do so by examining the social and cultural perspectives within which the music curriculum develops. The chapter also provides some specific guidelines and working strategies for classroom practice which suggest how equality may be fostered within the statutory framework of music in the National Curriculum.

The various aspects discussed are presented under a sequence of headings which begins with Introduction to Music at Key Stages 3 and 4, followed by Music, Culture and Freedom; Music and Disability; Music and 'Race'; Music and Gender; Music and Sexuality; Improvisation and Equality; and, finally, Sound Plans.

INTRODUCTION TO MUSIC AT KEY STAGES 3 AND 4

Music in education has travelled a long way since the 1960s and, in many ways, the National Curriculum document published in January 1995 (Music in the National Curriculum, Revised Statutory Orders) provides an unprecedented window of opportunity for teachers and students alike. The emphasis on Performing and Composing (Attainment Target 1), which has twice the weighting of Listening and Appraising (Attainment Target 2), makes it very clear that, above all, music is a practical subject, that thinking *in* the medium of music is the primary target, whilst thinking *about* the medium of music is a secondary target, though equally important as an activity. But in the Programmes of Study, this weighting is defined even more clearly since in the box headings to each Key Stage it states unequivocally: 'Pupils' understanding and enjoyment of music should be developed through activities that bring together requirements from both Performing and Composing and Listening and Appraising wherever possible' (DFE, 1995:2, 4 and 6).

In other words, teachers are expected to use *integrated* teaching methods, and students are to be encouraged to develop listening and thinking skills whilst engaged in the primary musical acts of improvising, composing and performing. Students are also to be taught critical skills in response to musical encounters which are charged with that experiential energy unique to music, the language of feeling. If music is lacking this authentic, affective glow then it will fail to ignite their enthusiasm and, as a curriculum subject, will be consigned to the doldrums of boredom and apathy.

Performing and composing are activities which make immediate contact with the world of organized sound. A musical form represents patterns of feeling which should engage the interest and emotions of students of all abilities and from a diverse range of cultural backgrounds precisely because, ideally, they resonate with the student's own patterns of feeling and response, and are not imposed from an externalized, possibly alien, cultural source. The American music educator Thomas Regelski has termed this function of music its 'individualising abstraction': 'The primary process in music is the individualising abstraction which imparts the sense of profundity and significance that is the purpose of such experience and the general attraction of music for most people' (Regelski, 1986:195). Herein also lies the power of music to promote equality or, at the very least, a sense of unity. Take a group of students from a wide range of social class backgrounds, a variety of ethnic roots, a range of ability and mixed gender; provide them with a template of learning in the form of a group project which involves improvising or composing music; set them to the task with a practical demonstration of the skills required (not forgetting the essential warm-up exercise); provide them with the necessary resources in terms of instruments (which may include electronic or digital technology): and the results? When successful, such a method will produce an original piece of music in which all the participants can have an equal share and which can be expressive of a shared sense of creative development and social purpose. (Unlike other forms of discourse, music works – can *only* work – when all the parts are in agreement.) The students may then begin to appraise their work, developing a shared language of criticism where necessary, appropriately prompted by the teacher. They may wish to record or notate their work, or improvise another piece on the same basis. Whatever the outcome, ideally they will have a sense of ownership and a feeling of having shared in the development of their own musical culture. They may then go on to appreciate other musics and other cultures, having gained some insight into the root process.

But what kind of music are we talking about? Music, like the rest of culture, does not exist in a vacuum: encoded in its seemingly abstract forms are the myths, dreams and aspirations of whole groups and sub-groups of people. And, also in keeping with the rest of culture, these musical forms are in a constant state of flux and renewal. Music in education might be expected therefore to play a vital role in this process of renewal, of cultural regeneration. When we look closely at the development of musical culture in the twentieth century we can detect a gradual move, a shift in emphasis away from the lionized figure of the composer, away from the hierarchies of the patronage system and towards greater musical autonomy on the part of individuals (Attali, 1977). If the education system is going to reflect and serve such social and cultural evolution then the promotion of equality must provide one of the foundation principles of any school's policy document for music. There may have been a time when those with a disability, or what may have been conceived as a lack of talent, might have been considered incapable of participation in practical or creative music-making. Such times should be past. Musical forms can now be heard as a common language, a participatory medium to which all, regardless of 'race', gender or ability should have equal access. Such a policy will inevitably need to address repertoire – content. The European canon, once the bedrock of school music, will no longer suffice, can no longer be heard, innocently, as a superior music by virtue of its apparent complexity and 'high art'. Other musics – Afro-Caribbean, Asian, improvised forms, dance music, popular idioms, jazz, blues etc. – can be seen to stand equal to the works of Bach, Beethoven and Verdi and to provide ample and exciting material for classroom study. This is the window of opportunity which the National Curriculum endorses – indeed, demands – and which sets it apart from subjects which, by virtue of their aims to prepare students for life, need to be eurocentric.

MUSIC, CULTURE AND FREEDOM

The radical idealism of many music teachers and educators over the past three and a half decades has often been in conflict with traditional notions of what constitutes a musical act, and for whom music exists. Until relatively recently the curriculum, as represented by examination syllabuses as well as day-to-day practice, was centred upon the mainstream of the European classical tradition, a canon of works representative not only of the imaginative geniuses (almost exclusively male) whose products were central to the curriculum, but also of the prevailing cultural mode and all that this meant in terms of economic growth, colonial expansiveness and male hegemony (Shepherd, 1991; McClary, 1991). Furthermore, the notion that music could be encoded with such social and cultural messages has been heavily resisted by a musical establishment only too ready and willing to preserve its elitist position in both a cultural and an economic sense. The forms of music, particularly the symphonic opuses which stem from the 'great tradition' have been called 'synthetic-analytic' (Vulliamy and Lee, 1987), describing a degree of intellectualism which renders their inner structures inaccessible to all but the chosen few whose background and training provide them with the necessary mental equipment to compose, perform and analyse; this, despite the fact that, for most people, music provides direct access to their feelings as well as a sense of social and cultural identity.

Music teachers have often found themselves strung between polarities, having in most cases received a training which is steeped in classical practice only to find themselves in classrooms populated by as diverse a mix of students as is to be expected within the pluralist society we inhabit. To what kind of demand does the music teacher respond – that of the weight of their own cultural heritage and the historical responsibility for its preservation? There are the immediate demands of their students, most of whom are intuitively aware of the power that music has to carry

177

the feelings and cultural aspirations of a diverse range of social groups.

Two recent debates spring to mind which perfectly demonstrate this dilemma. In February 1996 it was reported in the *Independent* that Nick Tate, the head of the Schools Curriculum and Assessment Authority (SCAA), was maintaining that students needed to be taught a clear *qualitative* difference between the music of Schubert and that of the pop groups *Blur* and *Oasis*. Somehow, it was being argued, it needed to be made clear to students that, by some unspecified absolute measure of quality, the Austrian composer had the edge on the Britpop songwriters. In contrast, and more recently, the composer Malcolm Williamson (the Master of the Queen's Music, no less) offered support to the people of Aldeburgh who had resisted the idea of erecting a statue to honour their late composer-resident Benjamin Britten, considered by some to be one of the greatest British composers of our time. Williamson described Britten's music as 'ephemeral and unlikely to stand the test of time'. The people of Aldeburgh in the meantime had apparently favoured honouring a deceased GP and his dogs! Predictably, Williamson came under the immediate fire of Britten's many supporters among academics, opera-lovers and critics, for whom Britten represents the epitome of British cultural excellence.

In both these cases we can detect resistance to the notion that 'great' music is of *relative* value. There is reluctance on the part of many academic musicians to judge music on the basis of its social meanings, even to the point of denying that music has such meanings. This need to hold onto *absolute* aesthetic values is understandable, especially in times such as ours when, in the wake of Dunblane, child abuse scandals, the murder of a headteacher outside the gates of his school, the seeming collapse of order in a West Yorkshire school and numerous other traumatic events, we are, as a culture and as a nation, deeply concerned about morality and desperate to fix upon some cultural and moral absolutes. Yet it seems to me impossible to listen to the music of Schubert without also taking on board the peculiar aesthetic which inhabits the spirit of early romanticism as well as the distinct flavour of the central European peasantry, which is etched into the melodic contours of his songs; and, in the case of Britten, who can doubt the *gentrification of passion*, the quintessential Englishness of his music? Compare this with the 'louche' tones of

Jarvis Cocker and then decide which of the two more authentically defines the cultural mode of postmodern twentieth-century Britain. The point I am making is that if we are truly to identify cultural *absolutes*, it is pointless, if not dishonest, to draw the line too narrowly, or at a level which suits a cultural minority but may be meaningless to the rest of us.

Some will argue that such discussion is irrelevant to the *intrinsic* qualities of the music, whatever these may be. But my arguments are not prompted by an ideological position: rather by the pragmatic demands of the contemporary classroom in which an authentic musical experience is one which carries a recognizable *emotive* charge for the student. When all is said and done, what constitutes a musical culture? Is it the notated, handed-down jewels of the classical canon? Or is it the roughly fermented home-brew played by a rock band at the local on a Friday night?

Milton Keynes may not strike us as a town with a flourishing musical culture in the way that, for example, Birmingham is now considered to have. Yet Ruth Finnegan (1989) discovered there a wealth of music-making, particularly composing activity, at all levels, many of which would not necessarily be labelled 'composition' by established musical custom. In my own area of West Sussex, music at a community level is flourishing and many local rock or blues bands insist upon playing their own music rather than presenting cover versions of chart toppers – is this what happens to performing and composing once our students leave the classroom? Is this the purpose of the National Curriculum emphasis on these attainment targets? Ideally, yes.

What must be clear is that by *empowering* young learners to make their *own* music, we offer them an *equal* role in the development of a musical culture and at the same time ensure that their own expressive needs are, potentially, fulfilled. Moreover, it is at Key Stages 3 and 4, according to Swanwick (1988) that students are more than prepared to engage in imaginative play, striking out for an individual tone of expressive activity which, whilst referring to an earlier stage of development, seeks to celebrate the developing identity of the adolescent. And, it must be stated, this identity is being simultaneously felt through an emerging sense of social positioning (class), gender and sexuality, 'race' (ethnicity) and intellect (ability). All of these will be reflected through musical experience.

MUSIC AND DISABILITY

Music has an extremely important role to play in the education of students with special educational needs. It is worth reflecting that, where music is concerned, we all have degrees of disability. Highly trained instrumentalists are often at a loss when it comes to improvising, having become dependent on notated forms, while the self-taught musician often feels inadequate when faced with a score. Students with physical disabilities such as cerebral palsy will be able to participate fully provided that the teacher is willing to accommodate them through whatever technical resources are available. Feet may need to be tied to drum pedals, beaters tied to the arms, or instruments looped over forearms. Digital keyboards which require minimal physical effort, or sequencers, will provide opportunities for individual exploration and achievement. In group work, it will be necessary to improvise, allowing space and time for students with physical disabilities to make their sounds at appropriate places.

Two recent examples show the results that can be achieved. In the first, a teenager with cerebral palsy had taught himself to play the theme from the film *Exodus* on his keyboard, albeit at a pace which seemed painstakingly slow at first hearing. However, by using his music as a kind of *cantus firmus* (a repeated melody used as the basis for musical decoration in early music) it became possible for each note of the melody, as it appeared, to be decorated by the rest of the group, improvising on tuned and untuned percussion instruments. The results were unique and satisfying. Abandoning an authentic rendition in favour of an original approach demonstrated just how much can be learned from the limitations imposed by disability.

In the second example, a mixed ability group was working on a vocal improvisation. One member of the group with moderately severe multiple disabilities, including partial sight and hearing, instinctively placed her fingers on the teacher's throat in order to feel the vibrations of the larynx. Initially taken aback, the group was, however, encouraged to adopt the same procedure and, by the end of the session, all had experienced vocal sounds in this tactile fashion. This is a technique I have since introduced into both disability awareness training and also into vocal improvisation work with non-disabled groups, with positive results.

Students with learning disability can also function on equal terms with the non-disabled provided it is understood that whilst a teenager may have a *mental* age of 6 or 7 this does not mean that the *feeling* age is at a similar level. Music is the language of feeling, its structures are accessible to all and it is important therefore to acknowledge this in dealing with older students. During a music and drama session at a special school I was struck by a comment from a 14-year-old student with moderate learning difficulties who exclaimed in the middle of a vocal and instrumental improvisation, 'This is better than baa-baa black sheep'. A diet of nursery rhymes is clearly inappropriate for students of this age: whatever their cognitive difficulties, their affective responses are often surprisingly (or unsurprisingly) mature.

MUSIC AND 'RACE'

Musical history is all about synthesis and integration: where one music has been allowed to influence another, the adoption of practice always results in a newly emergent form. Nowhere is this more clearly demonstrated than in the history of jazz. The modal, religious chants and ritual drumming of the West Africans transported as slaves to the Americas became intermingled with the tonal forms and the instrumental traditions of the New World, which had its roots of course in European marches and church chorales. The two musics became entwined and the resultant mix became what the great jazz drummer Art Blakey described as the one truly original art form to emerge from the United States. Whether or not we agree with this, there is no doubt that the influence and permeation of jazz in the field of rock music, popular song, show music, musical theatre, film music and the recording industry has been a dominating factor in the history of twentieth-century music. More recently, the music has found its way back to Africa, resulting in popular forms of urban African music such as Hi-Life and Soukous.

For the music teacher working at Key Stages 3 and 4 it has become necessary to acknowledge such cultural pluralism and to guard against the inherent dangers of promoting one kind of music at the expense of another. A school is in itself a valuable resource for cultural integration and so one might expect to find examples of practice which encourage students to make their own music out of whatever they have inherited in terms of shared, diverse influences. Of course, the picture is not this simple. Particular musics are encoded with the ethnic flavours of particular groups and the purity of particular traditions may be jealously guarded. Reggae and its associated forms, for example, is very much the preserve of urban Afro-Caribbean sub-cultures and is, of course, deeply encoded with the spirit of Rastafarianism.

Some forms of music may even have a pronounced racist, sexist and homophobic flavour (such as the more aggressive forms of urban rap). In Germany, under the Third Reich, traditional folk songs were appropriated by the Nazis and fitted to anti-Semitic and pronouncedly chauvinistic texts (Meier, 1992). This created a real problem for schools after the war since any kind of singing of traditional songs immediately recalled the ideologies of the pre-ceding period. In a democratic system where students' feelings are also taken into account, a teacher will quickly learn what kind of material is unsuitable. In the 1950s, my own secondary school was still quite happy to use the *National Song Book* or similar anthologies which, as I remember, included patriotic songs from the Boer War which today, as then, would be greeted with disdain and incomprehension by most school students.

MUSIC AND GENDER

Is it possible to discuss musical forms as if they are in any sense gendered? Is there such a thing as a feminine cadence or a femi-nine turn of phrase or a modality which can be interpreted as female rather than male? If the answer to any of these questions is 'Yes' then we might expect such labels to be as socially con-structed as other gendered distinctions. But can there be said to be any direct relationship between the dominance of men in the composing and directing of classical music and the actual forms in which that music is cast? And can we find a similar relation-ship between the enormous influence of women in the early history of jazz and the structural patterns of, for example, the blues?

John Shepherd (1991) and Susan McClary (1991) have both argued for the existence of such links. The notion that the goal-directed structures of tonal music, with their precisely constructed hierarchies of harmonic functions, represent the hierarchical, male-dominated structures of European religious, political and cultural history is convincingly argued by both these (and other) writers. Without going into detail, it is fairly obvious, even to the casual observer, that male conductors and composers still far outweigh in number their female counterparts, even in the present time, when women are taking up more places in politics and industry. Until recently, female musicians were banned from some major European orchestras. And, as McClary (1991) has pointed out, you will find on library bookshelves numerous offprints from the *New Grove Dictionary of Music and Musicians* with titles such as 'Masters of the Late Romantic Era'.

We may or may not agree with the notion that the actual structures of music can somehow be encoded with gendered messages, but there can be no argument that the same tradition that produced the elegant rationality and tonal dialectic of sonata structure in music also provided a form of male hegemony in political and cultural life that has only been seriously challenged in modern Western societies in the present time. Yet the tradition that produced blues, jazz and formed much of the background to modern popular traditions was, in its infancy, dominated by powerful women (such as the voodoo queens of New Orleans) who lived within a very different kind of social order. Shepherd's argument, essentially, is that the patterns in the music and the patterns of political life must be connected since they grow from the same roots. This is not to imply that musical form is socially determined. I would agree with Shepherd that '. . . social process knows no strict or prime causation. And, since creativity is an integral part of the social process, there can be no ultimate and complete explanation for the particular form that a (musical) symbol takes' (Shepherd, 1977:100).

So, without laying down strict causal laws we can say that the classroom both reflects and, potentially, influences cultural positioning, in music as in any other area of the curriculum. The music teacher is in a very powerful position therefore in raising awareness of these issues and in guiding practice. *Music in the National Curriculum* makes it very clear that students should be taught to 'relate music to its social, historical and cultural context' as well as 'identify how and why musical styles and traditions change over time and from place to place, recognising the contribution of composers and performers' (DFE, 1995:7(6b) and 7(6d)).

This relates to the Listening and Appraising of music. In

Performing and Composing music, students of both sexes will, it is assumed, be given equal opportunities to contribute in a variety of ways – directing groups, arranging and writing pieces, improvising and so on – and it may be necessary to combine this work with a reminder of the valid contributions made by women to music, from Hildegard of Bingen to Madonna.

MUSIC AND SEXUALITY

The musical experiences of young people are inevitably charged with sexual imagery. This is nothing new in musical experience: from Monteverdi's *Poppea* through Mozart's *Giovanni* or *Così*, via Berg's *Lulu* to Madonna, music and sex have been unequivocally linked. Since the war, the explosion of youth culture has spawned a never-ending stream of artists whose music and lifestyles often sit uneasily with the kind of moral and cultural values characterized by traditional teaching and curricula.

Furthermore, many artists have not merely challenged authority ('lay off of my blue suede shoes') but have challenged the social norm altogether. When Lou Reed sings of the 'wild side', there is no hint of judgement; rather a celebration of the underbelly of society. When Joan Armatrading sings 'I wanna girlfriend and a boy for laughs', there is a celebration of bisexuality; when David Bowie adopted his alter-ego ('Ziggy Stardust') it was not to reinforce the norm but to get in touch with an androgynous 'other'; and when Jimmy Somerville burst onto the scene with The Communards in the 1980s, it was to promote the notion that, despite AIDS, it was OK to be gay.

Faced with these social and musical realities, what does the teacher do? To ignore this aspect of music risks alienating those students to whom popular music means as much as football or clothes. To endorse diverse sexualities or populist flavours invites a charge of moral relativism. In my view the answer is to be found in what might be termed *responsible empowerment*. By this, I mean inculcating in students an awareness of their own capacity to express musically whatever moves them emotionally, whatever engages them sexually or whatever they aspire to spiritually.

The National Curriculum is significantly silent on specifics, the word *sex* appearing nowhere in the music document. However, when students are asked to 'compose music for specific purposes' this points to a functionality which must travel beyond the utilitarian into the expressive; and where they are required to 'analyse changes in character and mood, taking account of their intentions and the comments of others' it would be irresponsible not to take into account the importance of music in relation to sexuality and to accommodate this aspect in planning and preparation.

IMPROVISATION AND EQUALITY

In the preceding discussions I have talked a lot about *empowerment*. I now want to suggest some methods which will empower students to create their own musical forms as well as providing them with insight into musical processes in more general terms. Improvisation is a much-misunderstood term. Often, it spells a quick-fix solution to a problem or something undertaken without adequate preparation. As so often is the case, this popular usage of a term and a process tells us more about the cultural climate than about the term itself. In essence, improvisation merely means *unforeseen*, a process of which the outcome is as yet unknown. As such, it describes perfectly the act of creation and thus seems to me to express the essential musical act. Furthermore, a predicted result both imposes a ready-made aesthetic and runs the risk of excluding those whose ability, background or individual sensibility may not fit a pre-ordained pattern.

Improvisation provides an ideal strategic tool for ensuring equality in composing and performing. And collective (group) improvisation can produce not merely enjoyable and satisfying musical results but will have all sorts of other social and moral pay-offs – group bonding, sense of shared purpose, respect for others' musical ideas and therefore emotional space, sense of social cohesion and identity and, above all, a shared creative spirit, a sense, albeit abstract, of direction. Improvisation offers every single participant, regardless of ability, 'race', social class, gender or sexuality an opportunity to contribute. Above all, improvisational play offers a quality of experience which is peculiar to the arts and which is especially powerful in music. Group improvisation is also a *whole lot of fun* and the following ideas are offered as much in a spirit of conviviality as intended pedagogic tools.

Sound Plans

These plans are all examples of what I term *Holding Forms*.[1] The holding form is a framework within and around which a piece may develop, a template for improvisation. The holding form strikes a balance between a prescribed structure and a free-for-all. It also provides, ideally, an expressive as well as a structural basis around which students may improvise.

Sound Plan 1 – Rhythmsearch

1. The group sits in a circle.
2. Everyone begins lap drumming together.
3. Anybody is allowed to bring the drumming to a stop by making any sound and/or gesture (e.g. raising the arms and calling HO!).
4. This should result in sound punctuated by silence and will thus establish a basic structural principle (i.e. music is the organization, with intent, of sound and silence).
5. The group is then instructed to alternate right and left hands in a regular pattern of twos (LLRR/LLRR/LLRR etc.) to produce a continuum of regular pulse.
6. Again, anyone may bring this to a stop. When one player restarts the pulse, everybody joins in.
7. The players are now instructed to create individual rhythmic patterns by making spaces in the pulse (e.g. LL-R/LL-R/LL-R/LL-R etc.). Try to maintain a quality of attentiveness between the players so that they pick up on each other's rhythms.
8. Next, replace the lap drumming with vocal sounds (beep-beep/bap-bap/beep-beep/bap-bap). Again, make up rhythms by leaving gaps.
9. Introduce further ideas, e.g. holding on to sounds to produce long *bees* or *baas* or doubling the pulse to produce *billy billy billy billy*.
10. Transfer the rhythmic ideas produced in this fashion to tuned and/or untuned percussion instruments or keyboards if they are available. By varying the tempi and the vocal scat sounds a whole variety of different rhythmic patterns can be developed which may form the basis of numerous and varied pieces.

Sound Plan 2 – Chanting

1. Choose four short phrases in any language. Your students can supply these. Chant the phrases over and over until they turn into tunes (this should happen spontaneously). Then allow each student to choose (silently) one of the chants. After a count of three, everyone chants together, moving around the room until they have teamed up with others chanting on the same text. Repeat with a variety of texts.

2. A variation of this involves supplying each student with a work card on which is printed a text for chanting (try to ensure an even number of cards for each text). For example:

   Work Card 1 – *All the rivers run into the sea.*

   Work Card 2 – *You never miss the water 'til the well runs dry.*

   Work Card 3 – *Water, water everywhere.*

   Work Card 4 – *It's raining, it's pouring.*

3. With eyes closed, or perhaps blindfold, the students move slowly around the hall chanting their own text and listening out for others chanting the same. Team up into groups accordingly, as before.

4. The chanting can now be transferred to instruments resulting in three or four contrasting pieces based upon the texts.

5. Chants can be built up using a call-and-response technique, for example:

   Teacher: *don't*

   Students: *DON'T*

   don't care ... DON'T CARE

   don't care, didn't care ... DON'T CARE, DIDN'T CARE

   don't care, didn't care, don't care was wild ... DON'T CARE ETC.[2]

6. In a circle again, everybody thinks of an action associated with physical work (e.g. sawing, chopping wood, digging, hoovering). Everybody moves together, making up a chant to fit with the movement. For a variation, everyone makes the same movement and the teacher sets up a call-and-response chant to go with it (Day-o ... DAY-O/Day-day-do ... DAY-DAY-DO etc.).

7. Here is an easily remembered lyric:

   OH DEAR OH DEAR OH DEAR OH DEAR OH DEAR OH DEAR OH DEAR (x3)

OH DEAR OH DEAR OH DEAR OH DEAR OH DEAR OH
BLINKIN' DEAR

This can be chanted with movement. Each student walks in
time to the chant, in a straight line but all in different directions. Change direction on each line. Chant on the spot . . . OH
DEAR (2, 3, 4) OH DEAR (2, 3, 4) OH DEAR (2, 3, 4) etc.
without moving, and then begin the whole lyric/movement
again, each starting individually. This can form the basis of a
collective improvisation, playing freely with the suggested
melodies within the chant and adding percussion instruments
when appropriate.

Sound Plan 3 – Drumming

1. On laps, or desks, or even drums (if you can get enough
   together), set up a 2 + 2 pattern (two left-hand strokes followed
   by two right-hand strokes) using the hands (more immediate
   and less noisy than beaters). If the children experience co-ordi-
   nation problems with this, try chanting *Beep-beep, Bap-bap* at
   the same time. This may help to keep the hands in time.
2. Repeat the exercise, leaving out occasional beats. Repeat,
   leaving out more and more beats until total silence is
   achieved. Repeat again, making up lots of different patterns.
3. Start with lots of different patterns and see if everyone can end
   up on the same pattern.
4. Sit in a circle and pass drumming patterns around in any direction. Three adjacent students in the circle drum their patterns.
   When the fourth starts drumming the first drops out. Repeat
   this process all the way around the circle.
5. Here are some more drumming patterns to chant and play:
   Billy doo dap doo da/Billy doo dap doo da etc.
   Taka tak/Taka tak/Taka tak/Taa –/Taka tak/Taka tak/
   Taka tak/Taa etc.
   Bap – Bap – shaka tak tak –/Bap – Bap – shaka tak tak etc.
6. Everyone begins drumming together. If necessary, the teacher
   can keep time by beating out the pulse on a pair of claves. The
   students drop out one at a time, in any order, until one is left
   drumming solo. After about ten seconds, everyone joins in
   again and the process is repeated until everyone has played a
   solo.

Sound Plan 4 – Time Holes

1. Begin with time holes that are silent. The teacher says, 'GO' and, after about twenty seconds or so, says 'STOP'. This is a time hole.
2. The players can now begin to fill the time holes with sounds. Start with one short sound per player using any available sound source. Each player may make her or his sound only once within the span of the time hole.
3. Any player may control the time hole by saying GO and STOP. But no one may say GO until the previous player has said STOP. The lengths of the time holes may vary from around twenty seconds to a full minute or even more.
4. Move on to making their sound more than once within the time hole but attempting to make each sound in such a way that they do not sound simultaneously with any others. In this way it is possible to build up patterned sequences of sounds in the time hole.
5. Allow the single sound to double into a duplet. Once one player has played a duplet, all players may do so.
6. If using pitched instruments such as xylophones or keyboards, it may be necessary to limit the choice of pitches to create particular modes.
7. Continue the sequences from Stage 4 but allow them to overlap increasingly until all players are improvising freely.

CONCLUSION

Within the constraints of this book it would be impossible to present a full range of practical classroom activities. Furthermore, music, by its very nature, makes special demands on the teacher: the real essence of the subject can never be conveyed in print, only through practical demonstration can anything authentic be absorbed. The suggested publications listed below will convey some idea of the kinds of approach which reflect the principles outlined above. In summary these are:

1. respecting cultural and class backgrounds;
2. avoiding the imposition of an alien aesthetic;
3. being aware of those aspects of our own musical traditions

which militate against equality (such as the predominance of male influence in the classical music world);

4. understanding that musical quality resides not in levels of skill but in levels of imagination (this is of particular relevance to groups with special educational needs);
5. placing the emphasis on techniques which serve the development of the individual expressive imagination;
6. facilitating a kind of music-making, such as group improvisation, which promotes the collective imagination, thus placing emphasis on commonality of feeling.

The National Curriculum provides wide scope for interpretation. Where, for example, it states that 'Students should be given opportunities to . . . listen to, and develop understanding of music from different times and places, applying knowledge to their own work' (1995:7), this is in full recognition of the diversity of cultural needs that exist in British schools. It is very much up to the individual teacher to decide, through sensitive awareness of students' needs and cultural backgrounds, on the choices to make in respect of style, form, complexity and meaning in music. It will also mean using teaching techniques which either draw upon the widest possible range of styles or, as in the case of many improvisational forms, avoid cultural finger-printing altogether.

RESOURCES

This list, far from being exhaustive, is intended to demonstrate the kinds of teaching materials which reflect the principles outlined above. The major resource for music is to be found in live and recorded performances.

Addison, R. (1987) *Bright Ideas: Music.* Leamington Spa: Scholastic.
Bean, J. Oldfield (1991) *A Pied Piper.* Cambridge: Cambridge University Press. Specific to special needs children.
Binns, P. and Chacksfield, M. (1983) *Sound Ideas.* Oxford: Oxford University Press. Various titles aimed at music making in a variety of styles.
Burnett, M. (1980) *Pop Music Topic Book.* Oxford: Oxford University Press. Useful projects.
Catherall, E. (1989) *Exploring Sound.* Hove: Wayland.
Davies, L. (1985) *Sound Waves: Practical Ideas for Children's' Music Making.* London: Bell and Hyman.
Dunbar-Hall, P. and Hodge, G. (1991) *A Guide to Rock and Pop.* London: Science Press.

Farrell, G. (1990) *Indian Music in Education.* Cambridge: Cambridge University Press.

Floyd, L. (1980) *Indian Music.* Oxford: Oxford University Press.

Gilbert, J. (1991) *Topic Anthology.* Oxford: Oxford University Press.

Griffin, C. (1985) *Music Matters.* London: The Dryad Press. A variety of titles and a wide cultural reference in this series.

Holdstock, J. (1986) *Earwiggo up, Earwiggo down: Pitch Games.* Tadcaster: Ray Lovely Music. Excellent material for students with special educational needs.

McNicol, R. (1993) *Sound Inventions.* Oxford: Oxford University Press.

Paynter, J. (1982) *All Kinds of Music.* Cambridge: Cambridge Educational. A diverse set of ideas and resources covering a wide range of styles and cultures.

Paynter, J. and Aston, P. (1970) *Sound and Silence.* Cambridge: Cambridge University Press. A seminal book of creative classroom projects. More relevant than ever 25 years after publication.

Pepper, D. (1982) *High Low.* London: A & C Black. Useful project work.

Pugh, A. (1991) *Women in Music.* Cambridge: Cambridge University Press. A simple history of the role of women in music from Hildegard of Bingen to the present day. Sets the record straight.

Stevens, J. (1987) *Search and Reflect.* London: Community Music. Invaluable improvisation handbook.

Storms, G. (1981) *Handbook of Music Games.* London: Hutchinson.

Various. *Mango Spice, Phantasmagoria, Sing for Your Life, The Singing Sack, Tinder Box etc.* London: A & C Black. An invaluable resource of songs in all styles and from many cultural and ethnic sources.

Vulliamy, G. and Lee, E. (1982) *Popular Music: A Teacher's Guide.* London: Routledge.

BIBLIOGRAPHY

Attali, J. (1977) *Noise, the Political Economy of Music.* Manchester: Manchester University Press.

DFE (1995) *Music in the National Curriculum.* London: HMSO.

Finnegan, R. (1989) *The Hidden Musicians, Music-Making in an English Town.* Cambridge: Cambridge University Press.

McClary, S. (1991) *Feminine Endings, Music, Gender and Sexuality.* Minneapolis: University of Minnesota Press.

Meier, S. (1992) Children's Music in the Third Reich. Unpublished PhD thesis, University of London.

Regelski, T. A. (1986) Concept-learning and action-learning in music education. *British Journal of Music Education,* 3:195.

Shepherd, J. (1977) *Whose Music? A Sociology of Musical Styles.* London: Routledge.

Shepherd, J. (1991) *Music as Social Text.* Cambridge: Polity Press.

Swanwick, K. (1988) *Music, Mind and Education.* London: Routledge.

Vulliamy, G. and Lee, E. (eds) (1987) *Pop, Rock and Ethnic Music in Schools.* Cambridge: Cambridge Educational.

Witkin, R. W. (1974) *The Intelligence of Feeling.* London: Heinemann Educational.

NOTES

1. For the origin of this term see Witkin, R. W. (1974) *The Intelligence of Feeling.* London: Heinemann Educational. Chapter 8.
2. The full text of this anonymous ditty goes like this:

> Don't Care didn't care
> Don't Care was wild,
> Don't Care stole plum and pear
> Like any beggar's child.
>
> Don't Care was made to care,
> Don't Care was hung.
> Don't Care was put in a pot
> And boiled 'til he was done.

CHAPTER 9

Art[1]

Dave Allen

ART IN THE ENGLISH SCHOOL CURRICULUM: A HISTORICAL SURVEY

As in the legislation for the National Curriculum, 'art' in this chapter encompasses all the visual arts, including art, craft and design and all the lens-based and digital means of producing images. In the chapter I will argue that equality in art is bound up with the kind of images which young people are producing or learning about. In order to construct the argument, I propose to take a historical perspective on the development of art in the school curriculum. I shall begin, however, in the present.

The statutory Order for Art in the National Curriculum identifies two attainment targets. While the two are best seen as interdependent, they are commonly associated with different processes and educational aims. The first, 'Investigating and Making', generally encompasses the ways in which students produce their own artworks, a practice which has always been central to the teaching of art and design. The second is concerned with 'Knowledge and Understanding' of art in its various forms, which has its roots in art history and what has more recently been described as critical studies.

The processes which are central to 'Investigating and Making' are, with some justification, often linked to the liberal and 'progressive' developments in education which occurred in the middle decades of this century. Their origins, however, had a far more pragmatic basis. For example, Macdonald (1970) records how in the 1830s the British government became concerned with the quality of design in British manufacturing and the capacity of British industry to compete with foreign markets. In 1835 it intervened for the first time in art education to establish a Select Committee which, in the following year, recommended the establishment in London of a Normal School of Design, as well as grants to provincial schools, the formation of public galleries and museums, and the encouragement of public art.

While the origins of mass public art education lay in vocational or economic rationales, it is important to acknowledge that, from the start, the type of art education on offer was also determined by social class. While the children of 'ordinary' people were required to follow a form of art education which prepared them for industrial work, Macdonald records how the academics of the nineteenth century were offered a classical, fine-art education and they considered that 'design for industry was the lowest branch of ornament, even below the hand crafts'.

A dry and rather 'scientific' approach to general art education can be identified in the drawing books of the nineteenth century which contained diagrams, ornaments, objects and landscapes to be copied. Drawing, in particular, was at the heart of the early teaching of art and design because, as Carline (1968) and Macdonald (1970) suggest, it was 'absolutely necessary in many employments, trades and manufactures' (Carline:51).

Today, drawing continues to dominate but the nineteenth-century vocational rationale is no longer appropriate. Drawing is instead seen as the best way of developing a general visual perception and it also offers respectability – as art has become more 'experimental', the ability to draw 'properly' is often considered the most reliable criterion of genuine artistic skill. In addition this primary skill is often felt to be the source of real expression in art. For example, in the early 1980s, Her Majesty's Inspectorate examined fourteen secondary school art departments and observed that '*All* schools saw the thorough teaching of drawing as both a prime objective and a key which unlocked the door to a distinctive and convincing expression on the part of the students' (DES, 1983:62).

Despite these changes, it might be argued that the nineteenth-century pragmatic rationale for art education was revived with the initial inclusion of art within that broad area defined as tech-nology in the early stages of the National Curriculum. While that impulse seems to have lost ground, the more recent development of GNVQs in Art and Design, available from Key Stage 4, is also part of the history of art *and design* education. Whenever art is identified as an 'expressive' art alongside subjects like drama and music, it is worth remembering its role in the economic prosper-ity of the nation and the consequent level of funding it receives for the large number of young people who follow it post-16.

This pragmatic, vocational rationale for art education, estab-lished in the mid-nineteenth century, remained a powerful influence into this century. However, art was also an attractive subject to supporters of more liberal, child-centred pedagogies, not least because it was free from some of the constraints and expectations of 'core' subjects like mathematics and (eventually) English or science. What emerged was a freer approach to art edu-cation which came to be known as 'Child Art'. The growth of 'Child Art' in the middle decades of this century undoubtedly achieved a great deal for generations of young people and its main rationales, advocates and achievements have been well docu-mented by Carline, Macdonald and others. Significantly for the argument being developed here, the progressive practices of 'Child Art' were nurtured by what Dick Field (1970) described as a 'life-giving relationship' between art, artists and art education.

One of the main points about this 'life-giving relationship' is the way in which teachers' awareness of art practices is reflected in the kinds of tasks they present to their students. This is not sur-prising since the overwhelming majority of secondary school art teachers are practitioners – quasi-artists – and likely to be inter-ested in historic and contemporary practices which they translate into tasks for their students. Carline records such links, as long ago as the start of this century, between the progressive art teacher Franz Cizek and the 'impressionist painters of the Munich "Secession"' (1968:163), as well as the importance of Gauguin's views of civilization for Cizek's theories of art educa-tion. Carline also recorded evidence of modernist painters including Matisse, the Fauves and the German Expressionists reciprocally drawing upon these new practices in children's art to inform their own work.

Perhaps the most influential art teacher in Britain to derive ideas from modernism was Marion Richardson. Carline records the impact of her students' work on Roger Fry, who had been responsible for staging British exhibitions of the work of Cézanne, Gauguin, Matisse and Rousseau before the First World War, and how Richardson was 'equally impressed' by the work on show in Fry's exhibitions (1968:168). The exchange of ideas and practices between these artists and teachers led directly to changes in the artroom. During the inter-war years, Carline observed, this 'new school of thought' encouraged 'sensibility', drawing on the child's 'inner experience'. He also suggested that 'technical competence was of minor consideration' (1968:171) in contrast to the emphasis on technique in many nineteenth-century activities.

These two historical approaches – one derived from a nineteenth-century economic and vocational imperative, the other from the more liberal 'Child Art' movement – were very different in kind, although the two approaches both focused on students making their own images and objects. Only the first of the two attainment targets in the Statutory Order does that, since the second, 'Knowledge and Understanding' seeks to inform young people's understanding of historical and contemporary cultural practices. That is a very different aim.

John Bowden, Senior General Inspector (Art) in Harrogate, and an adviser or inspector for art education for a quarter of a century, recently acknowledged the significance of this change when he pointed out that knowledge and understanding or 'critical studies' has constituted the major change in recent art education. Otherwise, he suggested, 'art education has not changed a great deal in schools in the past thirty or forty years' (Bowden, 1996:13).

Given the assumed link between 'Child Art' and progressive education, this is a fairly dramatic claim from a very experienced art educator – has art teaching become conservative without anyone noticing? Can it be much as it was in 1967, or even 1957? Perhaps we might split the difference, and try 1962. Khrushchev and Kennedy ruled the world, Burnley and Spurs were the great English football sides, the Beatles were yet to record, young men were still doing National Service and no one had landed on the moon or dug tunnels under proposed motorways. There was almost full employment in Britain and just two television channels. In the art world, American abstraction ruled, although 'pop' was pulling some rude faces at the seriousness of late modernism.

In state secondary schools, most young people still followed a path determined by the results of a selective examination, and that path meant contrasting curricula. Nevertheless, everyone did the three Rs, which included 'traditional' mathematics; there were no computers or calculators and technology was called woodwork or domestic science. Some teenagers still studied Latin or Greek but few studied drama other than in extra-curricular sessions. In the artroom these same young people made pencil drawings of plants and objects or 'imaginative' paintings of figurative compositions, using colour cakes and sugar paper.

At the time, this practice was relatively new and art had a significant role in 'progressive' pedagogies typical of a growing liberal education. Yet the visual innovation and progressive pedagogies of the mid-twentieth century have been overtaken by major changes in artistic practice, in the social, political and economic life of the country and in the aims and organization of education, especially since the Education Reform Act of 1988. And art education? If Bowden is right it has changed 'little', except for critical studies.

Bowden is not alone in this view, for the National Curriculum Working Group (1991) reported on the dominance of drawing in artrooms as confirmation that, despite the increasing use of 'new' technologies in other parts of schools and in adult arts practice, art teaching has largely retained a traditional approach to the use of materials. The same report included the following evidence from HMI surveys: 'In most schools the activities and aspects of art and design covered consist largely of drawing and painting, with some ceramics, printmaking and work in textiles. Apart from ceramics there is very little three-dimensional work' (1991:2.8).

More optimistically, the Working Group suggested in paragraph 2.2 of this Report that the 'wide range' of practices in art education reflect the 'diversity' of professional artists and designers, and it offered a list which included graphic and product design, fashion, jewellery, photography, film and video, theatre design, the use of computers, and 'other new technologies'. Despite this, the Group found that 'most secondary schools give inadequate attention to the appreciation and critical judgment of work by artists and designers . . . Very few include a study of the work of designers, despite the importance of design in the world of work' (1991:2.12). So even in the 'growth' area of critical studies there were concerns over the range of study.

Nevertheless, progress has clearly been made since 1970, when

Macdonald's comprehensive historical survey concluded with just three paragraphs on the 'appreciation and history of art and design'. These identified a long-standing 'resistance to academic studies by art teachers', and the consequent preference for appreciation over history, despite the enthusiasm of 'many . . . students and schoolchildren . . . (for) the history of art, design and architecture' (1970:375). It is interesting that MacDonald records how the first examinations in art history (in 1858) contained questions that were too difficult for the teachers and were attempted by 'less than fifteen percent' of candidates (1970:375). It may be that to some extent the development of critical studies in recent years continues to reflect the interests and capacities of art teachers as much as the needs or preferences of students. In this respect, Bowden (1996) suggests

> there is no evidence that secondary schools are any more prepared to teach critical studies than primary schools . . . In secondary schools though these teachers are usually trained artists, they very often have limited art history knowledge themselves . . . They are also very resistant to changing the curriculum. (1996:16)

I have referred to Field's description of the 'life-giving relationship' between art and art education and, in particular, between early modernism and the growth of 'Child Art'. Despite this link, the growing influence of psychology and 'progressive' pedagogues on art education created something of a gap between adult art and its role in schools. For example, the curriculum guidelines produced by Hampshire Local Education Authority (1986) drew attention to the value of 'educating the child *through* art' (1986:23) but also suggested that 'studying the work of professional artists can be seen *only* as a method of teaching established values and recognising generally accepted criteria about art' (1986:138, my emphases). This view of the potential of critical studies is limited because it fears that the study of art will influence children and encourage them to be merely imitative.

Such fears were prevalent twenty years ago, but a more positive attitude to what was most often called critical studies developed in the early 1980s, largely due to a National Curriculum project led by Rod Taylor, then the art adviser for Wigan LEA. Taylor's project was jointly sponsored by the Arts, Crafts and Schools Councils and he supported it with energetic, missionary work. Despite the example from Hampshire, many art advisers supported his initiative, as did the National Society for Education in Art and Design (NSEAD), SCDC's national 'Arts in Schools Project' and the public examination boards which identified critical and contextual studies as an element of the new GCSE. By the late 1980s, critical studies was a subject whose time had arrived: supported by further conferences and publications (especially Thistlewood, 1989) the subject was eventually included as a compulsory attainment target in the Statutory Order.

In terms of issues of equality, critical studies immediately enables teachers to address the key issue of representation, by making it possible to ask of any work 'What is being shown here?', 'Who is choosing to show it?', 'Why are they showing it in this way?'. Asking such questions also takes us beyond the idea that a work is the product of one person since the exhibition of any kind of visual work depends on an infrastructure of institutions, organizations and individuals. The question 'Who is choosing to show it?' therefore refers not only to the artist who makes the work but also to all the individuals and organizations who make it structurally and economically possible to see work.

The work in question will cover a range of practices encompassing all contemporary visual imagery. The categorization of this work can be a useful pedagogical practice, asking students 'What kind of work is this?'. In art education at secondary level and beyond, categories are most often defined in terms of discipline, or medium deployed, so that painting is different from ceramics, print-making from photography, or two-dimensional from three-dimensional. Dividing practice in this way emphasizes certain kinds of practical skills and enables a predominantly formal, cross-disciplinary visual 'language' to develop (line, tone, shape, colour, etc.). What is interesting about an approach which addresses questions of equality is that this very often cuts across these traditional divisions. For example, the major Hayward Gallery exhibition 'The Other Story' displayed work by 'Afro-Asian' artists working in post-war Britain as a consequence of 'the mass emigration of Africa, Asia and the Caribbean to the West' (Araeen, 1989:9) and the art revealed a range of visual practices including painting, video, installation, sculpture, film, print-making. The question of nomenclature for these artists is a contentious one (see Cole, 1993), for where Araeen used the term 'Afro-Asian', Chambers and Joseph (1988) produced the first 'history of Britain's Black visual artists' (1988:4). Kwesi Owusu

(1986) in a discourse on black art and the black community identified 'the essential unity of the two main components . . . the
AfroCaribbean and the Asian', but added:

> To be BLACK is not merely a matter of skin colour. It is a state of
> consciousness, of what Frantz Fanon would have called 'combat
> breathing': a living, interminable challenge to Imperialism in the
> metropolis. This state of consciousness articulates the dialectics of
> race, sex and class within the context of the exploitative and
> endemic racism of capitalist social relations. (1986:21)

Such a definition cuts across the categories of media or form.
Similarly, as Berger (1972) demonstrated, any consideration of
images of women may well include paintings by Rubens, Picasso
or Watteau but should also examine magazine advertisements,
classical sculpture, Hollywood cinema or fashion photography.
Such juxtapositions of everyday and unfamiliar imagery can be a
useful way of extending young people's ideas about the visual.

I am suggesting here that critical studies is an important area for
opening up questions of equality in the classroom – mainly, but not
exclusively, through issues of representation. Critical studies has
taken a considerable hold on the art curriculum over the past decade
so that in 1993 Stanley was able to write that it 'has now become
part of the orthodoxy of art and design education' (1993:317).
Nevertheless, it tends to remain subservient to the business of
making art. For example, Thistlewood (1992) drew attention to Rod
Taylor's project work as introducing 'practice-informing values and
criteria' to the subject, yet recorded that despite the growth of critical studies in recent years, its principal purpose has been to serve
'the interests . . . of "making" or practice"', Thistlewood wondering
whether it can become 'an independent subject'.

In the original Order for Art in the National Curriculum,
Strand 7 (Attainment Target 2) required students to apply 'knowledge of the work of other artists to their own work'. This
disappeared from the revised Draft Proposals (1994) which
emphasized that while this was still 'recognised as important to
students' understanding and practical skills', the 'skills of critical
evaluation' now had 'greater emphasis' (1994:ii). Even this caveat
is missing from the Revised Order, so while critical studies has
become an accepted, indeed expected, part of art teaching, the
pedagogical purposes may be changing. The study of art is becoming as valid as the study of literature – a practice in its own right.

It is therefore possible that a new and more autonomous critical studies might draw more on contemporary theory, including theoretical reference to issues of representation and the circulation of images.

The aim of Taylor's work was to redress a perceived imbalance in the subject and to draw greater attention to the importance in art education of what the Project variously described as the 'contemplative aspects – verbal communication judgement, rigour, knowledge, broader context (and) critical awareness and understanding' (1986:xi). Yet there are two senses in which this new development perpetuated expressive, student-centred pedagogies which were, in part, the legacy of 'Child Art' and, more broadly, 'progressive' education. First, the early expectation that critical studies would inform and therefore 'improve' students' own expressive work; second, as Stanley (1993) suggested, 'the most welcome aspect of critical studies has been its insistence on privileging the student's own account and analysis of art . . . *the personal response*' (1993:317, my emphasis). Hughes (1993) argued that students must be introduced to the appropriate 'framework of discourse' and 'techniques' for understanding, but even this apparently more rigorous aim was to 'empower' students 'to make meaning for themselves' (1993:287).

Promoting the importance of the 'personal response' is clearly a legacy of liberal pedagogies: they are not ideologically unproblematic, and make a number of assumptions about the purpose of critical studies. I am happy to argue for developments in the critical analysis of visual artefacts, but less so with that well-established tradition of the personal response; rather, my focus is on a newer practice emerging from structural analysis, critical theory and inter-disciplinary work (including media education). This newer approach acknowledges that any critical response is in part 'personal', constructed from and reflecting a range of personal, social, political, economic and historical contexts, but it does not seek to privilege the personal over those other contexts. The challenge seems to me to be to retain those elements of a liberal pedagogy where self-expression in production and criticism are useful and significant, while developing considerably the flexibility of such criticism to deal with a full range of visual work, including an awareness of how such work is circulated and used to support or promote particular interest groups and ideologies.

Only in such ways can criticism be utilized for a pedagogy of equality, and to date that has not happened. For example, Mason and Rawding (1993) drew on Thistlewood's definition of critical studies to suggest that British art educators have generally concentrated on 'aesthetic presence (and) formative processes' but have been less strong on 'spiritual, social, economic and political causes' or 'cultural effects' of art (1993:357). In other words teachers seem to be most interested in the appearance and production of art and less in what it means in a broader context. Perhaps this was because, as Brazier (1985) observed, the strongest influence on the teaching of 'art history' in schools was derived from 'antecedents in nineteenth-century German scholarship' with its 'stylistic or iconographical preoccupations' (1985:1–2). Mason and Rawding, however, suggested that the emphasis on appearance was the consequence of 'a lack of theoretical coherence at the heart of critical studies' (1993:358). It may also be because *making* art remains the dominant practice in most artrooms and, as Bowden argues, too much of this remains as it was in the 1950s and 1960s. In particular the Order for Art has promoted the formal analysis and production of art (the 'elements' of line, tone, shape, etc.) over matters of content or representation.

Given such preoccupations it is perhaps not surprising that the majority of works studied in the classroom appear to be drawn from examples of early European modernism – particularly works which demonstrate painterly or expressive concerns – since these can be fairly easily understood *visually* and may well impact on the dominant medium of the artroom: paint. Work which might be described as conceptual or issue-based, or work in new or mixed media, appears less frequently. Since I have written extensively about this elsewhere (e.g. Allen, 1994) I do not propose to pursue the issue here in any detail but here is one example: a table of artists named in the various reports and proposals which led to the Order for Art (Table 9.1). It shows how a 'canon' of increasingly ancient, male painters was recommended to schoolteachers, while living artists, especially women and those working outside the fine art tradition, were increasingly excluded.

While this largely conservative 'canon' was being enshrined in the Order, other *non-statutory* examples were concerned with a broader range of 'visually communicated information' including 'family photographs, cards, teacups, illustrations, buildings,

Table 9.1 Artists named in various reports and proposals

Publication	Total	Pre-1900	Twentieth century (*living*)	Designers	Women
Working Group	26	9	15 (5)	2	7
Proposals	25	10	6 (1)	9	5
Consultation	37	25	12 (1)	-	2
First Order	38	25	13 (2)	-	2

African tribal art, computer images, comics, TV commercials, photographic montage, postage stamps, computer animation, T-shirt motifs, body ornament, kites, Aboriginal dream maps, wall-hangings'. Here we suddenly have de-personalized examples so that whereas men like Rembrandt, Constable or Monet produced specific works of art with titles, other kinds of visual artefacts simply appear, produced either through a largely mysterious industrial process, or by 'other' kinds of people who live in African or Aboriginal tribes. Two of the (living) women artists named in the first Working Group report, Sonia Boyce and Maud Suiter, are high-profile black British artists working in 1990s Britain, and both of them address as a central concern matters of existence, experience and representation. It is in these issues that questions of equality reside in the classroom. Neither escaped the first 'cull', their names disappearing from the examples, discouraging teachers from seeking out their work to use it in the classroom. The specificity of their practice and the processes by which they came to work as artists would have been very interesting as a subject of study, and far more focused than something called 'African Tribal Art'. It also has far more to do with Britain in the 1990s. Their names were included in the first report because a small number of educators, curators and critics had some influence on the process at that stage. As soon as the politicians and bureaucrats of the day got their hands on the process, the opportunity to encourage teachers to engage with such work was discarded.

So I am suggesting that neither in most practical work, nor in the artefacts examined in a critical studies context, is much space given to the kind of challenging artwork to be found everywhere over the past quarter of a century, despite Field's recognition that this should be a 'life-giving relationship'. Thematic and issue-based work, addressing itself to a massive range of political, social and economic questions bound up with equality, work in new media and technologies, mixed-media work, installation and performance art are all vital and vibrant practices which most schools simply ignore in favour of the old practices of painting and drawing. Similarly, art education has always had a very uneasy relationship with the imagery of popular or mass culture despite the ubiquitous nature of that imagery and the regular contact young people have with television, domestic photography, graphic novels, computer games, advertising and other kinds of familiar media. Schools simply appear to assume that these vital, daily visual experiences have nothing to do with them, believing instead in a somewhat mysterious process which enables delicate paintings of cheese plants to lead to visual literacy in the twenty-first century.

If art education is to shake off this conservatism and address itself to vital contemporary issues, including equality, it must again forge that 'life-giving relationship' with contemporary visual arts practice. That will include drawing and painting, but in future as no more than an equal partner in the world of image-making, alongside a range of two- and three-dimensional, still and moving images. It must also involve a broad range of work across fine art, popular culture, advertising and the media.

To summarize this theoretical and historical section then, I am arguing that questions of equality can only be addressed in the artroom by focusing increasingly on the broadening of conceptual and practical processes. The conceptual issues are enshrined in those previous questions such as 'What is being shown here?', 'Who is choosing to show it?', 'Why are they showing it in this way?' and 'What kind of work is this?'. The questions have all been fairly freely adapted from work in media education (e.g. Bowker, 1991) because they enable art teachers to extend the more limited range of questions most often asked in critical studies. Nevertheless, a firm understanding of the questions can do more than improve work in critical studies: it will also raise issues for the makers of visual artefacts, including students.

CLASSROOM PRACTICE

In terms of classroom practice, I am arguing that visual arts education in the twenty-first century must address itself to the rapidly expanding field of visual imagery, including, but moving beyond, a narrow focus on painting and drawing. In particular, art teachers must provide more opportunities for students to produce and study mixed-media, lens-based, digital, computer-based and moving imagery as a part of the *normal* art lesson. This work should proceed on the basis that all good art teaching recognizes the essential link between making and understanding art, and that the kinds of questions derived from media studies work (above) can form the basis of all processes of planning, making, analysing and evaluating art. Questions like 'What is being shown here?', 'What kind of work is this?' can be asked by students of their own work during the process of planning and making, as well as by them of the work of other artists.

In part, such an approach is dependent upon art teachers providing students with a broad range of images, as part of their critical engagement with the work of other artists. This will require a 'jackdaw' approach to publications and broadcasts, collecting articles, tapes and reviews to be available in the classroom and, as I have suggested, this must extend beyond the history of drawing and painting to include contemporary practice in art *and* design. Occasionally a particular show like *Sensation* at the Royal Academy (1997), or the annual Turner Prize, will provide extensive press coverage and secondary school students can be encouraged to help in collecting articles about such shows. Similarly, students will often have access to examples of current design through publications like *I-D* or *The Face* and will often be willing to bring them to school to complement traditional collections such as *The Great Artist.*

Examples of this kind of work will be a good place to start addressing questions of equality, particularly through the representation of age, gender, ethnicity, ability/disability and sexuality. In addition, examining how artists and the media represent issues can provide an excellent starting point for students' own image-making in addressing issues which are often important to them by adolescence.

The central problem, however, is that many art teachers

sustain work in traditional media because that is what they know about and are good at. In the near future one assumes that generations of art teachers will emerge who take for granted the advantages of new technologies and new media. In addition, one hopes (rather than assumes) that schools will recognize the resourcing implications of making students visually literate for the twenty-first century. Allied to the kind of conceptual framework hinted at in the questions above, this can enable serious consideration of issues of equality. In the meantime, can current art teachers be helped to extend the traditional media and processes of the classroom? One place to look might be the Statutory Order. I have suggested that the identification of two complementary attainment targets was a positive step in developing the art curriculum, but Table 9.1 also shows how the development of the Order tended to be rooted in an increasingly conservative view of the nature of art and design.

More recently, the School Curriculum and Assessment Authority (1996) produced a booklet entitled *Consistency in Teacher Assessment: Exemplification of Standards. Art: Key Stage 3* which is an almost perfect example of what I have been arguing against. The booklet offers examples of students' work 'chosen to illustrate the standard associated with achieving the expectations in different aspects of the end of Key Stage descriptions' (1996:5). It is full of traditional projects, with titles like Local Environment; Line, Shape and Texture; Plant Forms; The Human Figure; Design for Gift Bag; Facial Image; Metamorphosis; Shoreline; and most of the images show examples of work which which is figurative or 'realist'. A small proportion are of 'abstract' patterns or colour exercises. The claim that the 'examples cover a fairly broad range of media' (1996:5) is acceptable only as long as you discount any lens-based, electronic or digital images, or the kind of installation, performance and mixed-media work characteristic of so much twentieth-century practice. The 'content' of the work hardly ever addresses any difficult issues, while one exception, an image entitled 'The Pain of War', is so generalized as to seem a cliché. It is also interesting to note that this image appears in a section entitled 'Graphic Design', suggesting that such issues are not for the fine artists.

In this respect then the booklet is a good place to start by encouraging teachers to think of alternative ways of developing the range of skills and understanding which address contemporary concerns and issues. I have already suggested that this can be supported by referring on a regular basis to the work of other artists, particularly where examples of such work are available in the classroom. A second strategy might be to reject the general topics and titles which students are given, in favour of more specific topics. Sometimes this requires a simple linguistic adjustment such as 'The Bully' instead of 'Bullying', sometimes a larger change so that 'The Pain of War' might become 'Belfast' or 'Bosnia' (demanding media awareness), while 'Metamorphosis' becomes, perhaps, 'My Adolescence'.

At this point, with a change in the kind of topic and greater awareness of contemporary art and design, it is entirely possible to sustain drawing and painting as an important practice. However, since John Berger published his highly influential *Ways of Seeing* (1972), painting has been tied to particular issues of power and privilege. It is essential therefore that students are encouraged to explore other media; the 'new' photographic and digital technologies must become a key feature of work in the artroom, but this will not occur overnight. In the meantime I wish to propose one broad practice as a solution to introducing new work in schools: collage.

At its simplest, as a practical activity, collage is the process of sticking together a variety of visual elements in terms of content, texture, colour, tone, etc. In addition, I am arguing for a broader concept of collage which embraces many characteristic practices of the twentieth century. The concept owes much to Poggi's *In Defiance of Painting* (1992), although this chapter moves beyond her chosen remit to artefacts of the mass media in cinema, television, journalism and advertising, and also encompasses painting. Collage is therefore posited as a means of responding to the contemporary context without denying the value of much 'traditional good practice'.

Poggi suggested that the 'invention' of collage by Picasso, Braque and others (circa 1912) instituted 'an alternative to the modernist tradition in twentieth-century art' in that it emphasized 'heterogeneity' rather than 'stylistic unity' and would 'subvert' the distinctions between various 'forms of expression' (1992:xiii). Here again I wish to suggest that in its heterogeneity collage was able to provide the most appropriate vehicle for artists to examine questions of equality through their work. Poggi also argued that collage 'led to the further recognition of a link between the signs of "high" art and those of mass culture', a challenge which art education must address more adequately. There is little sign of it in the SCAA document.

Although Poggi focuses on Cubism and Futurism, she also reminds us that since the early years of the century, many artists have made 'collage, photomontage and assemblage an integral part of their art-making process' (1992:257), and she lists Duchamp, Tatlin, John Heartfield, Kurt Schwitters, Hannah Höch, Joseph Cornell, Jasper Johns, Robert Rauschenberg, Barbara Kruger and Mary Kelly as examples covering a period from the early years of the century to the present day. She adds that 'the coexistence of images, words and objects is now a familiar feature of twentieth-century art' and observes how this is even more important in the context of 'mechanical reproduction and . . . a commodity culture' (1992:257). If so, is it happening in artrooms? If not, why not?

I reproduce names here as a guide to teachers who may be interested in exploring a wide range of collage work (and there are many others), but I would emphasize that the list above is partial, limited to the fine arts and the world of the avant garde. In fact, collage (and montage) are everywhere, they are common visual practices of the late twentieth century, not merely in the world of art, but in almost every aspect of visual (and other) culture including advertising, magazine layout and, increasingly, television. For example, a form of collage known as montage is the process by which sequences of moving images are constructed and broadcast every day on our television and cinema screens. Collage work in the classroom challenges the dominant assumption of school art that, through a realist kind of painting and drawing, students may move inexorably towards the capacity to represent the world 'as if' through a window – a slice of life. Collage reminds us that visual representations are constructions and that, however unified, they are the products of an essentially fragmented experience: they emphasize difference and diversity which are at the heart of positive views of equality.

This chapter does not contain a wealth of suggestions for collage work in the classroom, in recognition that secondary school art teachers require more than tips on new 'activities'. Collage and issue-based work in any media, technology or dimensions, needs to be tied to good artistic practice and an understanding of the conceptual basis of such work.

The crux of this chapter is my suggestion that Field was correct about the 'life-giving relationship' between art and art education, and that therefore the best way to revitalize art teaching and enable it to address questions of equality is by finding artists who themselves seek to do that, or finding images which demand our attention in terms of equality. Some of the latter, in particular, may be highly suspect or problematic, but by using the kinds of questions identified previously it is possible to enable students to produce informed, critical analyses of a range of images. They, in turn, can then produce alternative representations and other images to challenge stereotypical or hostile images and artefacts currently in circulation. In this way, the work of *both* attainment targets can become genuinely 'critical' studies, and young people can come to recognize the importance and power of images in contemporary culture.

NOTE

1. This chapter was completed prior to the publication of the Secretary of State's Proposals (DFEE, 1999) following the review of the National Curriculum in England. These proposals are currently subject to public consultation. With respect to art teaching, they propose two significant changes to the existing Order as it is described in the following chapter:

   1. The subject previously called art 'has been redesignated as art and design'.
   2. 'The number of attainment targets has been reduced from two to one to integrate the practical and theoretical aspects of the programmes of study'.

   Neither of these changes affects the major arguments of the chapter but the proposals and any subsequent changes should be borne in mind especially when reading the opening section.

BIBLIOGRAPHY

Allen, D. (1994) Teaching visual literacy: some reflections on the term. *The Journal of Art and Design Education*, 13(2). Oxford: Blackwell.
Araeen, R. (1989) London: The Hayward Gallery, South Bank Centre.
Berger, J. (1972) *Ways of Seeing*. London: BBC and Penguin.
Binch, N. and Robertson, L. (1994) *Resourcing and Assessing Art, Craft*

and Design: Critical Studies in Art at Key Stage 4. London: NSEAD.

Bowden, J. (1996) *Round Midnight Papers.* Unpublished.

Bowker, J. (ed.) (1991) *Secondary Media Education: a Curriculum Statement.* London: BFI.

Brazier, P. (1985) *Art History in Education: An Annotated Bibliography.* London: Heinemann.

Carline, R. (1968) *Draw they Must.* London: Edward Arnold.

Chambers, E. and Joseph, T. (1988) *The Artpack.* London: Haringey Arts Council.

Cole, M. (1993) 'Black and Ethnic Minority' or 'Asian, Black and other Minority Ethnic': a further note on nomenclature. *Sociology*, 27(4).

DES (1983) *Art in Education 11–16.* London: HMSO.

DES (1995) *Art in the National Curriculum.* London: HMSO.

Field, D. (1970) *Change in Art Education.* London: RKP.

Hampshire LEA (circa 1986) *Guidelines for Art Education Five to Eighteen.* Winchester: Hampshire County Council.

Hughes, A. (1993) Don't judge pianists by their hair. *The Journal of Art and Design Education*, 12(3).

Macdonald, S. (1970) *The History and Philosophy of Art Education.* London: University of London Press.

Mason, R. and Rawding, M. (1993) Aesthetics in DBAE: its relevance to critical studies. *The Journal of Art and Design Education*, 12(3).

National Curriculum Council Art Working Group (1991) Interim Report. London: DES.

Owusu, K. (1986) *The Struggle for Black Arts in Britain: What Can We Consider Better Than Freedom.* Comedia.

Poggi, C. (1992) *In Defiance of Painting: Cubism, Futurism and the Invention of Collage.* New Haven, USA: Yale University Press.

Schools Curriculum and Assessment Authority (1994) *Art in the National Curriculum Draft Proposals.* York: SCAA.

Schools Curriculum and Assessment Authority (1996) *Consistency in Teacher Assessment: Exemplification of Standards. Art: Key Stage 3.* York: SCAA.

Stanley, N. (1993) Objects of criticism: a contribution from the new museology. *The Journal of Art and Design Education*, 12(3).

Taylor, R. (1986) *Educating for Art: Critical Response and Development.* London: Longman.

Thistlewood, D. (ed.) (1989) *Critical Studies in Art and Design Education.* London: Longman NSEAD.

Thistlewood, D. (ed.) (1992) *Histories of Art and Design Education: Cole to Coldstream.* London: Longman NSEAD.

Various Artists (1989) *The Other Story: Afro-Asian Artists in Post War Britain.* London: The Hayward Gallery, South Bank Centre.

Waldman, D. (1992) *Collage Assemblage and the Found Object.* London: Phaidon.

CHAPTER 10

Physical education

Gill Clarke and Gareth Nutt

Through the use and knowledge of the body and its movement, physical education makes a unique contribution to the education of young people.

(Department of Education and Science, 1991a:5)

To date, developments in National Curriculum Physical Education (NCPE) have been premised upon notions of entitlement to a broad, balanced, relevant and differentiated curriculum. However, as Evans *et al.* (1996) note, since the introduction of NCPE, opportunities to address issues of equity have been subsumed by texts that reinforce a very narrow and 'traditional' definition of the subject, and appear to have done little to prompt teachers to reflect upon their practices. The task that should be confronting teachers has been defined by the Department of Education and Science's (DES, 1991b) view that equality of opportunity in physical education (PE) requires:

an understanding and appreciation of the range of students' responses to femininity, masculinity and sexuality, to the whole range of ability and disability, to ethnic, social and cultural diversity, and the ways in which these relate for children to physical education. (DES, 1991b:15)

PE should encompass and celebrate cultural diversity, but in doing so it is essential to recognize the responsibilities that, as educators, we have, in order to challenge practices that perpetuate inequality and oppression and reinforce the unjust consequences of the social worlds we inhabit. PE has the power to create awareness and challenge individual attitudes, thereby increasing the possibilities for change and the prospect of a more equal and just society. However, it should also be recognized that working towards equality of opportunity and equity in PE is a complex and challenging process involving far more than merely offering equal access to what is increasingly becoming a range of competitive (predominantly team) activities (see The Department of National Heritage, 1995, 1996). Therefore, this chapter focuses on a range of issues and strategies that seek to challenge and transform the assumptions and inequities that may currently exist within PE. It is underpinned by the belief that 'unless a common curriculum is supported by other forms of organisational, curriculum, pedagogical and assessment innovations the resulting changes in how children think about and act towards each other may be insubstantial' (Evans, 1989:85).

CURRICULUM CONTENT

Notwithstanding the proposals for the review of the National Curriculum for the year 2000, the statutory framework for National Curriculum Physical Education is currently determined by:

- End of Key Stage Descriptions (EKSD) for every Key Stage (KS).
- Introductory paragraphs for the Programmes of Study (POS) for every Key Stage.
- General requirements relating to all Key Stages.

The context for learning is defined by the following areas of experience: athletic activities, games, gymnastic activities, dance, outdoor and adventurous activities, and swimming. Beyond the requirement that games constitutes a compulsory element of PE programmes at Key Stages 3 and 4 (KS 3/4), what teachers choose to teach, how they choose to teach and what organizational principles they adopt is left to their professional discretion. However, as Evans *et al.* (1996) suggest, 'Although this appears to 'liberate' teachers and schools, it also effectively means that achieving breadth and balance in the NCPE rests with the "accident" of a teacher's interests and predisposition and the level of support and resources schools can offer in the implementation of NCPE' (1996:7). Breadth, in this instance, refers to a curriculum that will bring all students into contact with each selected area of activity in sufficient depth to gain an appreciation of what it can offer, together with the different kinds of specific learning experiences each one can provide. Inextricably linked with breadth is the requirement that the curriculum should demonstrate an appropriate balance of areas of activity and avoid duplication and overlap. A balanced PE curriculum will ensure that each activity area is given sufficient attention in relation to the others. However, OfSTED (1995:11) reminds us that a balanced PE programme is 'about more than merely equalising time available between different aspects of the course: the choice of content and the use made of the time is important'. Thus, where some learning experiences are similar in different activity areas, it may be appropriate to sample from these. For instance, there is a need to offer a balance in terms of competitive/co-operative elements, individual/team or group activities and technical/creative experiences.

Furthermore, it is important to ensure that all activities planned for young people within PE have a clearly identifiable educational content and coherence whereby differing learning experiences do not appear as discrete and unconnected elements. Young people should be progressively challenged to learn something of value and not simply encouraged to engage in trivial and monotonous pursuits. PE should take into account previous learning, readiness for particular experiences, interests, aptitudes and achievements, with due regard given to the cultural significance of the chosen activities. For instance, it is important that activities are included in the curriculum which are neither euro- nor ethnocentric. Young people should be taught to recognize the universality of PE, since much can be learned from exploring and celebrating others' cultural traditions. But, in doing so, care must be taken to avoid 'tokenism' and the portrayal of activities from other cultures as some exotic alternative to 'our' ethnocentric traditions.

However, much current practice suggests that PE teachers are resistant to diversity and change. For instance, the consequence of their 'autonomy' appears to be that NCPE is, in the main, translated into a set of separate and distinct areas of activity that not only perpetuate a separate and different curriculum for boys and girls, but also 'openly accords the highest status to that area that has long dominated the PE curriculum in state schools, namely, competitive team games' (Evans *et al.*, 1996:7). Furthermore, within this area of experience, the hegemony of invasion games (e.g. hockey, football and basketball) is reinforced over net/court (e.g. tennis, badminton and volleyball), target and striking/fielding activities (e.g. cricket, rounders and golf) while at the same time preserving the hierarchical status of activities which have traditionally been defined as male pursuits. The following section explores this issue in more detail.

COMPETITIVE GAMES AND THE SCHOOL SPORT AGENDA

The compulsory emphasis accorded games in the PE curriculum would appear, in many cases, to have compromised notions of breadth and balance (see OfSTED, 1995). Indeed, if we relate this structural reinforcement of compulsion to a 'sporting agenda' that has gained momentum since the launch of *Sport: Raising the Game* (Department of National Heritage 1995 and 1996; Burgess 1997), then some important questions need to be resolved; not least by a Labour government from whom it is hoped that an inclusive policy of participation and excellence will emerge from its manifesto commitment to a 'Sporting Nation'.

For instance, within all these documents PE and sport continue to be inadequately defined, with what could be seen as an almost blatant disregard for the relationship that exists between them. To declare an intention to focus on sport without locating it within the broader remit of physical education's contribution to schooling is to represent a partial and distorted picture about what really goes on in schools, and what opportunities and priorities physical educators should have. Moreover, despite discourses that seek to 'locate sport at the centre of school life' (see DNH, 1995), the importance of PE to a young person's development and the centrality of the PE teacher's impact on the learning process continue to be systematically ignored, in favour of a view that it is both desirable and beneficial for all to be involved in competitive sport; much of which occurs in the form of extra-curricular opportunities. This is not to deny that competitive sport can be both a relevant and enriching experience, but if competitive games and school sport are to be accorded centrality it is necessary to recognize the implications of such a policy for young people's experiences in PE.

In this connection, it is important to acknowledge that males and females may well perceive and experience PE and sport differently. This is particularly so in activities where the competitive emphasis is stressed. Significantly, the *Sport: Raising the Game* documents (DNH, 1995, 1996) did little to dispel these concerns since they continued to place largely traditional male competitive team games at the heart of weekly life in every school. This intention was declared by the former Prime Minister, John Major, in his letter of introduction to the original policy statement (DNH, 1995), when he wrote 'Competitive sport teaches valuable lessons which last for life. Every game delivers both a winner and a loser. Sportsmen must learn to be both.' However, this view is not without its problems since it is well documented that competitive team games are anathema to many young women and men who are 'turned off' by such activities (see Scraton, 1992). Research by Clarke and Gilroy (1996), investigating the impact of *Sport: Raising the Game* on teachers' professional practice in secondary schools, reveals concerns about the 'lessons' that competitive sport transmitted to children. Some teachers comment:

> . . . competitive sport can give very negative messages to young people, i.e. behaviour of players and their bad attitudes to officials and others. Competitive sport shouldn't just be justified in order for young people to be able to cope with success and failure in life! (1996:17)

> In PE we often kid ourselves that *all* the values of competitive sport are *positive*. In reality there are occasions when sport reinforces *negative* values – e.g. bullying (physical and mental), sexual inequality . . . (1996:17–18)

Additionally, the teachers thought boys and girls possibly responded differently to competitive sport. Some remarked:

> The majority of boys enjoy competition – adrenaline rush and are keen to get started – most want to win. There are some girls who

respond in this way but I believe these are the minority. Girls in general enjoy sport but are less bothered whether they win or lose. Some boys are fanatical about competitive sport and it is very important to them. (My) impression is, girls, mostly, do not rate it so seriously . . . so important.

In mixed groups girls can be put off by boys being overtly competitive. Girls are far more competitive in single-sex groups. (1996:20)

Successful teaching of competitive team sport requires teachers to give positive encouragement to all and in particular to girls who, as illustrated above, may not respond to competitive sport in the same manner as their male peers, or in the presence of them. Additionally, it is imperative that the games and sports selected are drawn from not only those that have traditionally been associated with the male gender. For example:

- In selecting the content for KS3/4, it is important that our selection does not convey messages that function to reinforce stereotypical perceptions about 'race', gender, social class, sexuality, religion and ability.
- Teachers should promote activities which are non-gender specific, which challenge gender specificity or to which students attach no gendered label. To this category belong games like korfball, handball and tchouk ball (see Useful Addresses for sources of further information). Considered use of modified game forms such as new image rugby, pop lacrosse and mini-soccer should also be encouraged, particularly as they have been designed by their respective National Governing Bodies to accommodate boys and girls of all abilities: a view Russell (1992) confirms in advancing the merits of mini-soccer as a game 'for all youngsters regardless of ability. It is intended for girls and boys, and young footballers with disabilities and learning difficulties' (1992:6).
- Teachers should employ mixed-sex games courses covering the principles of play of invasion, net/court and striking/fielding games within the contexts of 'gender-neutral' activities such as hockey, softball and tennis. However, it is important that young people in mixed-sex groups can relate to the task, for feelings of security are more likely to induce confidence in their work.
- The teaching of single-sex groups should not be ruled out. The participation of girls in football and rugby, and boys in netball

and dance can challenge traditional labelling, particularly if staffing initiatives also encourage young people to question any preconceived ideas they may have.

- Teachers should recognize that within the constraints imposed by resources (staffing, time, expertise, cost, etc.) and facilities, it is possible to provide option programmes that look to extend the range of opportunities for young people to gain success and enjoyment.

However, even traditionally non-gendered activity areas such as swimming may require attention since it should be recognized that:

- Muslim girls may require to be taught swimming separate from boys and to be supervised by a female teacher/attendant.
- Muslim children, in general, may have to negotiate communal nakedness, a concept alien to their culture (Sarwar, 1991).

Furthermore, there is a need to recognize that an emphasis on competitive games can limit opportunities for young people to experience physicality in a supportive and sensitive environment if concerns with winning dominate. If PE is to play its part in enhancing the positive life experiences of all young people, we must strive to ensure that the environment presents opportunities to acquire the knowledge, skills and understanding necessary to value various forms of physical activity as integral features of their lifestyles. Additionally, it needs to be acknowledged that all the desired qualities of leadership, initiative, creativity, determination and teamwork attributed to competitive sport can be gained in various ways and from other activities within PE. We must also be aware that an over-emphasis on competitive games within the PE curriculum can restrict and dilute the importance and opportunities accorded other areas of experience. Dance, for example, has a special contribution to make to a curriculum for equality insofar as it offers young people opportunities to be creative, expressive and to work collaboratively. Similarly, health-related exercise (HRE) has done much to challenge the 'prevailing orthodoxy' of competition by seeking to re-conceptualize attitudes towards sport, the body and physical activity. The place of HRE, in particular, invites critical analysis since the consultation and implementation of the NCPE advocates that the essential knowledge, skills and attitudes associated with this dimension of the PE curriculum should be made available to all young people by means of a 'permeation' model.

THE 'PERMEATION' OF HEALTH-RELATED EXERCISE

HRE has emerged as a significant innovation in PE, but although it has attracted considerable attention, it has not always been able to articulate a clear and unambiguous rationale. Nevertheless, it seeks to present a form of activity which:

> emphasises human similarity and not dissimilarity, a form of activity which is not competitive and measured, a form of activity which expresses values which are indeed unmeasurable, a form of activity which is concerned with individual well-being and satisfaction rather than with comparison. In such a view of sport, differences between the sexes would be unimportant, unnoticed. (Willis, 1982:143)

References to HRE within the revised orders are found in:

- End of Key Stage Descriptions for every Key Stage (EKSD).
- Introductory paragraphs to the Programmes of Study (POS) for every Key Stage.
- General requirements relating to all Key Stages.

It is envisaged that health-related issues should permeate the curriculum throughout KS 1–4 rather than being designated as an area of activity in its own right. The challenge is to find ways of accommodating HRE within the structures defined by the revised orders. Such a process invites a critique of the values and assumptions underpinning decisions which impact upon the content, organization, teaching and assessment of HRE initiatives. The following represent possible models for the delivery of HRE:

- Integrated within the areas of activity.
- Focused HRE modules/units of work in PE.
- A combination of integrated and focused modules.
- Partly in PE and partly in other curriculum areas such as Personal and Social Education (PSE).
- Totally in other curriculum areas.

Because physical activity is so much at the centre of what we do as physical educationalists, initiatives that seek to 'theorize' HRE are often viewed with some scepticism. Hence PE's apparent reluctance to 'relocate' the teaching of HRE totally or partially into other curriculum areas such as a school's PSE programme. Of the models noted above, there appears to be an understandable view that a combination of integrated and focused modules is the most compelling means of 'permeating' the essential knowledge, skills and attitudes associated with HRE. But whether this strategy will enable PE teachers to move beyond issues of optimizing 'functional capacity' to embrace the socio-cultural dimensions of enquiry outlined in this chapter is doubtful. Indeed, Sparkes (1989) reminds us that although trends and developments in HRE have extended teachers' thinking in terms of curriculum content and teaching styles, they have largely failed to 'probe deeper into the ideological roots of the curriculum process and the manner in which this prevents children gaining a more coherent understanding of health in our society' (1989:61). Therefore, it might be necessary to explore cross-curricular initiatives that, for instance, utilize the complementary strengths of PE and PSE specialists. Issues such as body image, sexuality and drug abuse (see Christmas *et al.*, 1996), covered during PSE sessions (and perhaps delivered by PE specialists), might be addressed in ways that could bring greater coherence to students' perceptions, experiences and ability to make informed decisions about their future lifestyle choices. As one of us has suggested:

> it is time to bring our strengths and expertise in from the margins and to occupy a position of greater curricular centrality. This will have profound organisational implications but the benefits could have a powerful impact on the personal identities and lives of the young people we come to work with. For too long the role of the PE teacher has been ignored, understated, prone to caricature and marginalised. The contribution the subject can make in helping young people come to terms with the complex social worlds that confront them is considerable and needs to be acknowledged; not least from PE professionals themselves. If we are to continue to make bold claims about PE's impact upon the personal and social development of the young people we work with questions have to be asked about our curriculum design, teaching and assessment. (Nutt, 1996:4)

CURRICULUM ORGANIZATION AND GROUPING

All young people should have access to a programme of PE that covers the EKSD and POS appropriate to their age. A minority of young people may experience some difficulties, but this should not form the basis for exclusion from any component of NCPE. Everyone should have the opportunity of working with others of varying levels of ability and aptitude so that they can learn to appreciate and value the different types of achievements and individual contributions that all can bring to the learning process. Such a commitment must recognize that equality of educational opportunity is not simply determined by 'access to the same'. Sensitive lesson planning, organization and teaching methods are necessary factors in enabling young people to realize their full potential.

Thus, a commitment to equal opportunity and equality requires consideration of curriculum grouping strategies. The key principle underlying decisions of grouping in PE must be that all students have the same opportunities to realize their potential. Hence OfSTED's (1995) conclusion that 'Neither mixed nor single gender grouping is appropriate in every case, but careful review of the attitudes and achievements of different groups of students was a feature of the work of the best secondary physical education departments' (1995:6).

Paradoxically, it could be argued that the prevailing uncertainties surrounding grouping have functioned to make segregation and separatism deeply institutionalized features of the curriculum. Whilst these strategies do not have to compromise the principle of equality of opportunity, care must be taken to ensure that they do not reaffirm gender stereotypes, perpetuate myths and reinforce a 'diluted' experience for young people. Teachers may therefore need to acquire the pedagogical skills and competencies that will allow them to reorganize not only the forms of knowledge presented to students, but also to bring a more flexible approach to their grouping within lessons. This reflects Evans' (1989) conceptualization of co-educational PE that refers to situations where:

> . . . a variety of organizational grouping practices and accompanying curriculum and pedagogical changes prevail, the object of

which is to bring the sexes together under conditions which always are sensitive to those predispositions (abilities, physical strengths, cultural attitudes and expectations) which can so easily and often set children apart. (1989:86)

Thus, sensitivity to the context in which the activity is taking place is crucial. For instance, Clarke *et al.* (1997) have pointed to dance as an area that requires the careful consideration of pairing and partnering if we are to challenge conventional role expectations. Additionally, an awareness of issues relating to contact between students of different sexes and the same sex within some religious and cultural groups needs to be developed (Daley, 1991). Given that decisions will be context-specific, some potential difficulties may be overcome by utilizing a variety of strategies (see Clarke *et al.*, 1997) of which these may form a part:

- setting according to ability (which will allow for differentiation according to task/difficulty);
- friendship groups (which will allow students to work with particular friends chosen by themselves);
- random groupings (which will ensure groups associated on no particular basis).

In reaching these decisions, PE teachers must recognize that they have a duty to find ways of including young people with physical disabilities and/or learning difficulties into all areas of activity.

SPECIAL EDUCATIONAL NEEDS

Accommodating young people with special educational needs should be seen as 'an extension of good practice rather than the acquiring of new and distinctly different skills and techniques' (Utley and Sugden, 1994:12). Consequently, they should be treated in accordance with their individual needs with an emphasis given to what they can do, learn and achieve, for as Gill (1995) suggests 'If handled well and from a basis of knowledge about the students' ability, their needs and their learning style, there is sufficient scope in the Programme of Study for *all* students to be actively involved in a PE curriculum which is challenging, stimulating, of individual value and fun' (1995:30). However, there are a number of factors that must be considered if we are to offer worthwhile experiences for all young people. For example, teachers should:

- not make assumptions about ability. A young person's needs and abilities are more important than any category of disability;
- be aware of putting young people at risk.

Teachers should be prepared to provide appropriate support for young people. This may be in addition to any help provided by a Supportive Assistant (SA). It might include:

- Physical support within particular activities.
- Differentiation by task. All physical activities are made up of perceptual, cognitive and motor components, and therefore by reducing the demands in one or more of these areas it is possible to simplify tasks.
- Differentiation by outcome. Open-ended tasks in contexts such as gymnastics can encourage young people with special needs to explore the full potential of their abilities.
- Task adaptation/modification.
- Verbal and visual clarity of task communication and feedback, particularly with those with visual or auditory impairment.
- Sensitive and supportive encouragement. This might involve negotiating with the young person the exact nature and extent of their involvement in PE lessons. However, negotiations and adaptations must ensure that the young person's entitlement is not compromised. All activities must retain their integrity and respect the participant.

Certain contexts also offer young people with special needs a chance to participate on an equal basis to their peers. For instance:

- The water-borne environment is particularly helpful to many young people with disabilities.
- The creative and expressive contexts of gymnastics and dance offer real opportunities to excel since many of the key dance principles can be explored by young people with movement disabilities. Dance offers teachers the opportunity to explore the utilization of professional dance/theatre groups who work extensively with disabled dancers and who can present themselves as excellent role models.

- Grouping strategies should be flexible; additionally the scope for partner work is valuable in helping young people build confidence and increase the range of movements that are possible. The 'buddy system' or 'guiding systems' of working in pairs are strategies that can be of benefit to both the disabled child and any partner in providing physical and emotional support.
- Recognize that within the area of outdoor and adventurous activities there are many instances of the benefits to be gained by involving young people with special educational needs.
- Recognize that many national governing bodies of sport and other non-statutory organizations providing opportunities for young people with special educational needs offer detailed guidance and/or support (see 'Useful Addresses').

However, as important as these considerations may be, if issues are merely addressed by gaining access to the same and indulging in superficial change, the danger is that 'tokenistic' organizational changes will merely announce and reinforce the differences rather than drawing attention to the similarities and complementary competences young people bring to the social and physical setting. If we are to create real opportunities for young people in PE, decisions about content and grouping must be supported by fundamental developments in pedagogy and changes in ideology.

THE TEACHING AND LEARNING ENVIRONMENT

Effective learning involves a progression and shift of responsibility from teacher-directed work to young people becoming increasingly independent in their own learning. With the processes of planning, performing and evaluating embedded in the NCPE documentation it is clear that the objectives cannot be attained by solely employing didactic teaching approaches. Therefore, teachers must ensure that they use appropriate teaching approaches to match the learning objectives/outcomes they have set for the range of abilities and dispositions they confront. NCPE developments demand that teachers draw on a range of teaching styles (Mosston and Ashworth, 1986; Mawer, 1995) that may require individuals to:

- receive information – as in didactic and traditional teaching styles;
- work with peers – as in reciprocal teaching situations;
- solve problems – as in questioning and open-ended tasks;
- experience situations in realistic contexts – as in planning or negotiating individual programmes which may involve going out into the community. (Dudley Physical Education Support Services, 1993).

Nevertheless, although it is critical that tasks are well matched to a young person's stage of development and current level of skill, it is also important that we accept that much more is taught and learned than intended by the formal curriculum, and that a hidden curriculum acts as a powerful determinant in a young person's development. It is essential that teachers are sensitive to the messages that may be reinforced during the day-to-day trans-action of their work, and it is to these messages we now turn.

THE HIDDEN CURRICULUM AND PE

The effects of the attitudes and expectations of teachers, the preconditions for access, the interactions within mixed-sex, mixed-ability and multicultural groups, and the previous experi-ences and their relative ranges and levels of the skills, knowledge and understanding of the children, must also be considered (DES, 1991a:17).

Jewett and Bain (1985) describe the 'hidden curriculum' as the unplanned and unrecognized values taught and learned through the process of schooling. Since it is questionable just how hidden this curriculum really is, a more appropriate term may be the 'implicit curriculum'. The following sections illustrate the ways in which powerful messages can be conveyed within the teaching and learning process.

PE: THE BODY ON DISPLAY

PE is clearly a unique subject within the educative system since it has as its focus physical activity through and by the body. As such, the way that the body is viewed and schooled is worthy of critical discussion. Traditionally PE has schooled the body into narrow, prescriptive and publicly sanctioned gender roles. Within these social and cultural practices a particular body type has enjoyed celebration, namely the mesomorphic athletic body. Thus many young people within PE have felt alienated not only from their bodies but also from the subject since they did not match up to these hegemonic bodily ideals. Moreover, young people are constantly subjected to pressures to conform to 'the cult of slenderness' (Tinning, 1990) through sylph-like images that dominate media texts about what it is to be fit, healthy and attractive to the opposite sex. As physical educators we need to ensure that our curriculum celebrates diversity and difference, promotes social justice and does not reinforce particular body images. To this end it is essential that we recognize the public nature of success and failure in PE, and the impact this may have on self-confidence and self-esteem. It has been well documented how pressures to conform have especially damaging effects on young people and impact negatively on their self-esteem: indeed research has shown that self-confidence is linked with continuing sports involvement (see Graydon, 1997). Hence, we have a moral responsibility to ensure that the curriculum on offer fosters feelings of self-worth and provides opportunities for all students to experience success.

In connection with this, it is important to recognize how PE and physical activity is viewed and experienced by boys and girls. Traditionally, male sport has been seen as being of more importance, and accordingly the rewards and expectations for male athletes have been greater than those for their female counterparts. We need therefore to reflect on these legacies and to question the impact of these practices on PE. For instance:

- A consistent approach is vital. There should be consistency in terms of both sexes receiving the same time allowance for PE each week, the allocation of time and facilities for extra-curricular provision, expectations regarding kit, safety and non-participation, and pre- and post-lesson routines (showering, lining up, etc.).
- Clothing needs to be safe and facilitate movement rather than being associated with traditional gender conventions. Students should be allowed to wear appropriate clothing that does not cause embarrassment and does not create distinctions between boys and girls (Harris, 1993).

- Clothing should be affordable and accessible to all (Wilkinson and Hunt, 1992).
- Attention should be paid to cultural practices when considering the type of clothing that is deemed appropriate. For instance, Muslim students should be permitted to wear clothing that safeguards their modesty and decency. If possible, changing facilities should be provided to accommodate privacy, e.g. the use of cubicles as well as the more conventional communal facilities.
- The question of the removal of jewellery is one that may affect Sikh children who would not be permitted to remove bangles. Considered and sensitive negotiation that opens up communication between the young person, the parents and the community is vital.

HETEROSEXISM AND HOMOPHOBIA

Traditionally, sport has been seen as the prerogative of men and the breeding ground for the development of hegemonic masculinity. In consequence, many of the characteristics associated with sport – strength, masculinity, aggression, competitiveness, physicality and so on – have been associated with the development of the male character. Women who entered the sporting terrain did so at their peril, for to excel at sport meant to run the risk of their (hetero)sexuality being questioned. Though much has changed, stereotypical concerns and ideologies around masculinity, femininity, sexuality and physicality still constrain and limit the participation and behaviour of both boys and girls within physical education. Boys, for instance, may fear suffering ridicule for being expressive within dance, for showing grace in gymnastics or disliking physical contact in some games; girls too may face censure and questions about their sexuality when they participate in games such as rugby and football, especially since for them the culture of femininity may be sharply at odds with the culture of physical education (see Scraton, 1987). The underlying implication here is that these behaviours are not 'normal' and carry penalties such as the application of the label 'sissy', 'fairy', 'poof' to boys, or 'tomboy', 'dyke', 'lezzie' to girls. Therefore the behaviour is likely to be censored and avoided in an attempt to prevent the recurrence of the label. It should be recognized that these labels are not only applied to students; they may also be applied to teachers. What is being illustrated here is the pervasive power of heterosexism and homophobia to define acceptable behaviour (see Clarke, 1995a, b; Griffin, 1989, 1992). As one of us has written:

> We need to recognise the messages that PE and sport convey, and how they police sexualities. We need to recognise the institutionalised heterosexism within the cultural practices of the subject: that is the rules, the dress code, the required behaviour and heterosexual displays. Through our practices and actions we need to take the stigma from the word lesbian (and gay) so that all women (and men) cannot be intimidated or controlled by its use. (Clarke, 1995a:14)

Therefore, the place of PE in the social construction of masculinity, femininity and sexuality needs to be carefully considered in the planning, content and delivery of lessons. Young people and teachers come to PE lessons with different degrees of experience and ability, with different interests and prejudices rooted in social constructions surrounding issues of social class, 'race', disability, age, sexuality, masculinity and femininity. To treat all young people the same does not necessarily constitute equality as it may ignore the very differences from which they can all benefit. We must therefore consider strategies to challenge the powerful reinforcement of divisive messages.

STRATEGIES FOR GOOD PRACTICE

The following strategies seek to extend the notion of inclusion by recognizing the socio-cultural diversity that young people bring to their work:

- Increase the number of female staff teaching traditionally male activities and male staff teaching traditionally female activities. This will send powerful messages not only to the students but also to colleagues, parents and governors.
- Project more positive active images of girls. Display a balance in posters illustrating both males and females.
- Utilize resources that celebrate cultural diversity.
- Provide opportunities to watch videos and live performances

of 'athletes' that challenge conventional stereotypes and, in particular, those surrounding ability, sexuality, 'race', social class and gender. PSE sessions and classroom-based examination classes may provide further opportunities for discussion.

- Identify role models to whom students may aspire. It is just as important that we present positive male role models in dance and those areas of activity traditionally defined as the 'female preserve', as female role models in football and those areas of activity traditionally defined as the 'male preserve'.
- Use non-sexist, non-heterosexist and non-racist language. This will require teachers to raise their awareness and sensitivity to the ways in which language defines their conceptions of 'race', gender, sexuality, social class and the impact that this has on their own practice.
- Avoid comparisons in performance related to gender.
- Use boys and girls for demonstrations and answers, to challenge and alter the traditional views regarding the capabilities of boys and girls in activities such as dance and gymnastics (Williams, 1989, 1995; Green, 1993). Boys should be used to demonstrate movements requiring artistry and flexibility just as girls should be used to demonstrate movements demanding strength and athleticism. As Williams (1995:31) recognizes:

> Gymnastics is often seen as a 'female' activity, characterised by the ability to perform cartwheels and the splits and requiring considerable flexibility. While it would be good to think that the primary school would overcome such ill-informed stereotyping and that students would transfer to secondary school and to Key Stage 3 aware of the potential of gymnastics to develop a variety of physical capacities, the reality is that Key Stage 3 students are likely to continue to arrive with inaccurate assumptions about the physical qualities needed to be successful in the gymnasium.

ASSESSMENT AND RECORDING

From 1997, in common with teachers of the other non-core foundation subjects, PE teachers have been required to summarize their assessment for each student in Year 9 who is reaching the End of Key Stage. Although assessment in PE will not be an exact science, it does involve making summary judgements using the EKSD. But it should not be seen as a 'bolted on' activity requiring the use of extra tasks or tests. Assessment should be viewed as an integral feature of the teaching and learning process. Teachers are expected to use their knowledge of a young person's work to determine the extent to which their performance relates to an EKSD. These indicate the standards which the majority of young people should have reached by the end of Year 9. The aim is for a rounded judgement which takes into account a young person's strengths and weaknesses in performance across a range of contexts (see the School Curriculum and Assessment Authority, 1997). However, although guidance in the form of an 'Exemplification of Standards' video and supporting booklet (SCAA, 1996) has been circulated, the evaluation and assessment of a young person's progress and performance needs careful planning if teachers are to avoid discriminatory practices.

Assessments should be free from racial and gender bias, and comparisons between girls and boys that perpetuate the promotion of male standards as the norm should be avoided. It is important that encouragement for achievement in PE is not given to students to the detriment of their overall educational attainment, nor should it be assumed that skill, for example, is determined by ethnicity or gender. The criteria developed and deployed for reporting and assessment should be relevant and applicable to the abilities of all young people. For instance, is flexibility valued as much as strength? Is balance and agility as important as speed and strength? It is essential that we know and understand about young people's previous PE experiences and achievements. Peer evaluation and assessment also require careful handling so as to avoid the perpetuation of racial or gender stereotypes with regard to performance. Any name-calling, racist, sexist or homophobic insults or abuse based on socio-economic background/social class must be challenged. Young people must learn and be encouraged to value, respect and be sensitive to the work of their peers. Finally, we may need to subject our own expectations about what students can do and understand to critical scrutiny.

Because so many forms of assessment in PE are based on subjective observations, it is essential that teachers' ideological perspectives, and stereotypical expectations of appropriate behaviour, should not be allowed to mediate the process of passing judgements on young people's capacity to participate and perform. As Evans (1989:86) suggests, 'Our assessment procedures should be capable of monitoring the strengths and weaknesses, the achievements and competence of children whatever their size, shape and sex'. Assessment should therefore:

- seek to exploit criterion referencing when young people are assessed against context-specific criteria or objectives. With criterion referencing teacher assessment depends on what young people can do and helps to establish what has successfully been learned in readiness for future development.
- not ignore that differences in a young person's performance may be related to variables such as experience, physiology and anatomical factors such as strength and size. As Evans (1989:86–7) points out: 'There is nothing contradictory, in my view, about making a commitment to a "Physical Education for All" equity and equality and then expressing the view or knowledge that there are times in the assessment of performance when sex, like gender differences, does matter greatly in PE as in other academic subjects'.
- avoid the invidious ranking of students, particularly those that for physiological or anatomical reasons favour one sex over the other (see Evans, 1989:86–7).

Similarly:

- assessment of performance should be differentiated;
- assessment of examination courses requires sensitivity to issues such as the presentation and style of resources (worksheets, photographs, role models, etc.) and assignments;
- language and illustrations should promote positive images for boys and girls in sport from a variety of backgrounds and ethnic groups;
- questions should provide differentiation in order to cater for groups of different abilities, experience and background.

EXTRA-CURRICULAR ACTIVITIES

Extra-curricular activities have always been viewed as 'part and parcel' of a PE teacher's work, and for those young people willing and able to take part, the provision of an extensive and well-balanced programme of activities has much to offer their development. Quite apart from initiatives generated by 'Sports-mark' incentives, a measure of the perceived importance of extra-curricular activities is gained if we note that, in future school inspections, OfSTED will:

> report on the sporting provision that schools offer to students outside of formal lessons, during lunch-times, in the evenings and weekends, paying particular attention to traditional team games . . . [and] on the student participation rates in sporting provision outside formal lesson time and the number of teachers that supervise that provision; report on the school's sports competition programme, both within the school and against other schools. (DNH, 1995:12)

Equality of opportunity, in terms of participation, should also apply to the activities that are on offer outside of the delivered curriculum, so it is important that policies and practices do not convey messages of privilege and exclusivity. Since value should be placed on both female and male participation, both sexes should have equal access to teaching resources, facilities and equipment (CAHPER, 1994). However, OfSTED's (1995) survey of participation revealed that 'boys taking part generally outnumbered girls in secondary schools by a ratio of at least two or three to one' (1995:12). Although it is difficult not to conclude that OfSTED's concern has been driven by the competitive sport agenda (DNH, 1995, 1996), their findings confirm the importance of developing strategies that encourage greater participation in extra-curricular activities by everyone.

In association with these extra-curricular programmes, teachers also need to check that displays, noticeboards and school bulletins are monitored for equity so that sufficient opportunities for all young people are adequately reflected, regardless of gender, social class, ability and ethnicity. The portrayal of positive female and male athletic role models should be encouraged, not least in those pursuits and areas of activity that challenge stereotypical perceptions. In association with these recommendations, PE teachers must not allow extra-curricular sport to be misappropriated by schooling's tendency to 'sidetrack' academic under-achievement, or to function as a social control incentive for the behaviourally disaffected.

With respect to ethnicity, nowhere has this been more graphically

described than by Carrington's (1982) exploration of the interrelationships between African-Caribbean school failure, the apparent
success of this group in school sport and their contemporary structural position in the social formation. All his conclusions merit
serious consideration in our dealings with all young people, irre-
spective of their background and biographies, but especially the
over-representation of African-Caribbean students in school sports
teams that Carrington saw to be, in part, the product of channelling
by teachers who have a tendency to view this ethnic group in
stereotypical terms, as having skills of the body rather than skills
of the mind. By encouraging these allegedly 'motor minded' students to concentrate on sport in school perhaps at some expense to
their academic studies and by utilising (particularly in the case of
disaffected, non-academic black males) extra-curricular sports
involvement as a mechanism of social control, teachers have inad-
vertently reinforced West Indian academic failure . . . (Carrington,
1982:61)

Furthermore, activities which involve undertaking off-site
and/or residential experiences may also raise some problems
relating to perceived value. We need to be aware that some
parents may accord little importance to extra-curricular activities, particularly games, whilst young people from some ethnic
minority communities may be committed to further academic
study or religious worship (Daley, 1991). There may also be the
problem of an 'ability to pay'. This should not figure, with funds
available for schools to cover those who are unable to help with
the 'voluntary contributions' essential in many cases for this type
of experience; yet there is the question of the stigma that may be
associated with having to seek assistance in this manner (see
Clarke *et al.*, 1997), and some parents may be reluctant to seek
help. Sensitive support is an essential requirement if we are to
enrich the opportunities of young people from disparate cultural
backgrounds and traditions and from socio-economically
deprived groups. PE teachers committed to developing extra-
curricular opportunities may need to broaden their knowledge of,
and be prepared to enlist, individuals/agencies to support the
further sporting development of the young people they teach.
Thus, school–community partnerships should be explored as a
means of increasing confidence, trust and understanding in the
shared desire to extend sporting experiences.

Brackenridge (1994) reminds us, however, that all young people
have a right to a safe, supportive and secure environment and that

extending sporting opportunities for young people should not expose them to incidents of sexual, physical or psychological abuse. A collaborative professional vigilance on the part of all physical educationalists, coaches, parents and support agencies will do much to secure an environment that will help enable young people to benefit from the many existing and developing opportunities currently occupying the sporting landscape (see NSPCC and NCF, 1995; NCF *et al.*, 1996).

CONCLUDING REMARKS

The concern of this chapter has been the recognition that all young people will bring to their learning of PE a range of abilities and dispositions with which they and their teachers can work. The overall aim within PE should be to create an environment whereby all young people are able to realize their potential and, moreover, since good quality PE is their right, it also requires that teachers continue to critically evaluate and reassess their pedagogical practices. In this way we may develop a deeper appreciation of the strategic positions we occupy and the powerful impact that our teaching has on the identities and sporting lives of the young people we come to work with.

BIBLIOGRAPHY

Ball, S. (1994) *Education Reform: A Critical and Post-Structural Approach.* Milton Keynes: Open University Press.

Brackenridge, C. (1994) Fair play or fair game: child sexual abuse in sport organizations. *International Review for the Sociology of Sport,* 3.

Burgess, E. (1997) Off to a flying start. *British Journal of Physical Education,* 28(3).

Canadian Association for Health, Physical Education and Recreation (CAHPER) (1994) *Gender Equity Through Physical Education.* Gloucester, Ontario: CAPHER.

Carrington, B. (1982) Sport as a sidetrack. In L. Barton and S. Walker (eds) *Race, Class and Education.* London: Croom Helm.

Christmas, D., Holmes, P., Nutt, G. and Woodward, D. (1996) Anabolic steroids in education: the role for the physical education professional. In L. Lawrence, E. Murdoch and S. Parker (eds) *Professional and Development Issues in Leisure, Sport and Education.* Eastbourne:

Leisure Studies Association.

Clarke, G. (1992) Learning the language: discourse analysis in physical education. In A. C. Sparkes (ed.) *Research in Physical Education and Sport: Exploring Alternative Visions*. London: Falmer Press.

Clarke, G. (1995a) Homophobia and Heterosexism in Physical Education: Can We Move Into A New Era? Paper presented at the Physical Education Annual Conference: Moving Into A New Era. 21–22 April, Twickenham, England.

Clarke, G. (1995b) Outlaws in sport and education? Exploring the sporting and education experiences of lesbian physical education teachers. In L. Lawrence, E. Murdoch and S. Parker (eds) *Professional and Development Issues in Leisure, Sport and Education*. Eastbourne: Leisure Studies Association.

Clarke, G. and Gilroy, S. (1996) Deconstructing the Sporting Text: Raising the Game. Paper presented at American Alliance for Health, Physical Education, Recreation and Dance National Convention and Exposition, 16–20 April, Atlanta, Georgia, USA.*

Clarke, G., Leigh, R. and Reed, S. (1997) Physical education. In M. Cole, D. Hill and S. Shan (eds) *Promoting Equality in Primary Schools*. London: Cassell.

Daley, D. (1991) Multicultural issues in PE. *British Journal of Physical Education*, 22(1).

Department of National Heritage (1995) *Sport: Raising the Game*. London: DNH.

Department of National Heritage (1996) *Sport: Raising the Game. The First Year Report*. London: DNH.

DES (1991a) *National Curriculum: Physical Education Working Group Interim Report*. London: DES.

DES (1991b) *Physical Education for Ages 5–16: Proposals of the Secretary of State for Education and Science and the Secretary of State for Wales*. London: DES.

Dudley Physical Education Support Services (1993) *Physical Education in the National Curriculum: Policy into Practice*. Dudley: LEA Publications.

Evans, J. (1985) *Teaching in Transition: The Challenge of Mixed-Ability Grouping*. Milton Keynes: Open University Press.

Evans, J. (1989) Swinging from the crossbar: equality of opportunity in the PE curriculum. *British Journal of Physical Education*, 20(2).

Evans, J., Penney, D. and Davies, B. (1996) Back to the future: education policy and physical education. In N. Armstrong (ed.) *New Directions in Physical Education: Change and Innovation*. London: Cassell Education.

Gill, S. (1995) Children with special educational needs. *British Journal of Physical Education*, 26(3).

Gilroy, S. and Clarke, G. (1997) Raising the game: deconstructing the sporting text – from Major to Blair. *Pedagogy in Practice*, 3(2).

Graydon, J. (1997) Self-confidence and self-esteem in physical education and sport. In G. Clarke and B. Humberstone (eds) *Researching Women and Sport*. London: Macmillan.

Green, K. (1993) Primary practice and the gender bias in PE. *Bulletin of Physical Education*, 29(1):31–6.

Griffin, P. (1989) Homophobia and physical education. *CAHPER Journal*, March/April:27–31.

Griffin, P. (1992) Challenging the game: homophobia, sexism and lesbians in sport. *Quest*, 44:5.

Harris, J. (1993) Challenging sexism and gender bias in PE. *Bulletin of Physical Education*, 24(1), Spring.

Jarvie, G. (ed.) (1991) *Sport, Racism and Ethnicity*. London: Falmer Press.

Jewett, A. E. and Bain, L. L. (1985) *The Curriculum Process in Physical Education*. Dubuque, Iowa: W. C. Brown Publishers.

Kirk, D. (1988) *Physical Education and Curriculum Study: A Critical Introduction*. London: Croom Helm.

Kirk, D. (1993) *The Body, Schooling and Culture*. Geelong, Victoria: Deakin University Press.

Mawer, M. (1995) *The Effective Teaching of Physical Education*. London: Longman Group Limited.

Milosevic, L. (ed.) (1995) *Gender and Physical Education*. Leeds: Leeds Education Publications and Promotions.

Mosston, M. and Ashworth, S. (1986) *Teaching Physical Education*. New York: Merrill Publishing Company.

NCF, NSPCC and Sports Council (1996) *Child Protection in Swimming*. Loughborough: Amateur Swimming Association.

NSPCC and NCF (1995) *Protecting Children: A Guide for Sports People*. Leeds: National Coaching Foundation.

Nutt, G. (1996) Anabolic Steroids in Education: The Challenge for the Physical Education Professional. Paper presented at the 'Drugs Issues for Educators' Conference, Gloucestershire Drugs Project, Cheltenham, March 1996.**

OfSTED (1995) *Physical Education and Sport in Schools: A Survey of Good Practice*. London: HMSO.

Runnymede Trust (1993) *Equality Assurance in Schools*. London: Trentham Books.

Russell, R. (1992) *Mini-Soccer Handbook*. London: FA Publications.

Sarwar, G. (1991) *British Muslims and Schools: Proposals for Progress*. London: Muslim Educational Trust.

Schools Curriculum and Assessment Authority (1996) *Exemplification of Standards: Physical Education Key Stage 3*. London: SCAA.

Schools Curriculum and Assessment Authority (1997) *Key Stage 3 Assessment Arrangements: Non-Core Subjects*. London: SCAA.

Scraton, S. (1987) 'Boys muscle in where angels fear to tread' – Girls' sub cultures and physical activities. In J. Horne, D. Jary and A. Tomlinson (eds) *Sport, Leisure and Social Relations*. London: Routledge and Kegan Paul.

Scraton, S. (1992) *Shaping up to Womanhood: Gender and Girls'*

Physical Education. Buckingham: Open University Press.

Sparkes, A. (1989) Health-related fitness: an example of innovation without change. *British Journal of Physical Education,* 20:60–3.

Stanworth, M. (1983) *Gender and Schooling.* London: Hutchinson.

Sugden, D. and Talbot, M. (1996) Physical Education for Children with Special Needs in Mainstream Education. National Training Programme Organised by Leeds Metropolitan University and the University of Leeds on behalf of The Sports Council. Leeds: Carnetion and the Cult of Slenderness: A Critique. *ACHPER National Journal,* 107.

Tinning, R. (1990) *Ideology and Physical Education: Opening Pandora's Box.* Geelong, Victoria: Deakin University Press.

Utley, A. and Sugden, D. (1994) Special educational needs and primary physical education. *Primary Focus,* Summer 1994.

Verma, G. K. and Darby, D. S. (1994) *Winners and Losers: Ethnic Minorities in Sport and Recreation.* London: Falmer Press.

Wilkinson, S. and Hunt, M. (1992) *Equal Opportunities and Special Educational Needs in Physical Education.* Hereford: Hereford and Worcester Education Department.

Williams, A. (1989) Equal opportunities and primary school physical education. *British Journal of Physical Education,* 20(4):177–81.

Williams, A. (1993) The reflective physical education teacher: implications for initial teacher education. *Physical Education Review,* 16(2).

Williams, A. (1995) Gymnastics at Key Stages 3 and 4. In PEAUK, NDTA, BAALPE and the Sports Council (1995) *Teaching Physical Education At Key Stages Three and Four.* London: The Physical Education Association of the United Kingdom.

Willis, P. (1982) Women in sport. In J. Hargreaves (ed.) *Sport, Culture and Ideology.* London: Routledge and Kegan Paul.

Wright, J. (1996) The construction of complementarity in physical education. *Gender and Education,* 8(1).

* Papers available from the author at the Research and Graduate School of Education, University of Southampton, Highfield, Southampton. SO17 1BJ. e-mail gmc@soton.ac.uk

** Papers available from the author at Faculty of Education and Social Services, Cheltenham and Gloucester College of Higher Education, Benton House, The Park, Cheltenham, UK. GL50 2QF. e-mail gnutt@chelt.ac.uk

USEFUL ADDRESSES

Arts Council of England, 14 Great Peter Street, London SW1P 3NQ.

British Handball Association, 40 Newchurch Road, Rawtenstall, Rossendale, Lancashire BB4 4QZ.

British Sports Association for the Disabled, Information Officer, Solecast

House, 13–27 Brunswick Place, London N1 6DX.

British Tchouk Ball Association, 14 Highfield Road, Sudbury, Suffolk, CO10 6QT.

Candoco – The Laban Centre for Movement (and Dance Company), Laurie Grove, New Cross, London SE14 6NH.

National Coaching Foundation, 114 Cardigan Road, Leeds LS6 3BJ.

National Dance Teachers' Association, 29 Larkspur Avenue, Charetown, Walsall, Staffordshire WS7 8SR.

National Resource Centre for Dance, University of Surrey, Guildford, Surrey GU2 5XH.

Race Apart, 19b Albert Road, Teddington, Middlesex TW11 0BD.

Scottish Sports Council, Caledonia House, South Gyle, Edinburgh EH12 9DQ.

Sport England, 16 Upper Woburn Place, London WC1H 0QP.

Sports Council for Northern Ireland, House of Sport, Upper Malone Road, Belfast BT9 5LA.

Sports Council for Wales, Welsh Institute of Sport, Sophia Gardens, Cardiff CF1 9SW.

Women's Sports Foundation, 305–15 Hither Green Lane, Lewisham, London SE13 6TJ.

Youth Sport Trust, Rutland Building, Loughborough University, Loughborough LE11 3TU.

CHAPTER 11

Modern foreign languages

Clifford Walker and Ian Newman

INTRODUCTION

The authors of this chapter believe that differences of attainment between individuals are not *primarily* the result of differences between those individuals. They tend, rather, to derive from differences in how the society in which they live values their characteristics and allocates access to appropriate resources. It is our attitudes towards people – to learners, teachers and their communities – which are disabling, not their socio-economic class, gender, 'race', sexuality or special educational needs. Attributing deficits to learners excuses low attainment as inevitable and blames under-achievement on the consumers of education rather than the providers. Furthermore, the authors regard monolingualism as a form of cultural and educational deprivation as opposed to multilingualism and its many advantages.

Mass modern foreign language teaching is a very recent development in England and Wales and is not yet complete. British government policy has failed to reflect the multiethnic and multilingual nature of British society and the wider European and world context. The National Curriculum for England and Wales is unnecessarily restrictive and arbitrary in its specification of which languages may be taught. Methodologies have been promulgated by some inspection and advisory services with little understanding of their origins and bases in theory and with insufficient regard for their appropriateness in the classroom context and their limitations within it. Methodology must be adapted to learners, not learners adapted to methodologies. Language use in the classroom needs to reflect and build on learners' own experience of language.

Using the modern foreign language as the means of communication in the classroom can help students to engage more effectively with learning opportunities and develop useful communicative capacity in the target language, i.e. the language which they are trying to learn. If communication in the classroom is to be meaningful for learners, it needs to reflect their own purposes. Studying another curriculum area through the medium of the modern foreign language provides a wide variety of contexts requiring authentic language use.

A SHORT HISTORY OF LANGUAGE TEACHING

Mass secondary schooling in England and Wales is no older than the 1944 Education Act. Some might date it back only as far as the raising of the school-leaving age to 16 in 1972/3 (DES, 1971). Others might argue that mass secondary schooling began with comprehensivization in the 1950s, 1960s and 1970s (Lawton, 1973; Holt, 1978), albeit that the change was incomplete and left approximately one-fifth of LEAs with some form of selection at 11-plus. This has been a gradual process, which is still far from complete and, indeed, is in danger of being reversed. The introduction of the Certificate of Secondary Education with Modes I, II and III, the General Certificate of Secondary Education and, more recently, the introduction of General National Vocational Qualifications, created landmarks in the process of increasing access to public examinations and enlarging the range of secondary school students' achievements, recognized and validated by the state.

Mass modern foreign languages education is even newer. Under the tri-lateral system of grammar schools, technical schools and secondary modern schools, introduced under the 1944 Education Act, the teaching of languages other than English was restricted almost entirely to the fortunate few who had passed their 11-plus examination (Phillips, 1988). 'Few' is a relative term. In a Welsh county it might be as many as 45 per cent of the state school population that passed their 11-plus. In a North of England county borough it might be as few as 10 per cent (Yates and Pidgeon, 1957). The languages taught were either *classical* or *modern*. The classical languages were Latin and, to a lesser extent, Greek. The modern languages were predominantly French and, to a much lesser extent, German.

> It [modern language learning] gained a foothold at the turn of the century because its advocates were able to suggest that it offered the same training of the mind as Greek and Latin and because the developing science of phonetics gave modern language learning an appearance of rigour sufficient to legitimate its place in both grammar and independent schools. (Hornsey, 1981:34).

After comprehensivization, languages other than English were initially restricted to upper sets, streams or bands containing those students who would probably have passed their 11-plus had it still been in place. Gradually, the teaching of modern foreign languages was extended to almost all students in the first three years of comprehensive schooling until the age of 14. By the late 1970s, 85 per cent of students in comprehensive schools were starting a modern language (Hawkins, 1981). Beyond 14, most lower-band male students did not continue the study of a modern foreign language (Phillips, 1988).

WHAT IS A MODERN FOREIGN LANGUAGE?

The French education system refers to *langues vivantes* or living languages. The British education system used to refer to *modern languages*. The National Curriculum refers to *modern foreign languages*. What constitutes a *foreign* language? First of all, it is foreign, i.e. it is from another country and does not belong in the United Kingdom. By association, speakers of foreign languages are foreign and do not belong here. By extension, learning to speak a foreign language is learning to do something that is foreign and does not belong here. Such a view appears to be based on the false premise that the UK is monoethnic, monocultural and monolingual, that monolingualism is normal and that multilingualism is abnormal.

The UK is not monoethnic and has not been monoethnic since at least the Roman invasion of England in AD 43. The UK contains the Celtic survivors of the Roman occupation, once British, now divided into distinct ethnic and linguistic groups: Cornish,

Irish, Scots and Welsh. Whereas Cornish is no longer the language of the Cornish people and exists only as an object of study, Irish Gaelic, Scots Gaelic and Welsh are living languages. While Irish Gaelic is an official language in the Republic of Ireland, a compulsory subject in all schools and the medium of instruction in some, it was at one time officially suppressed in Northern Ireland. Curtis refers to a 'stick which Irish schoolchildren had to wear round their necks: every time the child spoke in Irish, a notch was carved on the stick, and at the end of the day the child was punished for each offence. A similar device was used in Wales and Scotland' (Curtis, 1984:64). But Gaelic is enjoying a small-scale renaissance, especially within the nationalist community, bilingual street names having started to appear in some nationalist areas. GSSE entries with NICCEA in Irish Gaelic are increasing (Department of Education in Northern Ireland, 1994). Three state primary schools and one state secondary school teach in Irish and prepare students for examinations in the medium of Irish.

Scots Gaelic is the first language of approximately 80,000 people in the west of Scotland and the Western Isles. It is the medium of instruction in approximately fifty state primary schools, concentrated mainly in the Highlands and Western Isles. But there are also schools in some large cities, including Edinburgh, Glasgow, Perth, Dundee, Aberdeen and East Kilbride which teach in Scots Gaelic. Scots Gaelic is taught in approximately twenty state secondary schools. It is used as the medium of instruction for at least one other subject, such as history, in approximately ten state secondary schools. But problems of too few students opting for Gaelic, the limited availability of examinations in Scots Gaelic and a shortage of appropriately trained and qualified teachers do not permit any state secondary schools to deliver the whole curriculum through the medium of Scots Gaelic. However, Jordanhill College at the University of Strathclyde is endeavouring to improve the supply of Gaelic-medium teachers and student numbers are slowly rising in Scots Gaelic classes.

Monolingual English governments have suppressed the official use of all languages other than Norman French, Latin and English from 1066 until recently, and used schooling as a tool to this end. As an official report about Wales put it in 1840: 'a band of efficient schoolmasters is kept up at much less expense than a body of police or soldiery' (Curtis, 1984:64). After a long struggle, a bombing campaign and at least one fatal hunger strike, in 1967 the Welsh Language Act granted Welsh legal status in Wales. Welsh is said to be understood by approximately 20 per cent of the population of Wales (Katzner, 1995). Welsh is a National Curriculum core subject in Wales and the medium of instruction in some schools in Wales. There is a Welsh-language television channel: S4C. Whereas Welsh speakers had to use only English, even in court, they can now use Welsh in official communications. But the officially sanctioned use of Welsh is limited geographically to the *Principality* of Wales. A Welsh-speaking citizen of the United Kingdom is legally obliged to use English in England, Scotland and Northern Ireland. A Welsh-speaker is as *foreign* as a Punjabi-speaker in the rest of the United Kingdom:

> In May 1988 a British citizen of Pakistani descent appeared in court charged with social security fraud. Since he spoke limited English he requested a Punjabi interpreter. This request struck the judge as even more outrageous than the original offence: the man had lived in England for 23 years and should not have needed an interpreter. Accordingly, the judge made taking English lessons a condition of the man's probation, commenting to the court that 'a person who lives here has a duty to understand the language.' (*The Star*, 6 May 1988, quoted in Cameron and Bourne, 1989:15)

The situation would have been the same if the defendant had been a British citizen of Welsh descent. Welsh is a foreign language in England and, by implication, the Welsh or at least Welsh-speaking Welsh, are foreigners in England, Scotland and Northern Ireland.

Scots Gaelic is the medium of a small amount of television and radio broadcasting but cannot legally be used in official communications such as law courts, tax returns and applications for jobs in local and central government service. Scots Gaelic is regarded by Westminster as a foreign language and, by implication, Scots Gaelic-speaking Scots are foreigners even in Scotland. Irish Gaelic has similar non-status in Northern Ireland. Irish Gaelic and Scots Gaelic may not be taught as part of the National Curriculum in England and Wales. Welsh may be taught only in Wales:

> In 1967 Welsh gained equal validity only within the borders of Wales. Welsh speakers outside Wales had no claim for equal treatment. In other words, the whole discourse of language rights in the Welsh case is focused on territorial considerations, to wit, the existence of a region (historically a nation) to which the Welsh lan-

guage belongs. It is a discourse of national boundaries rather than one of national rights (as we can see very clearly from the fact that individuals travelling beyond the Welsh borders could not take their language rights with them). (Cameron and Bourne, 1989:16)

English, a variety of German, in the form of Anglo-Saxon or Old English, came to England with the Germanic invaders after the departure of the Romans around the year 450. Other languages spoken in the British Isles before and since then – Irish Gaelic, Scots Gaelic, Welsh, Cornish, Cumbrian, Manx, Norse, Latin and French – have been condemned eventually either to marginalization or extinction.

The UK is multiethnic and multilingual. A large number of languages are spoken by its citizens and its schoolchildren. The number depends on definitions of language and multilingualism. It is not unusual for a secondary school to have students from twenty or more speech communities. It is possible that within a single local education authority, as many as one-third of students surveyed could be multilingual, speaking between them as many as 87 languages (Couillaud *et al.,* 1985). Central government ignores the existence of speech communities speaking languages other than English except to publish some pamphlets in languages such as Urdu and Vietnamese, and provide Home Office money for Section 11 projects to teach their children English. Until 1993, Section 11 of the 1966 Local Government Act funded support for students from New Commonwealth countries only. Section 11 now allows local authorities to create posts to cater for the needs of all their Asian, black and other minority ethnic populations (Cole, 1993). Its view of multilingualism emphasizes *heritage* rather than *minority rights.* It is territorial and assimilationist. Section 11 regards languages other than English as alien. It alienates minority ethnic children from their own communities and cultures. It leads them to regard their own mother tongues as somehow less than languages, and their own often high-level multilingualism as something of which to be ashamed rather than proud. Despite the existence of a large body of strong evidence that literacy is best acquired in a learner's mother tongue and can then be transferred to literacy in other languages with relative ease, Section 11 money cannot be used on developing mother tongue literacy. As far as successive governments have been concerned, non-English languages are *foreign* and so are people who speak them.

British governments have regarded the UK as monoethnic and monolingual, or at least believed that it should be so. The National Curriculum is predicated on the notion that the UK is and should remain a single monoethnic and monolingual society and, hence, that monolingualism is normal and multilingualism is abnormal. The existence of minority ethnic and speech communities is ignored and undermined, rather than celebrated and supported, except where it is quaint and of value to tourism, as in London's *Chinatown*. The Arab, Chinese, French, Italian, Jewish, Spanish and, more recently, Bangladeshi, Indian, Pakistani, African, Caribbean and other communities have had to create their own schools and other institutions. The fortunate few have received assistance from the governments of the countries from which they or their ancestors had emigrated to the UK (such as France, Italy and Spain). They have almost always done so without help from central government, but sometimes with support from an enlightened local government such as the London Borough of Islington which has subsidized the *Federazione Italiana Lavoratori Emigranti e Famiglie*. Most, possibly all, have had to face varying degrees of popular racial prejudice and institutionalized racism. Families have commonly felt pressurized to deny as far as possible their origins, culture and language and to raise their children as monoethnic and monolingual British, knowing nothing else and unable to communicate with their own grandparents, aunts, uncles and other relatives. Some schools have told families not to speak their own languages at home because it will prejudice their children's success at school: their children have been forbidden to speak their mother tongues in class. Many children have grown up ashamed of their ethnic origins, ashamed of their own parents and embarrassed over levels of multilingualism that can, in fact, exceed the linguistic competence of their own modern foreign languages teachers (graduate and postgraduate trained), and which in almost any other circumstances would be regarded as a great achievement, worthy of praise and academic recognition.

It is hardly surprising that governments which have devalued centuries of indigenous multilingualism, and excluded it from its planning of education, should also devalue and exclude more recent multilingualism, especially when associated with African and Asian cultures which they have disdained (with a few exceptions such as the entrepreneurial *enterprise* stereotypically attributed to Cantonese and East African Indian communities).

WHAT IS A LANGUAGE?

The inclusion of languages other than English in the National Curriculum is to be welcomed. At long last, all, or very nearly all, students in Key Stages 3 and 4 are entitled at least nominally to be taught a language other than English. 'Languages for all' is official policy. It is a pity, to say the least, that monoethnic and monolingual central government has imposed a restriction upon which languages may legally be offered as a first modern foreign language in England and Wales under the Education (National Curriculum) (Modern Foreign Languages) Order 1991. Only languages in list one enjoy this status. They are Danish, Dutch, French, German, Modern Greek, Italian, Portuguese and Spanish: the national languages of Denmark, Netherlands, Belgium, France, Luxembourg, Germany, Austria, Greece, Italy, Portugal and Spain. The national languages of Finland, Ireland and Sweden are excluded. It is an interesting list. Europe is profoundly multilingual. Even if dialects and recently introduced languages are ignored, the members of the European Union are multilingual and most of them grant official recognition to more than one language. Belgium recognizes Flemish (Dutch) and French. France has Basque, Breton, Catalan, French, German, Italian and Provençal speaking communities. Italy contains Albanian, German, Greek, French, Italian, Rhaeto-Romanic, Sardinian and Slovene speaking communities and recognizes French, German, Italian and Slovene officially. Spain has Basque, Catalan, Castilian, Galician and Valencian speaking communities and recognizes their languages officially. But the National Curriculum, i.e. the National Curriculum for England and Wales, ignores completely the enormous linguistic variety not only of its own people but also of its fellow member states of the EU. It includes only the big languages. The National Curriculum regards England as monoethnic and monolingual and the rest of Europe's nation states as being the same. Not even the reality of the ethnic and linguistic diversity of its neighbours is allowed to disturb the UK government's belief that nation states are monoethnic and monolingual. In Italy, for example, even Slovene-speaking students can attend Slovene-medium schools and sit public examinations in Slovene. The National Curriculum for England and Wales specifically forbids the use of languages other than English in England, and English and Welsh in Wales as the medium of examination.

This equation of belonging to a nation and speaking a particular language would appear absurd in many parts of the world, including many countries in Europe (Cameron and Bourne, 1989).

List two contains languages which may only be offered if at least one of the languages in list one is already offered to all students in Key Stages 3 and 4. They form an even more puzzling list: Arabic, Bengali, Chinese (Mandarin or Cantonese), Gujerati, Modern Hebrew, Hindi, Japanese, Punjabi, Russian, Turkish and Urdu. They are deemed to be languages of commercial or cultural importance. They are certainly heterogeneous. All the languages in list one are Indo-European, and represent three of the nine branches of the family. Danish, Dutch and German are Germanic, as is English. French, Italian, Portuguese and Spanish are Romance. Greek is Hellenic.

Only six languages in list two are Indo-European and therefore related, albeit distantly, to English: Bengali, Gujerati, Hindi, Punjabi, Urdu and Russian. The first five are Indic languages spoken in India, Bangladesh and Pakistan and related to Sanskrit, Marathi, Bihari, Rajastani, Oriya, Assamese, Kashmiri, Nepali, Sindhi and Sinhalese. Arabic and Hebrew are Afro-Asiatic languages closely related to Maltese, three Aramaic and six Ethiopic languages, and more distantly to six Berber and seven Cushitic languages (including Somali), Coptic and Hausa.

The prescription of which nineteen languages may be studied as a foundation subject in Key Stages 3 and 4 in England and in Key Stage 3 in Wales contrasts unfavourably with the situation in Scotland where there is no prescription but merely guidance (SOED, 1993). The Secretary of State for Scotland

> believes that the great majority of students should continue the study of at least one modern European modern language through to S3 and S4. He accepts, however, that in certain circumstances students and their parents may prefer to pursue the study of another language, for example, Gaelic, an Asian language or a Classical language. The Secretary of State would prefer to see these or other languages studied in S3 and S4 alongside a modern European foreign language but where parents and students are persuaded that they do not wish to follow this course and their preferred alternative is available within the school he would not wish these preferences to be frustrated. (SED, 1990:1)

What constitutes a modern European foreign language is not

defined but it is indicated that the category will normally comprise French, German, Italian, Spanish and Russian (SED, 1989). However, the DFEE is said to be reconsidering the situation as far as England is concerned. It appears that Irish Gaelic will be added to list one in September 1999 and that Finnish and Swedish will be added in September 2000. It also appears that list two may be expanded to include any language which is deemed capable of being taught according to the National Curriculum Modern Foreign Languages Programmes of Study. In other words, the MFL will still only include the big languages associated with great literatures and other high, rather than popular, cultures.

METHODOLOGY

Languages occupy a unique position in school curricula: whereas many, perhaps most people live from birth to death with only a low level of knowledge and skill in subjects such as mathematics, history or geography, almost everyone possesses a high level of linguistic knowledge and skill in at least one language. Virtually everyone learns to communicate in some form of language. It may be in Bengali, British Sign Language or a variety of Twin-Speak. Verbal communication is a universal characteristic of *homo sapiens* and the defining characteristic of *homo loquens.* Everyone speaks; but a large proportion of the world's population neither read nor write and many of their languages are rarely, if ever, written down.

The universality of human language learning has led some researchers to propose that human beings possess a specific, innate propensity for learning languages which is different from the mechanisms used for other learning (Chomsky, 1976), the existence of which would entail a genetically transmitted pre-adaptation to the learning task, which is species-specific (Wells, 1985). Furthermore, much of humanity does not merely learn one language. Multilingualism is not a universal or defining characteristic of humankind but it is probably the attribute typical of the majority of the world's population. In many countries, it is commonplace to speak a local language, a regional language and a national language. In Europe, including Britain, many students use a language at home which is not used by their school or the wider community. But successful classroom-based learning of modern foreign languages is far from universal even for students who are already multilingual.

A much greater proliferation of methodology in language teaching than in any other subject can be attributed to a combination of features: the universal human first language acquisition; the postulated existence of a Language Acquisition Device (in which some general information about language structure is programmed in the genetic code and therefore available to the child before she begins to puzzle out the structure of the speech she hears around her) (Chomsky, 1965); widespread multilingualism and the potential utility of language learning.

Language teaching has been prey to fads and fashions. Methodologies have been peddled by inspectors and advisers who understood little of their origins and even less of their limitations. The widespread adoption or otherwise of a particular methodology has often had little to do with utility in the classroom (Richards, 1984; Widdowson, 1990):

> The history of language teaching is the history of ideas about what language is and how languages are learned. The application to language teaching of theories concerning the nature of language and language learning has led to a succession of different instructional methods. While differences between methods often reflect opposing views of the nature of language and of language learning processes, the reasons for the rise and fall of methods are often independent of either the theories behind those methods or their effectiveness in practice. To understand the role of language theory, instructional theory, and implementation factors in methods is to know their 'secret life' and at the same time to discover the limitations of the 'methods syndrome' in curriculum development. (Richards 1984: 7)

Methodologies have drawn on various fields such as linguistics and psychology for their inspiration, but their relevance is limited:

> I am, frankly, rather sceptical about the significance, for the teaching of languages, of such insights and understanding as have been attained by linguistics and psychology. Certainly the teacher of language would do well to keep informed of progress and discussions in these fields and the efforts of linguists and psychologists to approach the problems of language teaching from a principled point of view are extremely worthwhile, from an intellectual as well as a social point of view. Still, it is difficult to believe that either lin-

guistics or psychology has achieved a level of theoretical under-standing that might enable it to support a 'technology' of language teaching. (Chomsky, 1965, quoted in Allen and Van Buren, 1971:152)

Teachers of languages should be familiar with research into potentially relevant fields, for example First Language Acquisi-tion (Aitchison, 1989; Fletcher and Garman, 1986; Wells, 1981, 1984, 1985), and Second Language Acquisition (Ellis, 1985; Light-brown and Spada, 1993), Language Description (Aitchison, 1995; Fromkin and Rodman, 1993; Widdowson, 1996), Phonology (O'Connor, 1973), Sociolinguistics (Giglioli, 1972; Hudson, 1996; Saville-Troike, 1982; Trudgill, 1974), Discourse Analysis (Brown and Yule, 1983; Stubbs, 1983), Semantics (Lyons, 1995), Pragmat-ics (Levinson, 1983) and Speech Act Theory (Austin *et al.*, 1975; Searle, 1969). Such research should be used critically by teachers, to inform their teaching (Stern, 1983; Widdowson, 1990). Unfor-tunately, the training of language teachers has too often neglected such areas, and frequently does not even provide any critical framework through which to approach such research. Neverthe-less, language teachers only expect research to inform their teaching, not tell them how to teach. 'The theoretical disciplines provide a reference for establishing principles of approach, they cannot determine techniques' (Widdowson, 1990:10). The limited success of methodologies, including the Direct Method, Functional-Notional Syllabuses (Wilkins, 1976), The Silent Way, Counselling-Learning, Suggestopedia (Stevick, 1980), when deployed uncritically in the school classroom, results from a failure to understand their premises and the consequent failure to weigh their advantages and disadvantages.

Most curriculum development in modern foreign language teaching in the UK since the introduction of comprehensive schools has focused on differentiation and how to teach languages to an increasingly large proportion of secondary school students. A modern foreign language has been compulsory in Key Stage 3 in England and Wales since the 1988 Education Reform Act and became compulsory in Key Stage 4 in England in 1996. Modularization, graded objectives, differentiated papers, profiling and computer-assisted language learning have all been aimed at making the languages curriculum more accessible to those low-attaining students who would have been in secondary modern schools 30 years ago. The focus of these developments has been lack of ability in the students and lack of engagement by them in learning tasks. The reasons for failure have been located in the students, hence the serious doubts raised by some modern language teachers as to the advisability of making a modern foreign language a part of the core in Key Stage 4. Attributing deficits to learners excuses low attainment as inevitable and blames under-achievement on the consumers of education rather than the providers. This type of deflection avoids any address to issues of social class, 'race', gender and sexuality, which are concealed by confusion with handicap and special educational needs. Sir Ron Dearing's compromise GCSE short courses, although initially welcomed by the doubters referred to above, are related more to the issue of space in the KS4 curriculum than any dilution of GCSE standards.

It would be fair to say, however, that GCSE syllabuses and subsequent updating of GCE A-level syllabuses and assessment have been crucial in the expansion of language teaching to parts of the population never reached before. The traditional emphasis in post-16 language studies, especially at A-level, on the *great works* of literature has been discontinued as a compulsory component of courses. Élitist cultural and literary bias has, thus, been modified or given option status; relevance to contemporary everyday life is emphasized. Speaking and listening are given equal status with reading and writing. Communicative content, range, fluency and meaning achieved can be rewarded in final exams. Grammatical accuracy is simply one of the criteria used for marking spoken or written texts. Regional varieties of languages, such as Latin American Spanish, are now deemed acceptable at both GCSE and A-level.

APTITUDE, 'THE GOOD LANGUAGE LEARNER' AND LEARNER TRAINING

What do languages, music and PE have in common? They are all subjects in which traditionally few students have succeeded. The blame for this widespread failure has been placed on the unsuccessful learners themselves. Subject-specific aptitudes have been posited. Successful learners are deemed to possess the *ear, talent, aptitude* or *gift*. Unsuccessful learners are deemed not to; deficits are attributed to learners. Research into language aptitude has been prompted by large organizations, such as the US armed forces and the US foreign service, in order to select who is most likely to succeed in language learning and avoid the expense of training those who are less likely to succeed. Language aptitude tests are commercially available. The Pimsleur Language Aptitude Battery (Pimsleur, 1966), the Modern Language Aptitude Test (Carroll and Sapon, 1959) and the York Language Aptitude Test (Green, 1976) are among the best known. Correlational studies into their predictive validity suggest that they can forecast as much as half of the range of language learning success (Green, 1977). These studies, however, generally use ethnically and culturally homogeneous groups of learners exposed to conventional Western teaching methods (Skehan, 1986). Their ability to predict successful language learning by ethnically and culturally heterogeneous groups exposed to African and Asian teaching methods is less clear. Aptitude testing is anti-egalitarian and against social justice. The challenge is to make language education accessible, not to limit access.

A slightly more sophisticated approach to improving the success of language teaching has been to examine learner behaviour rather than inherent traits. The Good Language Learner Project (Naiman *et al.*, 1978) contrasts the behaviour of 'good' and 'bad' language learners:

> This study, as well as other language teaching research, has confirmed the conviction that strategies and techniques form only a part of language learning. It is therefore important to relate them to personality and motivational factors in the learner, and to other less obvious aspects of the learning process . . . Certain personality and cognitive style factors are related to success in language learning. The present study identified two such factors as important: tolerance of ambiguity and field independence . . . Positive attitudes to language learning appear to be a necessary but not a sufficient condition for success . . . Regardless of learner differences in our view the following emerge as essential for successful language learning:
> 1. The learner must be active in his approach to learning and practice.
> 2. The learner must come to grips with the language as a system.
> 3. The learner must use the language in real communication.
> 4. The learner must monitor his interlanguage.
> 5. The learner must come to terms with the affective demands of language learning. (Naiman *et al.*, 1978:99–103)

The validity of these findings for learners of different 'race', social class, gender, sexuality, special educational needs, culture, educational experience and learning purpose (Widdowson, 1983) does not appear to have been demonstrated. They may merely be a reflection of what is relevant to success with particular methodologies. The findings might be thought to offer 'bad' language learners some useful guidance on how to emulate 'good' language learners; they attribute deficits to the consumers of education rather than providers. Teaching should be adapted to learners, not learners to teaching.

Learner training aims to build on *the good language learner* and related research to train learners to behave in ways which more closely resemble the behaviour of successful language learners. Three strands are identified. The first is learner independence:

> Training for Learners of English has as one of its aims to enable learners to take responsibility for their own learning. In other words, it aims to develop learner independence/autonomy. (Ellis and Sinclair, 1987:2)

The second strand is the successful language learner:

> In recent years there has been a great deal of research carried out by, among others, Naiman, Rubin, Stern and Wenden into the personality traits, cognitive styles and strategies of the successful language learner. These characteristics have been generalised, as far as this is possible and include the following: Successful language learners
> - are willing and accurate guessers;
> - have strong motivation;
> - are often not inhibited;
> - are prepared to attend to form;
> - practise;
> - monitor their own speech and that of others;
> - attend to meaning. (Ellis and Sinclair, 1987:2)

The third strand is training learners:

> We define learner training as a learning situation in which the teacher plays an instrumental role in helping the learner discover how to learn successfully. Dickinson and Carver have defined three main areas of training to help learners prepare for autonomy, namely:
> - psychological preparation e.g. confidence-building activities;
> - methodological preparation e.g. helping learners to understand

metalanguage and methodology;
* practice in self-direction e.g. giving learners opportunities to make choices about their learning. (Ellis and Sinclair, 1987:3)

The whole approach of learner training, while well intentioned, reflects mainstream Western, white, middle-class, male, heterosexual culture, together with elements of fashionable teaching methodologies such as communicative approaches, counselling learning, the monitor model and self-access learning. Aptitude testing rejects learners. The 'good language learner' approach stigmatizes learners. Learner training adapts learners to teaching. All three attribute deficits to learners rather than to methodology.

'RACE' AND MULTILINGUALISM

Language also means culture and philosophy
(Antonio Gramsci,
Selections from Prison Notebooks [1929–35] 1971:349)

Methodology is not culture-free; it is not neutral. No single methodology is equally relevant to or effective for all learners. There is no universal methodology of teaching languages or any other subject which can be applied without reference to the learners to whom it is applied. One of the authors, Clifford Walker, was present at a conference in Edinburgh in 1989 when a lecturer criticized Arab students of English for concentrating excessively on learning explicit grammatical rules, and memorizing word lists instead of trying to communicate. Clifford suggested to the lecturer that he was not only expressing a racist sentiment but was also violating a fundamental pedagogic principle: *start where the learner is* (Walker et al., 1995). Clifford went on to say that he could imagine that Arab teachers of Arabic to Europeans in the Middle East could equally complain that Europeans devote too much effort to syntactically and lexically inaccurate and difficult-to-understand attempts to communicate. An Arab teacher of English from the Middle East stood up immediately and said 'Exactly. Why do you in the West believe that your methodologies must be superior to ours and insist on imposing them on us?'

The international, post-colonial methodological imperialism of the British Council, the United States Information Agency, the

Alliance Française and other 'aid' agencies, uncritically imposing the latest gospel of language teaching on the Third World, is echoed by the methodological imperialism of inspectors and advisers apparently uncritically imposing the latest gospel of language teaching on schools and their students:

> Bilingualism is often blamed for a whole range of negative phenomena. However, closer analysis shows that it is not the existence of the individual's two languages that causes this negative behaviour, but a whole range of other social and psychological factors, especially society's view of the status of the languages, its treatment of the bilingual acquiring them, and the self-image which the bilingual develops during this process. (Dodson, 1983, quoted in Couillaud, 1985:377)

Western educationalists would do well to be more sceptical towards the methodologies and techniques which they espouse and promote, especially for learners who do not share their culture, languages or educational experience. The West can learn a good deal from the best contemporary practice of teachers in some 'developing' countries (Little, 1988).

LANGUAGE AND VARIETY

There are differences *between* languages; there are also differences *within* languages. They vary in syntax, vocabulary, phonetics, phonology and discourse structure. Every speaker belongs to a network of speech communities (Gumperz, 1968). Each speech community is distinguished from others by its membership and its speech. The factors governing language variation are many and include geography, socio-economic class, education, occupation, religion, ethnicity, gender, age, sexuality, status, role, speech event, purpose, setting and context (Saville-Troike, 1982; Trudgill, 1974). The most familiar variation within languages is geographical, stigmatized by the term 'dialect': 'A great culture can be translated into the language of another great culture, that is to say a great national language with historical richness and complexity, and it can translate any other great culture and can be a worldwide means of expression. But a dialect cannot do this' (Gramsci, 1971:325).

In Britain, there are clear differences in levels of *acceptability*, once a dialect is heard outside of its primary geographical area. Whereas some dialects enjoy considerable prestige, others are clearly and widely stigmatized. There is also widespread awareness of socio-economic class variation within languages, stigmatized by the term 'slang'. The varieties associated with property-owning and professional speech communities are deemed more acceptable and enjoy greater prestige than varieties associated with economically disadvantaged speech communities. The former vary less across geographical ranges, and are perceived as national standards suited to communication between speech communities and imposed on other speech communities when communicating with élites and when engaged in communication managed by élites. Non-standard varieties are considered inherently inferior and less capable (Labov, 1969), and (typically) to be unsuitable for use in written communication and education. The National Curriculum permits their use but relegates them to second place behind Standard English. Modern foreign language teaching focuses on the teaching of standard languages and uses Standard English as its starting point. This double use of standard varieties places speakers of non-standard varieties at a disadvantage. It takes as its starting point a language variety used by a minority of the population, and obstructs access to the modern foreign languages curriculum.

Language varies with gender. Women's language tends more closely towards that of higher socio-economic classes than that of their male partners. Women's use of language with each other is different from men's use of language with each other. But in communication between men and women, women sometimes have to use man-made language (Spender, 1980). Standard languages are male languages and the language varieties used in modern foreign language materials are male varieties (Spender, 1980). Sexist terminology and stereotypical role models are pervasive (NICC, 1993a, 1993b) in modern foreign languages teaching as elsewhere (Harris, 1992). Nevertheless, female students have generally been more inclined than males to study languages, and study them more successfully:

> Learning French was even associated with 'refinement' and it is curious that this association has persisted into the 1970s when Burstall found that, whereas the parents of primary school boys saw no vocational advantage for their sons in learning French, the

parents of girls seemed to accept it as a worthwhile 'finishing' pursuit for their daughters. (Hornsey, 1981:34)

As modern foreign language learning is increasingly of interest to male learners, who perceive career advantages in multilingualism arising from the internationalization of business, its focus is shifting from literature-based and conversational approaches towards vocational approaches and languages for specific purposes, such as General National Vocational Qualifications in Travel and Tourism and Business Studies and National Vocational Qualifications (De Sudea, 1988).

Language tends to vary with the age of the people using it. Young people's use of language resembles more closely the language attributed to lower socio-economic groups than that of their parent(s). Young people not only differ from their elders in their lexis, syntax, phonetics and phonology, but also in the topics and communicative purpose of language: they engage in different communicative acts from their parents and the structure of their discourse is different. The communicative purposes, communicative events and discourse structures in which schoolchildren engage in their mother tongues are rarely reflected in the modern foreign languages materials and teaching to which they are exposed. The language which they are taught is typically adult language. While it may be argued that they are being prepared for adult life, the learning experiences and processes through which they are to benefit in order to prepare them for adult life must take the learners' previous experience and current knowledge and skills as their starting point on which to build learning.

The social contexts in which modern foreign languages materials and teaching are contextualized are similarly predicated on high prestige models which do not match the experience of most students. The standard white, middle-class families, living in national capitals, which are almost ubiquitously described in teaching materials, are not familiar to children of minority ethnic, working-class, homosexual, single-parent and provincial families. The lack of social contexts with which many children can identify acts as a positive barrier to their engagement in learning activities.

If students are to believe some of the textbooks they use in their modern language lessons . . . a typical mum cooks a lavish meal in the kitchen, while dad repairs the car/plays golf; . . . a typical home is at least semi-detached with a minimum of three bedrooms; . . . a typical holiday consists of driving the family car to a three-star hotel in a luxury resort. (Harris, 1992:3)

Some more recently published materials, which schools are too often unable to afford, have begun to address these issues. Women are no longer portrayed as negatively as they once were but materials are rarely anti-sexist and still use sexist language. Such narrow social contextualization outside the experience of some learners compounds the barriers erected against them by the use of language varieties beyond their experience.

SPECIAL EDUCATIONAL NEEDS

Effective access to the learning of languages other than English is only now being permitted to students with special educational needs in secondary schools. Although few, if any, students in mainstream schools are subject to an exemption from the National Curriculum requirement that a modern foreign language be taught to all in Key Stage 3, it is frequently sacrificed to what are perceived as more pressing curriculum or pastoral priorities: 'Historically languages have been one of the most popular subject areas from which to withdraw students for individual or small group support' (Keise, 1992:156).

Withdrawal from mainstream lessons is still commonplace, even if less widespread than before. It can be appropriate and beneficial. Modern foreign language lessons are likely to be sacrificed because they are still perceived as an élite subject which only became compulsory for all students entering Key Stage 4 in 1996/7. It is considered by many teachers and families to be beyond the capacity of students with special needs, whom they may consider unable to articulate their own mother tongue sufficiently well. They believe that, for children who arrive at secondary school with a reading age below what is necessary to permit them ready access to most learning materials, it is better to set fewer targets, and attain them, than aim to deliver almost everything but attain almost nothing.

An emotion approaching despair has been evident in language departments of some schools, over how to deliver a modern foreign language to all students in Key Stage 4, especially in single-sex boys' schools. Some trialed special small sets are in preparation. For students with limited literacy, a focus on oral skills recommends itself, although they will need to take papers in reading and possibly writing to be awarded a GCSE pass. A focus on effectiveness rather than accuracy is already commonplace. Indeed, an almost total emphasis on lexical and holophrasic capacity (Widdowson, 1983) rather than syntax would seem to be desirable. This would enable the achievement of imprecise but reasonably effective communication, even if it requires more co-operative and well-disposed interlocutors than most. The content could be limited to a small modular core of essential notions and functions – similar to the Council of Europe's 'Threshold' and 'Waystage' syllabuses (Trim, 1973) – based on the most important aspects of areas already covered, combined with a few other useful items, recycled in a notional-functional spiral which revisits and revises without repeating activities which have been undertaken previously (Wilkins, 1976).

Making a modern foreign language accessible to students with emotional and behavioural difficulties in Key Stage 4 is likely to be even more demanding. Most of them will have developed strongly negative attitudes towards language learning and will lack the self-discipline required by pair-work and small-group oral and information-gap communicative activities. The target language needs to become the vehicle for content and activities which build on their own experience and interests and achieve a face validity for such students. For example, an entire one-term Spanish scheme of work for disaffected boys in Year 11 can be produced around the subject they say interests them most: football. It can link Spanish-medium classroom activities with Spanish-medium practical instruction and coaching on the football field.

However, the broadening of the scope of disapplication from the National Curriculum MFL requirements in Key Stage 4, in order to permit *work-related learning*, introduced in September 1998, is likely to mean that such groups will not be studying a language other than English post-14. The opportunities to prepare them for life in an increasingly globalized world will be diminished. Furthermore, the progress made in recent years to increase familiarity with languages other than English as a tool to raise their profile and prestige and to combat racism against the people who use them is likely to be reversed. *Languages for All* 11–16 will have been only a brief interlude in the predominantly élitist history of language teaching.

LEARNING PURPOSE

All language education requires content. Any meaningful use of language involves reading, writing, listening to or talking about something. Traditionally, the content of language teaching has been the culture, geography and history of the peoples whose mother tongue is being taught, and the countries in which they live. More recently, the content of language teaching has included aspects of the daily life of native-speaking children and tourism. Such content served language teachers and their students well when language teaching was a privilege reserved in the main for those lucky enough to pass their 11-plus examination and enter grammar schools. The purpose of modern language teaching was often little different from the purpose of teaching classical languages (Phillips, 1988). It was intellectual: the acquisition of knowledge about the language, not the ability to use it as a means of communication. Even at universities, the ability of many dons to communicate in the language was limited to the ability to read the most prestigious literature written in the language. Some were unable to speak the language or write an informal letter in it. Even now, school inspectors have such little faith in university language teaching that they insist on 'testing' the spoken competence of teachers with good honours degrees from top universities at job interviews. Rarely is the subject knowledge of teachers of other subjects, already certified by their qualifications, submitted to assessment of such questionable validity.

The utility of teaching modern foreign languages for primarily intellectual purposes has been brought into question where the ability to use the language as a means of communication is required either for a job or to facilitate further study. Ever more companies and occupations are requiring the ability to use at least one modern foreign language as a means of communication, and are including them in specifications for recruitment and promotion (Walker and Newman, 1988). It has also become a requirement for entry into various university faculties in many countries, where research and teaching materials have not been published in their indigenous languages. Such consumers of the ability to use a modern foreign language as a means of communication have discovered that traditionally taught knowledge about a language is not sufficient to permit everyday or occupational use of the language.

The utility of teaching modern languages for primarily intellectual purposes has also been brought into question where modern foreign languages have been included in the curriculum of almost all secondary school students in comprehensive and secondary modern schools. It has been difficult to engage many low-attaining students in the traditional content and activities of modern foreign language lessons. They have not been interested in learning about the high cultures associated with the language. Many have not been particularly motivated by pretending to communicate in the role-play activities which have been introduced to differentiate the curriculum and help make modern foreign languages more accessible to a wider range of students, especially post-14 in National Curriculum Key Stage 4.

LANGUAGE IMMERSION AND EXTENSION

Why is learning languages apparently so easy for children outside lessons and so difficult in lessons? One part of the answer is that learning languages informally outside the classroom is not as easy as it is often imagined to be. The chatty toddler is only part of the way to learning what is required for adult communication (Wells, 1985). Years of our lives are devoted to learning our first language(s). Adults living abroad still find themselves learning the local language(s) after a decade or more of residence, work and study. Another part of the answer is that studying a language formally in the classroom is different from learning a language informally outside of it. Less time is available: rarely more than three hours per week, 38 weeks per year for five years, making a total of less than 600 hours. Much of this limited time may be lost to activities in the mother tongue. Even less time is likely to involve using the target language as a means of communication rather than as an object of study and the focus of an exercise.

Classroom-based learning of modern foreign languages needs to be different from informal learning of modern foreign languages if it is to compensate for the time-intensive nature of the task. It is probably useful to be told about the German case system rather than having to infer it oneself, a task that would tax a trained descriptive linguist. But, because the learning processes that are used in formal classroom teaching are different from those which learners have developed in learning their first language(s), students are unable to apply their existing language learning skills to classroom-based learning. *Start where the learner is* has been widely accepted as a maxim of good teaching (Walker *et al.*, 1995). By making it difficult for learners to apply their linguistic knowledge successfully, and deploy language learning skills in language lessons, we violate this maxim and increase the magnitude of the learning task.

Students already know how to learn and use at least one language. They use the language, make errors, learn from their errors and develop an *intermediate competence* or *interlanguage* which gradually approximates more closely to the target language (Dulay and Burt, 1974). Formal teaching of vocabulary, grammar, pronunciation and the like can help learners, particularly older learners, to accelerate their language learning. But opportunities are also needed to use the language and develop their own interlanguage. Using the target language as a means of communication in the modern foreign language classroom can help students to engage more effectively with learning opportunities and develop useful communicative competence in the target language. Providing opportunities for *authentic* use of the target language in the classroom is difficult. Studying another curriculum area through the medium of the target language provides a wide variety of contexts requiring authentic language use. It allows students to make better use of the extensive experience gained in learning their first language(s), and to apply it to the task of learning a modern foreign language in the classroom (Widdowson, 1978).

The use of non-native languages as the medium of instruction in schools, especially in secondary schools, is widespread in many countries. In some cases the native language community is too small to support the production of school materials, or there is no single common language available to a multilingual community. In other cases the intention is purely the attainment of high levels of competence in the second or foreign language. This has been termed *cross-curricular foreign language teaching, bilingual teaching* and *immersion education*. In the British Isles many monolingual English-speaking families have chosen monolingual Gaelic-medium, Irish-medium and Welsh-medium schools for their children, so that they will be bilingual.

Immersion education evolved famously and on a large scale in Canada in the early 1960s in response to the tension between its Anglophone and Francophone communities and the persistent failure of foreign language teaching in schools. It provided a radical alternative programme aiming to guarantee advanced levels of bilingualism for children from monolingual backgrounds, and to create a more homogeneous community, while maintaining the same academic aims and objectives as the mainstream curriculum. The distinctive feature of immersion programmes is the use of the target language as the medium of instruction in most or all subjects, in contrast with the conventional language classroom where the focus tends to be on the language itself and its formal aspects in particular. This feature has been described as originally constituting a *useful expedient* (Stern, 1983) for the pioneers of immersion since it offered the opportunity to simulate direct bilingual experience, ensured substantial contact time with the target language and economized on teaching time by extending language education into other subjects. Evaluation studies suggest that immersion education has been successful in numerous Canadian schools (Swain and Lapkin, 1982).

In the UK full immersion education is, as far as the authors are aware, only available at independent schools, aimed in the main at expatriate communities, such as the Lycée Charles de Gaulle and Colegio Vicente Cañada in London, and the European School at Culham in Oxfordshire. Immersion education for all is not a practical proposition, but *language extension* can be. The term has been used to describe programmes which teach only a small proportion of their curriculum through the medium of a second or foreign language. There have been a small number of these in British mainstream state comprehensive schools in the past eight years, most of which have used French as the medium of instruction. But there is no reason – other than government policy – why other languages, including *community* and *heritage* languages, should not be used as the medium of teaching and learning in extension programmes. Their number is growing and likely to continue growing, especially in the recently proposed language colleges. A Bilingual Sections Association (the BiSA) was founded in 1995 to bring together schools offering immersion and extension in the UK.

LANGUAGE AWARENESS

Virtually all human beings possess an enormous amount of knowledge about and skills in one or more languages. This knowledge, already possessed by learners, can be of great use in learning other languages. Language extension and immersion programmes can make it easier for learners to apply their knowledge and skills to learning further languages. But a great deal of their vast amount of knowledge about their language(s) and how they learnt them is inchoate and not readily available to conscious examination. The difficulty experienced in trying to reflect on their own-language learning, and use, creates further difficulty in applying experiential skills to the task of learning other languages.

Left to their own devices, most learners will not be able to apply much of their linguistic knowledge and skills effectively in the languages classroom, even in extension and immersion programmes. First of all, help is required to make their knowledge explicit, and available to systematic reflection and analysis. Linguistics, the systematic study of language, is one of humankind's most ancient and successful endeavours. Teaching language learners about theoretical linguistics is unlikely to have a positive impact on their success in the languages classroom. But, teaching them about the history of English and other languages they speak – about language families and how they are related to other languages, different writing systems, what languages have in common and how they differ, how languages are used, how language varies between speech communities, how languages change over time – all this can have a positive impact on their success in the languages classroom. The approach can also have a positive impact on learners' self-esteem and their ability to use the languages which they already know more effectively.

Students from all minority ethnic and majority ethnic groups can benefit from learning their own and each other's history. All too often, even minority ethnic students either know little of their own people's history or only know it through the experience of the white majority. They are unaware of the position of their language(s) in the world, of who speaks the same language(s), when and why. Some are unaware of the literatures written in their language(s) and the cultures, histories and values which they mediate. Sometimes people do not even know the names of the languages which they speak. Language awareness programmes can help to empower learners of all 'races', classes, genders, sexuality and needs to use knowledge about themselves as a foundation for further learning, in particular language learning, especially in classrooms where target languages offer opportunities for authentic communication because they are used as a medium of teaching and learning.

BIBLIOGRAPHY

Aitchison, J. (1989) *The Articulate Mammal.* London: Routledge.

Aitchison, J. (1995) *Linguistics: An Introduction.* London: Hodder and Stoughton.

Allen, J. P. B. and Van Buren, P. (1971) *Chomsky: Selected Readings.* Oxford: Oxford University Press.

Austin, J. L., Sbisa, M. and Urmson, J. O. (1975) *How to Do Things with Words.* Oxford: Oxford University Press.

Brown, G. and Yule, G. (1983) *Discourse Analysis.* Cambridge: Cambridge University Press.

Cameron, D. and Bourne, J. (1989) *Grammar, Nation and Citizenship: Kingman in Linguistic and Historical Perspective.* London: Institute of Education, University of London.

Carroll, J. B. and Sapon, S. M. (1959) *Modern Language Aptitude Battery.* New York: The Psychological Corporation and Harcourt Brace Jovanovich.

Chomsky, N. A. (1965) *Aspects of the Theory of Syntax.* Cambridge, Massachusetts: MIT Press.

Chomsky, N. A. (1976) *Reflections on Language.* London: Temple Smith.

Cole, M. (1993) Black and ethnic minority or Asian, black and other minority ethnic: a further note on nomenclature. *Sociology,* 27(4):671–3.

Corder, S. P. (1981) *Error Analysis and Interlanguage.* Oxford: Oxford University Press.

Couillaud, X., Martin-Jones, M., Morawska, A., Reid, E., Saifullah Khan, V. and Smith, G. (1985) *The Other Languages of England.* London: Routledge and Keegan Paul.

Curtis, L. (1984) *Nothing But the Same Old Story: The Roots of Anti-Irish Racism.* Belfast: Sásta.

DENI (1994) *Language Studies: A Report by the Inspectorate.* Belfast: Department of Education, Northern Ireland.

DES (1977) *Modern Languages in Comprehensive Schools.* London: HMSO.

DES (1971) *Circular No 8/71.* London: HMSO.

De Sudea, I. (1988) Pre-vocational courses from 14 onwards. In D. Phillips *Languages in Schools: From Complacency to Conviction.* London:

Centre for Information on Language Teaching and Research.

Dodson, C. J. (1983) Living with two languages. *Journal of Multilingual and Multicultural Development*, 4(6).

Dulay, H. and Burt, M. (1974) You can't learn without goofing: an analysis of children's second language errors. In J. C. Richards (ed.) *Error Analysis*. London: Longman.

Ellis, G and Sinclair, B. (1987) *Training for Learners of English: Learning How to Learn English*. Cambridge: Cambridge University.

Ellis, R. (1985) *Understanding Second Language Acquisition*. Oxford: Oxford University Press.

Fletcher, P. and Garman, M. (eds) (1986) *Language Acquisition*. Cambridge: Cambridge University Press.

Fromkin, V. and Rodman, A. (1993) *An Introduction to Language*. Orlando: Harcourt Brace.

Giglioli, P. (ed.) (1972) *Language and Social Context*. Harmondsworth: Penguin.

Gramsci, A. (1971) *Selections from Prison Notebooks*, ed. and trans. Q. Hoare and G. Nowell Smith. London: Lawrence and Wishart.

Green, P. S. (1976) *York Language Aptitude Test*. York: University of York Language Teaching Centre.

Green, P. S. (1977) Testing for language aptitude. *Journal of the National Association of Language Advisers*, 8.

Gumperz, J. (1968) The speech community. In P. Giglioli (ed.) (1972) *Language and Social Context*. Harmondsworth: Penguin.

Harris, V. (1992) *Fair Enough? Equal Opportunities and Modern Languages*. London: Centre for Information on Language Teaching and Research.

Hawkins, E. (1981) *Modern Languages in the Curriculum*. Cambridge: Cambridge University Press.

Holt, M. (1978) *The Common Curriculum: Its Structure and Style in the Comprehensive School*. London: Routledge and Keegan Paul.

Hornsey, A. (1981) Why a modern language? In J. White *et al.*, *No, Minister: A Critique of the DES Paper 'The School Curriculum'*, London: University of London Institute of Education.

Hudson, R. A. (1996) *Sociolinguistics*. Cambridge: Cambridge University Press.

ILEA Afro-Caribbean Language and Literacy Project (1990) *Language and Power: Language Materials for Students in the Multilingual and Multiethnic Classroom*. London: Harcourt Brace Jovanovich.

ILEA Research and Statistics Branch (1987) *Catalogue of Languages Spoken by ILEA School Students*. London: ILEA.

ILEA Working Party (1984) *Equal Opportunities – Gender: Guidelines for Teachers of Languages*. London: ILEA Languages Centre.

Katzner, K. (1995) *The Languages of the World*. London: Routledge and Keegan Paul.

Keise, C. (1992) Languages. In K. Myers (ed.) *Genderwatch! After the*

Education Reform Act. Cambridge: Cambridge University Press.

Labov, W. (1969) The logic of non-standard English. In P. Giglioli (ed.) (1972) *Language and Social Context.* Harmondsworth: Penguin.

Lawton, D. (1973) *Social Change, Educational Theory and Curriculum Planning.* London: University of London Press.

Levinson, S. C. (1983) *Pragmatics.* Cambridge: Cambridge University Press.

Lightbrown, P. M. and Spada, N. (1993) *How Languages are Learned.* Oxford: Oxford University Press.

Little, A. (1988) *Learning from Developing Countries.* London: Institute of Education.

Lyons, J. (1995) *Linguistic Semantics: An Introduction.* Cambridge: Cambridge University Press.

Naiman, N., Frohlich, M., Stern, H. H. and Todesco, A. (1978) *The Good Language Learner.* Toronto: Ontario Institute for Studies in Education.

Newman, W. I. (1986) Implications of Immersion Education for Foreign Language Teaching in School. Unpublished MA dissertation. London: Institute of Education.

NICC (1993a) *Equal Opportunities in the N. I. Curriculum: Gender Equality (Primary).* Belfast: Northern Ireland Curriculum Council.

NICC (1993b) *Equal Opportunities in the N. I. Curriculum: Gender Equality (Post-Primary).* Belfast: Northern Ireland Curriculum Council.

O'Connor, J. D. (1973) *Phonetics.* Harmondsworth: Penguin.

Phillips, D. (1988) Thirty years of language teaching theory, practice and policy. In *Languages in Schools: From Complacency to Conviction.* London: Centre for Information on Language Teaching and Research.

Pimsleur, P. (1966) *Pimsleur Language Aptitude Battery.* Harcourt Brace Jovanovich.

Richards, J. C. (1984) The secret life of methods. *TESOL Quarterly,* 18 (1).

Saville-Troike, M. (1982) *The Ethnography of Communication.* Oxford: Basil Blackwell.

Searle, J. R. (1969) *Speech Acts.* Cambridge: Cambridge University Press.

SED (1989) *Circular No. 1178.* Edinburgh: Scottish Education Department.

SED (1990) *Circular No. 2/1990.* Edinburgh: Scottish Education Department.

Skehan, P. (1986) The role of foreign language aptitude in a model of school learning. *Language Testing,* 3(2).

SOED (1993) *The Structure and Balance of the Curriculum 5–14.* Edinburgh: The Scottish Office Education Department.

Spender, D. (1980) *Man Made Language.* London: Routledge Keegan Paul.

Stern, H. H. (1983) *Fundamental Concepts of Language Teaching.* Oxford: Oxford University Press.

Stevick, E. V. (1980) *A Way and Ways.* Rowley, Massachusetts: Newbury House.

Stubbs, M. (1983) *Discourse Analysis: The Sociolinguistic Analysis of Natural Language.* Oxford: Basil Blackwell.

Swain, M. and Lapkin, S. (1982) *Evaluating Bilingual Education: a Canadian Case Study.* Clevedon, Avon: Multilingual Matters.

Trim, J. L. M. (1973) Draft outline of a European unit/credit system for modern languages. In *Systems Development in Adult Language Learning.* Strasbourg: Council of Europe.

Trudgill, P. (1974) *Sociolinguistics: An Introduction to Language and Society.* Harmondsworth: Penguin.

Walker, C. A. and Newman, W. I. (1988) Promoting languages for non-specialists. *Inner London Education Authority Languages Centre Bulletin,* Summer: 6–11.

Walker, C. A., Newman, W. I. and Chambers, F. (1995) What teachers believe. *Educational Research,* vol. 37, no. 2, Summer 1995.

Wells, G. (1981) *Learning Through Interaction: The Study of Language Development.* Cambridge: Cambridge University Press.

Wells, G. (1984; 1985) *Language Learning in the Pre-School Years.* Cambridge: Cambridge University Press.

Widdowson, H. G. (1978) *Teaching Language as Communication.* Oxford: Oxford University Press.

Widdowson, H. G. (1983) *Learning Purpose and Language Use.* Oxford: Oxford University Press.

Widdowson, H. G. (1990) *Aspects of Language Teaching.* Oxford: Oxford University Press.

Widdowson, H. G. (1996) *Linguistics.* Oxford: Oxford University Press.

Wilkins, D. A. (1976) *Notional Syllabuses.* Oxford: Oxford University Press.

Yates, A. and Pidgeon, D. A. (1957) *Admission to Grammar Schools.* London: National Foundation for Educational Research.

PART 3

KEY STAGES 3 AND 4: RELIGIOUS EDUCATION, SEX EDUCATION AND GNVQ

CHAPTER 12

Religious education

Ruth Mantin

THE HISTORICAL AND POLITICAL LEGACY OF RE IN BRITAIN

A discussion of the ways in which religious education (RE) can promote equality in the secondary school classroom needs to consider the distinctive challenges presented by this area of the curriculum. Amongst these are the perceptions of RE and the history of RE in Britain. These are linked and together they determine the popular view of RE in schools.

When the state took over full responsibility for the nation's education in 1944, 'Religious Instruction' (as it was then known) was the only compulsory subject on the curriculum. The explanation for this lies in the government's need to reach a compromise with the churches who had previously been responsible for many schools, especially primary schools, in the prevailing ethos in Britain at the time. In the aftermath of the Second World War, there was a popular view that providing children with 'Religious (i.e. Christian) Instruction' was the best way of ensuring that the horrors of the Second World War would not be repeated (Wedderspoon, 1966:19–20). An extract from one of the earliest Agreed Syllabuses illustrates the assumptions underlying the inclusion of 'RI' in the curriculum and the ways in which these were linked to nationalistic, ethnocentric and patriarchal aims.

> The aim of this syllabus is to secure that children attending the schools of the county . . . may gain knowledge of the common Christian faith held by their fathers for nearly 2,000 years; may seek for themselves in Christianity principles which give a purpose to life and a guide to all its problems; and may find inspiration, power, and courage to work for their welfare, and for the growth of God's kingdom. (Surrey County Council Education Committee, 1945)

It is possible to exercise some degree of 'cultural relativity' when considering the socio-political role of 'Religious Instruction' in 1944. It is, however, important to appreciate that many of the ideological imperatives which determined educational policy with regard to religious education in the 1940s were still operating when the Conservative government engineered the 1988 Education Act. Even today, the subject carries with it the idea that the teacher has to be 'committed', i.e. Christian. Many RE teachers have experienced the temptation to lie when someone asks about their occupation. The alternative usually means enduring jokes about vicars or coping with an uncomfortable lapse in the conversation. RE suffers the stigma of not really being an academic subject but, at best, an attempt to provide certain values and beliefs and, at worst, an attempt to indoctrinate children.

The history of religious education in this country is in many ways a justification for such a view. Furthermore, in the debates surrounding the Education Act in 1988, right-wing politicians continued to argue for the importance of the subject on the basis of 'our Christian heritage'. Their perception of RE seems to have changed little from that of the extract quoted above from 1945. There still persists the belief that without the inculcation of Christian belief in the young, their sense of values would suffer and result in the erosion of values in our society.

MULTI-FAITH, PHENOMENOLOGICAL APPROACHES TO RE

Amongst specialists in the subject, however, RE has changed dramatically between the two Education Acts of 1944 and 1988 and beyond. Major influences in the development of the subject have been the secularizing influence of the late twentieth century, the growing plurality of British society and changes in educational philosophy since the 1960s. An important breakthrough came with a report from a Schools Council Project on Religious Education in 1971. The working party involved was chaired by Ninian Smart, who had just initiated the first-ever Religious Studies degree (as opposed to Theology) at Lancaster University. The working party argued that a 'confessional' approach to RE – that is, attempting to nurture children into Christianity – was inappropriate in a school curriculum. They claimed that the only legitimate reasons for religious education's inclusion in the curriculum were educational ones; and they presented such educational arguments on the basis of students' need to understand religion as an aspect of the human experience without, in any way, being expected to accept or reject any particular religious belief. They were, in effect, applying to the school curriculum the same approach demonstrated in the Religious Studies degree. This approach was given the rather unwieldy title of the 'phenomenological' approach because it advocated the attempt to understand religion, in its diversity of expression, as a phenomenon of human experience. The working party made it clear, however, that such understanding could not be achieved by simply knowing the facts and figures about religious phenomena. In order to understand a diversity of world-views, they argued, one needs to exercise 'imaginative self-transcendence' (Schools Council, 1971:22). In this way, students are asked to enter into an understanding of the experiential dimension of a diversity of religious traditions, in the same way that art or music requires them to understand the experience and motivations of artists and musicians. The aim of religious education then became that of understanding religious traditions on their own terms and, in the process, developing the skills to make informed judgements about religious phenomena. Following from this development, the Shap Working Party on World Religions in Education[1] was formed to promote effective, multi-faith RE. As a result, the nature of the subject underwent a radical transformation – at least among the specialists and theorists. This 'revolution' had not, however, touched many classrooms over twenty years later!

RE AND THE 1988 ACT

The 1988 Education Act seemed an ideal opportunity for the educational and non-confessional nature of the subject to be confirmed. Unfortunately, however, this opportunity was lost. The debate about the subject excluded educationalists other than those connected to the Church of England. It was dominated by right-wing politicians whose insistence upon the predominance of Christianity in religious education reflected their concern to transmit in schools an ideology of 'British heritage' and 'British culture' which excluded a recognition of plurality and diversity. The resulting legislation was again a compromise. On the one hand, there was some recognition of the educational and multi-faith status of the subject – it was, at least, now referred to as religious education. On the other hand, however, the syllabuses were still to be agreed locally, rather than nationally; parents and teachers were still given the right to withdraw from the subject; and it continued to be linked with compulsory daily collective worship, thus conveying the government's understanding of the subject as playing a confessional role. This compromise was expressed in the wording of the Act: 'New locally agreed syllabuses must reflect the fact that religious traditions in Great Britain are in the main Christian whilst taking account of the teaching and practices of other principal religions in Great Britain' (Education Reform Act, 1988:8). Behind this compromise lay attempts by right-wing politicians, especially in the House of Lords, to create legislation to ensure that RE was inculcating Christian beliefs and values (Alves, 1991). These politicians had even more influence on the law governing Collective Worship. Despite a wealth of research indicating that Collective Worship had no educational role in state schools, and despite calls for the abolition of daily compulsory worship coming from several Christian organizations, the Conservative government succeeded in retaining and even strengthening the legal requirements for compulsory daily worship in schools. Furthermore, they included the statement that it was required to be 'wholly or mainly of a broadly Christian character'. (Education Reform Act 1988:7(1) and (2)). There is not space in this chapter to explore all the implications of the requirements for Collective Worship. For many theorists in RE, it is essential to emphasize the distinction between religious education, an educational subject on the curriculum which is the responsibility of the RE teacher, and Collective Worship, which is the responsibility of the head-teacher and governors. In all the relevant publications resulting from the 1988 Act, however, the last Conservative government made it clear that they understood them to be 'joined at the hip'. This is one of the many ways in which that government revealed their intentions to reinstate the confessional and ethnocentric aims of RE. John Hull, editor of the *British Journal of Religious Education* at the time and a Christian theologian, has been an influential critic of government policy on RE and Collective Worship (Hull, 1993). He represents the views of many, including those within Christianity, who reject the attempts of right-wing politicians to 'hijack' Christianity in order to promote their own ideology. There is now a Labour government but, at the time of writing this chapter, we are still awaiting a change in policy with regard to RE and Collective Worship.

The historical and political legacy of religious education in this country, and the debates still surrounding its role and purpose, illustrate some of the challenges facing teachers of RE who wish to engage in an education which promotes equality. Further challenges are presented by the nature of religion itself. The Conservative government's policy in promoting religious education in order to convey a sense of 'British Christian heritage' is just one small example of the many ways in which religion has been used by those in power to control and exploit others. Religion is a powerful medium of social discourse; it can operate to legitimize a particular view of society, often to perpetuate situations of injustice and oppression. Some of the most obvious examples of this are the roles of religion in maintaining slavery, colonialism, apartheid, the caste system and the subordination of women. As the feminist writer Budapest has expressed, most succinctly: 'The easiest and most efficient way for small numbers to oppress large numbers of people is to sell them a religion' (Christ and Plaskow, 1989:271).

There remains, therefore, a pressing need to justify the place of religious education in the secondary school curriculum at all, let alone its role in promoting equality. Nevertheless, the argument of this chapter is that if taught as an educational subject, religious education has the potential to make an important and distinctive contribution to students' education, to their understanding of the ways in which power operates to marginalize and dominate others and – significantly – to the promotion of equality. In making this argument I intend to address two central aspects: first, the presentation of a diversity of religious traditions, cultures and groups; and second, the acknowledgement of the students' own world-views in relation to those of others. This includes a consideration of both the content of the subject and the means of students' learning. In both cases, the emphasis is on the importance of process rather than product.

As has already been indicated, one of the most significant developments in religious education in the last 25 years is the change of content, from solely Christian to multi-faith. Along with this came a change in the perception of the values the subject was expected to instil in its students. For example, one of the last Agreed Syllabuses to be produced before the 1988 Education Act claimed that the aim of RE was: 'To acquire knowledge of and gain understanding of, and respect for, the beliefs of others. To help to develop positive attitudes towards, and a sensitive understanding of, the demands of living in a multi-faith society' (London Borough of Brent, 1986).

Many specialists in religious education are proud of the 'pioneering' work done in multi-faith RE in the 1970s. They feel, with some justification, that by celebrating diversity religious education makes a distinctive contribution to an education which challenges discrimination on the bases of 'race', culture or ethnic background. In 1985, the Swann Report *Education For All* cited religious education (when taught from a phenomenological and multi-faith perspective) as having 'a central role in preparing students for life in today's multi-racial Britain and can also lead them to a greater understanding of the diversity of the global community. RE can also contribute towards challenging and countering the influence of racism in our society' (Swann, 1985:496).

We need to remember, however, that the Swann Report was criticized by anti-racist educationalists for promoting a 'multi-cultural' education which failed to address the need to understand the processes by which racism is created, institutionalized and perpetuated. As part of such a multi-cultural education, multi-faith RE can, therefore, contribute to the misguided theory that racism is the result of ignorance rather than misinformation. At its worst, multi-faith RE can be presented in terms of 'us' and 'them' and thereby actually reinforce tokenist, ethnocentric, stereotypical or even racist attitudes. While acknowledging these dangers, this chapter would nevertheless want to claim that a multi-faith RE which fulfilled the ideals of the phenomenological approach advocated by Ninian Smart and others back in the 1970s still has much to offer an education which promotes equality.

Unless schools present students with a diversity of world-views and cultures in ways which affirm and celebrate such diversity, they are engaging in 'racism by omission'. The inclusion of a variety of religious traditions in the curriculum signals to the students that they are worthy of attention. The alternative is to convey a powerful message of silence which declares that only one culture – the dominant culture – is to be acknowledged. In order to ensure that a multi-faith religious education contributes to rather than undermines the promotion of equality, we need to consider certain criteria when approaching the teaching of religious traditions.

Approaches to teaching world religions

When teaching a religious tradition, we need to ensure that we are representing it accurately in all its diversity and not stereotyping it according to one viewpoint within the tradition or to assumptions and preconceptions from outside.

When presenting Islam, for example, we need to be conscious of the legacy of slander and misunderstanding between the Muslim world and the West (Tames, 1982). This heritage has resulted in a form of discrimination now recognized as 'Islamophobia'. Muslims frequently point out that Christian 'extremists' are perceived and portrayed as being on the margins of Christianity whereas any example of violent behaviour exhibited by Muslims is regarded as the 'norm' of Islam. The danger is, of course, that the more messages young British Muslims receive that their tradition is being threatened then, understandably, the more defensive they become. Religious education therefore needs to show that Islam embraces many different viewpoints and forms of expression. Students need to appreciate that the word 'Islam' comes from the word for peace and that, from a Muslim perspective, peace, harmony, forgiveness and justice are central to the distinctive nature of the Muslim world-view (Brine and Riyami, in Erricker, 1993:56–8). The most common approach to an introduction to Islam is through a study of 'The Five Pillars' – Faith, Prayer, Fasting, Charity and Pilgrimage. Such an approach tends to reinforce rather than challenge the stereotype of Islam as a legalistic, judgemental and restrictive religion. Futhermore, most Muslims do not use the phrase 'The Five Pillars'! A discussion of the meaning of 'peace' (Hunt, in Erricker, 1993:98–100) or an exploration of the symbolism of Islamic art would be a much more appropriate approach to understanding Islam on its own terms.

Likewise, when approaching Judaism, we need to be fully aware of the difficulties involved in presenting an understanding of Jewish perspectives when most of us have been conditioned by a culture based on Christianity. The Christian scriptures were written at a time when Christianity was forging its identity in opposition to its parent religion. The debates reflected there have been used to fuel and justify anti-Judaism ever since. Jesus was a Jew, as were the disciples and first Christians. As Christianity emerged as a new religion it needed to assure the Roman Empire that it was not a threat. In the gospels, therefore, the blame for Jesus' death is moved away from the Roman authorities – despite the fact that crucifixion was a punishment administered only by them – and towards the Jewish community. The name 'Judas' comes from the Greek word for 'the Jews'. The fact that the Jewish community has been persecuted and oppressed for centuries, and the history of the Holocaust and the current resurgence of Neo-Nazi movements across Europe, make a discussion of these issues an essential aspect of an education for equality. A religious education which provides an understanding of Judaism on its own terms, and consciously counters the misinformation which sustains anti-Judaism, makes an important contribution to such an education.

The complex relationship between Christianity and Judaism – for instance, the fact that they share some of the same scriptures – presents particular challenges to the process of presenting Judaism on its own terms (Cole and Mantin, 1994:76–8). Just the use of the term 'Old Testament' projects onto Judaism the Christian belief that the 'testament' or covenant at the centre of the Jewish world-view has been invalidated and superseded by the 'New Testament' brought by Jesus. The phrase 'Old Testament' should, therefore, never be used when discussing the Jewish scriptures within a Jewish context. The debates between Jewish Christians and non-Christian Jews which are reflected in the Christian scriptures present Judaism as a legalistic religion which cannot provide salvation and cannot allow for forgiveness or atonement. This view still determines the way in which many RE teachers understand contemporary Judaism. The writings of Judaism itself, however, present a very different perception of

Judaism then and now. Salvation is not dependent upon the keeping of laws but is given by God. The keeping of *Torah* – usually translated as 'Law' but actually meaning something much wider than this to encompass a whole way of life – is the Jewish community's response to God's act of grace. This is expressed in the joyful and exuberant manner in which the giving of *Torah* is celebrated by the Jewish community.

The voices of different groups within the traditions must be heard. This is, for many reasons, especially important when presenting Christianity. The Conservative government's use of the concept of 'our Christian heritage' is just one in a long list of examples of the ways in which Christianity has been used to sanction the dominant culture since the fourth century when Emperor Constantine appropriated Christianity to serve his political ends (Kee, 1982). Paradoxically, however, central Christian doctrines present a belief in God as incarnate in a Person who identified with those on the margins of society, with the poor, the despised and the dispossessed. This Person rejected all attempts to invest him with political power but was arrested, humiliated, flogged and put to death by torture by the ruling powers. As a result, many Christians have experienced Christ as the embodiment of the stuggle against inequality and injustice. This inherent paradox in the Christian tradition is one of the reasons for its remarkable diversity. It is therefore important that RE teachers resist the pressure, applied by right-wing politicians, to use the teaching of Christianity as an aspect of dominant discourse. In order to present an accurate and educationally valid understanding of the Christian tradition it must be shown as a world religion which embraces a wide diversity of 'race', class, culture, sexuality and ethnic identity. Likewise, British Christianity should not be presented, exclusively, as a white, middle-class phenomenon. There is a growing collection of resource material which can be used to reflect the fact that religious traditions in this country are in the main Christian through an exploration of black British Christianity. Some examples are given at the end of this chapter. (Further illustrations of possible approaches to the teaching of Christianity within the context of an education for equality are presented later in this discussion.)

We need also to ask ourselves whether we are teaching about 'living' religions, portraying contemporary communities, or just a record of past history. We have to monitor carefully whether, within the limits of our own perspective, we represent religious traditions in an equally fair manner or convey value judgements in our teaching. When used to carry a sense of 'them' and 'us', multi-faith RE can reinforce rather than challenge ethnocentric attitudes. If teachers try to 'explain' religious traditions by comparing them with aspects of Christianity, they are often conveying the view that Christianity is the norm against which all other religions must be judged.

The accusation of 'idolatry' is still levelled at Hinduism by many Westerners and, in particular, by Christians. We need to ensure that Hindu practices and beliefs are approached from within the context of the Hindu world-view. An exploration of Hindu religious art and symbolism, or the implications of teachings about reincarnation and *karma*, are appropriate ways into understanding Hinduism. Similarly, Buddhism needs to be introduced through an appreciation of its teaching and world-view. Buddhist teachings about the importance of the mind and the rejection of 'belief' in favour of experience often appeal to students. A discussion of the causes of suffering, or the view that everything is subject to change, can provide an interesting and valid introduction to Buddhist teaching and practice. A consideration of the distinctive perspective of Sikhism is of particular interest to those RE teachers who wish promote equality because of its emphasis on issues of equality and social justice. At the end of this chapter I will provide some suggestions for resources for this 'perspective-led' approach to multi-faith RE.

For those engaged in developing anti-oppressive education, however, a religious education which fulfils the ideals of a phenomenological approach to the study of religion still presents us with a dilemma. We are concerned with all forms of discrimination on the bases of not only 'race' but also gender, social class, ability and sexual orientation. How, therefore, are we to reconcile our aim to present religious traditions on their own terms with the fact that most of these traditions include implicit assumptions or explicit teachings which directly contradict the aims of an education which promotes equality? How are we to respond to the religious teaching that men and women are ontologically different with regard to such qualities as 'authority'; that homosexuality is an aberration or 'sin'; that poverty should be the object of charity rather than an issue of social justice and that people with disabilities should be shown compassion rather than granted their civil rights? To recognize the potential conflict between anti-oppressive teaching and the phenomenological approach which encourages imaginative empathy, is to avoid the suggestion that to understand a position is to condone it, and also to avoid the suggestion that to appreciate another's world-view on their own terms is to exclude the possibility of critical analysis and evaluation. I would like to suggest a response to this dilemma which does not deny the reality of its challenge, nor betray the ideals of a phenomenological approach to the study of religion. At the same time I would argue that this response provides students with a further understanding of the ways in which power operates to marginalize and oppress others. This opportunity is offered by the importance of an understanding of story and narrative in the study of religion.

The phenomenological approach to the study of religion made an important contribution to religious education by demonstrating the importance of the mythological dimension of religious traditions. In doing so, it emphasized the distinction between 'myth', as commonly used to indicate a falsehood, and 'myth' as a technical definition, meaning a narrative expression of reality. In this technical sense, therefore, the 'truth' of the narrative lies not in its historicity but in the extent to which it expresses 'the way things really are'. As a result, RE now emphasizes the importance of story in humankind's search to make sense of the world. The aim of RE includes helping students appreciate that there are many different ways of seeing the truth, expressed through many different stories. This central aspect of RE can make a distinctive contribution to an anti-oppressive education because a further exploration of the role of story, symbol and language can involve students in the process of understanding how power operates in society, power which creates and sustains inequality. They can be shown that the story which is told the most and with the most authority can determine the way in which the world is understood so that 'history is told by the winners'. Those who have power can prevent others from telling their stories, can render them 'invisible' or 'demonized'. The reclaiming of their stories, history and world-view is therefore a vital aspect in the struggle of all marginalized groups to claim their right to equality (Christ, 1995). When this approach to RE is emphasized, the very fact that religion is often used as the sanction for oppressive structures can be used to facilitate the exploration of the processes by which a dominant group can subordinate others. Furthermore, this exploration is undertaken within the religious traditions and is therefore a legitimate aspect of the religious diversity to be explored in the classroom. A good example of this is the development of Liberation Theology in Christianity.

The feminist study of religion

The exploration of story can also benefit from the feminist study of religion which has made a distinctive contribution to an understanding of the power of narrative, symbol and language. Feminist scholars of religion have provided particular insight into the role of story and language in humanity's understanding of self, reality and patterns of domination. In their critique of traditions as androcentric,[2] feminist scholars lay special emphasis on the means by which language not only reflects but can actually create our perceptions of reality. As one feminist theologian argues:

> The feminist critique of religious language is an extremely sophisticated one, for it is based on a recognition of the fundamental importance of language to human existence. With Ludwig Wittgenstein, feminists would say 'The limits of one's language are the limits of one's world' and with Martin Heidegger, 'Language is the house of being'. We do not so much use language as we are used by it. Since we are all born into a world which is already linguistic, in which the naming process has already taken place, we only own our world to the extent that the naming that has occurred is our naming. (McFague, 1982:8)

Feminist scholars of religion cite the exclusion of women from the process of story-telling and naming as the means by which they have been denied not only authority and leadership but their very personhood, their very be-ing.[3] At the most basic level, therefore, the feminist critique of religious traditions calls for a reclaiming of herstory: 'We have learned that our stories have been dominated by the fathers, Augustine, Moses, Muhammad, Shiva and that we must reclaim the mothers too: Hildegard, Vashti, Rabia and Devi, if those stories are to be complete' (Harris and Moran, 1989:45). This reclaiming of stories does, of course, have implications for the resources and content of RE and I will discuss some relevant examples of classroom practice later in the chapter.

A religious education which promotes equality needs to ensure that its presentation of religious communities includes *all* their members – whatever their gender, 'race', ethnic identity, sexual orientation, social class, physical or mental ability. The analysis of story, however, goes further than this and raises the question of why and how certain groups could be marginalized and rendered 'invisible' in the first place. To engage students in the reclaiming of suppressed stories is to involve them in the stuggle against oppression because 'To exist humanly is to name the self, the world and God . . . The liberation of language is rooted in the liberation of ourselves' (Daly, 1985:8).

The feminist study of religion, however, has implications not only for women but for all marginalized groups. Its critique of patriarchy, sexism and androcentrism in religious traditions is undertaken not simply to reverse patterns of domination and give power to women but to challenge the structures of power themselves. A feminist analysis of language is undertaken within the context of a challenge to all dualistic modes of thought. Feminist scholars of religion argue that the male/female dichotomy is the 'prototype' for all forms of oppression, and they provide a critique of androcentric language which defines maleness as the norm of humanity. By the same process, they reject any world-view which perpetuates a dualism of the 'Absolute' and the 'Other', through which one group – be it male, white, Christian, wealthy, ruling class, able, heterosexual, or human – is presented as the Absolute over and against the Other, onto which all the negative aspects of a dualistic perception of reality are projected (Ruether, 1983:20). Feminist scholars of religion are now aware that many of their early assumptions about 'women's experience' were ethnocentric and universalist. The powerful critiques provided by black feminism or 'womanism' (as it is termed by Alice Walker), and by women from the so-called 'developing world', have made feminist theory address more carefully the issue of difference (Plaskow and Christ, 1989).

In its awareness of the enormous influence of language on perceptions of reality, and the role of narrative in constructing and sustaining structures of oppression, the feminist study of religion seems to share some of the concerns of postmodernist thought. A growing number of secular feminist thinkers are identifying themselves as postmodernist, though often on their own terms, 'blurring boundaries without burning bridges' (Braidotti, 1994:4). The central area of debate between feminists and postmodernists is the acceptance of 'thorough-going relativism' and the nihilistic implications of the theories of the latter, which deny any political agency.

It is, of course, important for the advocates of anti-oppressive education to acknowledge the contribution of postmodernist thought to an understanding of the structures of power, and to the importance of acknowledging difference, but the very fact that contributors to this book are arguing for an education which promotes equality means that they are not prepared to ascribe the same degree of relativity to all 'metanarratives'. There is a very real danger that postmodernism's denial of the validity of any overarching theories or ideas which can explain or effect social transformation could benefit those who profit most from the existing structures of domination, injustice and repression (Cole and Hill, 1995, 1996; Hill *et al.* (eds) 1999). Cole and Hill provide a compelling argument for the necessity of an anti-oppressive education to affirm a metanarrative of radical democracy:

> . . . the danger lies in the fact that postmodernism, by definition, lacks the enlightenment project of 'emancipation in a general sense'. In addition, in its rhetoric of resistance as opposed to a structural analysis of and prescriptions for social change, it undermines progressive social theory and plays into the hands of anti-socialist and indeed anti-feminist forces. (Cole and Hill, 1996:47; see also Kelly, 1999)[4]

A 'HERMENEUTICS OF SUSPICION' IN THE CLASSROOM

The challenge to systems of oppression made by the feminist study of religion can be used by religious education to provide a distinctive opportunity for education to help students construct their own critiques of dominant discourse. The feminist scholar Elisabeth Schüssler Fiorenza has developed a methodology, originally applied to biblical interpretation, which she terms a 'hermeneutics of suspicion' (Schüssler Fiorenza, 1983:9). This methodology already has considerable influence within and beyond the feminist study of religion and, I would argue, has implications for an education for equality in the secondary school curriculum. Schüssler Fiorenza argues that, because all religious texts are written from an androcentric perspective, they must be approached with suspicion and the interpreter must 'read the silences' in order to reclaim those who have been excluded from their stories. Schüssler Fiorenza developed her ideas from the work of liberation theologians such as Metz, and speaks of the power of 'dangerous memories' (Schüssler Fiorenza, 1983:31). These memories are 'dangerous' to those in power because they provide the oppressed classes with an alternative and challenging world-view, in which the patterns of domination are not just 'the way things are'. A 'hermeneutics of suspicion' can therefore be applied to stories to challenge the ways in which they demonize, marginalize or render invisible any marginalized group. Religious education can introduce students to the processes involved in a hermeneutics of suspicion by approaching stories with questions such as 'Who is telling this story and why?', 'Who is missing from these stories?'. By exploring the ways in which these debates are taking place within religious traditions, RE can at the same time provide students with the approaches involved in identifying and challenging the ways in which structures of oppression are created and sustained.

Here are some examples of material which could be used in the classroom to fulfil these aims. They relate to material which is suggested in many Agreed Syllabuses and/or link in with material covered in other parts of the curriculum, such as history and geography. Due to the absence of a National Curriculum for RE, however, there remains some possible flexibility about the precise year in which these activities could take place.

Year 7 – The Whales' Song (Sheldon, 1990)

'The Whales' Song' , written by Diane Sheldon and beautifully illustrated by Gary Blythe, provides students with an opportunity to explore the power of 'dominant discourse' and to appreciate the influence of 'metanarratives' upon the operations of power at an appropriate level. This remarkable book is multi-layered in its appeal and, whilst it can be used at Key Stage 2, presents issues which are suitable for discussion at Key Stage 3. It is a story about the power of story, and begins with the central character, Lily, listening to the stories of her grandmother. She learns that once the ocean was filled with whales who were the most wondrous creatures you could imagine. Her grandmother tells of how she would offer gifts to them and receive something in return;

sometimes they would sing to her. The grandmother's story is interrupted by the angry remarks of Uncle Frederick, who provides a very different story. He claims that whales were important only 'for their meat and blubber' and tells the grandmother not fill Lily's head with 'nonsense'. Lily is left to discover for herself which of these stories is 'true' when she has her encounter with the whales, listens to their song and hears them call her name.

In exploring the ideas presented by this book, students can appreciate the ways in which different stories reflect different world-views, and the ways in which these can be used to sanction and maintain structures of oppression. The story told by Uncle Frederick has made the most impact on recorded history, and conveys the assumption that humans have the power to dominate and exploit the 'natural' (non-human) world. The acceptance of this story means disaster for the whales, indeed the entire planet. The grandmother offers an alternative story, now being heard by a growing number of people, which defines the positive interdependence of all forms of life, and therefore the necessity of mutual respect.

Year 7/8 – Christian hunger cloths

The teaching of Christianity presents particular challenges for any RE teacher and especially one concerned with the promotion of equality. Most teachers and students bring a great deal of 'luggage' with them when approaching this subject (Cole and Mantin, 1994:7–20). As has already been discussed, this subject carries a legacy of attempts to impose a 'Christian heritage' rather than engage in an educational exploration of the largest and most powerful religious tradition in the world. The Christian 'hunger cloths', now available from several sources (more details at the end of this chapter), provide excellent resources for a presentation of Christianity which engages students in effective religious education and in reflection upon issues of social justice. The hunger cloths are produced each year at Lent and distributed by organizations such as CAFOD and Traidcraft. Their themes reflect the concerns of Liberation Theology and most of them come from the so-called developing countries.

The Haiti hunger cloth is particularly appropriate for Key Stage 3. In bright and bold images, a black, Haitian Christ is shown crucified on the Tree of Life. Spreading from the branches of this tree are biblical images which depict the current political struggle for social justice in Haiti. Jesus is shown to be present in all these images, suffering with the victims of state oppression. In exploring the symbolism of the images presented here, students can develop their understanding of such complex Christian doctrines as Incarnation, Redemption and Atonement. At the same time, however, they are also presented with a view of Jesus at the centre of political struggle against oppression. For many students, just the representation of Christ as black will present an immediate challenge to their preconceptions.

In a Latin American hunger cloth, Jesus as Risen Lord is depicted in the midst of those engaged in the struggle for human rights, including street children and Amerindian indigenous peoples. In the background are scenes which express the conquest and exploitation of the American Indians by Europeans, and the resulting poverty and injustice. This representation of Christ provides a very different story from that presented by those who wish to equate Christianity with the *status quo* and with the values of the ruling classes.

Year 9 – Native American world-views and the message of Chief Seattle

An exploration of Native American spirituality lends itself to cross-curriculum projects in Humanities in Key Stage 3. It also allows students to explore alternative narratives and the suppression of stories by those in power. The message of Chief Seattle provides an excellent insight into the world-view of Native Americans and provokes discussion of the value (now recognized) in a spirituality which was suppressed by the white Europeans in the name of 'civilization'. Accounts of Chief Seattle's words are reproduced in several sources but a particularly evocative version is provided by the picture book *Brother Eagle, Sister Sky* (Jeffers, 1992). This version also uses inclusive language.

Year 10 – Women in Islam

As already discussed, RE teachers need to approach the study of Islam with great care and sensitivity in order to counter the stereotypes and misinformation provided by the media. Condemnation of the treatment of women in Islam is too often the result of racism rather than feminist analysis. This important issue can, however, be explored from within a Muslim perspective whilst also engaging students in a hermeneutics of suspicion. Many Muslim women argue that they have more freedom and respect within Islam than women can experience in a Western culture which exploits and threatens them. A growing number of female Muslim writers, however, are challenging the processes by which the authority due to women in the *Qur'an* and the example of the Prophet has been denied by the supression of history and the patriarchal interpretation of texts. The work of Fatima Mernissi (Mernissi, 1991, 1993, 1996) is helpful here, and can be adapted to provide source material for the students. The issue of women and religion is being addressed by a growing number of new publications on ethical issues in a variety of traditions. Some suggestions for resources are given at the end of the chapter.

RE, EQUALITY AND STUDENTS' OWN EXPERIENCES

The relationship between an education which promotes equality and the exploration of narrative also includes the students' own stories. The work of the 'Children and Worldviews' research project[5] argues for an approach to RE whereby children are able to voice their responses to religious concepts on the basis of their own experience. Although this research is currently undertaken with primary schoolchildren only, its findings have enormous implications for the secondary school. Publications emerging from this research – such as Clive Erricker *et al.* (1997), *The Education of the Whole Child* – claim that the imposition of religio-political attitudes upon the structure of the curriculum limits the breadth and depth of the students' learning. Elsewhere, Clive Erricker (a director of the 'Children and Worldviews' project) affirms the relevance of exploring religious stories with children who have a secular world-view (see Erricker, in Starkings, 1993). He argues that young people cannot engage in an informed analysis of religion unless they understand its role in humanity's attempt to make sense of its experience; furthermore, that the relevance of studying religious stories relates to the students' own experiences as well as the issue of equality.

Religion, Erricker argues, is a language expressed in terms of beliefs and practices. Religious traditions are the vehicles whereby 'big stories' about the world and human existence are maintained and conveyed. Within these stories are smaller ones, parables, myths, historical accounts and others which are the bricks from which the institutions of religion are constructed. If this enterprise were solely a religious one, it would be hard to justify the exercise of involving the students in studying it. But we all engage in this enterprise of establishing an identity and sense of belonging. We all map the world in this existential way. Beliefs, practices, rituals, objects of particular significance that act as icons, stories through which we relate ourselves to others are the concrete manifestation of our world – building and establishing meaning in our lives. We all live by and within stories. Religious traditions are libraries of stories which are acted out and lived out by those who inhabit them, but we all inhabit them somewhere by virtue of being human.

Thus the patterning of children's lives can engage with others who recognize and live out a story different from their own. Communication across these domains is not only fruitful but necessary for individuals and for societies because it promotes understanding, respect, self-reflection and positive challenge. Erricker identifies our primary educational concern as that of helping students develop the skills and attitudes by which they can do this.

In order to achieve these aims, Erricker maintains, we need to ensure that we are truly engaging with young people's experience. It is very easy to pay lip-service to the importance of starting from students' experience while in fact we are excluding and disempowering them. We need to consider who is actually setting the agenda for these explorations. Research undertaken by the 'Children and Worldviews' highlights these issues and illustrates the ways in which the curriculum denies students' own voices. The project therefore argues that the starting point for any exploration of religious narrative must be the students' own stories, their own attempts to make sense of the world, especially in the face of challenges such as conflict or loss. Only then can the process of religious education be justified in a secular world, and the integrity of the students be respected. In the introduction to the most recent Teachers' Handbook produced by The Shap Working Party (Erricker, 1993), this student-centred approach is aligned with a phenomenological approach which attempts to understand the distinctive perspective of each faith community on its own terms, whilst acknowledging the enormous diversity within that community.

CONCLUSION

I would like to conclude by arguing that this student-centred, phenomenological approach to RE, coupled with the insights of liberationist and feminist studies of religion, provides a distinctive contribution to an education which promotes equality and is actively anti-oppressive.

The twin requirements of empathy and critical reflection, so central to good religious education, align with the notion of equality. A phenomenological approach to RE entails empathizing with the view of the believer and attempting to gain an insider's perspective. This is an extremely subtle process involving not only our rational intelligence but also the capacity to reflect on our own understanding in a critical way and take ours and others' feelings into account. Properly deployed, this achieves much more than accurate factual knowledge because it is imperative we become aware of why people see the world differently, and how important commitment to these understandings is. It is not just a matter of knowing about different ideas or practices but recognizing and acknowledging different identities. As a result, just teaching about religions is no more than tokenism. We must radically re-assess the learning process we undertake so that perceptions and attitudes are changed. The oppression of any group is a result of seeing them as 'other', as less human than we are. If this attitude is not confronted it does not matter how much information is conveyed, nothing will change. It follows that a phenomenological approach is not value-free but heavily value-laden. These values are, most often, in direct opposition to the values traditionally harnessed to the political direction of our society. Despite its dubious history, therefore, religious education has the potential to be a highly political, subversive and progressive activity.

ACKNOWLEDGEMENT

I would like to thank Clive Erricker for his help in preparing this chapter.

RECOMMENDED READING

I recommend as the most useful book for any RE teacher wishing to address issues of equality and diversity whilst presenting religious communities from within their own perspective, Erricker, C. *et al.* (eds) (1993) *Teaching World Religions – A Teacher's Handbook* produced by the Shap Working Party on World Religions in Education, published by Heinemann. This handbook provides excellent insights into the distinctive world-view of a religious tradition, usually contributed by a member of that faith community, whilst also recognizing the diversity and dynamism of such a tradition. Articles also provide many practical ideas for and illustrations of a 'perspective-led' approach to RE in the classroom, some of which have been referred to in this chapter. The scope of the handbook includes far more than the six major religious traditions. It explores, for instance, Rastafarianism and New Age spirituality. There is also an extensive chapter on resources.

The following books raise important issues for the theory of religious education but do not fully endorse the approach advocated in this chapter:

Gates, B. (ed.) (1996) *Authority and Freedom in Religious Education.* London: Cassell.
Jackson, R. (1997) *Religious Education: An Interpretive Approach.* Sevenoaks: Hodder and Stoughton.

The following are recommended as teachers' introductions to the major world religions:

Cole, W. O. (1994) *Teach Yourself Sikhism.* London: Hodder and Stoughton.
Cole, W. O. and Mantin, R. (1994) *Teaching Christianity.* Oxford: Heinemann.
Cush, D. (1994) *Buddhism – A Students' Approach to World Religions.* London: Hodder and Stoughton.
Jackson, R. and Kingsley, D. (1982) *Approaches to Hinduism.* London: Murray.
Nasr, S. H. (1994; 2nd edn) *The Ideals and Realities of Islam.* London: Aquarian.
Unterman, A. (1996; 2nd edn) *Jews – Their Religious Beliefs and Practices.* Brighton: Sussex Academic Press.

The following are recommended as introductions to the feminist study of religion:

Christ, C. and Plaskow, J. (eds) (1989; 2nd edn) *Womanspirit Rising – A Feminist Reader in Religion.* San Francisco: Harper and Row.

Isherwood, L. and McEwan, D. (1993) *Introducing Feminist Theology.* Sheffield: Sheffield Academic Press.

Plaskow, J. and Christ, C. (eds) (1989) *Weaving The Visions – New Patterns in Feminist Spirituality.* San Francisco: Harper and Row.

RESOURCES FOR THE CLASSROOM

There are a growing number of good resources for multi-faith RE being produced for the secondary school. This list is not exhaustive but includes material I have found to be useful for RE which promotes equality.

Key Stage 3

Religions of the World (Macdonald)

This series was one of the first to present Christianity as a multicultural world religion. It is still a very good resource. The books are mostly written by members of the faith community. They are large and colourful and the visual images emphasize the diversity within the tradition, challenging stereotypical preconceptions. The series includes a sensitive approach to new religious movements such as the Rastafarians and Hare Krishna Movement.

> *The Buddhist World,* Anne Bancroft
> *The Christian World,* Alan Brown
> *The Hindu World,* Patricia Bahre
> *The Jewish World,* Douglas Charing
> *The Muslim World,* Richard Tames
> *The Sikh World,* D. Singh and A. Smith

Religions through Festivals (Longman: General Editor, Clive Erricker)

These books attempt to understand festivals from within the perspective of the religious tradition.

> *Buddhist Festivals,* Holly and Peter Connolly
> *Christian Festivals,* R. O. Hughes
> *Hindu Festivals,* Robert Jackson
> *Jewish Festivals,* Clive Lawton
> *Muslim Festivals,* Alan Brine
> *Sikh Festivals,* Davinder Kaur Babraa

Growing Up (Longman: Series Editor, Jean Holm)

These books attempt to present a 'child's-eye' view of what it means to be a member of a faith. They claim to draw on close contact and consultation with the faith communities. The text is rather dense and could benefit from more colour illustrations but provides some good use of children's quotations.

> *Growing up in Christianity,* Jean Holm and Ronnie Ridley
> *Growing up in Hinduism,* Jacqueline Hirst with Geeta Pandey

Growing up in Islam, Janet Ardava
Growing up in Sikhism, Andrew Clutterbuck

Discovering Religion (Heinemann: Sue Penney)
This series covers the six major religions. It has been recently revised to provide more colour and more emphasis on religions as living traditions.

Skills in Religious Studies (Heinemann: J. Fageant and S. Mercier)
Books 1 to 3 cover the six major world religions with a skills-based approach.

Interpreting Religions (Heinemann: General Editors, Judith Everington and Robert Jackson)
This is a new series, emerging from the ethnographic research undertaken by the Warwick RE Project in faith communities. The books focus on the lives of young people in the communities and invite the students to draw on their own experience to interpret and reflect on the evidence presented to them.

Key Stage 3/4
Seeking Religion (Hodder and Stoughton: Series Editor, J. F. Aylett)
These are colourful, well-presented books which claim to be 'planned to provide a truly multi-cultural mixed ability approach to RE'.
   The Buddhist Experience, Melvyn Thompson
   The Christian Experience, John Aylett
   The Hindu Experience, Liz Aylett
   The Jewish Experience, Liz Aylett
   The Muslim Experience, John Aylett
   The Sikh Experience, Philip Emmett

GCSE
Themes in Religion (Longman: Series Editor, Clive Erricker)
This series emphasizes the diversity and living impact of each religion.
   Buddhism, Lilian Weatherly
   Christianity, R. O. Hughes
   Hinduism, S. C. Mercier
   Islam, Alan Brine
   Judaism, Clive Lawton and Clive Erricker
   Sikhism, Roger Butler

Examining Religions ((Revised Edition) Heinemann)
   Christianity, Joe Jenkins
   Islam, Rosalyn Kendrick
   Judaism, Ayre Forte

Ethical Issues (Key Stage 4 and GCSE)
Moral Issues in Six Religions, W. O. Cole. Heinemann.
Contemporary Moral Issues, Joe Jenkins. Heinemann.
(This includes a sensitive approach to different expressions of sexuality and addresses issues of racism, sexism, disability and social justice.)
Beliefs, Values and Traditions, Anne Lovelace and Joy White. Heinemann.
(This includes a good exploration of the issues surrounding the role of women in Islam.)
Ethics and Religions, J. Rankin, A. Brown and P. Gateshill. Longman.

Videos
Through the Eyes of Children series – Pergamon.
What's it Like? series – Central (1993).
Worlds of Faith series – North South for Channel Four (1996–7).

RESOURCES FOR MULTICULTURAL CHRISTIANITY

Hunger Cloths can be ordered through Traidcraft or CAFOD or directly from: Miseor, Mozartstrasse 9, D-5100 Aachen, Germany.
Jesus Worldwide – a set of A3 posters depicting Jesus through Philippino, Cameroon, Haitian and Chinese art. Ordered through: Christian Education Movement, Royal Buildings, Victoria Street, Derby, DE1 19W. Tel: 01332 296655.
What's it Like to be a Christian in a Pentecostal Church? Central (1993) (a video presented through the experience of Afro-Carribean young people).

NOTES

1. The Shap Working Party on World Religions in Education consists of specialists in Religious Studies and RE from a variety of religious backgrounds and working in all stages of education. It has produced several publications to promote the effective teaching of world religions (this term includes Christianity). The group takes its name from the place in the Lake District where it first met in 1969. The working party produces a handbook and a calendar of religious festivals every year. For further information contact the journal editor, Alison Seaman, National Society's RE Centre, 36 Causton Street, London, SW1P 4AU.
2. The term 'androcentrism' is used by feminist thinkers to define the process by which maleness is presented as the norm of humanity.

3. The term 'be-ing' is an example of the adaptation of language initiated by the feminist thinker Mary Daly. Daly has been very influential in her analysis of the relationship between language, symbol and domination in the sustaining of patriarchy (Daly, 1985). She invents, reclaims and subverts words in order to expose their role in the oppression of women and to restore female power and authority. Daly often inserts hyphens into words to change or adapt their meaning. She uses the term 'be-ing' to emphasize her claim that the women's movement was allowing women to realize their full potential as self-affirming subjects and to refuse their male-defined role as 'beings' or objects.
4. For an alternative view which argues for the positive value of post-modern relativism for education in general and RE in particular, see Erricker, 1998.
5. The Children and Worldviews project is a collaborative project between Chichester Institute of Higher Education and King Alfred's College co-directed by Jane Erricker and Clive Erricker and funded by the Calouste Gulbenkinan Foundation. It explores the spiritual and moral development of children in primary schools by allowing them to give their own accounts of what is important and meaningful in their lives.

BIBLIOGRAPHY

Alves, C. (1991) Just a matter of words? The religious education debate in the House of Lords. *British Journal of Religious Education*, 13(3).

Braidotti, R. (1994) *Nomadic Subjects: Embodiment and Sexual Difference in Contemporary Feminist Theory*. New York: Columbia University Press.

Christ, C. (1995; 3rd edn) *Diving Deep and Surfacing*. Boston: Beacon Press.

Christ, C. and Plaskow, J. (eds) (1989; 2nd edn) *Womanspirit Rising – A Feminist Reader in Religion*. San Francisco: Harper and Row.

Cole, M. and Hill, D. (1995) Games of despair and rhetorics of resistance: postmodernism, education and reaction. *British Journal of Sociology of Education*, 16(2).

Cole, M. and Hill, D. (1996) Postmodernism, education and contemporary capitalism: a materialist critique. In M. O. Valente, A. Barrios, V. Teodoro and A. Gaspar (eds) *Teacher Training and Values Education*. Lisbon: Lisbon University.

Cole, W. O. and Mantin, R. (1994) *Teaching Christianity*. London: Heinemann.

Daly, M. (1985) *Beyond God the Father*. Boston: Beacon Press.

Education Reform Act (1988) London: HMSO.

Erricker, C. with Brown, A., Hayward, M., Kadodwala, D. and Williams, P. (eds) (1993) *Teaching World Religions*. Oxford: Heinemann.

Erricker, C., Erricker, J., Ota, C., Sullivan, D. and Fletcher, M. (1997) *The Education of the Whole Child.* London: Cassell.

Erricker, E. (1998) Spiritual confusion: a critique of current educational policy in England and Wales. *International Journal of Children's Spirituality,* 3(1).

Harris, M. and Moran, G. (1989) Feminism and the imagery of religious education. *British Journal of Religious Education,* Autumn.

Hill, D., McLaren, P., Cole, M. and Rikowski, G. (eds) (1999) *Postmodernism in Educational Theory: Education and the Politics of Human Resistance.* London: Tufnell Press.

Hull, J. (1993) *The Place of Christianity in the Curriculum: The Theology of the Department of Education.* The Hockerill Educational Fondation, 51 Pole Barn Lane, Frinton-on-Sea, Essex CO13 9NQ.

Jeffers, S. (1992) *Brother Eagle, Sister Sky. A Message from Chief Seattle.* London: Hamish Hamilton.

Kee, A. (1982) *Constantine versus Christ: The Triumph of Ideology.* London: SCM.

Kelly, J. (1999) *Postmodernism and Feminism: The Road to Nowhere.* In Hill, D. *et al. op. cit.*

London Borough of Brent (1986) *Brent Religious Education: Now and Tomorrow.* Wembley: London Borough of Brent Education Department.

McFague, S. (1982) *Metaphorical Theology.* London: SCM.

Mernissi, F. (1991) *Women and Islam.* Oxford: Blackwell.

Mernissi, F. (1993) *The Forgotten Queens of Islam.* Cambridge: Polity Press.

Mernissi, F. (1996) *Women's Rebellion and Islamic Memory.* London: Zed Books Ltd.

Plaskow, J. and Christ, C. (1989) *Weaving the Visions: New Patterns in Feminist Spirituality.* San Francisco: Harper and Row.

Ruether, R. R. (1983) *Sexism and God-Talk.* Boston: Beacon.

Schools Council (1971) *Working Paper 36 – Religious Education in Secondary Schools.* London: Evans/Methuen.

Schüssler Fiorenza, E. (1983) *In Memory of Her.* London: SCM Press.

Sheldon, D. (1990) *The Whales' Song* illust. Gary Blythe. London: Hutchinson.

Starkings, D. (1993) *Religion and the Arts in Education: Dimensions of Spirituality.* Sevenoaks: Hodder and Stoughton.

Surrey County Council Education Committee (1945) *Syllabus of Religious Instruction.* London: HMSO.

Swann Report (1985) *Education for All.* London: HMSO.

Tames, R. (1982) *Approaches to Islam.* London: Murray.

Wedderspoon, A. G. (1966) *Religious Education, 1944–1984.* London: Allen and Unwin.

CHAPTER 13

Sex education

Clyde Chitty

CONTEXT AND DEBATES

It has been extremely difficult for schools and teachers to maintain a consistent sex education policy over the past ten or more years. The Thatcher and Major administrations constantly meddled in this sensitive area of the curriculum as they sought to impose their narrow right-wing perspective on caring but often frightened professionals.

It is, of course, impossible to separate the policy changes that have affected sex education since 1986 from the general ideological project of the Far Right, within which the imposition of a prescriptive model of sexual and personal morality has played such an important part. As Rachel Thomson (1993) has observed: 'Sex education both constructs and confirms the categories of "normal" and "deviant" which it regulates, monitors and controls . . . Education reflects the dominant politics of a society's institutions and sex education reflects the sexual politics of those institutions' (1993:219). Schools have been seen by the Far Right as key sites for social engineering and social control and for the firm application of a particularly vicious form of moral authoritarianism.

Nowhere is opposition to all participatory and consciousness-raising models of education more clearly expressed than in the first pamphlet of the right-wing Hillgate Group, *Whose Schools? A Radical Manifesto*, published at the end of 1986. Here it was argued that all children should be taught respect for 'traditional' family values. They had to be 'rescued' from 'indoctrination in the fashionable causes of the Radical Left: 'anti-racism', 'anti-sexism', 'peace education' (which usually means CND propaganda) and even 'anti-heterosexism' (meaning the preaching of homosexuality combined with an attack on the belief that heterosexuality is normal). To this end, schools should be 'released from the control of local government', thereby 'depriving the politicised local education authorities of their standing ability to corrupt the minds and souls of the young' (Hillgate Group, 1986:4, 13, 18).

It was also in 1986 that the neo-Conservative wing of the Thatcherite Tendency found a pretext for launching a major assault on so-called progressive teaching practices. This came in the form of a whipped-up controversy over the alleged use by teachers of a picture book from Denmark called *Jenny Lives with Eric and Martin* (Bosche and Mackay, 1983).[1] This had been published in Copenhagen in 1981 and first appeared in the United Kingdom in an English translation in December 1983. It attempted to present a positive image of a young homosexual couple bringing up a five-year-old girl, the daughter of Martin. This was followed by stories in the *Sun* under the front page headline 'VILE BOOK IN SCHOOL' (6 May) and in *Today* under the headline 'SCANDAL OF GAY PORN BOOKS READ IN SCHOOLS' (7 May).

At the time of this 'controversy' over the availability of *Jenny Lives with Eric and Martin*, a new Education Bill was in the process of passing through Parliament. In the House of Lords a number of Conservative peers demanded action on sex education, claiming that the kind of teaching which condoned homosexuality as a 'valid' alternative to heterosexuality was not only undermining *traditional* family life and encouraging divorce, but was also linked with the increase in rapes, attacks on children and sexual crime in general. The fear engendered by the spread of HIV/AIDS was used to justify a Christian-heterosexual approach to morality and an attack on homosexual lifestyles. Baroness Cox, a member of the Hillgate Group, stated: 'I cannot imagine how on earth in this age of AIDS, we can be contemplating promoting gay issues in the curriculum. I think that it beggars all description' (quoted in Jeffery-Poulter, 1991:208).

The Education Secretary Kenneth Baker bowed to the pressure

from the Right, and a new clause was introduced into the Bill (Clause 46 in the resulting 1986 Education [No. 2] Act) requiring that:

> The local education authority by whom any county, voluntary or special school is maintained, and the governing body and head teacher of the school, shall take such steps as are reasonably practicable to secure that where sex education is given to any registered students at the school, it is given in such a manner as to encourage those students to have due regard to moral considerations and the value of family life.

It was the 1986 Education Act which removed responsibility for school sex education from local education authorities and placed it for the first time in the hands of school governors – a blatant attempt to provide sex education with supposedly 'conservative' gatekeepers. School governors were now required to consider whether or not sex education should be included in the school curriculum, and if they decided it should, to produce a written statement on the form and content of that curriculum. This policy statement should then be made available to parents. Although at this stage parents were not given the right to withdraw their children from sex education lessons, governors were given the discretionary power to allow students to withdraw if parents had religious objections.

The new framework for the provision of sex education in schools was then elaborated upon in DES Circular No. 11/87, *Sex Education at School*, published on 25 September 1987 (DES, 1987). According to the Introduction to this Circular, 'appropriate and responsible Sex Education is an important element in the work of schools in preparing students for adult life; it calls for careful and sensitive treatment'. Yet, as many have commented (see, for example, Baker, 1988; Davies, 1988), what was intended to be an authoritative statement of the government's position in the light of recent 'controversies' was, in fact, notable for its lack of clarity and its inbuilt contradictions. There is, for example, a world of difference between the beginning and the end of Section 19. The opening clearly has the hand of HMI on it. It calls for facts 'to be presented in an objective and balanced manner, so as to enable students to comprehend the range of sexual attitudes and behaviour in present-day society'. The final sentence of the Section, which states that 'students should be helped to appreciate the benefits of stable married and family life and the responsibilities of parenthood', is there to pander to the government's moralist faction. How teachers are expected to be 'objective' and at the same time 'help students appreciate something' goes unexplained. What is true is that the *dominant* tone of the Circular is narrow and homophobic. In Section 22 we read:

> There is no place in any school in any circumstances for teaching which advocates homosexual behaviour, which presents it as the 'norm', or which encourages homosexual experimentation by students. Indeed, encouraging or procuring homosexual acts by students who are under the age of consent is a criminal offence. (DES, 1987:4)

The Circular makes special mention of the so-called Gillick Ruling on the provision of contraceptive advice to girls under the age of 16. In the Gillick case, it will be remembered, the House of Lords ruled that, while it should be most unusual for a doctor to provide contraceptive advice and treatment to a child under the age of 16 without parental knowledge or consent, there *could* be circumstances where he or she would be justified in doing so. The Circular points out that such circumstances have no parallel in school education:

> The general rule must be that giving an individual student contraceptive advice without parental knowledge or consent would be an inappropriate exercise of a teacher's professional responsibilities, and could, depending on the circumstances, amount to a criminal offence. (*ibid.*:5)

The determination of Thatcher's ministers to appease the forces of moral authoritarianism was further emphasized by the inclusion of what was to become the notorious Section 28 in the 1988 Local Government Act. This amended the 1986 Local Government Act by laying down that a local authority shall not:

(a) intentionally promote homosexuality or publish material with the intention of promoting homosexuality;
(b) promote the teaching in any maintained school of the acceptability of homosexuality as a pretended family relationship.

As many commentators have pointed out, Section 28 was a key cultural and symbolic event in the recent history of sexual politics. Almost immediately it was realized that confusion existed around the educational relevance of the Section, in the light of previous legislation. Dame Jill Knight and the other sponsors of the measure had simply overlooked the fact that the 1986 Education Act had already removed sex education from the control of local authorities – a fact which the government was forced to concede in a Department of the Environment Circular published in May 1988:

> Responsibility for sex education continues to rest with school governing bodies, by virtue of Section 18 of the Education (No. 2) Act of 1986. Section 28 of the Local Government Act does not affect the activities of school governors, nor of teachers. It will not prevent the objective discussion of homosexuality in the classroom, nor the counselling of students concerned about their sexuality. (DOE, 1988:5)

Nevertheless, the symbolic power of Section 28 was to prove immense. One almost immediate effect was the banning of the 'Scene' drama *The Two of Us* by BBC Education which, when it was shown some years later prefaced by stern warnings of its content, had its final (happy ending) scene cut. The Section also increased the pressure on lesbian and gay teachers to remain closeted at work. A 1993 survey by Stonewall, the lesbian and gay lobbying group, indicated that teaching had become the most closeted occupation.[2] It also changed sex education curricula fundamentally in the matter of teachers' responses to HIV infection. Discussion of sexualities was often omitted completely, other than to make a connection between homosexuality and HIV. Anything other than an illusory ideal of monogamous heterosexuality became associated with illness and death, and this helped to create a climate in which homophobic bullying flourished, with many teachers feeling powerless to challenge it in the face of Section 28. A 1996 survey on homophobic violence, also by Stonewall, found that 48 per cent of respondents under 18 had experienced a violent attack and that 40 per cent of these attacks had taken place in school.[3]

Ironically the risk of HIV infection has often been seen to be greatest among the 16–25 age group; yet caring and committed teachers have often felt powerless to address the need for information. Of course, these efforts were also hindered by the unequal age of consent for male homosexual activity (set at 21 until 1994) which acted as a destructive barrier to advice and support for young gay men. During the age-of-consent debate in 1994, a spokesperson for the charity Barnardos made it clear that the current law prevented it from giving practical support and information even in contexts outside formal education. The effect of Section 28 combined with the unequal age of consent served to create problems for many teachers and students in secondary schools.

Section 28 was clearly meant to achieve the creation of a climate of paranoia around the teaching of sex education. As Rachel Thomson has observed, it played an important role in undermining the confidence and professionalism of teachers: 'The phrase "the promotion of homosexuality" had the insidious effect of constructing teachers as the potential corrupters of young people and of frightening teachers from saying what they thought was sensible and right out of fear of losing their jobs' (1993:225). As we have seen, the emerging crisis of HIV/AIDS made it easy for the moral lobby to insist that school sex education should be seized upon as an ideal forum for promoting a prescriptive and uncaring model of sexual morality. This approach was widely advocated on the Right despite all the evidence of its ineffectiveness as a means of promoting 'responsible' behaviour among young people. As Braeken and Wijnsma have suggested: 'From a preventive point of view . . . it is more effective to adopt a lifestyle approach, meaning that the education displays respect for different sexual lifestyles and the freedom of individuals to adopt their own lifestyle, focusing solely on the promotion of safer behaviours as an integrated part of these lifestyles instead of using the promotion of safer behaviours as a vehicle for hidden moral issues' (1989).

It was obviously convenient to establish a clear link between homosexuality and HIV disease and leave the privileged and assumed naturally superior status of heterosexuality unchallenged. As Ewan Armstrong and Peter Gordon have argued, gay men (together with prostitutes and bisexual men) could be identified as 'the bridges across which HIV would visit the (presumably as yet uninfected) heterosexual community' (1989:22). This identity was easy to establish because sexuality was seldom, if ever, adequately defined in any sex education or safer sex curriculum, and the implication was that gay men represented some sort of 'threat' to the health of the nation.

Such was the concern felt about the spread of HIV and AIDS that the government decided to undermine the powers given to school governors in the 1986 Education Act and provide a safety net of basic information about HIV infection for all students at the secondary stage. All the rhetoric about parental and governor control of the sex education curriculum could be abandoned (or at least modified) in the face of the HIV/AIDS threat. With the advent of the National Curriculum in 1988 (and with the first parts coming into effect from September 1989), some aspects of sex education, particularly the reproductive and disease components, were already included in the science curriculum. Then in 1991 the National Curriculum Science Orders were revised to include HIV/AIDS at Key Stage 3 (for 11- to 14-year-olds). The revision, made after consultation with key agencies in the field, recommended that HIV/AIDS was such a serious threat to public health that it could not be left to school governors to decide whether or not it should be taught.

None of this was unproblematic; and what is remarkable is that despite the climate of fear and censorship created by the government, a number of teachers refused to be intimidated by the numerous official pronouncements on sex education covering all its various aspects. Speaking, for example, at the World AIDS Day Conference in December 1991, Michael Marland, headteacher of North Westminster Community School in the London Borough of Westminster, reminded his audience that Section 1 of the 1988 Education 'Reform' Act specifically required the school curriculum to be concerned with 'preparing students for the opportunities, responsibilities and experiences of adult life'. How, he asked, could human sexuality be left out of such preparation? (see reports in *The Times Educational Supplement*, 6 December 1991; 10 January 1992). And this was just one example of using the government's own legislation to good effect. Others have made use of Section 19 of DES Circular No. 11/87 to argue that teachers have a duty to enable students to appreciate the range of sexual attitudes and behaviour in present-day society.

The more liberal and enlightened aspects of the 1987 Circular clearly posed very real difficulties for a government anxious to demonstrate that it was concerned about the moral health of the nation. Indeed, there was pressure on John Major's administration in 1993 to draft legislation *preventing* the inclusion of sex education in the school curriculum. Both John Patten, then Education Secretary, and his deputy Baroness Blatch were, it seems, greatly influenced by the campaign being waged by the 60,000-strong

Christian Action Research and Education Group and by the small fundamentalist Christian sect known as the Plymouth Brethren, who were anxious to ban all sex education in schools and also to remove all mention of the HIV virus and its transmission from the statutory National Curriculum (see Craigie, 1993). And James Pawsey, Conservative MP for Rugby and Kenilworth, was not alone in the Party in arguing that sex education should be banned, since it clearly encouraged premature experimentation among the young. For Mr Pawsey, the issue was quite clear-cut: 'Despite the growing emphasis on the teaching of sex, the rate of abortions continues to increase, and small wonder, for if we teach our children German, can we be surprised when they actually practise it' (Pawsey, 1980).

All this seemed to be at odds with the messages contained within the Department of Health White Paper *The Health of the Nation*, published in July 1992 (DOH, 1992), which emphasized the importance of sexual health and identified it as one of the key areas in which substantial improvement had to be achieved. With the number of under-age pregnancies fixed at that time at around 8,000 a year, the White Paper set itself the target of reducing this figure by 50 per cent by the year 2000. It also wanted priority given to lessening the incidence of HIV, AIDS and other sexually transmitted diseases.

Rachel Thomson has pointed out that there was a fundamental dichotomy between the approach of *The Health of the Nation* and that of policy documents emanating from the Department for Education. For example, the DFE White Paper *Choice and Diversity: A New Framework for Schools*, also published in July 1992, attempted to define the nature of the 'spiritual and moral development' of students – a quality that schools would be required to demonstrate to the newly reformed school inspectorate. Should school sex education be used as an opportunity to communicate knowledge and skills to enable young people to make their own informed decisions (the Department of Health approach); or should it be used as an opportunity to promote a particularly narrow vision of the world, of people and of sexuality? According to Thomson: 'These two approaches, sexual health and sexual moralism, were increasingly coming into conflict, the former stressing the distinction between sexually healthy and sexually unhealthy practices, the latter between the morally legitimate and the morally illegitimate' (Thomson, 1993:220).

Despite all the scare stories which appear in the media, it also seems to be true that the vast majority of parents support the provision of explicit and effective sex education in schools. A study by Isobel Allen for the Policy Studies Institute carried out in 1987 had found that 96 per cent of parents were happy with the sex education that was taking place in schools (Allen, 1987). More recently, in 1994, a major survey of 1,400 parents carried out by the Health Education Authority found that 94 per cent supported the general concept of sex education being part of the school curriculum. Just one per cent of parents said that they would like to withdraw their children from all sex education lessons. The vast majority was in favour of sex education taking place in primary schools where they wanted students to learn about growing up and personal hygiene. A total of 44 per cent thought reproduction should be taught to children in this age group. Subjects such as contraception, HIV and AIDS, sexually transmitted diseases, sexual relationships, moral values and family life could then be left to the secondary school. Around 80 per cent of parents wanted secondary schools to teach about HIV and AIDS, and only 5 per cent were implacably opposed to this. There seemed to be general confidence in the role of teachers in the whole area of sex education, although this was not shared by a quarter of Muslim parents and 17 per cent of Hindus (Young, 1994).

Another right-wing myth that needs to be shattered is that sex education in schools actually *encourages* early sexual activity. It may suit the Right's purpose to promote this lie, but all the evidence suggests that the countries with the most explicit sex education have had the lowest teenage pregnancy rates and that the better the sex education, the higher the age at which teenagers first engage in sexual activity. As far as the 15-to-19 age group is concerned, the 1993 figures for teenage pregnancy rates were 9 per 1,000 in Holland and 30 per 1,000 in Sweden, compared with 65 per 1000 in Britain (see Ferriman, 1993). Holland and Sweden are countries where sex education in schools is frank and unambiguous, which suggests that effective sex education serves to *postpone* unguarded sexual activity, rather than encourage it.

The 1993 survey *Sexual Attitudes and Lifestyles* interviewed 18,876 people aged 16 to 59. It found that the age at which the majority of 16- to 24-year-olds first had sexual intercourse was then 17, compared with 21 for those born 40 years earlier. It also found that sexual activity was lowest among those teenagers who gave 'formal teaching' as their main source of information about sex. According to Kaye Wellings, one of the Survey organizers: 'The data clearly belies the assumption that sex education in schools encourages young people to experiment earlier. In fact, it appears to postpone sexual activity' (see Johnson *et al.*, 1994). Other evidence suggests that school programmes which promote both postponement and protected sex if sexually active, are more effective than those promoting abstinence alone. School-based programmes are also found to be more effective when given before young people become sexually active and when they emphasize skills and social norms rather than mere knowledge.

RECENT GUIDANCE AND LEGISLATION

In April 1993, the Department for Education published the first draft of a proposed revision of Circular 11/87 (DFE, 1993a), in which a key passage in Section 19 appeared in a truncated version ('the Secretary of State considers that . . . the aims of a programme of sex education should be to present facts in an objective and balanced manner'), which no longer allowed for the recognition of lesbian and gay sexualities. But the ensuing process of consultation was soon overtaken by the government's own last-minute amendment to the new Education Bill passing through Parliament. This amendment became Section 241 of the 1993 Education Act.

As a result of this amendment, consideration of AIDS, HIV, sexually transmitted diseases and aspects of human sexual behaviour other than the biological aspects would no longer form part of National Curriculum Science. Governors of secondary schools were now required to provide sex education to all registered students and no longer had the power, granted to them by the 1986 Education Act, of deciding whether or not sex education should form part of the school curriculum[4] – although they were still required to develop a policy explaining *how* and *where* sex education would be taught, and to make that policy available to parents. Finally, and perhaps most controversially, parents now had the right to withdraw their children from all or part of the sex education programme in both primary and secondary schools.[5] Parents were not required to give reasons for their decision; nor did they have to indicate what other arrangements they intended to make for providing sex education for their children. Once a request for withdrawal had been made, that request had to be complied with until the parent changed or revoked it.[6]

Right-wing fundamentalists clearly hoped that large numbers of parents would exercise the option of withdrawing their children from 'compulsory' sex education classes. Teachers had to be 'punished' for their reluctance to provide sex education in the context of 'traditional' moral values and family life. According to Valerie Riches, Director of Family and Youth Concern, writing to *The Times* on 17 July 1993: The right to withdraw children from lessons must be maintained until the sex education lobby shows itself both willing and capable of promoting responsible attitudes towards sexual behaviour, marriage and family life.'

The sex education clauses of the 1993 Education Act were elaborated upon in a second draft circular published in December 1993 (DFE, 1993b) which eventually became Circular No. 5/94 *Sex Education in Schools*, published on 6 May 1994 (DFE, 1994). Much of the controversy surrounding these two documents focused on two key areas: the exact meaning of the term 'stable family life'; and the risks that teachers would take in giving contraceptive advice to girls under the age of 16.

The December draft circular again reproduced Section 19 of Circular 11/87 without reference to 'the range of sexual attitudes and behaviour in present-day society'. It stated in Section 7:

> The aim of schools' programmes of Sex Education should . . . be to present facts in an objective, balanced and sensitive manner, set within a clear moral framework. Pupils should accordingly be encouraged to consider the importance of self-restraint, dignity, respect for themselves and others, and sensitivity towards the needs and views of others. They should be enabled to recognize the physical, emotional and moral implications, and risks, of certain types of behaviour, and to accept that both sexes should behave responsibly in sexual matters. Last but not least, students should be helped to appreciate the value of stable family life, marriage and the responsibilities of parenthood. (DFE, 1993b:2)

Asked at the launch of the December draft circular whether all children should be taught that it was better for parents to be married, that heterosexuality was better than homosexuality and that fidelity was better than promiscuity, the (then) Education Secretary John Patten swiftly replied: 'Yes to all three.

Homosexuality is clearly undesirable; and parents should not choose to remain unmarried. We should also aspire to the ideal that if you get married, you stay married' (quoted in the *Independent*, 7 December 1993).

Section 26 of the 1987 Circular had taken a tough line on the question of the provision of contraceptive advice to girls under the age of 16:

> The general rule must be that giving an individual pupil advice on such matters without parental knowledge or consent would be an inappropriate exercise of a teacher's professional responsibilities, and could, depending on the circumstances, amount to a criminal offence. (DES, 1987:5)

And this stern warning was repeated in Clause 38 of the December draft circular (DFE, 1993b:9).

The Sex Education Forum asked Allen Levy QC for a ruling on this warning, and his advice was that the government's statement was unduly alarmist. On the release of his judgement to the press in February 1994, Rachel Thomson wrote:

> Allen Levy has concluded that a teacher is entitled to tell pupils where they can get confidential advice on contraception. That would not amount to aiding and abetting an offence if the teacher honestly intends to act in the young person's best interests. We agree it would probably not be appropriate at present for a teacher to go much further than this. (reported in *The Times Educational Supplement*, 18 February 1994)

In the event, the warning in Clause 39 of the final version of the Circular was toned down and seemed to imply that the issue might have to be tested in the courts:

> Particular care must be exercised in relation to contraceptive advice to pupils under sixteen, for whom sexual intercourse is unlawful. The general rule must be that giving an individual pupil advice on such matters without parental knowledge or consent would be an inappropriate exercise of a teacher's professional responsibilities. Teachers are not health professionals, and the legal position of a teacher giving advice in such circumstances has never been tested in the courts. (DFE, 1994:14)

Even in its revised form, this ruling is an issue of real concern for many teachers; moreover, the Department of Health is also thought to be worried that the Circular may serve to undermine its campaign to both reduce the number of under-age pregnancies and to combat the spread of sexually transmitted diseases. At around the same time, however, a survey carried out for the Health Education Authority showed that most teenagers under the age of 16 would not talk to teachers about contraception if they thought their parents would have to be told. While 84 per cent said it would be helpful to consult a teacher, only 31 per cent said they would do so if they thought their families would eventually find out (Meikle, 1994).

As a result of all this, the Association of Teachers and Lecturers (ATL) on behalf of an informal 'consortium' of concerned organizations, asked public law specialist Michael Beloff QC for a ruling on the issue. In a 65-page judgement, prepared in collaboration with Helen Mountfield, the ATL was advised that a teacher need not seek parental consent before giving a student counselling or advice relating to sexual matters. And if a girl reveals to a teacher that she is having under-age sex, the teacher is not necessarily obliged to inform the child's parents or the head-teacher of the school. According to the judgement:

> We do not consider that the advice in the Circular seeks to impose an absolute duty to break confidences; nor indeed is the Circular binding in law. Accordingly, we do not consider that a teacher is bound to follow Circular advice if, in the teacher's professional judgement, the child's best interests are better served by not doing so (subject to the parent's power to excuse from sex education lessons and the headteacher's power to direct). (ATL, 1994:40)

The judgement goes on to conclude that:

> Circular No. 5/94 is advisory only and has no special legal status. Teachers are not obliged to follow its advice . . . We do not consider that a teacher who gave a child under the age of sixteen advice relating to contraception, and who acted *bona fide* in what he or she honestly believed to be the child's best interests, would be likely to incur criminal liability. (*ibid.*:64–5).

It remains to be seen how the issue will be decided if it ever reaches a court of law.

CLASSROOM PRACTICE

How are secondary schools to set about implementing successful sex education strategies? A recent report from Peter Griffiths, HM Inspector, indicates that 1,600 inspections by registered inspectors and HM Inspectors in 1995 showed that 85 per cent of schools have a clearly defined sex education policy: 82 per cent at Key Stages 1 and 2 and 91 per cent at Key Stages 3 and 4. Nevertheless, it seems some schools are still not reviewing their policies and practices regularly, as was advocated by DFE Circular 5/94.

The recently published OfSTED Framework for Inspection requires Inspectors to report on each school's sex education policy and practice within the wider framework of health education and personal and social education. In Brenda Reid's view (Reid, 1996:6), this will serve to 'spur those schools on which have, as yet, not examined and reviewed these areas of practice'.

The 1990 NCC publication *Curriculum Guidance 5 – Health Education* argued that health and sex education were most likely to be successful when they were built on the best of current practice and did not present schools with an unfamiliar model (NCC, 1990:26). It put forward a number of possible timetabling options for both primary and secondary schools, which could include health education in the curriculum as:

(a) a subject permeating the whole curriculum;
(b) a separately timetabled subject;
(c) part of a PSE course/programme;
(d) part of a pastoral/tutorial programme;
(e) a subject arising from opportunities in other activities;
(f) by means of 'long-block timetabling' (e.g. 'sixth day' timetabling, activity week). (NCC, 1990:26–8)

It was accepted that some of these approaches, for example A, E and F, would be particularly relevant to primary schools.

The December 1993 DFE Draft Circular put forward four suggestions for covering sex education in the secondary school:

(a) as a discrete topic;
(b) within broader programmes of personal and social education;
(c) within the teaching of science;
(d) both in science and in other subject areas. (DFE, 1993b:5–6)

It emphasized that governing bodies must maintain a written statement of their policy on the provision of sex education, copies of which had to be made available to parents on request (*ibid.*:5).

It is, of course, important that sex education be supportive of, and responsive to, the needs of all students – and should therefore be sensitive to the diversity and development of sexual identities. *Curriculum Guidance 5* offered an excellent, developmentally appropriate curriculum for sex education in schools. It suggested that through sex education at Key Stage 3 students should:

(a) recognise the importance of personal choice in managing relationships so that they do not present risks, for example to health or to personal safety;
(b) understand that organisms (including HIV) can be transmitted in many ways, in some cases sexually;
(c) discuss moral values and explore those held by different cultures and groups;
(d) understand the concept of stereotyping and identify its various forms;
(e) be aware of the range of sexual attitudes and behaviours in present-day society;
(f) understand that people have the right not to be sexually active; recognise that parenthood is a matter of choice; know in broad outline the biological and social factors which influence sexual behaviour and their consequences;
(g) know how labelling and stereotyping can have a negative effect on mental health;
(h) understand the emotional changes which take place during puberty; understand differences in maturation and have a positive self-image. (NCC, 1990:16–17)

Then at Key Stage 4 students should:

(a) understand aspects of Britain's legislation relating to sexual behaviour;
(b) understand the biological aspects of reproduction;
(c) consider the advantages and disadvantages of various methods of family planning in terms of personal preference and social implications;
(d) recognise and be able to discuss sensitive and controversial issues such as conception, birth, HIV/AIDS, child-rearing,

abortion and technological developments which involve consideration of attitudes, values, beliefs and morality;

(e) be aware of the need for preventative health care and know what this involves; be aware of the availability of statutory and voluntary organisations which offer support in human relationships (for example: Relate);

(f) be aware that feeling positive about sexuality and sexual activity is important in relationships;

(g) understand the changing nature of sexuality over time and its impact on lifestyles (for example: the menopause);

(h)be aware of partnerships, marriage and divorce and the impact of loss, separation and bereavement;

(i) be able to discuss issues such as sexual harassment in terms of their effects on individuals. (NCC, 1990:18–19)

In a recent issue of *Sex Education Matters*, the quarterly newsletter of the Sex Education Forum, Caroline Ray argues that good sex education has three elements: it provides accurate information; it gives students the opportunity to practise social skills; and it gives students the chance to examine their own and others' attitudes and values in this area (Ray, 1995:10). She goes on to insist that sex education should be of high quality in terms of learning experience. This means that it has to be both effective and a positive experience for participants. To ensure that this is indeed the case, sex education should be delivered:

- by trained and confident staff;
- within environments that are supportive and safe for staff, visitors and students;
- in a way that is respectful of and responsive to difference;
- using methods which involve students actively in their own learning and encourage both the acquisition of knowledge and skills and the exploration of attitudes and values.

Caroline Ray is co-editor, with Dilys Went, of *Good Practice in Sex Education*, an excellent sourcebook for schools, published by the Sex Education Forum in June 1995. This provides many useful practical ideas for delivering an effective sex education programme in schools. It focuses on good practice in three areas:

1. providing a solid foundation for sex education to take place;
2. eliciting the support of parents, students, staff, governors;
3. ensuring high quality and effective delivery.

Also recently published, by the Camden and Islington Community Health Services NHS Trust, and constituting an excellent resource for teachers, is *Colours of the Rainbow: Exploring Issues of Sexuality and Difference* (Mole, 1995). This has already acquired a fair degree of notoriety in the popular press which, in the light of what has already been said in this chapter, serves merely to indicate what an excellent teaching pack it is!

There are also two excellent small-scale publications aimed particularly at young gay men. *True Colours* from the Terrence Higgins Trust and *Young Gay Men Talking* from the AIDS education charity AVERT provide basic information about choices and useful contacts and addresses in a clear format. *Young Gay Men Talking*, as its title suggests, also includes extracts from the life stories of gay youth which would be extremely useful both in provoking discussion and supporting individuals. These publications are available free in single copies and *True Colours* is also available through the National Union of Teachers and on the Terrence Higgins Trust web site (http://www.tht.org.uk).

AVERT has also published *Talking About Homosexuality in the Secondary School*, by Simon Forrest, Grant Biddle and Stephen Clift. Building on their research, which has shown that there is a 'general silence surrounding the whole subject of sexuality [which] has led in many schools to unacceptable levels of intolerance and bullying', the authors provide a thoughtful rationale and detailed strategies for confronting the issues of sexuality and HIV/AIDS education in the secondary school. They carefully map a process of talking with governors, parents/carers, school staff and students with the intention of opening up these areas for discussion and thereby contributing to a positive school ethos.

Talking About Homosexuality . . . also presents some ways of challenging homophobic bullying, which are developed in some detail by Jonathan Salisbury and David Jackson's excellent book *Challenging Macho Values: Practical Ways of Working with Adolescent Boys*. Salisbury and Jackson recount their experience of working with such boys in secondary schools in the Midlands, and provide a series of classroom strategies which they have used to challenge sexist and homophobic behaviour. They present a lot of useful material on the development of boys' sexualities and also on the 'gendered structure' of the secondary school, but their book is particularly interesting because they are ultimately so sympathetic towards the boys. Anyone looking for innovative and thought-provoking ways to challenge sexual harassment, bullying or anti-social behaviour by boys in the secondary school will be well advised to read this book.

CONCLUSION

The current Labour government committed itself in its election manifesto to the repeal of Section 28. The European Commission of Human Rights has already ruled that the unequal age of consent in this country violates Articles 8 and 14 of the European Convention on Human Rights. Although in the summer of 1998 the House of Lords rejected legislation passed by the House of Commons to equalize the age of consent, it seems unlikely that campaigners will abandon the struggle to create equality before the law for all young men and women.

As we approach the end of the millennium, the national picture with regard to the acceptance and celebration of sexual diversity appears, in fact, to be one of both progress and setbacks. In January 1999, the House of Commons once again voted to lower the age of gay consent to 16 (by 313 votes to 130, a government majority of 183); and, once again, this was followed by a House of Lords vote rejecting the proposal, though with a majority reduced from 168 in July 1998 to just 76.

Then, on a pleasant warm evening at the end of April, the third of the three London nail bombs was targeted at gays and lesbians and their friends drinking at the Admiral Duncan pub in Soho. Although it is true (and worrying) that several witnesses were frightened to give their names to journalists, the government response to this atrocity took the form of speaking up for the values of a liberal, civilized society. In a wide-ranging speech delivered in Birmingham at the beginning of May, the Prime Minister argued powerfully that an attack on any section of the community was an attack on Britain as a whole. In his words: 'When the gay community is attacked and innocent people are murdered, all the good people of Britain, whatever their race, their lifestyle, their class, unite in revulsion and determination to bring the evil people to justice.' He could have added that education itself has a vital role to play in defeating the sort of racism and homophobia that tolerates attacks on minorities and prevents us from creating a truly decent society based on respect for human diversity.

At the same time, there seems to be a new awareness by the Government of the role that effective sex education can play in reducing the number of teenage pregnancies. As we have already seen, this country has a very poor record with regard to this area of public health, and particularly in comparison with the situation that exists in all other European countries. The Government would like to see a 50 per cent cut in under-18 pregnancies by the year 2010; and discussion of responsible behaviour in human relationships is to form part of a PSE programme in schools as one aspect of a (not altogether liberal) package of measures announced by the Government in June 1999. Any programme of sex education at the secondary level should, of course, be designed to give all young people total control of their lives and, it is hoped, remove the risk of their being cajoled or intimidated into courses of action that will later bring hardship and distress.

ACKNOWLEDGEMENT

I would like to thank Viv Ellis for his comments on and substantive inputs to this chapter.

NOTES

1. A similar furore has recently accompanied the publication of a new teachers' resource book on homosexuality, *Colours of the Rainbow*. The front-page story in the *Daily Mail* on 2 March 1996 was headlined: 'Five-year-olds to get gay lessons'.
2. *Less Equal Than Others* available from Stonewall, 16 Clerkenwell Close, London EC1R 0AA (£5).
3. *Queer Bashing* also available from Stonewall at the above address (£6). See also *Playing It Safe: Schools and Sex Education* (forthcoming).
4. Governors of primary schools continue to have the responsibility to decide whether or not the school should provide sex education. In this sector of schooling, the situation established by the 1986 Education (No. 2) Act remains unchanged at the time of writing.

5. This does not apply to sex education which continues to form part of National Curriculum Science.
6. This provision even applies to students over compulsory school age. A student in this category who sought to challenge the parental decision would, if he or she could not resolve the matter with the parents, ultimately have to apply to the courts.

USEFUL ADDRESSES

AVERT, 11–13 Denne Parade, Horsham, West Sussex RH12 1JD. Tel: 01403 210202. e-mail: avert@dial.pipex.com.

Good Practice in Sex Education: A Sourcebook for Schools, edited by Caroline Ray and Dilys Went for the Sex Education Forum, is also published by the National Children's Bureau.

Sex Education Matters is the quarterly newsletter of the Sex Education Forum, published by the National Children's Bureau, 8 Wakley Street, London, EC1V 7QE.

The Terrence Higgins Trust, 52–54 Grays Inn Road, London WC1X 8JU. Tel: 0171 831 0330.

BIBLIOGRAPHY

Allen, I. (1987) Education in Sex and Personal Relationships, PSI Research Report No. 665.

Armstrong, E. and Gordon, P. (1989) Safer sex education – conflict today; tomorrow the world? *Forum*, 32(1), Autumn:21–2.

ATL (Association of Teachers and Lecturers) (1994) *Sex Education in Schools: Joint Opinion*, Michael Beloff and Helen Mountfield. London: ATL.

Baker, N. (1988) Facts versus morals. *Times Educational Supplement*, 22 April.

Bosche, S. and Mackay, L (1983) *Jenny Lives with Eric and Martin*. London: Gay Men's Press.

Braeken, D. and Wijnsma, P. (1989) Unpublished paper presented at the International Workshop on the prevention of sexual transmission of AIDS and other Sexually Transmitted Diseases, held in The Netherlands, 20 April–3 May.

Craigie, E. (1993) Knowing in the biblical sense. *Observer*, 11 July.

Davies, P. (1988) Sexuality: a new minefield in schools. *Independent*, 26 May.

DES (1987) *Sex Education at School (Circular No. 11/87)*. London: DES.

DFE (1992) *Choice and Diversity: A New Framework for Schools*. London: HMSO.

DFE (1993a) *Sex Education In Schools: Proposed Revision of Circular 11/87*. London: DFE.

DFE (1993b) *Education Act 1993: Sex Education In Schools*. London: DFE.

DFE (1994) *Education Act 1993: Sex Education in Schools (Circular No. 5/94)*. London: DFE.

DoE (Department of the Environment) (1988) *Local Government Act 1988 (Circular No. 12/88)*. London: DoE.

DoH (Department of Health) (1992) *The Health of the Nation: A Strategy for Health in England*. London: HMSO.

Ferriman, A. (1993) More sex in class, please. *Observer*, 7 November.

Forrest, S., Biddle, G. and Clift, S. (1997) *Talking About Sexuality in the Secondary School*. Horsham: Avert.

Hillgate Group (1986) *Whose Schools? A Radical Manifesto*. London: The Hillgate Group.

Jeffery-Poulter, S. (1991) *Peers, Queers and Commons: The Struggle for Gay Law Reform from 1950 to the Present*. London: Routledge.

Johnson *et al.* (1994) *Sexual Attitudes and Lifestyles*. Oxford: Blackwell Science.

Meikle, J. (1994) Poll kindles sex education row. *Guardian*, 30 March.

Mole, S. (1995) *Colours of the Rainbow: Exploring Issues of Sexuality and Difference*. London: Camden and Islington Health Promotion Service.

NCC (National Curriculum Council) (1990) *Curriculum Guidance 5 – Health Education*. York: NCC.

Pawsey, J. (1980) The sex education that isn't working. *Daily Mail*, 22 August.

Ray, C. (1995) Laying the foundations for effective sex education. *Sex Education Matters*, 6.

Ray, C. and Went, D. (eds) (1995) *Good Practice in Sex Education – A Sourcebook for Schools*. London: National Children's Bureau.

Reid, B. (1996) Sex education – governors' roles and responsibilities. *Parents and Schools (Campaign for State Education Newsletter)*, 87, February.

Salisbury, J. and Jackson, D. (1996) *Challenging Macho Values: Practical Ways of Working with Adolescent Boys*. London: Falmer Press.

Thomson, R. (1993) Unholy alliances: the recent politics of sex education. In J. Bristow and A. R. Wilson (eds) *Activating Theory: Lesbian,Gay, Bisexual Politics*. London: Lawrence and Wishart.

Young, S. (1994) Nine out of ten parents support sex lessons. *The Times Educational Supplement*, 4 November.

CHAPTER 14

GNVQ

Arleene Piercy and Glenn Rikowski

This chapter is primarily aimed at teachers in secondary schools who are undertaking the General National Vocational Qualifications (GNVQs). It starts out with a brief background to GNVQ and its relationship to the National Curriculum – which has recently undergone some modification with the advent of a GNVQ Part 1 pilot programme for Key Stage 4 in seven vocational areas from September 1997 (NCVQ/SCAA, 1996, 1997). Thereafter, the chapter highlights the unequal way GNVQ is often presented in schools as a qualification for the 'less able' or 'less academic' student. There is also some practical advice, suggestions and strategies for incorporating a concern with *social* equality in its many forms (class, gender, 'race' and ethnicity, sexuality, age, disability and special needs) into GNVQ. Examples of how to infuse GNVQ (focusing on leisure and tourism) with the values of social equality – with a sample assignment (in the Appendix) – are provided as indicators of how GNVQ can be used for designing learning activities which incorporate principles of equality, as well as giving students an academically rigorous learning experience.

Two key questions underpin this chapter: Is GNVQ doomed to be viewed as the perennial 'unequal partner' in relation to 'academic' GCSE and A-level courses – is 'parity of esteem' (Wolf, 1993) feasible?; can GNVQ be a vehicle for addressing social inequalities within the school and the wider society? These questions provide the underlying structure to the chapter which explores the potential of GNVQ for combating curricular and social inequalities.

GNVQ: ORIGINS AND PURPOSE

GNVQs were first announced in the Conservative government's White Paper, *Education and Training in the 21st Century* (DES, 1991), where it was stated that the government intended that GNVQ (together with NVQs) would replace other vocational qualifications and constitute the main national vocational provision for education and training. This clearly indicated the intention of the then Conservative government to become specifically involved in the 16+ curriculum in schools and colleges. GNVQs were introduced in 1992 and Pilot GNVQs were run for the 1992/93 academic year. By 1994/95, 184,000 students had registered for GNVQ courses (Education Committee, 1996:xiii). In his review of the National Curriculum in 1994, Sir Ron Dearing had advocated the setting up of GNVQ Part 1 courses in schools for 14–16-year-olds. These were introduced in 1995 – through pre-Pilots (Bamfield, 1996) – and school students now have the opportunity to study GNVQ Part 1 at Foundation (equal to two GCSEs at D–G grades) and Intermediate (equal to two GCSEs at A*–C grades) levels (NCVQ/SCAA, 1997:2). The GNVQ Part 1 should take up no more than 20 per cent of curriculum time at Key Stage 4 (Bamfield, 1996).

As Terry Hyland (1994a, 1995) has argued, the original government fascination with GNVQs was partly a result of criticisms – from employers, educationalists and researchers – of the behaviourist and reductionist approach of National Vocational Qualifications (NVQs) with their narrow focus on occupational competence. Many of these critics were arguing that with the focus on *occupational* competence, NVQs were not producing the 'flexible' and 'adaptable' workers required for a future of periodic unemployment, where workers would undergo one or more changes of career direction, and where attaining new skills would be at a premium (Taubman, 1994). Thus, there was a concomitant need for more general employability skills, and this was a weakness in the National Council for Vocational Education's (NCVQ) approach to preparing the workforce of the future through NVQs alone. Furthermore, as Hodkinson and Mattinson (1994:324) noted, the 1991 White Paper was also concerned with the fact that many young people did not want to lock themselves into working in a particular job, with the NVQ training riding on it, as they were still making up their minds about their occupational preferences.

The problem is where GNVQs stand in relation to A-levels and NVQs, and also how they relate to the labour market. Taking the latter issue first, GNVQs could be seen as 'general education' with a vocational bias (e.g. for students wishing to go into the business, leisure and tourism industries or into health and social care). In terms of how they relate to the labour market, they could be viewed as preparing young people for work in sectors of capital (particular industries – such as leisure and tourism, or engineering), larger fractions of capital (such as the whole of manufacturing industry), functions of capital (business and science GNVQs, for example) and welfare state sectors (e.g. health and social care). Thus, in terms of how they relate to the labour market, GNVQs can be disaggregated along at least four tracks. These tracks are grounded by their relations to forms or categories of capital, and from this perspective it is misleading to view all GNVQs as having the same relation to the labour market (Rikowski, 1998).

On the issue of where GNVQs stand within the educational firmament, the position is even more confused. As with the old BTEC courses, GNVQs have come to hold an uneasy position between preparation for work and preparation for higher education (HE). Second, where they stand and how they relate to both A-levels ('general education', for capital-in-general)[1] and NVQs (standardized occupational preparation) has been a topic of much debate. The general state of confusion can be viewed in the Dearing Report (1996) where, at one point, Dearing redraws the academic/vocational divide between A-level/GNVQ and NVQ rather than along the more conventional 'divide' of A-level and G/NVQ (Rikowski, 1997). Within schools – as opposed to colleges – the situation is slightly clearer, with the academic/vocational divide flowing along the A-level/GNVQ (including Part 1) fissure. It is our view that the rigidity with which the academic/vocational divide of the two tracks in the school system is implemented and maintained will heavily influence the progress of equality in our education system. The reasons and background for this will be addressed later in the chapter.

GNVQ AND CURRICULUM TRADITIONS

The curriculum tradition of GNVQ is closely aligned with that of the National Curriculum. It is based on aspects of the liberal humanist tradition[2] but with some underlying and contradictory technocratic assumptions. The liberal humanist approach to education, used by the universities and master craftspeople for centuries to transmit knowledge from 'master' to novice, has been at the centre of traditional learning. This was and still is a very male-dominated (patriarchal) approach. It embodies, within many of the organizations that revere it, an institutionalized discrimination, particularly against women, as it assumes that 'the technical' is a male domain of skill, knowledge and practice within education and work.

However, the liberal humanist approach was never historically available to the mass of the population, and the ever-increasing quantity of human knowledge makes it difficult to give the range of subjects it encompasses space in the National Curriculum. This has caused considerable difficulties in the implementation of both the National Curriculum and GNVQ. In addition, the liberal humanist tradition, with its patriarchal approach and élitist and controlling traditionalist emphasis – where only a few are deemed to be able to cope with a rigorous, academic and subject-centered education – does not take into account the developing needs of the twenty-first century. The different social, economic and global environmental situation we are facing necessitates a more practical problem-solving approach, and the addition of some of the aspects of a more technocratic approach appears to be a rather clumsy, inadequate attempt to address these problems.

In contrast to the liberal humanist tradition, the technocratic tradition outlined and advocated by Bobbit (1918, 1924) and Tyler (1949) is based on the assumption that we agree on the fundamental aims and objects of the programme. Hence, all learning can be reduced to statements of learning outcomes and an external drive to mould the learner in a certain way. From this perspective, clear objectives would be set within a technologically appropriate method, defining the learner's ability in terms of outcomes. When writing this type of curriculum we might use the term 'the student will be able to' in order to clarify what we hope to be able to identify or assess from the learning experience.

The dangers inherent in this type of curriculum are that the basic assumptions regarding the aims and objectives – and the pre-specified ends – can be fitted to meet the demands of any political project which is premised on the continuation of capitalist society, with little or no social or moral examination of these aims and objectives. This is the basic reason why both New Labour and the Conservatives ignore any real opposition to the basic principle of a National Curriculum; both are committed to the Thatcherite model of 'free' market economics on a global scale (Cole and Hill, 1997). Furthermore, there is also within the technocratic approach an inherent assumption that all learning can be reduced to a statement of learning behaviour and denying that other learning evidence may also exist and provide evidence of success (Golby, 1989). Therefore, New Labour and the Conservatives can both rest assured that students learn within a narrow predefined set of behaviours and outcomes which do not encourage diverse or critical thought (cf. Hill, 1997).

The assumption that all learning is pre-specifiable denies the possibility that an indefinite range of evidence may show that learners have expanded their knowledge/understanding and experience, particularly in the case of non-physical activity. For example, a student pursuing a project may produce an excellent report and have pursued an original line of enquiry in which he or she has achieved considerable understanding and insight, but because the enquiry has deviated from the stated learning outcomes that piece of work is not *valid evidence* for the qualification. In one example which Arleene Piercy came across, a day-release student (from school to the local further education college, studying GNVQ Business Studies) went on a six-week school exchange to India. The student produced an impressive diary/project of the trip with illustrations and photographs, but it proved to be extremely difficult to accredit the student for much of this work – apart from some key skills – because of the narrow pre-specified and ethnocentric nature (a concern with *British* leisure and tourism enterprises and experiences) of the GNVQ Leisure and Tourism curriculum.

The technocratic tradition makes the mistake of misrepresenting educational performance by reducing the range of evidence for it. This is true of GNVQ but is even more so with the NVQ. The aim of both is to mould the learner's learning to a predetermined shape. The important questions to ask are: 'Who is determining the shape of the curriculum, and for what purpose?' and, 'What groups or individuals may be disadvantaged by such a doctrinal approach?'. The technocratic tradition is most at home in industrial and military training and in politically repressive regimes, as it is a method which decides what is taught, how it is taught and, most importantly, what answers are *acceptable.*

The biggest danger of the technocratic approach for teachers is its ability to seduce us with simplicity and order. The *subject matter* of the curriculum becomes less important than the *objectives* of the curriculum. Furthermore, assessment of the 'worth of the curriculum' (Hirst and Peters, 1970) may not have been made. It is this threat to the knowledge base of the curriculum which concerns many academic specialists. Hirst and Peters (1970) viewed their 'forms of knowledge' as being 'timeless' but nevertheless tried and tested (throughout history) and therefore worthy to pass on to future generations. The inevitable problem with this is that a 'body of knowledge' is based on a set of assumptions generally acknowledged by the groups that hold power or sway in that community or culture. Teachers never pass on 'knowledge without (class and other) social interests', and 'disinterested knowledge' is always in some *relation* to the dominating social force within a historical epoch; in contemporary society, this compelling and oppressive force is *capital* and its human representatives (Postone, 1996; Rikowski, 1996).

Yet the technocratic approach is not totally devoid of merit. Its main advantages are that it has a clear prescription with outcomes which allow the academic and industrial worlds to 'understand' one another (and open each up to critical scrutiny) and have closer approaches to training and codes of ethics. The learning outcomes create the basis of a contract between the teachers and the student; the public at large has information available on what can be expected or achieved, and so has a basis of criticism.

GNVQ is based on that body of knowledge which a Conservative government quango, the National Council for Vocational Qualifications (NCVQ), has decreed is important to be transmitted to our young people. This knowledge has been defined in a unit-based, modular curriculum with elements and performance criteria (pre-specified learning outcomes) which must be evidenced by a portfolio of work which meets the elements' evidence indicators (continuous assessment) and the passing of some national multi-choice tests on certain mandatory units of study. The GNVQs were intended to have the same rigour and high standards as A-levels and GCSE and were described by the Education Secretary at the time, John Patten, as 'vocational A-levels' (in Nicolls, 1994:25). The aim was to provide students with a programme that had sufficient academic rigour for entry to higher education and would thus extend access to further and higher education through three pathways: the academic A-level route, the training route through NVQs (mostly delivered in the workplace) and a new middle vocational education GNVQ route.

The diagram below illustrates how the NVQ and GNVQ relate to the GCSE and A-level qualifications.

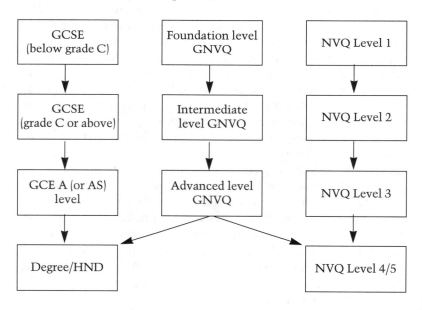

Figure 14.1 The Three Pathways to Higher Education

Theoretically, qualifications can be achieved through a combination of the three pathways, but this depends largely on local conditions, funding and links between the various agencies and the examination boards involved. In practice, the opportunity to learn through a combination of the three main pathways, combinations of GCSE/A-levels and Intermediate and Advanced GNVQ, is more likely to be available in a single institution of a large secondary school or further education or tertiary college.[3] The smaller secondary school would not have the money available to supply the wide range of staff specialisms needed, or have the staffing flexibility to cope with the additional pressures on the timetabling of groups. It would be difficult in smaller schools to offer a large range of options as the group numbers would make it difficult to justify economically. Some examinations boards of A-level and Advanced GNVQ have explored the possibility of developing common teaching materials to enable some areas of A-level and GNVQ Advanced to be taught together. Edexcel/ London Examination Board, for example, has reworked the Advanced Business Studies area with this end in view.

THE STATUS OF GNVQ AND EQUAL OPPORTUNITIES

Looking at the decision to institute a new vocational education route in isolation from other social and economic factors could be seen as an extension of the opportunities open to young people. Raffe (1985) puts forward the view that it is the *context* of the qualification, not the content, that gives it status. Universities and employers tend to judge a qualification on the type of people they think take it, not by the qualification itself, for:

> Courses introduced at the bottom of the education ladder acquire low status, and their students become stigmatized by employers and educational selectors as the less able, the less motivated and the less employable . . . Abler and 'better motivated' students are reluctant to enter such courses lest they too be stigmatized and lose their position in the educational (and subsequently occupational) hierarchy. (Raffe, 1985:20–1, in: Hodkinson and Mattinson, 1994:323)

Although a great deal of effort has been made to get higher education institutions to recognize GNVQ, the pattern of low status and recognition for vocational subjects and those who study them will continue whilst the historical divisions between academic and vocational education are perpetuated. This point is also highlighted by Andy Green in an article comparing PCET (Post Compulsory Education and Training) in England and France:

The fact that the Vocational *baccalaureate* shares a title with the other *baccalaureate* by no means gives it parity of esteem, but the fact that it belongs to the same integrated system means that students can and do transfer from one track to another. The very fact that the French system of PCET is predominately education-led and school-based gives it a certain unity, whereas English and Welsh system tends to polarise around the false dichotomies of 'Education' and 'Training'. (Green, 1995:63)

The emphasis on quality is continued in the equal opportunities statement on GNVQ for the examination boards and centres (BTEC, 1995). It is based on the National Framework for G/NVQ guidelines for standards and quality and, as with the National Curriculum, the responsibility for implementation lies with the school or college. Previously, equal opportunity policies were rarely if ever referred to or followed up beyond the submission stage but recently implemented key regulatory standards and quality criteria (produced by NCVQ and the Joint Council for Awarding Bodies published by NCVQ, in March 1995) should ensure that more specific monitoring of a centre's policies and implementation are carried out, particularly in the area of recruitment of staff and students, counselling guidance, support, accredited prior learning and external verification. The establishment of a key regulatory standard and quality criteria for developing equal opportunities policy at all points and levels in an organization does ensure that implementation can permeate throughout policy rather than be a statement tacked on to job advertisements or a brochure and then largely ignored. The equal opportunity requirements of a centre carrying out GNVQ are as follows:

- There is a centre policy on equal opportunities.
- There are systems for implementing the policy.
- Information, guidance, counselling and support are available to individual candidates. (BTEC, 1995:11)

The implementation of equality in GNVQ falls short in the same way that so many otherwise good policy decisions fall short: in the lack of resourcing, in particular of in-service teacher training. NCVQ and awarding bodies need to specify that all teachers undertake full training on equal opportunities legislation, approaches, implementation and monitoring, including that of curriculum materials and the needs of specific groups. There is also a need for equal opportunities training to feature in the training of assessors and verifiers, in order that they can monitor materials and organizations effectively.

VOLUNTEERS OR CONSCRIPTS? GNVQ IN SCHOOLS

The myriad of false assumptions that has existed since the feudal system between what is seen as 'academic' and what is seen as 'vocational', what is seen as 'training' and what is seen as 'education', lies at the heart of the social class system and the inequality of provision and opportunity in the United Kingdom. The study of subjects seen as directly work-related is still considered inferior in status to the more 'academic' studies and, what is more, is regarded as requiring inferior brain power. The major problems with the introduction of vocational GNVQ into the secondary sector still rests on this basic prejudice: it will be something for the 'non-academic students' to take. Furthermore, it is seen as a way of keeping students in the school to keep up the numbers on the roll and the unemployment figures down. Many teachers see it as a low-status area for which they do not always have the necessary subject knowledge, and is certainly a considerable extra burden on shoulders already overloaded with National Curriculum responsibilities.

The further tragedy, in terms of equality of opportunity for the 'less able' child, is that the GNVQ is a very demanding course which requires students with a high level of ability to research and organize. It requires a great deal of time for staff to organize, write materials and assess, and it needs a highly modularized structure to operate successfully. It is certainly not suitable for 'low-ability students', which is the main purpose for which it is being used in schools. Effort has been made to address this by the introduction of the Foundation level, although many schools and colleges do not have sufficient students to run both Intermediate and Foundation levels, so decisions about which is chosen are made largely on economic grounds.

Much of the marketing material, emanating from schools and sixth form colleges, now emphasizes that introducing GNVQ into their school or college offers an additional choice for students. We have yet to see any evidence to show that the 'more able' students are being encouraged to avail themselves of the vocational options. This was hardly assisted by comments to university tutors made at a conference in 1994 by the Chief Executive of NCVQ, who stated that preparing students for higher education was the principal job of A-levels, and that GNVQs were more concerned with employment (Targett and Tysome, in *Times Higher Education Supplement*, 25 February 1994). This immediately throws into question the whole feasibility of a three-track system (A-level/GNVQ/NVQ routes) of equal status. As with parental choice of school, it is usually only those children who have the money and prior attainment who really have any choice. The traditional bias is that the vocational choice is an option for the 'less academic' student.

As always, examination of these issues creates more questions than answers, questions such as: 'How do we break down these deep-seated historical prejudices?', 'How do we ensure that all in our society really have a choice?', 'Why are the National Curriculum and GNVQ largely ignored by the élitist fee-paying schools?', 'Who chooses what goes into the curriculum?'.

Three national educational policy decisions are important if we are to improve the equality of access and true choice in our education system. First, we must support and campaign for a one-track, modular, credit-based system, which could be used to break down the vocational/academic divisions and gender-based stereotyping in our schools and colleges. There has been some talk of a single curriculum and assessment framework in the government's Scottish 'Higher Still' plans, which has met with opposition and the fear that abolition of the élitist A-level would not be a popular New Labour measure: 'middle England' would feel betrayed. There have also been recent developments by the GNVQ awarding body Edexcel to break down the academic/vocational divide by pioneering parallel delivery support material and enable co-teaching of Advanced GNVQ Business and A-Level Business Studies. The National Union of Teachers' *14–19 Strategy for the Future*, launched in London on 29 November 1995, advocated similar reforms to the strategies outlined above.

Second, a major simplification of our curriculum is required with a modular credit-based system across the range of subject areas which would give more flexibility for students who have to move areas, or miss time at school for health or family reasons, enabling them to transfer credits they have achieved instead of failing perhaps two years' work, as is the case with many A-level students who have difficulties during their courses. Alternatively, as in the USA, students could combine study with working, which many do already (Rikowski and Neary, 1997). GNVQ has gone some way towards this with Unit-based assessment (GNVQ is organized in units of study which can be accredited as units of achievement in their own right), but unless the organization of the curriculum of both academic and vocational subjects is standardized across both the school and nationally, it will continue to result in less choice and flexibility available for students and more difficulties in timetabling for teachers.

Third, a larger proportion of the education budget should be spent on teaching rather than examination. The money allocated to GNVQ was mostly spent on over-complex assessment procedures and unnecessary assessor training for teachers, with very little going to teaching and resourcing of the courses. The cost of the GNVQ portfolio requirements, money for trips and work-experience expenses were passed on to parents and no provision at all made for students from economically deprived backgrounds.

Our arguments led inexorably to the conclusion that GNVQ cannot be a basis for curricular equality; it cannot become a vehicle for breaking down the academic/vocational divide. Perceptions of 'the vocational' as being primarily for relatively 'low-ability' children are underpinned by entrenched social class and national–cultural factors. Nevertheless, as well as working and arguing for equality of opportunity in the classroom as a *minimum* whilst, in our professional practice, working for the more fundamental goal of social *equality*,[4] it is important that we campaign, through teachers' unions and curriculum organizations, for a curriculum which does not rest on assigning students to distinct curriculum tracks which have lasting effects on educational and work trajectories and identities.

GNVQ AND SOCIAL INEQUALITIES

In this section we aim to show that, although GNVQ will not bring about curricular equality or 'parity of esteem' with the 'academic' GCSE/A-level track, it *does* have real potential for raising issues of *social inequality*. However, through considera-tion of Leisure and Tourism GNVQs we will show that this potential has definite limits. Thus, this section considers oppor-tunities for integrating the principles and practice of equality within GNVQ, and the limitations of GNVQ in terms of playing such a curricular role.

Our methods and ideas for underpinning GNVQ with a com-mitment to tackling social inequalities are expounded below in relation to Intermediate and Advanced Leisure and Tourism. We give this as an example, and would wish to argue that the under-lying principles of making social inequality *an issue* and *an aim* could, and should, be applied to all GNVQs. However, before pro-viding some specific examples of how GNVQ could be infused with the values of equality and equality of opportunity we embark on a brief discussion of some general and practical issues and concerns surrounding this infusion.

Introducing Equality into GNVQs

Legislation, national frameworks and school policies give a basic framework of rights and responsibilities in the area of equality but they do not create equality in our own lives or the lives of others. Our approach to equality has to permeate what we do and what we are.

The first stage of awareness is to realize we all have prejudices, some conscious and some unconscious, and try to deal with them. This should be the starting point with students. Trying to carry out specific lessons or role-plays on equality is often of limited success, particularly with the 'bags of hormones' we are dealing with in the secondary sector. The main reason for this is that students see it as irrelevant and divorced from their studies; or as preaching a particular view at them; or as an attempt to chal-lenge the prevailing ethos of their peers or family. Vocational education programmes can provide an ideal platform and many golden opportunities to integrate equality and equal opportunity awareness and education into the curriculum in an entirely natural way. The service industries, of which the leisure and tourist industry presents a good example, certainly offer plenty of opportunity as the essential core of the work is dealing with the needs of all people with respect to age, social class, ethnicity, gender, religion, sexual orientation, disability and special needs.

For example, Unit 1 of GNVQ Leisure and Tourism (both at Intermediate and Advanced level) allows for such a focus, as a concern with equality and realism could be contrasted to the drive for increased expansion and the economic contribution made by the leisure and tourist industry in recent years. In this light, the relatively poor pay and conditions, the long and unsociable hours of many service industry workers, particularly those in poorer European and 'Third-World' countries, become contentious and 'political' issues. The focus on work in GNVQs can be used to highlight *work-based inequalities* (of income, wealth and power) and the inequalities (gender, 'race', age, disability and sexual orientation) that flow from the power of employers and their managerial representatives in the recruitment process and in the organization of work. Most Units will offer occasions to incorporate equality and equal opportunity issues and projects or assignments. In addition to the possibilities suggested above, the two examples in the next sub-section will give further illustration, in more depth, of possible projects which would incorporate both the equality and special needs assessment requirements whilst addressing aspects of equality of opportunity and special needs.

Two examples from GNVQ Leisure and Tourism

This sub-section explores two extended and detailed examples of how GNVQ can incorporate a concern with the principles of equality and equality of opportunity. The first of these examples also points towards the *limits* of GNVQ as a curricular vehicle for promoting the values of equality and equality of opportunity.

Example 1
Unit 3 Intermediate Leisure and Tourism (*Customer Service in Leisure and Tourism*) offers an ideal focus to introduce class, ethnic differences, gender, disability and special needs and sexuality. The Customer Service Units are key mandatory units and have strong links to the other mandatory Units both at Intermediate and Advanced levels. They form the basic grounding for work in other units on marketing, planning an event, work experience and (advanced) human resources. The key principles of customer service are focused on the satisfaction of customers' needs, so in-depth understanding is required of the issues of social

class, ethnicity, gender, disability and special needs and sexuality, as students not only need to understand the various needs of their customers but also to prepare themselves for the practical application during work experience where they will often come face-to-face with people in all these situations on a daily basis. Having established the rationale for inclusion of equality and equal opportunity in this Unit, the next stage is to decide how it can be done.

Initial teacher input would provide an outline of the Unit, defining what customer service is, and raise awareness of the basic principles of catering for the needs of customers and the diversity of people situations they may have to deal with, including aspects of social class, ethnicity, gender, sexuality, disability and special needs. This can be followed by discussions and activities on the judgements and assumptions we make about people and why, including examples on the type of people who are on the receiving end of racism, sexism or discrimination on grounds of gender, disability, sexual orientation or special needs. Students can investigate the expectations that customers have of service givers by discussing, evaluating and writing down good and bad examples from their own experiences.

Teachers can give input on the various types of communication – with individuals, face to face, written, telephone, computer-based, non-verbal, listening skills – feeding back to check understanding and giving illustrations of how communication can be used to assist or hinder an interaction. The excellent Video Arts videotape titled *If Looks Could Kill* and the accompanying booklet could be used. The video tells the story of an unfortunate Mr Hapless and his various encounters with good, bad and indifferent service in an attempt to prepare for his holiday. He is finally driven to apparent suicide. The video ends with an unusual twist (which we will leave for you to discover) and a recap checklist of general principles to aid good customer service. Students can discuss (in small groups) problems of why 'good' service to one person is 'awful' service to someone else and the influence of our social class, sexuality, age, ethnicity, gender, and the effects that being able-bodied or disabled or having special needs have on our expectations. Questions, activities, and discussion could be instituted on our attitudes, fears, assumptions of people with disabilities, special needs, lesbians or gay men. Students need to be assisted to realize the necessity of an understanding of themselves and the development of tolerant, accepting and caring attitudes to giving good customer service. The principles of 'ideologically sound' customer service should be focused on supplying the needs of the customer in a fair and equitable way and the benefits of this to the organization. Students could devise their own Customer Charter ensuring they take into consideration serving the needs of women, disabled people, people with special needs, the working class, minority ethnic groups, gays, lesbians and bisexuals in addition to the increased customer concern regarding environmental issues.

On the basis of the Unit specifications, students should be expected to give reasons why good customer service policy and practice are of benefit to short-term profits, as well as the long-term social, economic and environmental future of the business organization. We would wish to make a number of points at this juncture, as the *limits* of GNVQ for combating social inequalities appear to have been reached.

First, the key issue for social equality is whether valuing human relations, well-being and solidarity is less or more important than the pursuit of 'business needs' – especially when the latter run counter to the former. With *niche* marketing, customization and other forms of flexible production, marketing and selling, the aim is to fragment and cut up social groups into market segments – to practically negate our common humanity. Firms basically want us to *buy* their products; our happiness, or relations with others and solidarity with them are only important when they express themselves in positive sales, or negatively in terms of boycotts, industrial action and other forms of production and sales 'disruption'.

Second, from a socialist perspective, the view of the Unit specifications is that profit is the main game, and that good 'customer service' and 'customer care' are mere means to enhancing profits. This debases notions of 'care' and 'service'; they are strewn before the altar of profit as workers are 'forced to care' in the pursuit of sales for their employers. It also seeks deliberately to create alienating social relationships, where the 'care' and 'concern' of leisure and tourism workers becomes un(sur)real in relation to the 'customers' and their 'needs'.

Third, it might seem that a 'concern' with the environment is being cynically manipulated to increase profit margins; we, as 'environmentally responsible' (Blairite) consumers, are being tagged as consumers of products from firms with a 'sound' environmentalist stance. All three issues point towards some of the *contradictions* involved in taking GNVQ as a curricular vehicle for promoting equality and equal opportunities. We need to alert students to such contradictions, and to use them as means for putting the spotlight on the 'world of work' whenever it throws up examples where human beings are forced to behave as 'capitalized' humans when they act in, and for, the interests of their employers.

Returning to Example 1, portfolio evidence can be supplied by video, drawings, charts, photographs, discussion notes, role plays, or written evaluations of the student's actual experience of dealing with customers from work experience or part-time work. The evidence indicators suggested by the exam boards mostly involve writing a report. This endless report-writing can become tiresome and could constitute an overload of written work, especially with students who find written work difficult, so using evidence from photographs, drawings, charts, computer print-outs, videos, discussion notes, written evaluation of work experience or part-time work can be a welcome change. It is not necessary for students to have a major assignment for every element, although it must be remembered that, in order to gain 'Merits' and 'Distinctions' the GNVQ planning and information-seeking and evaluation sheets need to be completed. Hence, a number of theme-graded assignments need to be included over the course as a whole.

Example 2

The Intermediate Leisure and Tourism Unit 8 deals with the environmental impact of leisure and tourism in the UK, and the Advanced Unit 1, Element 4, also has a particular focus on the environmental impact of the leisure and tourism industry. Therefore, these are ideal for investigation of the ecological aspects of the industry, and their implications for equality.

Leisure and tourism is a relatively new industry which developed – on a mass scale – after the Industrial Revolution and which provided, initially, cheap travel by train. By the 1960s cheap package holidays for the masses were available and by the 1970s affordable foreign holidays (first of all in Spain) were options for millions of British people. The industry was largely responsible for enabling working-class people to travel and afford a holiday.

The social change was reflected in popular songs from the 1930s onward such as 'Oh Mr Porter, What Can I Do?' (1930s) and Cliff Richard's recording 'Summer Holiday' in the early 1960s. The key ecological concept for students to understand, in relation to equality of opportunity whilst studying these units, is that mass demand both then and now has an ecological price to pay and it is usually those who can least afford it who suffer the consequences of poor health from pollution. More roads mean more vehicles and more pollution; more hotels mean more sewage and more waste.

The leisure and tourism industry generally has begun to develop an awareness of environmental and ecological issues, with companies specializing in 'green tourism' and airlines becoming involved in wildlife protection, and the GNVQ syllabus reflects this. The industry is also a major employer world-wide and is constantly faced with the balancing of economic and environmental considerations, and students should be made aware of this. These difficulties are particularly pertinent in areas of the developing world where tourist industries are still being established, along with the difficulties that pollution brings, the destruction of natural habitats and exploitation of labour.

At Intermediate level it is important initially for students to have first-hand experience of this in the United Kingdom, and an project based on the New Forest (the student handout for which is given later, in the Appendix) is a major assignment – well tried and tested, and GNVQ-verified – suitable for evidence for Unit 8. The assignment could also be adapted to any of the regional National Parks or areas of special scientific interest.

The New Forest Information Centre provides excellent materials including an environmental report *Living with the Enemy* (New Forest District Council, 1994), various videos, talks and visits to the Forest which will provide teachers with an adequate resource base for giving environmentally specific and equality input. Many environmental and equality issues occur naturally, as part of the study: for example, conflicts between the rights of access to common land and environmental damage; the rights of animals versus humans; car pollution from the volume of holiday traffic versus air and noise pollution for locals; tied cottages; rights of grazing. Experience and study of the New Forest Information Centre as part of the visit could provide evidence for Unit

3, Element 2 ('The provision of information as part of customer service'). This would enable students to cover work for two units on the same trip and provide the necessary links in understanding between the two units.

Following our detailed exploration of incorporating equality concerns within GNVQ, the next sub-section outlines some general ideas concerning how GNVQ can be used to raise equality issues.

General ideas for incorporating equality into GNVQ

The following examples indicate how aspects of equality may be incorporated in assignment work. Again, the ideas are framed in relation to Intermediate and Advanced Leisure and Tourism GNVQs.

1. For Unit 1, Intermediate ('Investigating Leisure and Tourism') an assignment could be used entitled 'An investigation of art and entertainment in the region: taking into consideration the needs of all the community groups'. This could include discussion on rave parties and their environmental, legal and safety aspects. It could also include a visit backstage to a local theatre and attendance at a performance of the students' choice. (This is an experience which many students will not get from their home backgrounds.)

2. For Unit 7, Intermediate ('Operational Practices') students could investigate the range of programmes in a local leisure centre, to identify which groups in the community are catered for. Students could be asked to make suggestions for activities, courses or promotions for the working-class community in general, for the minority ethnic communities, for women, for disabled people, for older people, gay, lesbian or bisexual communities or to make suggestions to improve the environment of the centre or institute by the recycling of waste.

3. An interesting cross-modular project for Unit 1 Intermediate and Advanced ('Investigating Leisure and Tourism') and Unit 3 Intermediate or Unit 6 Advanced ('Customer Service in Leisure and Tourism') could be based around a visit to a local airport, ferry port or major railway station and compiling a report on the facilities, including disabled access, price and type of food available, immigration procedures and language

assistance for those whose first language is not English and for visitors from abroad.

4. For Unit 8 Intermediate ('Environmental Impact'), work could look at the environmental impact of an airport (for example) on the local community, and any measures taken to minimize negative impacts.

5. For Unit 4 Intermediate ('Contributing to the Running of an Event') or Unit 8 Advanced ('Event Management') students could be encouraged to suggest ideas for projects or assignments, which would cover the elements and evidence indicators, with an equality theme. For example, a charity event or a sports event with an 'equality theme' could be considered. This might be a buffet and concert or disco incorporating menu choices to include religious, philosophic, ethnic and special dietary food requirements, with special planning and research to cater for musical tastes of various groups and individuals. Alternatively, a sports event for the disabled could be used.

The above ideas are just a few of the practical approaches to tackling social inequalities within the specific context of GNVQ Leisure and Tourism. In our view, many of them could be generalized to other GNVQs.

CONCLUSION: CURRICULAR AND SOCIAL INEQUALITIES

We have argued in this chapter that the academic/vocational divide will be maintained as long as the two-track (in schools) and three-track (post-compulsory education and training) curricular trajectories survive. We do not see 'parity of esteem' between academic and vocational forms of learning as being a possibility with the advent of GNVQ. On the contrary, the introduction of GNVQ has recreated, in post-compulsory education and training, a 'new tripartism' redolent of the 'old tripartitism' enshrined within the 1944 Education Act. Of course, in the 'old tripartite' English schooling system the fissures were more closely connected to specific social class positions. The 'old tripartitism' was openly and institutionally class-based. In the 'new tripartitism' the three educational trajectories – academic/vocational education/training –

are more opaque as they seem to refer to three forms of *learning*. Unlike the 'old tripartitism', where there was a clear *institutional* differentiation (the three types of school) linked to social class destinations, the 'new tripartitism' appears to be linked to learning within three curriculum tracks and these (especially in the case of sixth-form and FE colleges) *cut across* institutions. Thus, rather than corralling young people into three types of institutions, the 'new tripartitism' is superficially more 'open' and based on a greater degree of student 'choice'.

In the 'new tripartitism' the social class formation function of education is submerged beneath Dearing's three-track diagrams, hidden behind nationalistic rhetoric surrounding the National Education and Training Targets (NETTs), and camouflaged by the national drive to raise the quality of labour-power throughout the British national capital at the lowest possible cost. For us, one of the prerequisites for altering this tragi-comedy is to sweep away the academic/vocational divide and institute a *one-track* comprehensive system of education and training within the context of a national credit accumulation and transfer scheme and a common curriculum (also within compulsory education and post-school education and training, for 16- to 18-year-olds) where the 'academic' and the 'vocational' are *unified*.

The movement from a liberal humanist to a technocratic educational discourse simultaneously constitutes a turn away from a liberal humanist mode of thought, where it was at least possible to frame questions of value, aims and human goals, and a turn towards towards a technocratic discourse, where goals and aims are *given*, where capitalist social reality is assumed throughout, where only *technical* problems are considered (for example, how to operationalize a 'customer care' policy) and only the concomitant *technicist* solutions allowed. This *technicist* discourse underpinning GNVQ functions to expunge questions of social value, purpose and constitution from learning.

However, as GNVQ is supposed to be focused on the 'world of work' the social inequalities inherent within capitalist enterprises are fair game for teachers interested in making these inequalities *problematic*. Thus, the technocratic approach has to be overcome as teachers and students struggle to view the real, palpable social inequalities behind the technicist ether. The biggest danger in calling for the *unification* of the 'vocational' and the 'academic' curriculum is that the *foundation* of such a curriculum would be hewn out of a technicist discourse and technocratic approach to knowledge and skill, where the 'needs' of industry would predominate over critical insight into the constitution of capitalist society. Hence, the basis of such a unification, for us, is crucial. If this 'unification' is based upon a 'celebration of capital' which sits astride a curricular programme where students think through 'solutions' to the everyday, practical problems of businesses then, for us, this would constitute the degeneration of education into a mere tool of capital accumulation. Of course, it is doubtful whether businesses would take much notice of GNVQ students' 'solutions' to their problems, although this misses the point entirely: challenging the social inequalities embedded within the capitalist work environment and reconstructing and rethinking work within a discourse which privileges social equality would come a long way behind a concern with increasing capital accumulation and the competitiveness of British enterprises.

The latter is indeed the 'tragedy of labour', where the creative power and thinking of actual and future workers is subsumed under the goal of capital accumulation. It would be wrong, in our view, for education to play a leading role in this tragedy. Combating the technocratic approach to education and learning is a step towards ensuring that any future integration of the 'academic' and the 'vocational' curriculum does not rest upon a pro-capitalist foundation.

We are much more optimistic regarding GNVQ as a vehicle for combating *social* inequalities, those emanating from 'really existing capitalism' (gender, class, 'race', age, sexuality, disability, special needs, religious) rather than those emanating from the curriculum – and for posing awkward questions for those committed to ecological renewal. The examples provided, and the strategies suggested for infusing GNVQ courses with the values of social equality and ecological awareness, are indicators that GNVQ need not be 'written off' as a mere 'celebration of capital' and as a 'servant' to its 'needs'.

Our suggestions on how GNVQ can open up the 'world of work' to analysis and debate points towards a form of pedagogy which questions the existing forms of work organization, labour markets, recruitment processes and work values. When employers scream from the rooftops (well, from the educational press and mass media) that education should focus more on industry and its 'needs' – which are basically 'labour-power needs' (Rikowski, 1996) – a reply might also scream back along the lines that the inequalities of work, prejudice in the workplace and recruitment, and the power of big business, should indeed be *closely* studied by all school students. In a contemporary British educational context, devoid of a unified and common curriculum, we might also add that GNVQ is one of our best bets for providing young people with the opportunity to think critically about the organization of work and economy and the injustices emanating from social class, gender, disability, 'race', sexuality, age and other forms of social division. The current British context requires a critical pedagogical eye cast upon the 'world of (capitalist) work'. We believe GNVQ can play a significant role in making 'work' a source of political understanding for young people in Britain today.

NOTES

1. In Karl Marx's first volume of *Capital* (especially in the early sections), the analysis proceeds on the basis of 'capital-in-general' – the general, and most fundamental categories (commodity, value, use-value, exchange-value, money, labour-power, labour and capital) that ground and define capitalist society. In these deliberations, Marx was not interested in 'this or that capitalist', particular capitals (firms), branches of industry or competition between capitals. Rather, his task was to unfold the basic, structuring and systematic features of production based upon *capital*. This, at root, is production premised upon the value created through unpaid labour (also unpaid labour time) which is then used by capitals and their personal representatives (owners, managers) to further *expand* the level of value created in the next production cycle through utilizing the surplus-value (a surplus over and above the value represented by workers' *wages*) created by workers in the first production cycle. In this way, capital appears to be 'self-expanding' value. In reality, its expansion is based upon increasing the quantity of unpaid labour time, that part of the working day, week, month or year where the value created by workers in production does not enter into their wages, but is appropriated by representatives of capital for further production (see Chapter 1 for a fuller discussion of surplus value). Education for 'capital-in-general' is education which is not aimed, intentionally, at preparing young people for particular jobs, firms, branches of industry or one of the great fractions of capital (manufacturing capital, for example). Education for 'capital-in-general' can only be about preparing young people

for *work within the framework of capitalist society* – working in and through capital – which has at its goal the *accumulation of capital*, the ceaseless expansion of ever greater amounts of *surplus-value* (value based upon unpaid labour, unpaid labour time). Most compulsory education in contemporary Britain is basically education for 'capital-in-general'; though, with the advent of GNVQ, there has been an increased focus on education for sectors and fractions of capital. Of course, this is not to say that particular capitals do not draw upon skills, knowledge, work attitudes and personality traits partially developed within young people while they are at school. But this misses the point about the *intentionality* behind the process – which (setting GNVQ aside) operates mainly at a 'general' level of 'work preparation'. A-levels are an example of this; they only adventitiously prepare young people for working in particular capitals or sectors of capital. A-levels are basically, therefore, a form of education for 'capital-in-general'. The level of 'intentionality' is relatively 'weak' on the ground; teachers in schools and classrooms may well have other goals, perhaps more purely 'educational' ones, than mere preparation of young people for work in capitalist society. However, when we turn to examining education policy documents which express a need to prepare British young people for competition on the world economic stage, then, at this *policy* level, the 'intentionality' underpinning the process of socially producing young people as labour-power (people with the capacity to labour) takes on a 'stronger' form.

2. The liberal humanist tradition specifies 'knowledge' as the most important aspect of the curriculum and is defined as in the traditional areas of study in old established public schools and universities. The learner is considered an apprentice working alongside 'the master' learning the mysteries of the subject. The opposite curriculum approach would be the progressive approach where 'individual growth' is the central tenet and subject matter is only important in its importance for the child's understanding of the world – following Dewey (1915), and the progressive education movements in the States since the 1920s and the UK since the 1960s (Harris, 1994).

3. Tertiary colleges were set up from 1979 onwards in a number of local education authorities and administered under the further education sector on comprehensive principles. They provide academic sixth-form courses and vocational and practical courses for the 16- to 19-year-old age group. Under the regulations in existence at the time, sixth forms or sixth-form colleges were not able to offer this. The wide spectrum of ability levels they cater for enables them to attract sufficient numbers to offer a wide range of courses.

4. See Cole and Hill, Introduction to this volume, for more on the distinction between equality of opportunity and equality.

BIBLIOGRAPHY

Bamfield, E. (1996) GNVQ Manufacturing (Part One) at Key Stage 4: A Case Study Prior to a Pilot. MEd dissertation, University of Birmingham, School of Education.

Bobbit, F. (1918) *The Curriculum.* Boston, Mass: Houghton Mifflin.

Bobbit, F. (1924) *How to Make a Curriculum.* Boston, Mass: Houghton Mifflin.

BTEC (1995) *Policy Framework: Regulatory Policies and Quality Criteria.* London: Business and Technology Education Council.

BTEC/GNVQ (1995) *Getting GNVQs Right: Teaching, Learning, and Assessing.* London: Business and Technology Education Council.

Capey, J. (1996) *Review of GNVQ Assessment Grading.* July 1996 News Release. London: National Council for Vocational Qualifications.

Cole, M. and Hill, D. (1997) New Labour, old policies: Tony Blair's vision for education in Britain. *Education Australia,* 37.

Dearing, R (1996) *Review of Qualifications for all 16–19 year olds. Full Report.* Hayes: SCAA Publications.

DES (1991; Vol.1 of 2) *Education and Training for the 21st Century.* London: HMSO.

Dewey, J. (1915) *The School and Society.* Chicago: University of Chicago Press.

Education Committee (1996) Education and training for 14 to 19 year olds – volume 1. First Report on the Proceedings of the Committee, House of Commons, Session 1995–96, 14 February. London: HMSO.

GNVQ (1996) *Mandatory Units for Advanced Leisure and Tourism.* London: NCVQ Accredited, Business and Technology Education Council.

GNVQ (1996) *Mandatory Units for Intermediate Leisure and Tourism.* London: NCVQ Accredited, Business and Technology Education Council.

GNVQ (1996) *Option Units for Intermediate Leisure and Tourism.* London: NCVQ, Business and Technology Education Council.

Golby, M. (1989) Curriculum traditions. In B. Moon, P. Murphy and J. Raynor (eds) *Policies for the Curriculum.* London: Open University Press.

Green, A. (1995) Core skills, participation and progression in post compulsory education and training in England and France. *Comparative Education,* 31(1):49–67.

Harris, K. (1994) *Teachers: Constructing the Future.* London: Falmer Press.

Hill, D. (1997) Reflection in teacher education. In K. Watson, S. Modgil and C. Modgil (eds) *Educational Dilemmas: Debate and Diversity, Vol. 1 – Teacher Education and Training.* London: Cassell.

Hirst, P. and Peters, R. (1970) *The Logic of Education.* London: Routledge and Kegan Paul.

Hodkinson, P. and Mattinson, K. (1994) A bridge too far? The problems facing GNVQ. *The Curriculum Journal*, 5(3):323–36.

Hulme, J. (1996) The need: a flexible curriculum. Report on the NUT conference '14–19 Strategy for the Future: Road to Equality'. *The Teacher*, January/February.

Hyland, T. (1994a) *Competence, Education and NVQs*. London: Cassell Education.

Hyland, T. (1994b) GNVQs and the post-school curriculum. *Educational Change and Development*, 15(1):45–9.

Hyland, T. (1995) A Critical Study of GNVQ. Paper Presented at the University of Birmingham, School of Education, Post-16 Perspectives Seminar, 15 February.

Marx, K. (1867/1977) *Capital: A Critique of Political Economy – Volume I*. London: Lawrence and Wishart.

Moon, B. (1996; 3rd edn) *A Guide to the National Curriculum*. Oxford: Oxford University Press.

NCVQ/SCAA (1996) *Part One GNVQ: A Brief Guide for Parents*, Hayes: SCAA Publications.

NCVQ/SCAA (1997) *Part One GNVQ: A Brief Guide*. Hayes: SCAA Publications.

New Forest District Council (1994) *Living with the Enemy*. Poole: South Side Publishing.

Nicolls, A. (1994) GNVQs: Challenging the 'gold standard'. *Education and Training*, 36(1):25–8.

Postone, M. (1996) *Time, Labor and Social Domination: A Reinterpretation of Marx's Critical Theory*. Cambridge: Cambridge University Press.

Raffe, D. (1985) Education and training initiatives for 14–18s: content and context. In A. Watts (ed.) *Education and Training 14–18 Policy and Practice*. Cambridge: CRAC.

Rikowski, G. (1996) Education, globalisation and the learning society: towards a materialist analysis. Unpublished paper. University of Birmingham: School of Education.

Rikowski, G. (1997) After Dearing: the review of 16–19 qualifications. *Forum*, 39(1):19–21.

Rikowski, G. (1998) *Education for Industry: A Complex Technicism*. Unpublished paper. School of Education, University of Birmingham.

Rikowski, G. and Neary, M. (1997) Working schoolchildren in Britain today. *Capital and Class*, 63, Autumn:25–35.

Targett, S. and Tysome, T. (1994) Chief confuses GNVQ signal. *Times Higher Education Supplement*, 25 February.

Taubman, D. (1994) The GNVQ debate. *Forum*, 36(3):77–80.

Tyler, R. (1949) *Basic Principles of Curriculum and Instruction*. Chicago: University of Chicago Press.

Video Arts, *If Looks Could Kill*. 68 Oxford Street, London W1N 9LA. Tel: 0171 637 7288.

Wolf, A. (1993) Introduction. In A. Wolf (ed.) *Parity of Esteem: Can*

Vocational Awards Ever Achieve High Status? International Centre
for Research on Assessment, ICRA Proceedings – No.1. University of
London: Institute of Education.

APPENDIX

Handout for students on the New Forest Assignment
Intermediate Level option unit
Unit 8: Investigating the environmental impact of leisure and tourism

Scenario
You are working for the New Forest Information Centre and have been
asked to prepare a report on the environmental consequences of Leisure
and Tourism activities in the New Forest. You have been asked to pay
particular attention to three aspects:

1. the environmental issues,
2. the environmental impacts of leisure and tourism in the forest,
3. the measures to deal with the negative impacts of leisure and tourism
    activities on the Forest.

Task 1
Using your notes, textbook, information packs, learning resource centre
and local library, the New Forest Information Centre, and local TV and
newspaper reports, carry out research on the above three aspects using
your theme planning and information documents to assist and record
your progress.

Task 2
Write a report with the title 'Environmental Consequences of Leisure
and Tourism in the New Forest' using the following headings:

1   Introduction
2.   Key Environmental Issues
2.1   Access to the Forest
2.2   Wear and tear on the natural resources of the Forest
2.3   Conflicts of interest in the Forest
2.4   Conservation in the Forest
2.5   Preservation of the Forest
3.   Activities at the Forest
3.1   Land
3.2   Water
3.3   Sporting
3.4   Recreational
3.5   Cultural
4.   Economic

4.1 Employment
4.2 Income
4.3 Migration
5 Impact
5.1 Positive
5.2 Negative
6. Conclusion
7. Recommendations

You should include, where appropriate, maps, charts, diagrams, photographs or pictures to illustrate your report.

Aims of the assignment
- To identify the key environmental issues relating to leisure and tourism activities.
- To describe the environmental impacts on a locality.
- To describe the implications for a local environment of leisure and tourism activities.
- To process the information into a report.

Assessment
A plan of action to carry out research.
A correctly formatted report covering the areas outlined in the tasks.
Some illustrative material which adds to the interest and understanding of the report.

Name index

Subject index